INTRODUCTION TO "GNOSTICISM"

INTRODUCTION TO "GNOSTICISM"

ANCIENT VOICES, CHRISTIAN WORLDS

Nicola Denzey Lewis

BROWN UNIVERSITY

New York   Oxford

OXFORD UNIVERSITY PRESS

OXFORD
UNIVERSITY PRESS

Oxford University Press is a department of the University of Oxford.
It furthers the University's objective of excellence in research, scholarship,
and education by publishing worldwide.

Oxford   New York
Auckland   Cape Town   Dar es Salaam   Hong Kong   Karachi
Kuala Lumpur   Madrid   Melbourne   Mexico City   Nairobi
New Delhi   Shanghai   Taipei   Toronto

With offices in
Argentina   Austria   Brazil   Chile   Czech Republic   France   Greece
Guatemala   Hungary   Italy   Japan   Poland   Portugal   Singapore
South Korea   Switzerland   Thailand   Turkey   Ukraine   Vietnam

Oxford is a registered trademark of Oxford University Press in the UK and
certain other countries.

For titles covered by Section 112 of the US Higher Education Opportunity
Act, please visit www.oup.com/us/he for the latest information about
pricing and alternate formats.

Published in the United States of America by
Oxford University Press
198 Madison Avenue, New York, NY 10016

Library of Congress Cataloging-in-Publication Data
Lewis, Nicola Denzey, 1966–, author.
   Introduction to Gnosticism : Ancient Voices, Christian Worlds / Nicola Denzey
   Lewis, Brown University.
        pages cm
   Includes bibliographical references and index.
   ISBN 978-0-19-975531-8
   1. Gnosticism—Textbooks.   2. Nag Hammadi codices.   I. Title.
   BT1390.L49 2013
   299'.932—dc23
2012036710

Contents

CHAPTER 8. Two Valentinian Gospels: The *Gospel of Truth* and the *Gospel of Philip* 88

CHAPTER 9. The Thomas Literature: The *Gospel of Thomas* and the *Book of Thomas the Contender* 100

CHAPTER 10. Sethian Gnosticism: *Three Steles of Seth* 118

CHAPTER 11. In the Beginning: Two Creation Myths: *Hypostasis of the Archons* and *On the Origin of the World* 131

CHAPTER 15. Deconstructing the Divine Feminine: *Thunder: Perfect Mind* and *Trimorphic Protennoia* 191

CHAPTER 16. What Are Pagan Texts Doing in a Christian Library? *Discourse on the Eighth* and *Ninth, Asclepius,* and Plato's *Republic* 207

CHAPTER 17. Apostolic Traditions in Conflict: *Letter of Peter to Philip, Acts of Peter and the Twelve Disciples,* and the *Apocalypse of Peter* 218

Maps, Diagrams, and Timelines

Preface

If you're like many people, you might have heard about Gnosticism or even Nag Hammadi from somewhere—a television show, a magazine, a blog, a class at school. That curiosity leads you to your local bookstore, where you snatch up a translation of the Nag Hammadi library (NHL). You hope to find all the wonders of the universe revealed: the secret teachings of Jesus, the books that didn't make it into the Bible. You pay for the book in a rush, bring it home, open it up, start reading, and don't get very far. You find that even the most user-friendly text—the *Gospel of Thomas*, let's say—makes pretty much no sense, at least at times. This gospel promises to reveal Jesus's "obscure" sayings and indeed they certainly are obscure; most readers are quickly left scratching their heads. And that's just the *Gospel of Thomas*. By the time you reach a text called *Zostrianos*, you're utterly, utterly confused. The little introductory paragraphs that modern scholars provide are not very helpful, either, saying things like, "This text is a Barbeloite Sethianizing revelation dialogue with aretalogical passages." A what? At this point—not without justification—most readers just put the book down for good.

This book is designed to be a guide for the perplexed, written to help unlock the Nag Hammadi writings, discovered in 1945 and now widely available in various English print editions as well as free online. They are some of the most fabulously sophisticated, often beautiful, always thoughtful ancient writings that Christians of the second century and beyond composed, read, and circulated. These writings were, however, virtually always esoteric; they were not meant for the uninitiated, and they were not meant to be clear in their meaning for those who did not have eyes to see and ears to hear. At best, those who authored these texts believed they revealed things too sacred for profane readers. To understand them you need, at minimum, some knowledge of the Bible but also a good grounding in Plato and later Platonic philosophy, a knowledge of Jewish scriptures that are not in the Bible as well as reading techniques employed by Jewish scholars, a background in Roman history and Graeco-Roman magic, and enough language skills to understand the puns and wordplays in Greek, Hebrew, and sometimes Syriac and Coptic. As one of my undergraduates once said in our seminar on Gnosticism, looking down at a text wonderingly, "wow...the more you know, the more you know!"

I love this statement, because of the unintentional pun about Gnosticism, which was an ancient movement involving *gnosis*: salvific knowledge. It was all about what you knew and how you knew it. But the student was indeed right. The more you know, the more you find in these texts, and each reading brings more insight, provided you keep learning more about the background of these texts. The point of this book is to walk the uninitiated through these ancient writings without expecting that anyone will have a clue what a Barbeloite Sethianizing treatise is, but giving you enough points of contact with things you might be reasonably supposed to know about in order to unlock new worlds of meaning. I know I have done my job in the classroom when students blanch at a new Nag Hammadi writing, utterly lost at first, but by the end of the class they are all quite thrilled at their own brilliance.

This book is the product of more than a dozen years of teaching Gnosticism at Bowdoin College, Dartmouth College, and Brown University. It grew from my frustrations teaching Gnosticism to undergraduates, from having to tell them, time and time again, that when it comes to these materials, they are mostly on their own. While there have been in recent years a number of excellent books introducing nonspecialist readers to Gnosticism, there are fewer that guide readers through difficult texts. There are no books at all that walk readers through the Nag Hammadi Library, the most significant collection of so-called Gnostic writings in existence.

Since the NHL's discovery, teams of scholars in the United States, Germany, Scandinavia, France, Italy, and Canada have produced scholarship on Gnosticism of exceptional quality with exceptional speed, and part of the goal of this book has been to digest, condense, and produce for a general audience some of that work. I am humbled by the insights and learnedness of these scholars; what I have done here represents not a desire to take credit for the insights of others but to share it more broadly, as it deserves to be shared. Because of the nature of this book, there are neither footnotes nor extensive bibliographies; but it is important to acknowledge my debt to the very wonderful minds who have set themselves to understanding this material.

I chose to cluster NHL writings by theme or kind, rather than by addressing each tractate separately under a separate heading. Although every single one of the NHL writings is at least mentioned and placed into some sort of interpretive context here, not all of the NHL treatises are equally important or even interesting, and thus delegating each of the fifty-two writings its own paragraph of more-or-less even length seemed like the wrong approach. By clustering texts by theme, I encourage readers to think about similarities and differences within the corpus rather than considering each text in isolation. There are, however, a few exceptions to the "clustering" technique: some of the texts are so important and rich that they merit their own chapters (although they are often made reference to in other chapters when they are relevant). Thus there are separate, stand-alone chapters for the *Gospel of Thomas*, the *Apocryphon of John*, and the *Gospel of the Egyptians*, three key writings from the NHL that have forever altered our understanding of early Christianity.

There are a number of Nag Hammadi tractates that are not discussed in any detail in this volume: they include *Exegesis on the Soul*, *Eugnostos the Blessed*, the *Sophia of Jesus Christ*, *Dialogue of the Savior*, *Authoritative Teaching*, *Concept of our Great Power*, *Paraphrase of Shem*, *Second Treatise of the Great Seth*, *Melchizedek*, the *Thought of Norea*, the *Testimony of Truth*, the *Interpretation of Knowledge*, *Hypsiphrone*, the *Teachings of Silvanus*, and the *Sentences of Sextus*. The reasons for omitting these are various and complex, but suffice it to say that many of these are preserved only in very fragmentary form, and hence they are neither much read nor much studied. That said, I decided to sacrifice a comprehensive treatment of all the Nag Hammadi writings in favor of devoting more energy and attention to the most important texts in the collection. This decision is underscored by the practicalities of pedagogy, where most courses that examine this material necessarily confine themselves to the better known and better preserved NH writings. It remains my unfulfilled wish, however, that students will someday have a guide to the very most perplexing and obscure of these writings, and not just the ones that have become most famous.

This book is not a translation of the Nag Hammadi writings itself, but it is one that works *with* various translations of the NHL (including, at times, my own). It is designed to be read alongside whatever edition or translation a reader should choose. I also wanted to provide more of a detailed "walkthrough" of NHL texts than either general books on Gnosticism or brief introductions at the front of primary source collections can do. For that, students fortunately have three terrific collections of translations at their disposal:

1. James M. Robinson, ed., *The Nag Hammadi Library in English*. 4th ed. (Boston: Brill, 1998). This volume is the classic English-language translation produced by an international team of scholars in 1978, and it remains a wonderful resource. Each text is prefaced by a brief introduction, but these introductions are geared toward specialist readers, often containing technical vocabulary. All the translations in this volume, minus these short introductions, are widely available free on the Internet, albeit in an earlier (1988) edition. Since this is how many of my students find and access the NH writings, passages in this book are generally taken from the online editions so that students may easily find them.

2. Marvin Meyer, ed., *The Nag Hammadi Scriptures* (San Francisco: HarperSanFrancisco, 2007). More up-to-date than the Robinson edition, Meyer corralled the world's finest Coptic scholars to retranslate the NHL and provide introductions. In certain cases, these translations differ quite radically from the Robinson editions. The introductions, like the Robinson editions', are written for specialists but are far more detailed. This is therefore an indispensible volume for intermediate students and is highly recommended. When The *Nag Hammadi Scriptures* provides a particularly useful or accurate translation, I have used it here; these excerpts are marked accordingly.

3. Bentley Layton, *The Gnostic Scriptures* (New York: Doubleday, 1987). This book is an outstanding edition of a selection of Gnostic writings by a top scholar of Coptic and early Christianity. The texts in this volume are all Layton's own translations and thus share a few idiosyncrasies (e.g., Layton retranslates many titles, so a text that everyone calls *Hypostasis of the Archons* based on the Robinson edition, Layton calls *Reality of the Rulers*). Another shortcoming to the volume is that it is selective, offering selections of a variety of writings both in and not in the NHL. Nevertheless, I consider this book an indispensible resource for students at all levels. At times, I select key passages from *The Gnostic Scriptures* when, again, I feel they best reflect my understanding of the original text; these excerpts are marked accordingly.

In addition, there are a number of more professional English language critical editions of the NHL available for more serious students. While I have consulted them, I have not quoted them directly here. They remain key resources:

1. James M. Robinson, *The Coptic Gnostic Library. A Complete Edition of the Nag Hammadi Codices*. 5 vols. (Boston: Brill, 2000). This is a condensed, softcover edition of the Coptic/English critical editions originally released in thirteen hardcover volumes. For advanced students.

2. Each Nag Hammadi Codex has its own bilingual Coptic-English critical edition published

in the Nag Hammadi and Manichean Studies series with Brill, Leiden. These editions include lengthy introductions, notes, indices, and other important tools for advanced study.

3. Finally, some of the more popular texts (the *Gospel of Thomas* and the *Apocryphon of John*, notably) are published as freestanding studies with their own English translations, sometimes with Coptic provided. For these, consult the bibliography provided at the end of each relevant chapter.

A note on the use of the Bible: my own approach to NH is to refer to the New Testament (NT) frequently, because in my opinion, the writings of the NT were the most significant sources of inspiration for NH writers. I therefore believe that all the sources in the NHL were composed around the second century CE, with the exception of the *Gospel of Thomas* (possibly written earlier but revised in the second century).

Most of the biblical quotations here are from the Revised Standard Version (RSV). I believe that many students today who find the content of these texts to be alienating might be comforted, in a sense, to learn how these texts at Nag Hammadi made use of the NT. I don't presume a student's knowledge of the NT, but I do recommend it as background or even co-study. For those looking to read a good translation, I recommend Harold Attridge, ed., *The Harper Collins Study Bible* (San Francisco: HarperCollins, 2006).

I should mention one technical detail that may be confusing to beginner students; I use the term "New Testament," but only infrequently do I employ "Old Testament." I prefer the term "Jewish scriptures," or "Hebrew Bible," but there are times when I am citing the work of second-century writers that I use the term "Old Testament" because it more accurately reflects their way of thinking about the Jewish scriptures. It should also be said that the Jewish scriptures are much broader a category than just the writings of the Old Testament or the Hebrew Bible. Also, because Jews and Christians of the second century were using the Septuagint (LXX) (the Hebrew Bible translated into Greek), "Hebrew Bible" can be a misleading term.

Finally, I need to thank the many people from whom I have learned so much over the years. My intellectual godfathers—some of whom I don't know well, but all of whom are reflected in this volume—include Harold Attridge, Bentley Layton, Frederick Wisse, James Robinson, and Birger Pearson. Recent work by Gerard Luttikhuizen, Einar Thomassen, and Christoph Markschies has changed the field in important ways. I've been grateful for conversations over the years with John Turner, Anne McGuire, Ismo Dunderberg, April DeConick, Karen King, Marvin Meyer, David Brakke, and Louis Painchaud. Rising stars in the field—Tuomas Rasimus, Zeke Mazur, Mikael Haxby, Michael Kaler, Lance Jenott, Geoffrey Smith, Dylan Burns, Ben Dunning, Taylor Petrey, Minna Heimola, Bas Van Os, and Philip Tite—have also been wonderful conversation partners, and their excitement over this project has sustained me in significant ways. Other scholars not in the field of Gnosticism but significant conversation partners are Greg Snyder, Bob Royalty, AnneMarie Luijendijk, Pierluigi Piovanelli, and Charlie Stang.

This book has grown from my interactions over the years with undergraduate students, especially at Dartmouth and Brown; special thanks to Rebekah Junkermeier, Harry Huberty and Tim Baker at Dartmouth (all now graduate students at Harvard); Justine Ariel, Rita Bullwinkel, Michael Cohen, Obasi Osborne, George Miller, Christopher Canary, Steve Carmody, Susannah Kroeber, Ben Marcus, and Brown grad students Chandler Coggins, Heidi Wendt, Christopher Sweeney, and Stephen Young. While still in draft form, the students at Davidson College also offered cheerfully constructive comments on some of the chapters here. Of that group, special mention goes to Rebecca Ayscue, James Frankel, Melissa Hickey, Emily Romeyn, and Laura Thrash. Those who ploughed their way through the full manuscript of this book at the request of Oxford University Press and offered many suggestions and caught many errors did truly heroic duty, and I want to acknowledge them here: Ben Dunning, David Brakke, Caroline Johnson Hodge, Susan Marks, John Turner, David Zachariah Flanagin, Christopher Fuhrmann, and those who chose to remain anonymous: thank you. The Oxford editorial team, headed by Robert Miller, deserves an awed thanks for turning a manuscript into a book; a special thanks to the copy editor for her painstaking work. My husband Tal Lewis remained through this process all that an incredible partner should be and far more—I am forever grateful for his love and support. Finally, I owe my greatest debt to my own extraordinary teacher Elaine Pagels, who taught me about the All. I dedicate this book to the memory of two wonderful undergraduates whose pleasure they took in these texts stays with me even as I mourn their untimely deaths: Ariel Shaker (Harvard '10) and Paige Hicks (Brown '11).

Abbreviations and Signs Used in This Book

Adv. Haer.	Irenaeus, *Adversus Haereses*
BCE/CE	Before the Common Era/Common Era
BG	Berlin Gnostic Codex
ca.	circa
CT	Codex Tchacos
ff.	and following line or lines
MS	manuscript
NH	Nag Hammadi
NHC	Nag Hammadi Codex
NHL	Nag Hammadi Library
NHLE	James Robinson, ed., *The Nag Hammadi Library in English*
NHS	Marvin Meyer, ed., *The Nag Hammadi Scriptures*
NT	New Testament
Pan.	Epiphanius of Salamis, *Panarion*
pl.	plural
POxy	Papyrus Oxyrhynchus
Ref.	Hippolytus, *Refutation of All Heresies*
sing.	singular

Books from the New Testament and Hebrew Bible (Old Testament) are abbreviated according to standard abbreviations.

ABBREVIATIONS FOR NAG HAMMADI WRITINGS, LISTED BY CODEX ORDER

Prayer of Apostle Paul	PrApP		*Apocryphon of John*	ApJn
Apocryphon of James	ApocJas		*Gospel of Thomas*	GThom
Gospel of Truth	GosTruth		*Gospel of Philip*	GPhil
Treatise on the Resurrection	TreatRes		*Hypostasis of the Archons*	HypArch
Tripartite Tractate	TriTrac		*On the Origin of the World*	OrigWld

Exegesis on the Soul	ExSoul		Asclepius 21–29	Asclep.
Book of Thomas the Contender	BThomas		Paraphrase of Shem	PShem
Gospel of the Egyptians	GosEg		Second Treatise of the Great Seth	2ndTreatS
Eugnostos the Blessed	Eug.		Apocalypse of Peter	ApocPeter
Sophia of Jesus Christ	SJC		Teachings of Silvanus	TSilv
Dialogue of the Savior	DialSav		Three Steles of Seth	3StelesSeth
Apocalypse of Paul	ApocPaul		Zostrianos	Zost.
The First Apocalypse of James	1stApocJas		Letter of Peter to Philip	LPP
The Second Apocalypse of James	2ndApocJas		Melchizedek	Melch.
Apocalypse of Adam	ApocAdam		Thought of Norea	TNorea
Acts of Peter and the Twelve Disciples	ActsP12		Testimony of Truth	TestTruth
Thunder, Perfect Mind	Thunder		Marsanes	Mars.
Authoritative Teaching	AT		Interpretation of Knowledge	InterpKnow
Concept of our Great Power	ConGPower		A Valentinian Exposition	VE
Plato, Republic	Rep.		Allogenes	Allog.
Discourse on the Eighth and Ninth	Disc8th9th		Hypsiphrone	Hyps.
Prayer of Thanksgiving	PThanks		Trimorphic Protennoia	TriProt

SIGNS WITHIN PRIMARY SOURCE QUOTATIONS

Many of the Nag Hammadi writings are fragmentary and, where possible, have been restored by modern translators. Signs in quotations of translations indicate where material has been added, or where it cannot be reconstructed:

Square parentheses indicate a modern addition to a text [ ]

Square parentheses enclosing three periods [...] indicates a hole in the ancient manuscript

Round parentheses ( ) indicate an addition to a text

Alternate Names of Tractates

English translators of the Nag Hammadi writings often translate the titles their own way rather than standardizing. Sometimes this has to do with debates on how or whether a specific word should be translated (e.g., should a Greek word like *Allogenes* be translated or left in Greek?); sometimes a book has more than one title, so some use one title and others, another. For the sake of simplicity and consistency, I've used the titles of the NH writings from J. Robinson, ed., *The Nag Hammadi in English*. This is a widely available volume, and all the separate tractates in it can be accessed free on the Internet. Nevertheless, it's likely that even a beginning student of NH will come across other titles commonly used. This table shows, in the left-hand column, some titles used in the Robinson volume; on the right are the alternate titles by which these tractates are known and which students will sometimes find in other volumes and collections.

Apocryphon of John	Secret Book of John, Secret Revelation of John
Apocryphon of James	Secret Book of James
Apocalypse of Adam	Revelation of Adam
First Apocalypse of James	The First Revelation of James
Second Apocalypse of James	The Second Revelation of James
Thunder, Perfect Mind	Thunder: Perfect Intellect
Trimorphic Protennoia	First Thought in Three Forms, Three Forms of First Thought
Gospel of the Egyptians	Holy Book of the Great Invisible Spirit
Allogenes	The Foreigner
Three Steles of Seth	Three Tablets of Seth
Treatise on the Resurrection	Epistle to Rheginos
Asclepius	Perfect Discourse
Second Treatise of the Great Seth	Second Discourse of the Great Seth

A NOTE ON NUMBER REFERENCES IN NAG HAMMADI TEXTS

Scholars have devised a simple system for line citations in the NH writings, but it needs some explaining:

- The abbreviation NHC stands for "Nag Hammadi Codex," and it tells a reader from which codex or codices a particular writing comes.
- Codex numbers are traditionally written in upper-case Roman numerals.

When citing a specific passage or line, scholars use the folio or page number of the codex, followed by a line number from that codex.

To give an example, a full citation looks like this: *Gospel of the Egyptians* (NHC IV, 54:5). This means the line being cited comes from the version of the *Gospel of the Egyptians* in Nag Hammadi Codex IV (there's another copy of the same text in Codex III), page 54 of the codex, line 5. Most sources will use a comma to separate the folio and line number rather than a colon; I prefer to use the colon because it looks more like the chapter-and-verse citations we customarily use for biblical citations and is thus a bit less confusing. Technically, however, it should be pointed out that in the example above, 54:5 means page 54, line 5, rather than chapter 54, verse 5, as it would if it were a biblical text.

Modern critical translations of the Nag Hammadi writings, whatever language they are in, use the same folio-and-line citation, which is useful in comparing the different English translations available. Be aware, however, that the English versions of the NH texts found online are identical to the published versions in J. Robinson, ed., *The Nag Hammadi Library in English* (1988), except that they lack citation numbers, making them very challenging for doing serious scholarly work.

List of Nag Hammadi Tractates by Codex

I. (JUNG CODEX)

1. The *Prayer of the Apostle Paul*
2. The *Apocryphon of James*
3. The *Gospel of Truth* (1st copy)
4. The *Treatise on the Resurrection*
5. The *Tripartite Tractate* (Valentinian)

II.

1. The *Apocryphon of John* (1st copy—long version)
2. The *Gospel of Thomas*
3. The *Gospel of Philip*
4. The *Hypostasis of the Archons*
5. *On the Origin of the World* (1st copy)
6. The *Exegesis on the Soul*
7. The *Book of Thomas the Contender*

III.

1. The *Apocryphon of John* (2nd copy—translation 1 of short version)
2. The *Gospel of the Egyptians* (1st copy—translation 1)
3. *Eugnostos the Blessed* (1st copy)
4. The *Sophia of Jesus Christ* (1st copy)
5. The *Dialogue of the Savior*

IV.

1. The *Apocryphon of John* (3rd copy—long version. Copy of same Coptic translation as II.1)
2. The *Gospel of the Egyptians* (2nd copy—translation 2)

V.

1. *Eugnostos the Blessed* (2nd copy)
2. The *Apocalypse of Paul*
3. The *(First) Apocalypse of James*
4. The *(Second) Apocalypse of James*
5. The *Apocalypse of Adam*

VI.

1. The *Acts of Peter and the Twelve Apostles*
2. The *Thunder: Perfect Mind*
3. *Authoritative Teaching*
4. The *Concept of Our Great Power*
5. Plato, *Republic* 588a–589b
6. The *Discourse on the Eight and Ninth*
7. The *Prayer of Thanksgiving*
7a. Scribal Note
8. *Asclepius* 21–29

INTRODUCTION TO
"GNOSTICISM"

A Fourth-Century Christian Library

THE NAG HAMMADI CODICES

In 1945, a momentous event occurred for our understanding of early Christianity. A library of ancient texts, lost for 1,600 years, was rediscovered. Here's the story that scholars often tell about what happened that day. Outside the small town of Nag Hammadi in Upper Egypt, a man by the name of Muhammad 'Alī al-Sammān was out searching for *sabakh*, a manure-like fertilizer. Digging the soft soil in a mountainous area dotted with scores of caves once used as grave sites, the Jebel al-Tarif, 'Alī's fingers struck something that turned out to be a red earthenware jar. 'Alī thought perhaps he had found buried treasure. In fact, he had—but not the type he had wished for. Jiggling loose the pottery bowl that served as the jar's lid, he saw what he thought were flecks of gold, but these were only fragments of papyrus, turned gold with age. What he discovered inside the jar were some twelve or so **codices** or ancient books carefully written in **Coptic**—the last form of the language once spoken by the Egyptian pharaohs. Christian monks from the nearby monastic settlement of Chenoboskion had copied out the materials in these books some 1,500 years earlier by inking them carefully on papyrus.

'Alī took the books home and, determined to make some use of this otherwise useless find, turned them over to his mother, who tossed some of the aged and crumbling pages into the oven for kindling. Some weeks later 'Alī and his brothers avenged the murder of their father. They ambushed his murderer and (it is said) committed a horrific act of violence, hacking off his limbs, ripping out his heart, and devouring it on the spot. Fearing police investigation, 'Alī handed over the codices to a priest. A local teacher saw these codices and had one sent to Cairo to be appraised.

Once they reached Cairo, the codices ended up with individual antiquities dealers. The first, Codex I, was offered up for sale in New York and Paris. In 1951 Gilles Quispel, a professor from the Netherlands, urged the Jung Foundation of Zurich to purchase the codex for the birthday of the great depth-psychologist Carl Jung. The **Jung Codex** (Codex I) was eventually repatriated to Egypt and in 1956, all the **Nag Hammadi** codices were placed in the Coptic Museum in Cairo, Egypt, where they remain today. How much of this story is actually true remains unclear; certain salacious aspects of

MAP 1.1 Egypt and Nag Hammadi

the story (such as the gullibility of Egyptian peasants, or their act of cannibalism) certainly ought to make us suspicious. But whatever the true circumstances behind their discovery, the content of these ancient books were about to change our picture of early Christianity forever.

The NH manuscripts are in Coptic, which is an Egyptian language written not in hieroglyphs but in a modified Greek script (see Coptic Alphabet box on page 4). Coptic was the language of the Christian monastic culture that flourished in fourth-century Egypt, but it was not the language

FIGURE 1.1 The Nag Hammadi Codices

THE NAG HAMMADI CODICES AT A GLANCE

- 13 books or codices (sing.: **codex**)
- 52 writings, or 46 different works (6 are doubles or different versions we call **redactions** of the same text).
- 6 writings we had known before; others were completely unknown.

- Some are clearly not Christian texts (e.g., Plato's famous dialogue, *The Republic*), and some are difficult to classify by religious tradition.
- Written in Coptic but originally composed in Greek

in which the Nag Hammadi documents had originally been written. Although we do not have any of the complete originals of the NH documents, there are hints that the texts had been composed in Greek. To begin with, the documents use a high percentage of Greek loanwords; many of these were specialized terms from Greek philosophy, which simply did not exist in Egyptian languages. In certain passages, the scribes selected Greek words instead of Coptic words. Why would a scribe prefer

a Greek word over a Coptic word if he were writing in Coptic? Chances are he would have made this choice only if he were translating and felt that the Coptic word did not carry the same nuances or associations as the Greek word. Another clue that the texts were composed in Greek is that when we have two Coptic versions of the same text—as we do in the case of one of the most important documents from Nag Hammadi, the *Apocryphon of John* (*ApJn*)—they differ slightly from one

THE COPTIC ALPHABET

ⲁ	Ⲃ	Ⲅ	Ⲇ	Ⲉ	Ϛ	Ⲍ	Ⲏ
a	b v	g	d	e	s	dz	e ī
alpha	bida	gamma	daida	ei	so	zita	ita

Ⲑ	Ⲓ	Ⲕ	Ⲗ	Ⲙ	Ⲛ	Ⲝ	Ⲟ
th	i	k	l	m	n	ks	o
thita	jauta	kapa	laula	mi	ni	ksi	o

Ⲡ	Ⲣ	Ⲥ	Ⲧ	Ⲩ	Ⲫ	Ⲭ	Ⲯ
p	r	s	t	u	ph	kh	ps
pi	ro	sima	tau	he	phi	khi	psi

Ⲱ	Ⲩ	ϥ	ϧ	Ϩ	ⳉ	ϭ	†
ô û	š	f	x	h	dž	tš	ti
au	šei	fei	khei	hori	džaudžia	tšima	ti

Coptic has a few different dialects, the two most important of which are **Sahidic** and **Akhmimic**. We find both dialects used in different NH codices. Occasionally, we have the same text in two different Coptic dialects. Sahidic was the most common dialect for early Christian texts; Akhmimic flourished around the town of Akhmim in the fourth and fifth centuries but died out shortly after that. The use of Akhmimic at NH therefore helps us to date the texts in that dialect, since it survived for a relatively short period of time.

another. The simplest explanation for this is that two different translators, working independently, each came up with a slightly different translation of the same Greek document.

How did the NH codices end up being preserved? The most popular theory is that they were deliberately hidden there for posterity, sometime in the fourth century CE. The fourth century was a watershed era for the development of Christianity. At the beginning of the century, the Emperor **Constantine I** (306–336 CE) famously "converted" to Christianity following a dream or vision; the year was 312 CE, when his allegiance to Christianity won him a decisive victory over his enemy Maxentius at the **Battle at Milvian Bridge**. In 313 the Edict of Milan ended formal persecution of Christians and granted Roman citizens freedom to practice whatever religion they chose. Within a decade, Christians were granted legitimacy, community, power, the right to public assembly, and churches and basilicas. But their growing power also coincided with an increased need to police the boundaries between "licit" and "illicit" forms of Christianity. In the institutionalization and imperialization of the Christian Church, all those who dissented from a growing master narrative about Christianity were eventually silenced.

In 367 CE the powerful bishop of Alexandria, **Athanasius**, issued a formal document known as the *Festal Letter of 367* denouncing the use of certain Christian writings and outlining which books constituted proper Christian scripture—all that Christians needed for salvation. Athanasius's list of approved books closely resembles the list and order of books in the New Testament that Christians of today still use. Some suspect that it was around this time when cautions and prohibitions were being made against various writings, those not to be considered scripture. An unknown Egyptian monk made the choice at this time to preserve and hide the NH codices. Others think, however, that the codices were not so much hidden to preserve them for future generations as they were simply deposited in graves as a sort of "grave good"; it was not an unusual instance in late ancient Egypt to bury a book in a tomb, since books were luxury items that might demonstrate the prestige and wealth of their owner. Some even speculate that there was a connection between the writings in the NH books and a preoccupation about the nature of the afterlife; this is a major theme in many of the individual tractates in the Nag Hammadi collection.

THE NAG HAMMADI MANUSCRIPTS: SOME SPECIFICS

Although there are technically thirteen Nag Hammadi codices, what actually remains are twelve books, with eight pages (called *folia*) from a thirteenth book tucked inside the cover of the sixth codex. These eight pages form a complete text, the *Trimorphic Protennoia* (*TriProt*).

The codices are bound with leather, which had been tooled or decorated, and the most elaborate volume (Codex II) featured an *ankh* symbol (the ancient Egyptian hieroglyph for "life") on the cover. The covers were stiffened to make hardcover volumes by facing the inside of the soft leather covers with a material called **cartonnage**, a kind of papier-mâché made by gluing layers of older, leftover pieces of papyri writings together. A leather strap or thong held the codex closed. There appear to be two different styles of book covers—one more detailed than the other—which divide the codices into two different groups. Each group, we think, was assembled by a different monastic workshop, then at some point the two groups were collected together at Nag Hammadi.

If we match handwriting to determine which scribes were responsible for what writing, we know that a single scribe copied most of Codex I, but a different scribe copied the fourth writing in that book. This second scribe also copied the first and second writings of Codex XI. A third scribe was responsible for writings three and four of Codex XI and Codex VII; he also worked in a different Coptic dialect. We also know that at least three of the codices were made by scribes working in close proximity, because they left blank pages for each other to copy certain

texts. Codices IV and VIII apparently belonged together because they were copied by two scribes with nearly identical styles.

There are six writings for which we have duplicates, but none of those duplicates is in the same book. In addition, there are no duplicates in either of the two groups distinguished by different book covers. But one writing, which we call *On the Origin of the World*, is found in both Codex II and Codex XIII; both copies are nearly identical in wording and written with the same scribal hand. But at some point Codex XIII was torn apart, its copy of *OrigWld* discarded, and the remaining writing in that book inserted into Codex VI. We know that *OrigWld* was in Codex XIII because the last half-page is on the same page as the text someone was trying to preserve, and they could not keep this second tractate complete without including the half-page with the end of *OrigWld* on it. This tells us that there was some intentionality in the way that the texts were gathered, and that someone knew that it was unnecessary to have two copies of a single text in a single book. In fact, one of the scribes who worked on Codex VI included a note to say that he was concerned not to displease whoever had asked him to collect and copy the texts in the book by duplicating a text he already owned. Since there are duplications in the thirteen codices as a whole collection, however, this scribe probably wrote that note before all thirteen books were collected together.

WHY A CODEX OR BOOK?

In antiquity, Jewish communities and others collected texts in the form of scrolls or rolls (Latin **volumen** from "to roll," as in our English "volume") rather than books. But scrolls are not very practical. They are inconvenient for looking back to check a point, for instance. They are also unwieldy to stack and store, and difficult to fix once the ancient papyrus on which they were written had dried and split, which happened frequently as the scroll was constantly rolled and unrolled. Thus, between the second and the fourth centuries CE, the **codex** came to replace the scroll. These books could be carried conveniently, stacked a variety of ways for easy storage, and proved much more convenient for quick reference. Ancient Christians were early adopters of the codex form; by the fourth century all Christians relied on books (pl: *codices*) for their sacred texts.

Although the earliest books were waxed wooden tablets tied together, people soon found that **papyrus**—a plant from Egypt whose fibrous pith was sliced into thin strips, laid out into sheet form, pounded with a mallet, dried, and then written on—made a far better book. Papyrus was plentiful, renewable, cheap, and durable. An active scribal culture in Egypt kept papyrus books in production. Scribes were sometimes literate but often not; they worked as copyists and were paid by the line. By the middle of the fifth century, monks in monasteries had taken over most of the "freelance" scribal duties, and thus monasteries became centers where manuscripts were collected, copied, and then distributed to other monasteries for their libraries.

MAKING SENSE OF A COPTIC GNOSTIC COLLECTION

Much attention has been given to the individual texts contained in the Nag Hammadi library, but much less on how they came to be a "library" in the first place. At the front of this book is a table of the different codices and the individual texts that they contain. Were these texts compiled in the order in which we find them accidentally, or was there some larger organizing principle at work? This kind of study of the manuscripts as a whole is called **codicology**. There are some clues that we are dealing

with an intentional organizational plan. Codex I contains important texts, which probably circulated quite widely. An interesting thing about Codex I is that although many people assume that the NHL is Gnostic or **heretical**, there is nothing really heretical in this codex. Put simply, Codex I is the most un-Gnostic Gnostic collection in one volume.

There are other interesting patterns in the way that the individual volumes of the NHL are compiled. Codex V contains five treatises, four of which bear the title "**apocalypse**," so it is hard to imagine that this was an "accidental" collection. Codex VI contains many non-Christian writings, including a selection from Plato's *Republic*. Codex XI might reflect a possible liturgical order, meaning the volume was arranged so as to be useful for a community performing a religious service of some kind. Codex XIII, torn apart in antiquity, likely began with the

FIGURE 1.2 A page from the Berlin Codex, which contains the *Gospel of Mary*, the *Apocryphon of John*, the *Sophia of Jesus Christ*, and the *Acts of Peter*.

TABLE 1.1: Some Significant Coptic Gnostic Manuscripts in Brief

Codex Name	Find spot	Present Location	Date of Discovery or Acquisition	Language	Number of works	Approximate date
Berlin Codex	Akhmim, Egypt	Berlin, Staatsbibliothek	1896	Coptic, from Greek originals	Four: • *Gospel of Mary* • *Apocryphon of John* • *Acts of Peter* • *Sophia of Jesus Christ*	400–500?
Askew Codex	?	London, British Library	1773	Coptic, from Greek originals	Three: • *Pistis Sophia* • Untitled • untitled	350–400
Bruce Codex	Thebes, Egypt	Oxford, Bodleian Library	1769	Coptic, from Greek originals	Five: • *First Book of Jeu* • *Second Book of Jeu* • Untitled tractate • Untitled hymn • *The Passage of the Soul through the Archons of the Midst*	300–500
Codex Tchacos	El Minya, Egypt	Basel, The Maecenas Foundation for Ancient Art	1970s	Coptic from Greek originals	Four: • *Gospel of Judas* • *Letter of Peter to Philip* • *First Apocalypse of James* • *Allogenes* (not the same as the text of the same name found at Nag Hammadi)	ca. 300?

Apocryphon of John. If so, then four separate NH codices began with this same document. Finally, Codex IV seems to have been unnecessary if all the volumes were to stay together as a set, since it contains only two texts (**Apocryphon of John** and *Gospel of the Egyptians*), which were already in Codex III. This seems to indicate that the anonymous scribes put some attention into organizing the texts they received into categories.

HOW UNUSUAL IS IT TO HAVE THESE TEXTS?

Egypt's climate conditions mean that ancient manuscripts buried in the sand (or deposited in a jar as the NH codices were) can last virtually indefinitely. That said, we have remarkably few complete books from the same period, of the same general nature.

Those texts that exist are:

- The Berlin Codex (P. Berol. 8502) in Berlin's Staatsbibliothek. Discovered in 1896, it contains four separate works: the *Gospel of Mary*, the *ApJn*, the *SJC*, and the *Acts of Peter and the Twelve Disciples* (*ActsP12*).
- The Askew Codex (MS Add. 5114) in the British Library. Discovered in 1773, it contains three separate works: the *Pistis Sophia* and two untitled fragmentary treatises.
- The Bruce Codex (Bruce MS 96) in the Bodleian Library, Oxford. Actually two codices, these books were discovered in 1769. It contains six separate works: the *First Book of Jeu*, the *Second Book of Jeu*, an untitled tractate, an untitled hymn, and a brief passage describing the ascent of the soul through the **Archons** of the Middle.
- The **Tchacos Codex** (CT) in the Maecenas Institute, Basel, Switzerland. Discovered in El-Minya, Egypt, it contains four separate works: the *Letter of Peter to Philip*, *James* (identical with the NHL's *First Apocalypse of James* but more complete); the *Gospel of Judas*, and *Allogenes* (different than the NHL book of the same title).

HOW GOOD WERE THESE SCRIBES?

Fourth-century Egypt had what we call a scribal culture, in that there was an active trade in circulating, collecting, and copying manuscripts onto papyrus. Egyptian scribes were the best copyists in the ancient Mediterranean world, but they also worked under primitive conditions (imagine having no artificial sources of light beyond candles, and no eyeglasses, for example). Sometimes the scribes themselves were illiterate, or sometimes their Greek was not particularly good, so many failed to fully understand what they were copying.

Since it is such a well-known text, the brief fragment of Plato's *Republic* included in Codex VI provides us with a great opportunity to test how good the Nag Hammadi scribes were. We have enough adequate manuscript copies of this ancient text to recognize a bad one when we see it. And the copy we have at Nag Hammadi is a bad one. The scribe probably copied it because it was an ancient and edifying text, but he could not really appreciate or understand it. It is very possible that the copy the scribe possessed had been already corrupted by having been copied too many times. Taking Plato's *Republic* as a kind of cautionary tale, reconstructing the individual writings in the NHL is very difficult because we have neither a "control" copy in most cases (Plato's *Republic* is an exception) to compare our copy with nor, as in the case of New Testament manuscripts, a lot of copies of a single text to compare one against the other. When text is missing or corrupted, in most cases we cannot restore what was once there. Some of that material is gone forever.

WHO WERE THESE SCRIBES?

We know very little about the monks or copyists who worked on the NHL. James M. Robinson, the American scholar who headed the first translation project of the NHL into English, surmised that the codices might have come from a **Pachomian** monastery near where the books were originally found. Pachomian monasteries were great centers of copyist activity but not until after the fourth century, the earliest point at which the NHL could have been copied. Those who specialize in Pachomian monasticism doubt the hypothesis that the codices were copied there because (1) it is too early for Pachomian monks to have organized scriptoria, (2) the NH books themselves bear no traces of having physically come out of that setting, and (3) if they derived from a Pachomian milieu, they left no trace on the way that Pachomians thought and behaved as Christians.

Sometimes we are fortunate enough to hear directly from a scribe himself. This happens when a scribe signs his work or comments on what he has copied in the margins of the manuscript. If the comment comes at the end, this is called a **colophon**. We have a few colophons from NH. In Codex III one scribe identifies himself: "In the flesh my name is Gongessos [the Latin name Concessus]"; he continues, "but my spiritual [i.e., baptismal] name is 'Eugnostos.'" Another colophon says: "remember me also, my brethren, in your prayers: Peace to the holy ones and to the spirituals." (Codex II). This does not give us too much information, but the use of the term "spiritual" to refer to members of a fourth-century Christian community is somewhat unusual; it is actually a technical term from some of the NH writings themselves and, by the fourth century, had become associated with those the Church called "heretics." The fact that the scribe used such a word could imply that he was reading what he had copied and actually incorporating a much older vocabulary into his way of understanding the world. A final colophon in Codex VII reads: "The book belongs to the Fatherhood. The son himself wrote it. Bless me, O Father; I bless you, O Father, in peace, Amen." This, too, draws on language directly from the texts themselves, seeming to indicate that the scribes had some affinity for the ideas they were copying.

DATING AND LOCATING THE CODICES

One of our best ways to date manuscripts is to take a look at the cartonnage, the stiffening material from the book covers. Cartonnage can provide a solid date (such as from a dated letter reused to stiffen the cover), or else make reference to a historical event that took place on a specific date which we can then cross-reference (such as the date in which a bishop was appointed). In the case of the NHL, analysis of the cartonnage fragments produces three dates: 341 CE, 346 CE, and 348 CE. The kinds of documents used in stiffening the covers vary widely, from administrative and military rationing receipts to personal correspondence, and even a short fragment of the book of Genesis. Those who analyzed the cartonnage fragments concluded that the types of papyri fragments inside the covers probably came from a typical Egyptian town dump rather than from a monastery, suggesting that the covers of the books, if not the whole books themselves, were produced in an urban environment in the middle of the fourth century.

WERE THESE TEXTS REALLY GNOSTIC SCRIPTURE?

Today, the writings of the NHL are not accepted as scripture by any modern branch of Christianity. This is partly because the **canon** of books that most Christians consider scripture was fixed in antiquity, and even the discovery of new books cannot change the fact that the canon is closed. Some Christian churches, however, object to the nature of the NH writings as heretical; they see these writings as competing with the writings of the New Testament for the status of scripture as the holy, authoritative "word of God."

It is important to understand what many Christians often mean when they use the word "scripture." Scripture usually indicates a body of texts that a religion or group of people consider authoritative and sacred or "revealed" by a divine source to a human agent. In this sense, some of the Nag Hammadi texts (not all) certainly qualify as scripture. On the other hand, Christianity was still a new religion in the second century and as such did not yet have consensus on which writings constituted scripture apart from the **Septuagint** (the Old Testament, or the Hebrew Bible translated into Greek by and for Greek-speaking Jews in antiquity; also identified as LXX). As Christianity grew out of Judaism, it took with it the Jewish scriptures as authoritative and sacred. What we see happening among the Nag Hammadi documents is a shifting attitude toward Jewish scripture as "sacred." Christianity needed to define itself as different from Judaism, and part of the process of doing that necessarily involved rethinking the category of scripture. What was to differentiate Christianity from Judaism if they used the same sacred texts? The process of embracing some Jewish scriptures and rejecting others—or of developing a different way of interpreting Jewish scripture that was distinctively "Christian"—took time to develop. It was also a project with which all Christians of the second century were engaged.

In the broader context of the Roman Empire, it was fairly unusual for a religious group to have its own set of scripture. It was a feature of Judaism, to be sure, but other pagan religions had no sacred texts. Therefore it was not necessarily a "natural" choice for a religious community to orient itself around a collection of writings. However, Christianity as a movement involved the production of a very large number of writings. These were of varied sorts: letters to Christian communities, biographies or "gospels" of Jesus, sermons or homilies, and interpretations of Jewish texts, to mention just a few. The NHL gives us a good idea of how diverse Christian writings could be, and they also teach us which sorts of texts were more commonly circulated. For example, there are quite a few apocalyptic writings in the NHL and also many texts labeled "gospels," although those gospels do not share a common literary form.

Ultimately, the Nag Hammadi codices were not meant to function as alternative bibles, or an alternative to the Bible. While some people talk about them as scripture, this attributes a status to them that they did not have when they were written. (In fact, many of the New Testament writings did not at that time have the status of scripture.) There is a common claim among some modern Christians that the Nag Hammadi texts represent an "alternative" or "heretical" Bible, but this is not true. Unfortunately, this view is probably made worse from modern collections with such misleading titles as *The Gnostic Bible*. These writings were not meant to replace the gospels, or the letters of Paul, or the Hebrew Bible. They were to be read *alongside* those books, most likely to give inspired interpretation to them. In short, the Gnostics of the second century probably drew upon a very similar set of scripture as their opponents. What differed was their interpretation of those texts.

QUESTIONS TO CONSIDER

1. How might the discovery of the Nag Hammadi writings force you to think about early Christianity differently?

2. What reasons can you think of for the way the codices came to be deposited in the desert?

3. Look at the codices list at the front of this book. Do they appear, at face value, to be a random collection? Or can you detect any patterns from the titles?

KEY TERMS

heretical	Jung Codex	Pachomian	Sahidic	colophon
apocalypse	Athanasius	Coptic	codicology	Festal Letter of 367 CE
Apocryphon	redaction	papyrus	Battle of the Milvian Bridge	Tchacos Codex (also called the Codex Tchacos)
codex (pl: codices)	*volumen*	Constantine I	canon	
cartonnage	Nag Hammadi	Septuagint	Akhmimic	

FOR FURTHER READING

Doresse, Jean. *The Discovery of the Nag Hammadi Texts: A Firsthand Account of the Expedition that Shook the Foundations of Christianity.* Rochester, VT: Inner Traditions International Press, 1986. Now out of date in terms of scholarship, Doresse provides one of the earliest accounts of the discovery of the NHL, written for an interested general audience.

Meyer, Marvin. *The Gnostic Discoveries: The Impact of the Nag Hammadi Library.* San Francisco: HarperOne, 2005. A highly recommended introduction for beginning and intermediate students.

Websites

www.gnosis.org A site from a modern Gnostic church, this website has a wonderful text archive, which includes all the modern translations of the Nag Hammadi documents plus many other ancient writings. It is also searchable, which makes their archive an invaluable tool for research. Be aware that many of the site's essays are written from a non-academic perspective for people seeking to learn more about modern **Gnosticism**, or contemporary spiritual interpretations of ancient documents.

www.nag-hammadi.com A nice overview of the Nag Hammadi discoveries, in several languages.

Coptic Textbooks

Lambdin, Thomas. *Introduction to Sahidic Coptic.* Macon, GA: Mercer University Press, 1987.

Layton, Bentley. *Coptic in 20 Lessons: Introduction to Sahidic Coptic with Exercises and Vocabularies.* Louvain: Peeters, 2007.

2

The Problem with Gnosticism

The Nag Hammadi Library is usually characterized as a Gnostic library. What is **gnosis**, the Greek root word at the heart of Gnosticism? *Gnosis*, in Greek, means "knowledge." But it is not simply a matter of knowing things, or knowing about things (in fact, there's a separate Greek word for this kind of knowledge, *episteme*, from which we get the philosophical term "epistemology"). Gnosis is a special kind of insight into the nature of reality.

In the 1999 movie *The Matrix*, the hero Neo has a pivotal meeting with Morpheus, the man who is to change his life completely.

In a sort of surreal "fireside chat," Morpheus reveals to Neo the true nature of the world as Neo knows it:

> MORPHEUS: Let me tell you why you're here. You're here because you know something. What you know you can't explain. But you feel it. You've felt it your entire life. That there's something wrong with the world. You don't know what it is but it's there, like a splinter in your mind driving you mad. It is this feeling that has brought you to me. Do you know what I'm talking about?

> NEO: The Matrix?

> MORPHEUS: Do you want to know what it is? The Matrix is everywhere. It is all around us, even now in this very room. You can see it when you look out your window or when you turn on your television. You can feel it when you go to work, when you go to church, when you pay your taxes. It is the world that has been pulled over your eyes to blind you from the truth.

> NEO: What truth?

> MORPHEUS: That you are a slave, Neo. Like everyone else you were born into bondage, born into a prison that you cannot smell or taste or touch.

Morpheus's sentence, "It is the world that has been pulled over your eyes to blind you from the truth," could have come directly from the pages of an ancient **Gnostic** document. *Gnosis* is the recognition of that truth: that reality is deception; that we are enslaved in a prison that we cannot smell or taste or touch; and that there exists, apart from this deceptive reality, another place that is our true origin and source. *Gnosis*,

FIGURE 2.1 In this key scene from *The Matrix* (1999), Morpheus (Laurence Fishburne) begins Neo's (Keanu Reeves) awakening from the Matrix.

therefore, is the transcendental recognition that one does not belong to this world but instead dwells briefly in it. Like Neo, we also have a responsibility to "wake up" to reality, to save ourselves from the world that has been pulled over our eyes.

That an ancient concept like *gnosis* shows up in a popular Hollywood blockbuster like *The Matrix* seems to underscore a basic point: this ancient idea resonates with us today. In this sense, **Gnosticism**—the idea that *gnosis* is a necessary form of awakening from perceptual sleep—is also a philosophy that transcends place and time. There can be ancient Gnosticism and modern Gnosticism, or Christian Gnosticism and non-Christian Gnosticism. *Gnosis* is transcendent, because as an insight it links human individuals with a higher, eternal, purer, indivisible realm. Those who possess *gnosis* recognize that they are not of this world but of that other one, the existence of which remains invisible and imperceptible to the rest of us trapped in ignorance.

Most of us agree that Gnosticism is a philosophy, a way of thinking about the world. But here's where it gets complicated: the term "Gnosticism" is also used to describe an ancient movement or school. But as far as we can tell it was never known by the modern term "Gnosticism." In Greek, *gnostikos* was an adjective, but it applied to people in various ways—it could be an insult, or some people could approvingly describe themselves or an idea as "gnostic." Thus Gnosticism is kind of a slippery thing to talk about from the perspective of a historian rather than that of a philosopher. As a term, it only developed in the eighteenth century as a way of talking about a philosophical movement that had its birth in the second century.

In fact, one might ask, "is it fair to speak of Gnosticism as a movement at all?" As with any religion or movement ending with -*ism*, the word implies a kind of universal, generalized movement. The same is implied in such constructions as "*the* Gnostic myth" or "Gnostic understanding of scripture." In reality, there is, or was, no single

Gnostic myth, nor was there one single understanding of any ancient metaphysical system. The ancient so-called Gnostic texts all give variations on a singular theme; although there are similarities, part of what makes our work interesting is to discover the differences. It is in the differences between narratives and worldviews that we begin to learn most about the lively debates that characterized the world of the second century, the era in which these Gnostic ideas came to be most actively and widely debated.

What makes this textbook different from other books on NH is that it does not presume that the entire NHL is Gnostic. Many writings in it have nothing to do with the pursuit of *gnosis*; not all the ideas we find in it are Gnostic, either. So rather than imposing an inaccurate term on the various writings contained in the NHL, this book approaches the entire collection as a miscellany—a variety of Christian and non-Christian texts—some Gnostic and others not, which came together to represent a range of ancient voices.

DID GNOSTICISM REALLY EXIST?

A century ago, scholars were confident they knew what Gnosticism was. It was a timeless religious movement characterized by distinct features. These features were already outlined eighteen hundred years ago by a small group of early Christians, who considered themselves defenders of "right-minded" Christianity. According to these Christians, classic characteristics of the Gnostics included:

- Dualism: Gnostics distinguish between a higher, unknowable god and a lower, inferior god (called a **Demiurge**). They held that ancient Jews and Christians mistakenly thought this lower, inferior god was the god of the Old and New Testaments. The higher, unknowable god exists in the realm of Light; everyone else persists in darkness and ignorance.

- The lower, inferior god created humankind in conjunction with his seven angels. Thus humans are blind and ignorant because we are created in that image of a blind and ignorant god. Only those who possess *gnosis* differ from the rest of humanity, because they have awakened to their enslavement.

- An attitude of social revolt: Gnostics did not feel as if they needed to play by the rules, since the rules were established by ignorant beings. They considered themselves a spiritual elite, separate from the majority and from the rules that govern society.

- A rejection of the material cosmos: Gnostics felt that the visible and material world was an inferior creation of an ignorant god; they were only trapped in this lower cosmos but knew themselves to be from a higher source.

- A hatred of their physical bodies: Gnostics felt their bodies to be mere shells, inferior and often polluted receptacles of flesh that imprisoned their souls.

- Along with contempt for their physical bodies, Gnostics were sexually promiscuous in ways that more conservative Christians found repellent.

- Gnostics considered themselves to be "saved": thus Gnostics felt that they had no need to behave ethically. Because they considered themselves from a higher realm, they had no need to behave in ways that would lead to their salvation by avoiding sin. Nor did they need the guidance of bishops or the sacraments, or even to refrain from sinful or immoral behavior. This is a position called "predestination," and it has always been a controversial one, since it implies that a god "preselects" those who receive salvation.

It's important to repeat that this set of characteristics emerged from those who considered themselves the enemies of the Gnostics, those members of what was to emerge two centuries later as the dominant form of Christianity—the **Catholic Church**. But these characteristics rarely emerge from Gnostic texts themselves. Since Catholicism later either destroyed or suppressed virtually all of the Gnostic writings that once existed, all we have (or, more accurately, *had*) to understand Gnosticism came from anti-Gnostic polemics.

HANS JONAS AND GNOSTICISM

One of the most prominent scholars of Gnosticism to have emerged in the twentieth century was a German-born professor of philosophy, **Hans Jonas** (1903–93), who taught for many years at the New School in New York City.

In 1958 Jonas released a hugely influential study titled *The Gnostic Religion*, the English translation of his German two-volume work, *Gnosis und spätantike Geist* (1934–54). In this book Jonas drew on his training in German existentialism, which he had studied at the hands of two famous philosophers, Edmund Husserl and Martin Heidegger. Far from being repelled or scandalized by the Gnostics, Jonas considered Gnosticism a philosophical movement akin to existentialism and nihilism, both of which had emerged in response to various social and historical forces in play in antiquity. These forces produced a sort of spiritual crisis in which people

FIGURE 2.2 The German Jewish philosopher Hans Jonas penned one of the most influential studies of ancient Gnosticism, *The Gnostic Religion* (1958).

felt themselves to be alone in the cosmos. The classic Gnostic, therefore, was a loner intellectual with a sort of melancholy rebelliousness. Gnostics did not gather into communities; they did not have rituals (not group rituals, anyway); and they were anti-Christian in a profound sense. Gnosticism could be classified according to a series of typological characteristics: for example, it was dualistic, mythological in character, and "impious" in the sense that it broke the established rules for how people behaved in relation to the Divine.

Jonas did not see Gnosticism as a Christian **heresy** but as a separate religio-philosophical tradition that developed alongside Christianity, not from it. Gnosticism and Christianity were parallel movements. It was therefore possible to look for the pre-Christian origins of Gnosticism. An entire school of Gnostic Studies—particularly active in Germany and represented in the work of scholars such as Kurt Rudolph, developed with the intent to discover Gnosticism's origins and subsequent developments in the history of religions. To this school, "Christian Gnosticism" was only one form of a broader, more ancient trend of practicing personal salvation through gnosis.

Jonas's work has remained hugely influential; not only does it stand behind contemporary "Gnostic" movies such as *The Matrix*, it also guides some of the best modern scholars of Gnosticism. For instance, the German scholar Christoph Markschies has recently set out a number of defining characteristics of ancient *gnosis*:

1. The experience of a completely otherworldly, distant, supreme god.
2. The introduction of further divine figures (conditioned by this experience) or by the splitting up of existing figures into figures that are closer to human beings than the remote supreme god.
3. The estimation of the world and matter as evil creation and an experience of the alienation of the Gnostic in the world.
4. The introduction of a distinct creator God or assistant: within the Platonic tradition he is called "craftsman"—Greek *demiurgos*—and is sometimes described in Gnostic document as merely ignorant, but sometimes also as evil.
5. The explanation of this state of affairs by a mythological drama in which a divine element, one that falls from its sphere into an evil world, slumbers in human beings of one class as a divine spark and can be freed from this state.
6. Knowledge (*gnosis*) about this state, which, however, can be gained only through a redeemer figure from the other world who descends from a higher sphere and ascends to it again.
7. The redemption of human beings through the knowledge of "that God (or the spark) in them."
8. A tendency toward dualism of different types, which can express itself in the concept of God, in the opposition of spirit and matter, and in the concept of the human being as constituted of body plus soul (C. Markschies, *Gnosis: An Introduction* [Continuum Publishers, 2003: 16–17]).

Are Markschies's characteristics on the mark or overly generalizing? The only way to determine this is subjective: to work through the ancient writings themselves, and then to see whether or not Markschies appears to be right.

THE MESSINA DEFINITION

Following the wide release and popularity of Jonas's *The Gnostic Religion*, interest in Gnosticism began to grow worldwide. And then came the Nag Hammadi Library. Although the texts were discovered in 1945, it took some time after their discovery for the texts to be circulated and translated; few scholars read Coptic (the language of these texts) and World War II had disrupted a great deal of scholarship, particularly in Germany where biblical studies and theology had its strongest specialists. Slowly, however, a global effort to work on these texts began to coalesce.

In the Italian city of Messina in 1966, prominent scholars of Gnosticism gathered for a groundbreaking conference on the origins of Gnosticism (called, informally, the Messina Conference) to debate what this thing called Gnosticism was in the wake of Jonas's book. These scholars drew up a document called the **Messina Definition**, designed to define Gnosticism.

Once the Messina Definition was in place, two interesting things happened. First, scholars of Gnosticism were free to reexamine all the existing writings that had previously been defined as Gnostic (not to mention all the ancient figures who had also been defined as Gnostic), and to reevaluate whether these texts and figures now fit the new definition. If they still fit, then they could be safely be called Gnostic. If they did not they were something else, some *other* thing that

had not yet been defined or classified. The problem with this sort of scholarship is that it lets a modern definition drive the way we read, understand, and classify an ancient document rather than letting it stand on its own merit. Scholars created and defined what Gnosticism was, then searched ancient texts to find it (or not find it) there. Since this sort of activity is generally subjective, scholars disagreed on which texts fit the definition and which did not. Thus while a *definitional* consensus was reached, actual consensus in terms of which texts were Gnostic could no longer be reached. The consequence of this definition is that, still today, depending on the scholar you ask, you are likely to receive very different answers concerning which ancient text or figure is Gnostic, and which is not. For instance, consider table 2.1. Here, some prominent scholars of Gnosticism weigh in on whether they consider a selection of texts from NH to be Gnostic. As you can see, there is quite a range, and no consensus at all.

The second significant problem to emerge from the Messina Conference concerns how scholars work. While earlier generations of scholars tended to favor generalizations, creating lists of

THE MESSINA DEFINITION

"[Gnosticism is] a coherent series of characteristics that can be summarized in the idea of a divine spark in man, deriving from the divine realm, fallen into this world of fate, birth, and death, and needing to be awakened by the divine counterpart of the self in order to be finally reintegrated. Compared with other conceptions of a 'devolution' of the divine, this idea is based ontologically on the conception of a downward movement of the divine whose periphery (often called **Sophia** [Wisdom] or **Ennoia** [Thought]) had to submit to the fate of entering into a crisis and producing—even if only indirectly—this world, upon which it cannot turn its back, since it is necessary for it to recover the *pneuma,* a dualistic conception on a monistic background, expressed in a double movement of devolution and reintegration."

The Messina Definition was written by scholars for scholars, hence it is not very user friendly. The key idea that it expresses, though, is that Gnosticism is characterized by an underlying myth: that humans have within them a divine part that came from the higher realms, a part that we have forgotten. When this part or "spark" is awakened, we can recognize our own origins in these higher realms.

TABLE 2.1: Are the Nag Hammadi Tractates Gnostic? Some Scholars Consider the First Three Nag Hammadi Codices

CODEX I	Michel Tardieu	Jean-Pierre Mahé	Paul-Hubert Poirier	Clemens Scholten
Prayer of the Apostle Paul	Yes	Yes	Yes	–
Apocryphon of James	Yes	Yes	Yes	No
Gospel of Truth	Yes	Yes	Yes	–
Treatise on the Resurrection	Yes	Yes	Yes	–
CODEX II				
Apocryphon of John	Yes	Yes	Yes	–
Gospel of Thomas	No	–	Yes	No
Gospel of Philip	Yes	Yes	Yes	–
Hypostasis of the Archons	Yes	Yes	Yes	
On the Origin of the World	Yes	Yes	Yes	–
Exegesis on the Soul	No	–	Yes	No
Book of Thomas the Contender	No	–	Yes	No
CODEX IV				
Gospel of the Egyptians	Yes	Yes	Yes	–
Eugnostos	No	–	Yes	–
Sophia of Jesus Christ	No	–	Yes	–
Dialogue of the Savior	No	–	Yes	No

Table adapted from Michael Williams, *Rethinking Gnosticism* (Princeton, NJ: Princeton University Press, 1996), 47.

broad characteristics or general definitions, scholars nowadays are more likely to favor approaches that consider texts and figures on their own merits. This approach implies that *any* definition of Gnosticism is bound to be incorrect or unhelpful, since there are always too many exceptions to the rule for the core definition to be accurate.

RETHINKING "GNOSTICISM": MICHAEL WILLIAMS AND KAREN KING

In 1996 an American scholar of Gnosticism, Michael Allen Williams, wrote *Rethinking Gnosticism: Arguments for Dismantling a Dubious Category*, which essentially toppled the primacy of the Messina Definition. Gnosticism could not be defined usefully, he argued, because every single supposedly Gnostic feature could either be present or absent from any single supposedly Gnostic text. Williams used as his core corpus of writings the NHL. No one would doubt that these writings qualify as Gnostic, and yet they neither completely fit the Messina Definition of Gnostic nor do they exhibit the features that Hans Jonas and his predecessors had laid out. For example, consider Jonas's claim that Gnosticism has a "mythological character." There are a few key NH texts that have a markedly "mythological character," but many more that do not. The implications are significant: If the Nag Hammadi texts, which many scholars agreed were all Gnostic, do not fit the key characteristics or definitions of Gnosticism, what could? Williams's key point is that no ancient text actually reflects Gnosticism, and that is no surprise, because the term itself is a modern invention. Ultimately, Williams called for the term "Gnosticism" to be abandoned, at least as it applies to ancient documents.

In 2005, Karen King, another prominent American scholar, published a landmark study titled *What Is Gnosticism?* Like Williams, King argued persuasively that Gnosticism should be abandoned as a classification. She pointed out that the term was not used in the ancient world but was entirely a modern construction. What's more, Gnosticism was created as a sort of foil for "normative" or "mainstream" Christianity. It was little more than a fancy word for "heresy," defined against what mainstream Christianity was *not*.

King and her colleagues argue that there was no such thing as mainstream Christianity in the ancient world. Mainstream implies popularity, what everyone was doing. But we simply don't have enough data from the second century to evaluate what everyone was doing, or what the most popular form of Christianity was. What if a supposedly heretical form of Christianity had been the most popular? A useful example is the case of the popular and influential church leader **Valentinus**, who taught in Rome in the middle of the second century CE. There came to be, by all accounts, many Valentinian churches that followed his brand of Christianity, and Valentinus himself had only narrowly missed being elected bishop of Rome (a key position now known as the pope). Our information suggests that at least in certain places and certain times, **Valentinianism** might have been

so popular as to have been considered "mainstream." Nevertheless, his more proto-orthodox contemporaries branded Valentinus a Gnostic and later, he was considered a dangerous **heretic**. Consequently, many modern Christians aren't comfortable with the idea that Valentinianism might have been popular enough to have been mainstream, preferring to assume or argue that their own forms of Christianity have always been normative, dominant, or mainstream. Many Roman Catholics will say, for instance, that there has *always* been a Catholic Church, and that it was *always* recognized as the dominant form of Christianity. In the first Christian centuries, the Catholic Church had a fight on its hands against those pesky Gnostics who tried (and ultimately failed) to unseat it. This way of reading the historical evidence depends on seeing the Gnostics as limited, disorganized, and ultimately doomed to fail because they were arrogant elitists who did not understand the Truth. But that is not the only way of reading the evidence, and Karen King calls for us to be careful about what the ancient documents say and do not say.

Michael Williams and Karen King's call to abandon the terms "Gnostic" and "Gnosticism" have been tremendously influential in modern scholarship. In this book you will find the Nag Hammadi documents discussed as Christian or pagan, or having Platonist or Stoic resonances, or identified according to subcategorizations as **Valentinian** or **Sethian**, but you won't find any references to the texts or ideas in them as Gnostic. On the other hand, to abandon the term "Gnosticism" completely has caused headaches and inconvenience for modern scholars: we don't have many better words, and the use of these words is already deeply entrenched. You may hear bad jokes about how and why we study someone like Valentinus, "the artist formerly known as Gnostic." Yet we should persist in talking about Gnosticism only very carefully, because Williams and King are right: the term is a modern designation and, functionally, tells us very little about the ancient texts we are about to study.

THE YALE SCHOOL

Scholars still actively debate whether it is accurate to talk about ancient Gnosticism. Although Michael Williams and Karen King have been very influential, others have argued that it is indeed correct to talk about the existence of people who called themselves Gnostics (*Gnostikoi*). The strongest proponents of this view come from Yale University, thus the perspective is known informally as the "**Yale School**" of Gnosticism. The best representatives of the Yale School are the American scholars Bentley Layton and David Brakke and the German scholar Stephen Emmel. These scholars argue that there were in fact many people in the ancient world who saw themselves as possessing superior knowledge or gnosis, and for whom the pursuit of gnosis was a spiritual goal. Even though the terms "Gnosticism" or "Gnostic" are not found in the ancient literature, they note, the term "*gnosis*" appears frequently. Thus what ties together a variety of ancient writings is this emphasis on *gnosis* as a positive goal or achieved state.

The designation "Yale School" is somewhat misleading, in that it seems to suggest that those scholars who contend that Gnosticism and Gnostics did in fact exist are confined to those with a connection to Yale University. In fact, there are many outstanding scholars in North America and Europe who argue the same thing. Thus the term is best used colloquially and with some reservations.

HERESY VERSUS ORTHODOXY

Before we move away from debates around Gnosticism, Gnostics, and *gnosis*, there is another commonly employed set of words that are often leveled at the so-called Gnostics: heretics and heresy. Heretics are, by definition, Christians who have broken away from authoritative Christian beliefs and practices, sometimes called **orthodoxy**. The word comes from a combination of two Greek words, *ortho*, meaning straight or correct (think of an orthodontist, who makes teeth straight), and *doxos*, which means thinking or opinion. So people who are orthodox are, literally, "straight thinking."

In fact, Christianity of the second century had developed an orthodoxy, but it was not yet the dominant, agreed-upon, or imperially supported form of Christianity. The orthodox, or better, proto-orthodox, were one set of persuasive voices among others. But in that century, the proto-orthodox bishops drew boundaries between what they saw as the so-called right sort of Christianity, and what they perceived their opponents to be doing. They called these opponents heretics, from the Greek *haeresis*, which means choice or division. So heretics were, literally, splitters: people who diverged from what these boundary-drawers felt was right-thinking Christianity.

The terms "orthodoxy" and "heresy" are no longer as helpful as we once found them. On a basic level, to talk about Christian orthodoxy in the first few centuries is misleading because it can be so easily confused with Christian Orthodoxy (note the capital "O"), a formal division of Christianity that occurred much later. **Orthodox Christianity** is one of the chief branches of modern Christianity and the predominant form of Christianity in Eastern Europe and the Middle East. To keep from confusing second-century orthodoxy from later Orthodox Christianity, we might use the term "proto-orthodox" rather than "orthodox" or "Catholic" to talk about Christians whose views are still held as authoritative in modern Christianity.

A second problem with the terms "orthodoxy" and "heresy" is that they were developed by certain second-century figures to characterize themselves and differentiate them from outsiders. They are what sociologists and anthropologists call *emic* terms, labels developed only within a social group. In other words, many people might have considered themselves to be orthodox and others, heretics. The terms are subjective and therefore not very useful. The term "heretic" in particular came to develop strongly negative overtones. Many of the people who came to be labeled thus would have been shocked and offended by being called this by their opponents.

Those of us who work in Gnosticism are much more likely to be wary of past labels. We imagine a situation, instead, where those who some people called heretics comprised a strong and powerful majority in some areas, whereas the self-proclaimed orthodox were very likely a small and vocal minority who saw themselves as purists. In reality, we have no way of knowing how the vast majority of early Christians understood their religion. We have only a few voices and most of what they say counts as "history written by the winners." The discovery of the NHL only confirms our suspicions that the actual picture of Christianity in the Roman Empire must have been very different from the picture we get solely from reading the accounts of the self-proclaimed straight-thinking Christians.

In order to remember who was on whose side during the middle of the second century, leaders of the developing Christian orthodoxy developed a system of what we call **heresiology**—the study of heresy. These leaders penned important polemical works that often slandered other Christians, characterizing and mischaracterizing their form of Christian belief and practice as heretical. Here are some of our most important heresiologists:

- **Irenaeus of Lyons** (second century CE–ca. 202 CE), a bishop in Gaul (modern France). Author of the five-volume *Exposure and Refutation of Knowledge (Gnosis) So-Called* (we call it by its Latin title *Adversus Omnes Haereses* [*Adv. Haer.*]). Irenaeus's work on defining Gnosticism was (and remains) tremendously influential. Specifically attacking Valentinianism (see chaps. 6 and 7) and the source(s) of Gnostic heresy, Irenaeus preserved enough of his opponents' writings to allow us to reconstruct them fairly accurately. Until 1945, *Adv. Haer.* was our best surviving account of Gnosticism.

- **Hippolytus of Rome**, (ca. 170–236 CE), author of *Refutation of All Heresies* (*Refutatio Omnium Haeresium* [*Ref.*]). A complex figure, Hippolytus was anti-pope (or rival bishop) of Rome. He catalogues thirty-three Gnostic sects and systems, some of which he reproduces from Irenaeus, but some of which introduces new material.

- **Clement of Alexandria** (ca. 150–215 CE), author of the *Stromateis* [*Strom.*] or *Miscellanies*. Clement uses the term "*gnosis*" in a positive sense, while denouncing Gnostics as heretics. He also reproduces precious fragments of Gnostic writings otherwise destroyed, including excerpts of Valentinus's writings and of his student Theodotus.

- **Origen of Alexandria** (ca. 185–254 CE), author of *Against Celsus* (*Contra Celsum*). Origen, a sophisticated thinker, composed his treatise *Against Celsus* to refute the pagan philosopher Celsus's description of Christianity. Origen explained that the system Celsus knew was not orthodox Christianity but a form of heresy. *Contra Celsum* preserves some Gnostic writings that Origen reproduced in order to refute his opponent.

- **Epiphanius of Salamis** (ca. 376–400 CE), author of the *Panarion* ("Medicine Chest").

The *Panarion* identifies perceived heresies and treats them as if they were diseases to Christianity that needed to be cured, or more correctly, amputated. The *Panarion* also preserves important documents, including the Valentinian teacher Ptolemy's *Letter to Flora*, a female student in second-century Rome.

Sometimes the heresiologists got their hands on important Christian texts that are now otherwise lost, and in the process of refuting them, reproduced the original texts in their entirety. When this happens, those of us who study early Christianity feel very fortunate. Other times, heresiologists summarized Gnostic writings that they had before them, in which case we are reliant on the accuracy and truthfulness of those summaries, since the original writings are now lost. On one or two occasions, we have discovered the original writings that we can now check back against the summaries of the heresiologists; we have learned that often they did not do a bad job of summarizing the texts they found repugnant. But every now and then, the heresiologists tended to extremes in their polemic against heresy. Rather than simply describing practices different from their own in neutral terms, they often enough went for sensationalism. The two most frequent charges we find are:

(a) the heretic engages in highly immoral behavior, particularly of a sexual kind;

(b) the heretic worships demons/the devil/ practices witchcraft.

Here, for example, are some passages from Epiphanius's *Panarion* on the "Gnostics":

> They hold their women in common. And if someone from out of town belonging to their persuasion comes to visit, they have a signal for use by men unto women and by women unto men: the hand is held out, in greeting of course, and a tickling stroke is made in the palm of the hand, as to indicate secretly that the visitor is of the same religion as they. Thereupon, having recognized one another they hasten to dine. And they serve lavish meat dishes and wines, even if they

are in penury. Then, after a drinking party where so to speak they have engorged their veins with gormandizing, they turn to their frenzied passion.

> And husband withdraws from wife and says, speaking to his own wife, "Arise and have the love feast with your brother." And when the wretches have had intercourse with one another . . . in the passion of illicit sexual activity, then they lift up their blasphemy to heaven. The woman and the man take the male emission in their own hands and stand gazing toward heaven with the impurity in their hands; and of course they pray—I refer to the so-called Stratiotics and the Gnostics—offering what is in their hands aptly to the Parent of the Entirety. And they say, "We offer unto you this gift, the body of Christ (the anointed)" and then they eat it, partaking of their own filthiness. And they say, "This is the body of Christ (the anointed), and this is the Passover because of which our bodies feel passion and are constrained to confess the passion of Christ (the anointed)." (*Pan.* 26.4.1–7, trans. Layton, *Gnostic Scriptures*, 206–7)

So how do we account for something like this? Epiphanius does not present this as gossip or hearsay; he tells us that he has firsthand knowledge of these people. But was Epiphanius telling the truth about them? This is still an active debate among scholars. Here are some possibilities:

- Perhaps this is a stock form of slander. Accusations of witchcraft, cannibalism, and incest are fairly standard in many polemical writings, and this is what the ancient Romans accused proto-orthodox Christians of doing. It is also a common trope in American popular culture: think of the characterization of Appalachia in something like the famous American horror movie *Deliverance* (1972) (or, more recently, *Wrong Turn* [2003]).

- Perhaps this was a misunderstanding of some sort. When ancient Romans heard about the Christian ritual known as the Eucharist, they also heard rumors about Christians consuming the "body" and "blood" of their savior. Of course, this did not mean that Christians were cannibals, but Romans still misunderstood. Perhaps, in the same way,

Epiphanius misunderstood the symbolic dimensions of one group's rituals and took them literally.

- Given that Christianity was still in its experimental phase and there was no established way to do a ritual, perhaps some fringe group did indeed engage in rituals which we might find repugnant. However, the Gnostic documents that we have from Nag Hammadi in no way lead us to believe that those reading or using those texts engaged in ritual sex.

How do we know which one of these options is right? Unfortunately, we don't. But here are just some of the disciplines and tools we can draw on to help us make an informed guess:

- *Anthropology* teaches us about human behavior and offers us useful comparisons from other societies, including our own.
- *Sociology* teaches us about the construction of human communities, and the correlation between types of religious commitment and types of groups or communities.
- *Ritual Studies* teaches us about the dynamics of ritual and its function and forms within a group. It offers us a great deal of comparative material as well as theoretical models that can be helpful.
- *Textual criticism* teaches us how to read a text "between the lines," looking for things like models, form, and authorial intent.
- *Rhetorical criticism* teaches us about the use of formal speech, language, metaphor, imagery, exaggeration, and the impact of formal language.

This book draws on all these approaches, so readers will become practiced in reading NH scriptures in a way that unlocks more of their mysteries than if we were simply reading with the assumption that the heresiologists were always reporting fact about their enemies.

There are several things that we *can* say for sure about the people who were labeled heretics by those who considered themselves right-thinking Christians. First of all, they were well educated and participated in intellectual study groups. Second, they were city-dwellers, part of the urban fabric of the major cities of the Roman Empire. Third, they were probably fairly affluent, which we know mostly from their educational levels, since affluence and education went hand in hand.

IS THERE ANY TRUTH TO THE RECONSTRUCTIONS OF THE HERESIOLOGISTS?

The discovery of the NHL provides a perfect opportunity to examine the claims of the heresiologists, because for the first time in nearly 2,000 years, they give us the lost voices of those denounced as heretics. Here are a few of the most common charges against Gnostics or Christian heretics that the heresiologists leveled against their enemies, along with a new assessment of whether these charges were likely true or false, based on the new information that the NHL provides us:

1. The heretics are often women, or they use women to spread their heresies. A striking feature of the heresiologists' accounts is that the heretics either work with women partners (for instance, the arch-heretic Simon Magus led a group with his lover, a woman he named Helena for her similarity to the classic beauty Helen of Troy) or they geared their teaching toward women in order to lure them in (for instance, the heretic Marcus the Magician allowed women to preside over and participate in sacramental rituals).

   TRUE or **FALSE**? Probably **TRUE**. Nag Hammadi documents contain many positive estimations of women or feminine power (see *Thunder*; *OrigWld*; *HypArch*). Although this statement does not necessarily translate into a social reality where women are allowed to lead, we know of at least one authentic Gnostic document, Ptolemy's *Letter to Flora*, which provides spiritual and moral instruction to a woman. We also have tombstones for Christian women that allude to their involvement in certain Valentinian rituals and initiations. In short, many of the groups against which the heresiologists fought probably included women in their groups as students, teachers, and leaders. But there is no independent evidence that these heretics were involved with them sexually. More revealing is the charge—again, likely to be true—that heretics upset the proper Roman social order by giving strong positions to women.

2. The Gnostics rejected the need for martyrdom. **TRUE** or **FALSE**? Probably **TRUE**, but the issue is complex. As Christianity began to grow in the second century, some prominent Christians were arrested by Roman authorities for being seditious or for inciting revolutionary behavior against the Roman Empire. Members of the self-proclaimed orthodoxy insisted that Christian martyrdom was an important act of courage that brought salvation and glory to those who faced death in the arena. They also scorned the Gnostics for being cowardly and arguing that public martyrdom was unnecessary or, worse, completely wrong-minded. It seems to have been the case, however, that while certain Gnostic groups did not seek out martyrdom, others did; those who did not seek it nevertheless might have advocated choosing a voluntary death rather than being actively executed if they had been rounded up and arrested. Some of our NH documents clearly advocate how to die "properly" for those who had been arrested and were facing martyrdom (see *1stApJas*; *ApocJas*).

3. The Gnostics subverted proper Church authority. **TRUE** or **FALSE**? Probably **FALSE**, but again, the issue is complex. The key question

here is to what degree any sort of "proper Church authority" existed in the second century. If Christianity was illegal, underground, and took many different forms, and there were no churches or Bibles, can we really talk about "proper Church authority"? Can we really talk about "the Church," in fact? The term suggests a lot of things that simply did not yet exist as dominant and authoritative.

One common issue was **apostolic authority**. This doctrine implies that Jesus originally set up a ministry, deliberately founding a Christian Church and appointing his apostle Peter as its head. Peter then appointed his successor, and his successor appointed his own successor, and so on. **Apostolic succession** and the passing on of apostolic authority is the foundation of the Roman Catholic Church's papacy. In other words, the current pope receives his authority to be pope based on a claim of an unbroken line of authority that extends back to Peter and ultimately to Jesus.

It is certainly the case that all of these Gnostic groups did not trace themselves back to Peter through his apostolic authority. But they did trace themselves back to other apostles. Some favored Jesus's brother James (see *ApocJas*; *1st* and *2ndApJas*); some favored Mary Magdalene (*GosMary*); some favored Thomas (*GosThom*); others favored Paul (*HypArch*; *InterpKnowledge*; *ApPaul*) who, as it turns out, had never actually met the human Jesus and who thus complicated the idea of apostolic authority, since he claimed that he had received his commission to lead Christians directly from the risen Christ, not the earthly Jesus.

What all this means is that the Gnostics did subvert Church authority based on the claim that Peter was Jesus's successor. In the second century there was a spirited debate about which of Jesus's disciples was truly his successor. Some claimed Peter as the most significant; other groups of Christians traced their tradition back to other disciples.

4. The Gnostics reject Scripture.

   TRUE or **FALSE**? Probably more **FALSE** than true. Typically, Irenaeus (who makes this claim that the Gnostics rejected the authority of the New and Old Testaments) is being tricky here. Questions emerge: (1) Which Christian texts were considered scripture in Irenaeus's time? (2) Who decided which texts were Scripture and which were not? With the creation and circulation of the New Testament still two centuries away, Christians circulated a great number of texts. The only thing we learn here, therefore, is that Irenaeus had a different idea about which texts were authoritative to Christians and which were not. That said, the Nag Hammadi texts prove that the Gnostics knew and revered many texts that now have the status of scripture, including the Gospel of John and some of Paul's letters, including his First Letter to the Corinthians, Ephesians, and Colossians. The *Gospel of Truth*, for example, paraphrases or alludes to the gospels of John and of Matthew, Paul's letters to the Romans, Corinthians, Ephesians and Colossians, Hebrews, 1 John, and the Book of Revelation. The *GosTruth* may have interpreted these letters in a way that rubbed Irenaeus the wrong way, but it certainly proves that Gnostic authors used and revered some of these Christian scriptures.

5. The Gnostics considered themselves to be "saved" already.

   TRUE or **FALSE**? Probably **TRUE**, but then, other Christians (Irenaeus included) probably thought that *they* were saved too, just like many modern "born-again" Christians consider themselves to be saved. The issue for Irenaeus and his colleagues was that the Gnostic Christians considered themselves above morality, because they believed that there was no need to adhere to morality when they were, to pick up on a later phrase, "saved by nature." According to the heresiologists, that meant that Gnostics felt emboldened to be sexually promiscuous. Whether they were or not is difficult to

ascertain. But many so-called Gnostic texts—just like more so-called orthodox texts—were written by those who considered themselves to have found salvation and truth.

6. The Gnostics have crazy mythologies with endless stories of horrors in the heavens.

   TRUE or **FALSE**. Most likely **TRUE**, actually. Although Irenaeus reproduces quite a bit of Gnostic **cosmology** and mythology, we did not know how accurately he was doing this until we found some of the texts he was apparently using. Their complex mythological and cosmological narratives mark out some of these Gnostic texts from other Christian traditions (see *GosEg*; *ApJn*; *HypArch*; *OrigWld*). At the same time, mythologies and accounts of horrors in the heavens are not in every NH text; we also find negative assessments of the heavens in non-Gnostic writings, including, for example, the book of Revelation in the New Testament.

MODERN CHRISTIANITY AND ANCIENT GNOSTICISM

Modern Christianity is a highly diverse religious movement, and there is not only one perspective on ancient Gnosticism and its value or validity. Some more liberal churches actively embrace newly discovered Gnostic texts like the *Gospel of Thomas*. Others, like the Roman Catholic Church, see the value in some Gnostic texts as helping us to reconstruct the history of Christianity but do not consider a Gnostic text such as the *Gospel of Thomas* as within the **canon** or list of approved Christian writings; thus they are more or less dismissive of them. Other more conservative churches consider Gnosticism still to be a dangerous and foolish heretical movement. These churches reject ancient Gnostic texts outright, presenting them as writings that were meant to supplant the gospels of the New Testament. In truth, they were not; all our Christian Gnostic texts were written *after* the New Testament gospels, and they often refer in positive terms to the gospels. The Gnostic texts were meant to supplement, not to supplant, the four New Testament gospels. Other conservative churches point out that the so-called Gnostic gospels, such as the recently discovered *Gospel of Judas*, offer no new reliable, historical information about Jesus; thus they are useless. However, these gospels do not purport to be historical documents but are faith-based, just as virtually all Christian texts are faith-based.

The point of this book is not to argue that the NH writings can teach us about Jesus and his disciples. Neither is it to argue that the NH writings are (or were intended to be) as important to the history of Christianity as the New Testament. There are other arguments, however, to be made in favor of studying them. First, the NH documents have a great deal to tell us about early Christianity. Second, this new set of writings can help us to see multiple sides of a history that had been, up until 1945, one-sided; as the Catholic Church became the dominant form of Christianity in the fourth century, it systematically silenced the voices of all others. Third, this new collection of writings enlightens us about what ancient Gnosticism was and was not. Finally (and most importantly) this book approaches the NH writings from a novel point of view. While most people call the NHL Gnostic, or a collection of Gnostic texts, or an example of Gnosticism, this book works against that view. This is not just because the terms "Gnostic" and "Gnosticism" have been shown to be problematic but because the NHL is in fact a selection of ancient writings. Some of its writings talk about *gnosis*; others do not. Some contain ideas that would have been deemed heretical; others do not. Just as not all of these writings are Gnostic, not all are Christian. Thus it is important to recognize the NHL as a glimpse into an ancient book collection—a miscellany, eclectic mix of documents. To be able to fully appreciate these writings, we first need to look more closely at the different worlds of the Roman Empire, the setting for early Christianity.

QUESTIONS TO CONSIDER

1. What do you think about the modern move of some scholars to abolish the terms "Gnostic" and "Gnosticism"? Does it make sense to you?

2. How would the existence or nonexistence of an actual group of Gnostics change your reading of an ancient text, which exhibited the characteristics of what we now call Gnosticism?

3. Consider the selection in this chapter from Epiphanius of Salamis's *Panarion*, where he describes a group of people he calls Gnostics. What do you make of what Epiphanius is doing? Do you believe his account? Why, or why not?

KEY TERMS

Apostolic Succession	canon	Yale School
Sophia	**Origen of Alexandria**	**Messina Definition**
Ennoia	**Hans Jonas**	heretic
gnosis	heresy	heresiology
orthodoxy	**Sethian**	**Epiphanius of Salamis**
Orthodox Christianity	**Hippolytus of Rome**	**Valentinian**
Irenaeus of Lyons	apostolic authority	**Demiurge**
Catholic Church	**Clement of Alexandria**	

FOR FURTHER READING

Brakke, David. *The Gnostics: Myth, Ritual, and Diversity in Early Christianity*. Cambridge, MA: Harvard University Press, 2010. A significant new study arguing that there were indeed ancient Gnostics. For advanced readers.

Harris, John. *Gnosticism: Beliefs and Practices*. Brighton: Sussex Academic Press, 1999. A good, readable introduction for beginning to intermediate students.

Jonas, Hans. *The Gnostic Religion*. Boston: Beacon, 1960. This is a classic study, but one that was produced before the discovery of key Gnostic texts, many of which obviate Jonas's claims.

King, Karen L. *What Is Gnosticism?* Cambridge, MA: Belknap Press of Harvard University Press, 2005. One of the US's top scholars of Gnosticism takes on the question in this study that largely dissects the modern construction of ancient Gnosticism by figures such as Hans Jonas.

Markschies, Christoph. *Gnosis: An Introduction*. Translated by John Bowden. London: T. & T. Clark, 2003. A short treatise that can be helpful to intermediate students.

Pearson, Birger. *Ancient Gnosticism: Traditions and Literature*. Philadelphia: Fortress, 2007. A basic introduction for beginners, offering brief summaries of a wide variety of texts.

Roukema, Reimer. *Gnosis and Faith in Early Christianity: An Introduction to Gnosticism*. Harrisburg, PA: Trinity Press International, 1999. Both an introduction to Gnosticism and an a theory of its origins, this English translation of the Dutch original might be interesting for more advanced students, particularly those intrigued by the connections between Gnosticism and Platonist philosophy in the ancient world.

Rudolph, Kurt. *Gnosis. The Nature and History of Gnosticism*. San Francisco: HarperOne, 1987. A very readable introduction, although now somewhat dated and in need of revision.

Williams, Michael Allen. *Rethinking Gnosticism: Arguments for Dismantling a Dubious Category*. Princeton, NJ: Princeton University Press, 1996. A very useful study that both challenges earlier mischaracterizations of Gnosticism and proposes an alternate way of classifying Gnostic texts.

For more on The Matrix and Gnosticism

Flannery-Dailey, Frances, and Rachel Wagner. "'Wake Up!' Gnosticism and Buddhism in *The Matrix*." *Journal of Religion and Film* 5/2 (2001). Online at http://www.unomaha.edu/jrf/gnostic.htm.

For a general take on Gnosticism

Smoley, Richard. *Forbidden Faith: The Secret History of Gnosticism*. San Francisco: HarperOne, 2007.

3

The Roman Empire

RELIGIOUS LANDSCAPES

It is a fair guess that whoever composed the *Apocryphon of John* in the middle of the second century would not have recognized the world in which a lone monk carefully copied out that text on yellowed papyrus pages two hundred years later. Those two centuries saw vast, seismic shifts in the Roman Empire, and at the epicenter of those shifts was Christianity, which grew from a small, largely underground movement to become the dominant religion. How did it all happen?

The rise of Christianity has fascinated historians for a very long time, and different theories have been offered as to why Christianity was as successful as it was. This chapter provides a broad look over Roman social landscapes, looking at the factors that shaped Christianity, honing it with a complex interplay of forces. Let's start with the biggest possible picture: the Roman Empire as an entity.

An empire is a political structure built around an emperor, who acts as a sole and despotic ruler. It replaced the Roman Republic, which was a form of democracy but was in fact an **oligarchy**, a political system where a few elite citizens govern as representatives of the people. The first Roman emperor was Octavian, who single-handedly changed everything.

EMPEROR AUGUSTUS

When Octavian defeated his last rival for power, Mark Antony, at the Battle of Actium, he became the sole and self-proclaimed ruler of the territory that Rome held, which included almost the whole Mediterranean world.

Octavian took the title **Augustus** and ruled for forty eventful years (27 BCE–14 CE). Augustus ordered widespread reforms on law and morality; he reintroduced ancient priestly offices and reasserted religious law; he pressed for aggressive expansion of the Empire, and he funded new building campaigns, literally transforming the urban landscape. During his rule, fine new Roman roads connected cities and aqueducts carried fresh water into them. A burgeoning economy based on slavery, agriculture, and trade made Rome wealthy and stable.

Under Augustus, a new and distinctive collective Roman identity took shape. A fondness

TIMELINE 3.1 The Roman Empire of the First to the Second Centuries

	History of Hellenistic and Roman Times	History of Christianity
4 BCE		**4 BCE** The Birth of Jesus
		4 BCE—30 CE Life of Jesus
1 CE	**14–37** Tiberius, emperor	**27–30?** Public Ministry of Jesus
	37–41 Caligula, emperor	**30?** Crucifixion of Jesus
		30–120 Oral Traditions of Jesus and initial spread of Christianity throughout the empire
	41–54 Claudius, emperor	**31–32??** Conversion of Paul
		34–64 Paul's missionary activities
	54–68 Nero, emperor	
	68–69 Year of four emperors	
		49 1 Thessalonians, Paul's earliest letter and the earliest surviving Christian writing
		49–62 Paul's letters
	69–79 Vespasian, emperor	**64** Death of Paul and Peter
		65–70 Gospel of Mark
	79–81 Titus, emperor	
		80–85 Gospels of Matthew and Luke
	81–96 Domitian, emperor	
		80–110 Deutero-Pauline Epistles, Pastoral Epistles, General Epistles
		90–95 Gospel of John
	96–98 Nerva, emperor	**95** *I Clement*
		95–100 Book of Revelation

TIMELINE 3.1 *Continued*

	98–117 Trajan, emperor	
100 CE	**117–138** Hadrian, emperor	**100** The *Didache*
		110 Letters of Ignatius
		100–130 Rise of Gnosticism
		110–120 *Gospels of Thomas and Peter*
		120–140 *Shepherd* of Hermas, *Apocalypse of Peter*
		130 *Epistle of Barnabas*
		130–150 Rise of Marcionites; *Gospel of Judas*
		155 *Martyrdom of Polycarp*

FIGURE 3.1 Augustus, the first of Rome's emperors.

for military discipline was combined with an aggressive policy of expansion through foreign domination. Enemies were subjugated, and disobedience to the Roman Empire was not tolerated. Traditional values—conservatism, honoring the ways of the ancestors, and patriarchy, and—were further supported by Augustan policies.

By the second century—under the emperor Trajan—the Empire reached its farthest extent and was at its strongest, militarily and politically. The successive reigns of what the Renaissance political theorist Nicolo Macchiavelli called the Five Good Emperors ushered in a time of prosperity and stability.

These emperors had relatively good social policies; in addition (unlike some of their predecessors) they were all relatively sane. These emperors had to deal with Christians, but there are some indications that they did so in a relatively even-handed manner, never calling for the systematic rounding up and executing of Christians, although many Christians

THE FIVE GOOD EMPERORS

Roman emperors were a notoriously unstable lot. Augustus had failed to put into place a principle for imperial succession, so it was unclear how, at the death of one emperor, another would be put into place. Some emperors inherited the position through family ties (often adoptive family); some were acclaimed by senators; others were put there by the Roman army. Sometimes more than one emperor was proclaimed at once. Most of the time, imperial reigns after Augustus were brief and prematurely cut short by assassinations. However, in the second century, the Empire more or less stabilized, even thrived under the generally beneficent rule of what we call the Five Good Emperors. This was the era during which most of our Nag Hammadi texts were written.

were indeed put to death under their reigns. They were not tyrannical despots so much as canny and effective leaders, and in the case of the Antonines, they were known for their love of education and philosophy. Under the three emperors of the Antonine dynasty, Greek learning experienced a renaissance, and the cities of the Empire were full of the impressive buildings, schools, and libraries that came to characterize the Roman Empire of the second century.

ROMAN SOCIAL STRUCTURE

At the top of the social hierarchy stood the Emperor and others of an upper social class who were subject to special privileges and held the highest possible status. Beneath them were two levels of elites, the senatorial class and the equestrian class. Both classes possessed certain privileges (for example, front-row seats at public entertainments, important posts in government administration, superior status before the law, and more humane punishments if they committed crimes) and a great deal of power and wealth. They also had restrictions on whom they could marry and whether their status could be passed down through the family or acquired. By the second century, some of these restrictions had been relaxed and there was more fluidity to the social structure, but a marked division still existed between elites and non-elites.

Beneath the elites stood a large free population—merchants, traders, builders, tradespeople, farmers, and the like. These people had been freeborn, that is, they had never been slaves. They were of a slightly higher status than freedpeople, who had been slaves but then either won, earned, or bought their own freedoms. The freedpeople class was transient, however, since one was not born into that status and it lasted only one generation. The children of freedpeople were freeborn, and thus automatically of a higher status than their parents; they were Roman citizens with rights. Nevertheless, we tend to know a lot about freedpeople, because they were so happy with their new achieved social status that they enthusiastically broadcast their lives, leaving us with quite a few texts, literally scores of funerary monuments, and not a small amount of art.

It is virtually impossible for us to calculate what percentage of the population was slaves. Most people came to be slaves by bad luck. They could have been prisoners of war, or their impoverished birth parents might have abandoned or sold them because they could not afford to raise them. Slaves were not considered to be people; they were things. They could not marry, for instance, and any children they might bear were not considered theirs but could be taken and placed elsewhere as

MAP 3.1 The Roman Empire: Central and Eastern Provinces

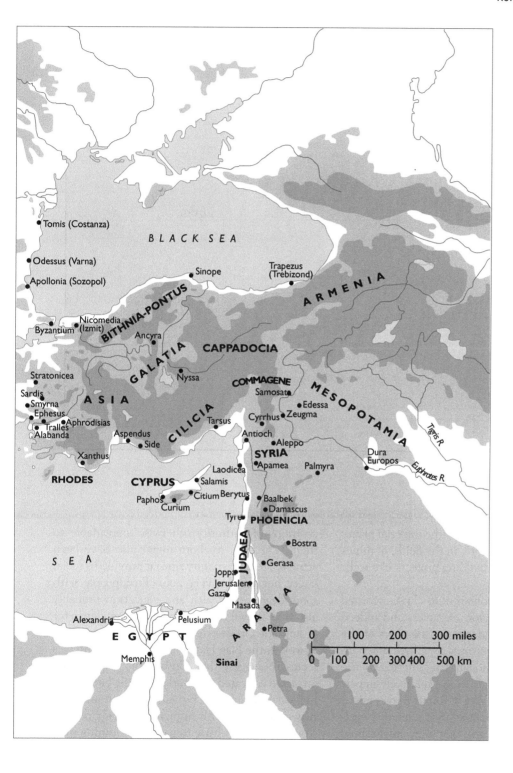

BLACK SEA

Tomis (Costanza)

Odessus (Varna)

Apollonia (Sozopol)

Sinope

Trapezus
(Trebizond)

ARMENIA

BITHNIA-PONTUS

Nicomedia
(Izmit)

Byzantium

Ancyra

GALATIA

CAPPADOCIA

Nyssa

COMMAGENE

Samosat

MESOPOTAMIA

Stratonicea

Sardis

Smyrna

Ephesus

Aphrodisias

ASIA

Tralles

Alabanda

Xanthus

Aspendus

Side

CILICIA

Tarsus

Cyrrhus

Edessa

Zeugma

Antioch

Aleppo

SYRIA

Apamea

Palmyra

Dura
Europos

Tigris R

Euphrates R

RHODES

CYPRUS

Laodicea

Paphos

Curium

Citium

Salamis

Berytus

Baalbek

Damascus

SEA

Tyre

PHOENICIA

Bostra

JUDAEA

Gerasa

Joppa

Jerusalem

Gaza

Masada

ARABIA

Alexandria

Pelusium

EGYPT

Petra

Memphis

Sinai

0   100   200   300 miles

0   100   200   300 400   500 km

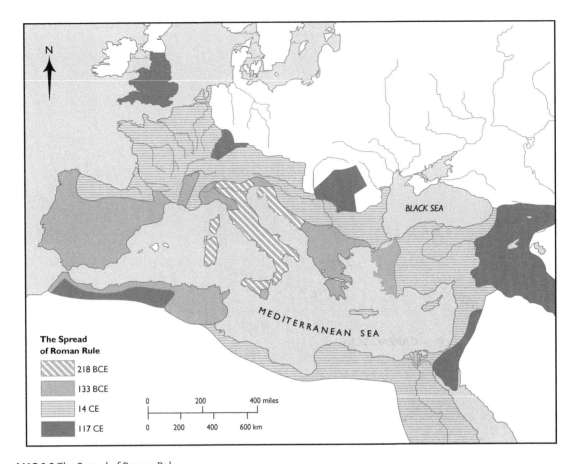

MAP 3.2 The Spread of Roman Rule

needed. Slaves worked within the imperial places and the homes of the elite, in the fields, in mines and factories, and on building projects like walls and aqueducts.

Members of the Roman elite classes scorned Christianity as a religion of slaves, and indeed there is no secure evidence for members of the highest classes converting to Christianity in the first century, although Paul's letter to the Romans addresses wealthy and relatively upper-class Christians in the city of Rome. Slaves might have been drawn to Christianity's relative egalitarianism, which meant that they might hold

positions of authority otherwise unavailable to them. The poor freeborn might also have been attracted to Christianity since it provided a social safety net for the very poor. Freedpeople with some degree of wealth and education probably also were drawn to Christianity; our evidence for prominent Gnostic teachers such as Valentinus as well as the Nag Hammadi writings themselves seems to suggest that Gnosticism in particular attracted educated and worldly people but not the highest Roman elite. But since Christianity was new and treated with suspicion by many people, Roman elite had little to gain from joining such a movement until it was officially sanctioned in the fourth century.

RELIGIOUS CONTEXTS IN THE ROMAN EMPIRE

For a long time, scholars assumed that Romans were not religious people; they had no sacred texts, no system based on faith or belief, and no real word for "religion." Yet scholarship has changed considerably over the years, and classicists have devoted increasing attention to defining and understanding Roman religion on its own terms. Indeed, the Romans seem to have been extremely religious people; it is fair to say, though, that they were not religious in the sense that ancient Christians or Jews were religious. Still, what we might call "religion" was everywhere in the Roman Empire.

State Religion and Civic Cult

The primary way one would be "religious" in a Roman context was to participate in imperial and civic religion. The emperors were considered "sons of God" or "sons of the gods" and were afforded a special status. Dead emperors (and sometimes their wives) could be deified or transformed into deities, then honored in temples dedicated in their names. Different groups (called "colleges") of priests developed to serve the imperial cult, primarily by offering sacrifices at the temples.

Civic religion was not always centered on emperor worship, but it did usually involve sacrifice. A sacrifice might be a pinch of incense thrown on an altar, or it might involve the slaughter of animals. One of the most elaborate sacrifices, the *suovetaurilia*, called for the sacrifice of a bull, a ram, and a pig to the god Mars to bless and sacralize the land (see fig. 3-2).

Sacrifices were conducted outdoors in front of temples, with a host of ritual experts and assistants present. Priests were usually male (there were a few notable exceptions, such as the Vestal Virgins). They could either be professionals or else an upper-class man could serve as

FIGURE 3.2 One of the most elaborate animal sacrifices for religious rituals, the *suovetaurilia*, called for the slaughter of a pig, a ram, and a bull.

a priest of a certain cult on a certain day or set of days.

Besides sacrifice outside temples, there were other forms of public religion one might see on a Roman street or marketplace. There were religious processions and religious holidays. "Colleges" of priests were experts at interpreting omens such as the flight paths of birds. People prayed to the gods at outdoor shrines. They flocked to healing temples of Aesculapius to stay overnight and receive a dream visit from the god. They visited tombs of the dead to honor or worship their ancestors, bearing gifts of honey or wine. People celebrated coming-of-age rituals for their sons, bringing them to the Temple of Mars Ultor where boys would mark their symbolic passage to manhood by donning the toga of adult males. They sought out oracles at famous temples dedicated to Apollo or other deities. In the Roman Empire, religion was, in fact, everywhere.

Private and Domestic Religion

Religion was also part of homelife. Traditional family cults—led by the father and, differently, the mother of the household—worshiped local deities called the Lares and Penates in small shrines included within every household. Rituals inside the home included leaving offerings of incense and flowers before the Lares, Penates, and other images of deities associated with the family, and lighting lamps each evening. Unfortunately, much of what happened in the Roman Empire that we might call "domestic religion" is simply difficult to ascertain, because it consisted of small everyday actions and rituals that were not often recorded. Nevertheless, the site of the home as a kind of religious or ritual space meant that Christians, meeting in private homes, already had some ideas and a model for what religious behavior within a household might be like.

Freedom of Religion

Generally speaking, the Romans believed in freedom of religion. You could worship whom or whatever you pleased. There was no concept of adhering to only one deity, so you might worship many gods, depending on the occasion and your own family traditions. Certain gods were associated with certain social classes (for example, the god of the woods, Silvanus, was traditionally revered among country dwellers and peasants, but not so much among the elite). Other gods were gender specific: the goddess Mater Matuta, for instance, had only female devotees.

Freedom of religion in the Empire meant that if you were an immigrant, it was taken for granted that you might import your own religion and practice it in a new place. There were, therefore, shrines of non-Roman gods in many Roman cities, and these were freely visited. In fact, some foreign deities had a certain allure, and both immigrants and native Romans frequented their cults. Judaism was generally popular and respected as a religion; it was well known throughout the Empire, and Jews were respected for their "foreign" ways without fear of persecution.

OTHER RELIGIONS IN THE ROMAN EMPIRE

- *Judaism*: An ancient religion, Judaism had been around longer than Rome itself; there were Jewish communities in many cities of the Empire, some of them sizable. Jews of the Diaspora (that is, Jews outside their ancestral lands) were **Hellenized**; their first language was Greek, and they read their own sacred scriptures in a Greek translation called the **Septuagint** (LXX). In parts of the Roman Empire, notably the cities of Antioch and Alexandria, Jews were recognized as a kind of "distinct society" with some degree of autonomy. At the same time, the Jews in the Roman province of Judaea (early twenty-first century Israel and Palestine) revolted against Roman rule, such that the Romans destroyed the central focus of ancient Judaism, the Jerusalem Temple, in 70 CE. Another Jewish revolt under Trajan (115–117 CE) took place in Alexandria, and a third major revolt under Hadrian (135 CE) led to the transformation of Jerusalem into a Roman city renamed Aelia Capitolina and the expulsion of all Jews from the city. Jews and pagans had, to put it mildly, a complicated relationship, and the degree of tension between the two varied across time and place. On the whole, however, Jews were a large enough minority that they far outnumbered Christians in the second century, and they were a visible enough group that their practices and **monotheistic** devotion was known and respected. Still, in the second century, following two centuries of war with Rome, Judaism was in a period of change. It would soon emerge again in the form of early rabbinic Judaism, the precursor to the modern form of the religion. Judaism offered to its adherents a life lived ethically in close relationship to a single God. It was unusual, in the context of the Roman Empire, in that the Jews followed a monotheism, the details of which were outlined in the first five books of the Hebrew Bible, the Torah. Being Jewish meant adhering to laws and commandments that marked them as different from pagans, whether in following dietary laws, observing the Sabbath and specific holy days, circumcising male children, or refusing to participate in polytheistic worship. Finally, many (but not all) Jews also awaited the arrival of a messiah, whose arrival would usher in a new era of promise and restoration.

- ***Mystery Cults.*** Apart from official Roman cults with formal priesthoods, temples, and rites, there were also religions that were open to a variety of people and which had a very different flavor from official Roman cults. The rites of these religions were celebrated secretly, and people had to be initiated into them. Once they were initiated, they swore to secrecy what they had seen and experienced. The oldest of the mystery cults was the famous Eleusinian Mysteries (so called because they were celebrated in the town of Eleusis, Greece). People flocked from all over to be initiated into the rites of the goddess Demeter. By the second century, Romans who could afford it became initiates at Eleusis, but there were also many other options closer to home. The mystery cults had such a widespread appeal that as Christianity developed, it often presented itself as a sort of mystery cult, drawing on a distinctive vocabulary. The Christian sacraments of baptism and Eucharist/Lord's Supper, for instance, were often termed "mysteries" and those who celebrated them, "initiates." So although Christianity was not itself a mystery cult, Christians sometimes drew on that language to talk about Christianity, perhaps to make their religion seem more appealing to Romans already looking for something like a mystery cult.

- *Mithraism.* One of the most prevalent Roman mystery cults was Mithraism, based around the god **Mithras**, a Roman deity with Eastern associations (see fig. 3-3). By the second century, Mithraic shrines—virtually all of them subterranean and used to celebrate secret initiatory rites and banquets—could be found across the Empire. A popular idea is that Mithraism was Christianity's biggest competitor, but Christianity evidently had an edge

FIGURE 3.3 At the center of a Mithraeum stood a *tauroctony* or "bull-killing" cult image like this one. The god Mithras slaughters a bull; beneath, the dog, snake, and scorpion (like Mithras and the bull) represent constellations in the night sky. Thus this image is a coded "map" of the cosmos.

on Mithraism, since Mithraism accepted only male initiates.

Remarkably, many churches in the later Roman Empire came to be built on top of Mithraic shrines. In the city of Rome, for instance, there are such shrines under the churches of San Clemente, Santa Prisca, and San Stefano Rotondo. These churches were not built until hundreds of years after the Mithraic shrines had fallen into disuse, so it is not a simple case of a Christian holy site replacing a pagan one; however, there was probably some intentionality to the decision to build a church on what had, at one point, been space dedicated to Mithras.

• *Isis and Serapis.* Since before the Empire, Romans had a fascination with Egypt, and by the second century there developed a kind of "Egyptomania" in Rome. Roman domination of Egypt meant that the worship of **Isis** and Serapis, Isis's consort Osiris in Roman guise, reached the Empire as an exotic new religion. Isis's all-male priests were recognizable from their shaved heads and white linen garments; Isis temples were often quite large and featured cisterns or pools filled with "Nile water" to create an Egyptian atmosphere. Romans could be initiated into Isis's or Serapis's mysteries, although we are left without much information about what they really were. Certainly a degree of bodily purity and asceticism was involved. Although Christianity as a whole does not pick up on much from these Roman-Egyptian cults, some of the language on inscriptions to Isis is quite reminiscent of passages from Nag Hammadi texts, notably *Thunder: Perfect Mind.*

ELEMENTS OF ROMAN LIFE THAT AFFECTED CHRISTIANITY

Other elements of life in the Roman Empire were not directly concerned with religion, but nonetheless they impacted the growth and development of Christianity.

- *The desire for upward mobility.* Although it was hard to get ahead in Rome because of the clearly defined class structure, many people desired to rise above the status into which they were born. Religion could offer a safe place for the socially ambitious to shine. Some Christians, in particular, claimed that they were all equal "in Christ," no matter what their social status (Gal 3:28). Slaves could head Christian assemblies; women could teach men, at least in some Christian contexts.

- *Expansion of Empire.* The second century was a time of rapid growth; by 111 CE the Empire reached its farthest geographical extent, from Portugal and Britain in the West to Eastern Syria in the East, and from the Danube in the North to the south of Egypt and Tunisia. This expansion meant population shifts as people came to Rome from all the borderlands and kingdoms outside the Empire, challenging Romans to define and redefine what it meant to be "Roman." It meant that Romans in general became accustomed to and tolerated strange customs and behavior, including religious behavior.

- *Absence of social services.* Rome was not really a "Big Government" sort of place, so it offered few social services. There were no hospitals, no social welfare programs, and no safety nets for people who needed them. Those who were sick needed the help of family members; without family, there was no one to care for you. A similar situation occurred for widows or foreigners in a city. People with shared concerns often bonded together into groups called *collegia*; these *collegia* could be occupational (e.g., the college of carpenters or barrel makers could get together to share work and set fair prices) or based on other concerns: there were burial societies, which required their members to pay annual dues (often something like a few jugs of wine) in order to insure getting a proper funeral and burial. Some scholars have suggested that Christianity was very much like a *collegium*; Christians banded together based on a shared social need, such as caring for the poor and the sick.

- *Conservatism and Tradition.* Romans were traditionalists and had great respect for ancient traditions. Christians had to balance the desire to claim that their religion had an ancient Jewish foundation (remember that they are using the Jewish scriptures as their sacred text) with the fact that many were Gentiles, not Jews, and did not see themselves as Jews exactly, although they used Jewish scripture, followed some (but not all) Jewish practices, and followed Jesus, who was himself Jewish. The fundamental issue, from the perspective of the Roman Empire, was not one of how Jewish the Christians were, but one of newness: as Christians moved away from Jews and Jewish practices, they became, in the eyes of Romans, a "new religious movement," which tended to garner suspicion in the Roman Empire.

- *Village-level or "traditional" practices.* Not all religion in Rome was about imperial cult or civic religion. In villages, towns, and households, people had their own ways of honoring their gods. Some of these practices included magic and divination (summoning the gods) through the use of spells, curse tablets, and amulets. These practices were widespread and crossed religious boundaries; Christianity did not stop these practices but often became incorporated into them, such that we find a lot of Christian magical spells and amulets. There are actually a lot of interesting points of contact between Nag Hammadi texts and the celestial beings that are featured on magical amulets and tablets; we shall see some examples later on in this book.

• *Active Trade Networks*. Trade and commerce brought interactions between groups and peoples over a huge geographical expanse. From the Silk Routes, for instance, came not just goods but travelers, including the unexpected: Hindu ascetics from India or Buddhist monks from India and China. Ideas also traveled along trade routes, such that ports and key cities along trade routes were very cosmopolitan. Sometimes new ideas and practices were assimilated; other times they were met with conflict.

The Empire was an enormous place, and there was room in it for all kinds of different religious movements to flourish. Christianity fared better than most, as it happened, because it offered useful types of "goods" to a community of spiritual shoppers—Romans were drawn to different religious options, picking and choosing from a thriving religious marketplace. Why precisely Christianity continued to grow, and how, is the subject for chapter 5.

QUESTIONS TO CONSIDER

1. Considering that Jesus was put to death and that the Jewish Temple in Jerusalem was destroyed in 70 CE, does it surprise you to know that Romans theoretically practiced freedom of religion? Why, then, do you think that Jesus and his fellow Jews came into conflict with Rome?

2. Can you think of connections between the different Roman social classes and the kinds of religious groups that they sought out? Does it make sense to you that a slave might have been drawn to a different religious community than a member of the elite?

3. Scholars sometimes draw a distinction between Roman civic (i.e., public) religions (such as emperor worship) and "personal religion" (such as Mithraism). Do you think "personal religion" (including Christianity) offered something that civic religion did not? And what would that have been?

KEY TERMS

oligarchy	Augustus	Hellenized
Septuagint	Mystery cult	Mithras
Isis	monotheism (monotheistic)	

FOR FURTHER READING

Beard, Mary, John North, and Simon Price. *Religions of Rome*. 2 vols. Cambridge/New York: Cambridge University Press, 1998. This sourcebook/textbook combination is indispensible for the student of Roman religion.

Lane, Eugene, and Ramsay MacMullen, eds. *Paganism and Christianity 100–425 CE: A Sourcebook*. Minneapolis: Augsburg Fortress, 1992. A collection of ancient texts on religion in the ancient world.

MacMullen, Ramsay. *Paganism in the Roman Empire*. New Haven: Yale University Press, 1981. A clear introduction to Roman religion. For intermediate students.

Meyer, Marvin. *The Ancient Mysteries: A Sourcebook*. San Francisco: Harper & Row, 1987. An anthology of ancient texts on the mystery cults, with useful introductions.

4

Christianity in the Second-Century Empire

AN OVERVIEW

Imagine that we are back in the second century, the time when many of the ancient texts in this book were written. What was Christianity like then? Christianity was still a relatively small religion, making up only a miniscule percentage of the population at the beginning of the century. It was new, and it was also an underground movement. No one in 150 CE imagined that within two hundred years, Christianity would become the dominant, legal religion of the Roman Empire. It is, however, easy for us to take the growth of Christianity as a foregone conclusion and give to it a centrality in the second century that it did not have.

It can be helpful—and surprising—to start with what Christianity *lacked* in the second century:

- a fixed, agreed-upon scripture
- a fixed, universal ecclesiastical hierarchy
- a pope
- a doctrine of the dual humanity and divinity of Jesus
- a formal, universally recognized creed

- a doctrine of Original Sin
- consensus on the nature of the Trinity
- consensus about the resurrection
- consensus about whether women might be leaders or priests
- cathedrals or churches

Given that all these things had not yet developed or reached their final, official form, now so much a part of the fabric of many modern churches, it is inaccurate to think of any Christian text as heretical or any person as a heretic, even though we do sometimes find the language used in ancient Christian documents as one group or individual levels it at another. Such a label indicates a diversion from a consensus or an established, universal religion. Simply put: Christianity was not yet that kind of movement.

Christianity, as a minority religion, faced a number of challenges as it strove to gain a foothold in the Roman Empire. The main thing that a new religious group needs to thrive is people willing to join. But conversion in antiquity is not something we understand, primarily because we lack hard evidence for this time period. Imagine the situation: Romans allowed freedom of religion, so in theory people could worship any god they liked; Roman authorities, though, were also concerned about keeping the peace in such a large and diverse empire. Thus Romans placed restrictions on, for example, the right to private assembly (meaning that groups of any religion or association risked trouble if they gathered together without making their intent well known). Romans also were worried about dissidents or revolutionaries stirring up people against the masses. Given that they had put Jesus to death and considered him a dangerous criminal, anyone proclaiming this executed criminal to be a god— *the* God—might run a similar risk of being arrested, questioned, and even put to death. In fact, some of Jesus's own disciples had been killed for their public preaching and teaching.

HOW DID CHRISTIANITY WORK?

Rather than through any grand public sermonizing or miracle working, Christianity likely grew through more intimate networks. Here are a few different likely scenarios: imagine you have been raised in a pagan household, but you are friends with your neighbor who is a Christian. You are impressed by how friendly his fellow Christians are, and how they take care of the sick and elderly in the community. You decide you want to know more. Or imagine you have been raised in a pagan household, but you're a slave. Your life is quite miserable, but you know other slaves who tell you about their Christian beliefs. They tell you they are part of a new community "in Christ" where there is no distinction between slave and free, and even slaves can have responsibility and dignity. Or imagine you are a newcomer to a city, arriving by ship. You know no one in the city, but you meet some workers at the dock who offer you a safe place to sleep and a warm meal. They invite you to stay with them and teach you about their beliefs and practices. Or imagine that you're an upper-class young woman. You have been promised in marriage since the age of eight to a man much older than you. You're now fourteen, and your family decides you are ready to be married. But your slave tells you about Christianity and

---

THE ROMANS ON CHRISTIANITY

Most important Romans—literary figures, men of letters—largely ignored the phenomenon of Christianity altogether. The first indication of Christianity's spread we have is from Pliny the Younger to Emperor Trajan, dated 111 CE, around eighty years after the death of Jesus himself. Pliny thinks Christianity is what he calls a *superstitio*: "superstition," and at least potentially dangerous to the Roman order (Pliny, *Letters* 10.96). Around the same time, Tacitus mentions Christians in his *Annals*:

> They got their name from Christ, who was executed by sentence of the procurator, Pontius Pilate, in the Reign of Tiberius. That checked the pernicious superstition for a short time, but it broke out afresh—not only in Judea, where the plague first arose, but in Rome itself, where all

the horrible and shameful things in the world collect and find a home. (*Ann.* 15.44)

The biographer Suetonius, for his part, also thinks of Christianity in the same terms: he calls the Christians "a body of people addicted to a novel and mischievous superstition." Innovation was not a quality highly prized by Romans, particularly in the religious sphere. Once the Christians move away from being identified with the Jews, they lose the respect accorded to the Jews on account of the antiquity of Judaism. Christians were therefore placed in a tough spot: Did they want to appear more Jewish, or more Roman, or more distinct? The NH writings reveal some of these key problems as Christians tried out a variety of new identities in relation to the Empire.

how young women can remain unmarried and are protected, and financially supported as esteemed virgins. Or imagine that you are a pagan man but are very drawn to what you see happening at the Jewish synagogue across the street from your house. People there worship an ancient and powerful God, and they take care of each other in a way otherwise unknown in the Empire. You can convert to Judaism, but that means doing things like following kosher food laws (difficult in many situations) and you would need to be circumcised as an adult convert, without benefit of anesthetics and antibiotics. But someone tells you about Christianity, where you can worship the same god, have the same benefits of a community, yet not have to follow food laws or be circumcised. In any of these cases, what would you choose?

By the second century, then, Christianity was growing and had widespread appeal for many people, particularly the weaker or disenfranchised members of society. Still, for a movement to grow, you need more than converts. You need money, organization, respectability, patronage—in short, you need leaders. One of the chief problems in this religious movement was how to attract educated or wealthy people. It is easy to see what appeal Christianity might have had for a slave, but it is harder to see what appeal a largely illegal underground movement might have had for upper-class educated people—especially men—who had specific civic religious duties upon which their lives and livelihood depended. They had much to lose by affiliating themselves with a movement most respectable Romans considered a "pernicious superstition."

If you were an upper-class male, chances are that Christianity would not have held much appeal. A range of religious options was open to you. If you had been well educated, as you would have been, and chanced upon many Christian writings—the gospels of the New Testament, for example—or even a Jewish and Christian sacred text like the book of Genesis, you might have found them disappointing. They are written

simply, without the highest and most sophisticated ideas to which you had been exposed. You might still have found them compelling, but you probably would not consider them very learned.

Still, you might have encountered Romans who were nevertheless considering Christianity to be an intellectual movement, based on study and not that far removed from the respected life of a philosopher. These Christians might have shared their writings with you: they combined ancient Greek myth, philosophy, number theory, astronomy, textual interpretation, wordplay, and a marked concern for interesting things like the origins of the cosmos. As a thinking person, you might well have been caught up in what these Christian intellectuals were doing. These were the ones disdained by the heresiologists as the "Gnostics," or those bragging about possessing *gnosis*.

ACCOMMODATION VERSUS NON-ACCOMMODATION: A CHRISTIAN DILEMMA

Christians, whatever they believed, faced an identical issue: How to live in a proper, and safe, relationship to the Roman Empire? Christianity was small; it flew "beneath the radar," so to speak, because aspects of it garnered scorn and suspicion from outsiders. It was not yet centralized, not yet one thing. And thus as Christians grappled with the issue of how to fit in, the movement itself reached an impasse. Christians could do either of two things:

1. Accommodate to the Roman Empire (the model of adaptation and survival).
2. Choose not to accommodate to the Roman Empire (the "alternative society" model).

Christians actively debated which of these options was viable, but the issue was actually very complex. Did Christianity include all people, or just some? Should it create an alternative society—one with Christian rules and principles that were in direct contravention to the broader society in which one lived—or could Christianity and the Roman Empire be reconciled? It was clear that Jesus had not capitulated to Roman society but had accepted a brutal death, so in a sense, rebelling against the Empire was the "Christ-like" thing to do. Or was it?

It might be useful to think of the situation of a modern immigrant moving to the United States. Many immigrants come here to start a new life, and they are proud and anxious to be Americans; they want to embrace elements of American culture. In some ways, it is also expected of immigrants that they will assimilate: learn to speak English, swear the Pledge of Allegiance, raise their children to respect and honor American values reflected in the Constitution including patriotism, and freedom of expression. Becoming American in the fullest sense also offers immigrants a modicum of safety and respectability: they blend in, and they play by the rules. In other words, assimilation offers positive "goods" to immigrants. Some goods are concrete: becoming citizens gives them rights and entitlements. They are entitled to a voice in politics; they are entitled to legal employment and safety nets like welfare or unemployment insurance if they are out of work; their children can count on a free public education, and so on.

The situation in the Empire was somewhat similar. Something called the **Pax Romana** ("Roman Peace") meant that if you were Roman (particularly a Roman citizen), you were entitled to all the benefits that the Empire brought, and there were many. In return for all the things that being Roman gave you, you had to swear allegiance (think of saying the Pledge of Allegiance today), you had to play by the rules, and you had to show that you were a friend of Rome, not an enemy. You did this by offering sacrifices and participating in civic religion. And you would want to do this (or want to be seen doing this), because the Roman Empire came down brutally and swiftly on its enemies.

Again, Christianity in the second century was not well known, and from a Roman perspective, it was a bit shady and probably not "Roman" enough. Christians could be regarded with suspicion, the perception being that they did not "play by the rules." For one thing, they worshiped as a deity someone whom the Romans had put to death for sedition. For another, they refused to offer sacrifices, and for this act of "impiety," the Romans often called them "atheists" because they did not honor the gods of the Empire.

Christians therefore had a choice. They could assimilate, or they could be anti-Rome as some perceived Jesus to have been (even if Jesus actually *had not* been anti-Rome, the Roman administration still clearly perceived him to be, since they executed him). We might therefore imagine a kind of divide emerging between a Christian pro-assimilation faction and a Christian traditionalist faction. This is one useful way of moving away from the old, established "orthodox" versus "heretic" division of early Christianity. Traditionalists (later called by modern scholars the "orthodox" or the "proto-orthodox") tended to place a high value on those who supported an idea of Christianity as anti-Rome. They rejected all forms of pagan worship as idolatry, all Roman culture as sinful and polluting, and all forms of Roman authority as demonic. They composed scathing treatises against all elements of Greek and Roman life. Most strikingly, if the Roman Empire intervened in their lives, say, arresting them to investigate what they were doing, traditionalists advocated that the only proper response was to choose to die as a martyr in public defiance of Roman authority.

The pro-assimilation Christians were radically different. They maintained that being Roman and being Christian were not mutually exclusive terms. Greek and Roman culture, after all, brought many good things, like science, philosophy, and law. Imagine how intellectually impover-ished people would be if all our knowledge of science derived from the Hebrew Bible or the New Testament: not to demean those writings, but they are not primarily scientific treatises. These assimilationists sought to draw out from Graeco-Roman culture elements that could enrich Christianity—from models for living a virtuous life to models of conceptualizing God as One.

People who have been labeled Gnostic were often really best characterized not as Gnostic at all, but as pro-assimilation. Put differently, many of the complaints that the heresiologists leveled at the so-called Gnostics were that they considered tradition important but not so important as being experimental about blending Christianity and Roman traditions. In fact, we see this quite plainly in the heresiologists' fury that Gnostics rejected the idea of martyrdom. Rather than choosing to oppose the Roman Empire publicly, these pro-assimilation Christians found no problem with pledging their allegiance to the Empire instead and saving their devotion to Christ for a more private or domestic venue. Remember that there was always freedom to worship whomever you chose; the Romans had problems only with those who defied Roman laws and customs.

This all is a bit of oversimplification, of course. A better way to look at it is that in this experimental century, different groups spanned the spectrum of traditionalist to assimilationist. Heresiologists/the orthodox tended to one end of the spectrum, and the Gnostics to the other. But thinking of things this way tends to get to the heart of the ancient debates and explains how heated these issues became. It also moves us away from considering the self-appointed orthodox heresiologists as the dominant, normative or "mainstream" form of Christianity. We do not actually hear from the Christian mainstream; we hear from the radical traditionalists who reshaped and ultimately won the debate about how Christianity should look. In fact, if mainstream Christianity were that extreme and the actual situation had been that polarized, the movement might not have survived; everyone would have been rounded up by

the Romans and put to death as dissidents, and the Empire would have inexorably stamped out Christianity's existence. But Christianity was built by those who chose not to go to death, but to go home to their families instead—to have and raise children, and to raise those children in their new faith. And the Romans, for their part, were happy enough to let people go about their business, even if it involved worshiping a deity that might have raised some eyebrows. This, in fact, was how Christianity grew over the course of two centuries.

REGIONAL CHRISTIANITIES

Christianity in the second century was not one entity; it was hundreds of things—various groups with different ideas, different practices, different texts they found inspiring and inspired. Sometimes, specific forms, schools, or branches of Christianity emerged in urban contexts (Christianity in this period was primarily an urban phenomenon). Here are a few profiles of significant cities in the Roman Empire and the distinctive types of Christian groups that functioned there:

Profile #1: Alexandria

A Greek city in Egypt, **Alexandria** was named after Alexander the Great, who founded the city in 331 BCE. It was the second biggest city in the Empire after Rome and very cosmopolitan. Alexandria was home to a large, settled Jewish community. Although by the second century the memory of the pharaohs had grown distant and incomplete, Alexandrians also had a fondness for making connections with Egypt's past. A port city, Alexandria proudly possessed one of the seven ancient wonders of the world, its famous Pharos or lighthouse. Constructed in 280 BCE and around 400 feet tall, it was for more than a thousand years one of the tallest buildings in the world.

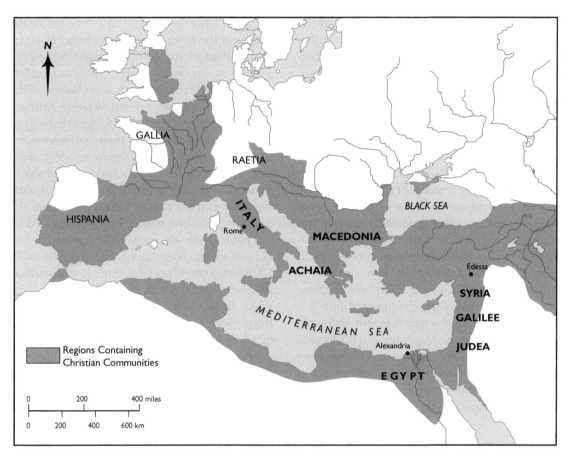

MAP 4.1 By the end of the fourth century CE, Christian communities could be found all through the Mediterranean basin. Major centers were Rome, Alexandria, and Edessa.

Alexandria was also a place for learning, with a library that was world famous. Built during the time of Alexander the Great, it was still functioning during the Roman Empire. The library's mandate was to collect all the world's knowledge; its halls were full of scrolls placed on rows upon rows of shelves. Since the city was an international trade hub, it was (so the story goes) a rule that any book to arrive in the city from a ship would be copied, the copy placed in the library, and the original returned. Thus, this library guaranteed that the city of Alexandria became the primary place for both learning and book production in

the Empire. The library also provided research stipends for scholars to come from all over the world to study the collection. As a research institution, the library was where cutting-edge work in literature was done; it was a major center for Homeric studies, for example. It was not just a major center for literature, either: it also specialized in the sciences, including physics, biology, mathematics, and astronomy.

Christians of Alexandria in the second century were probably cosmopolitan and urban. Many would have been highly educated. Indeed, when we find writings from Nag Hammadi that are particularly learned and which seem to draw on Jewish and Greek philosophical elements together (*OrigWld* and *Eugnostos* are key examples) scholars suggest they were composed at Alexandria—the most likely intellectual environment to have produced sophisticated work that knitted together different cultural influences.

By the fourth century, Egyptian monasticism had become distinct; although monasticism was based in the desert rather than the city, even the cities witnessed the presence of groups of Egyptian monks. These monastic circles were deeply, even radically, **ascetic**. They believed the body was something to be mastered, and women in particular were to be avoided. At the same time, Egyptian monasticism could sometimes stand in tension with the more orthodox or ecclesiastical framework of Alexandria, where the chief authority was the bishop. It is in this environment of fourth-century Egypt that the Nag Hammadi books were copied and eventually disseminated, although we do not know when precisely, or where precisely, this happened. Nor do we know, unfortunately, who copied them, and for whom.

Profile #2: Rome

The city of **Rome** was the Empire's thriving center. At its height, it had a population of around a million people. The presence of the emperor in the city from the first through the third centuries gave Rome a certain distinctive flavor as the Empire's most significant and sacred ceremonial center. Examples of thriving civic religion—temples, sacrifices, shrines and priests—were everywhere. Only in Rome could you find special sacred areas marked out that connected Romans with their ancient roots, just as there were priesthoods and priestly colleges in the city that existed only there.

As a bustling hub, Rome had its share of immigrants settling from other parts of the Empire, many of whom came from the eastern part of the Empire and spoke Greek as well as Latin and brought their own cultural and religious traditions. There

had been Christians in the city since before the middle of the first century, as we know from the apostle **Paul**'s letter to the Romans in the New Testament. The apostle **Peter**, on whom Jesus had laid the mantle of succession, was also one of the early Christian figures revered by later Christians in the city. Both Peter and Paul were buried just outside the city walls after their martyrdom, and Christians visited their graves as an act of devotion. Christians in the city had also had significant run-ins with imperial authorities; around the year 64 CE when a fire had ravaged Rome, the emperor Nero had some Christians rounded up and put to death as scapegoats for causing the fire. For that reason, Nero became hated and feared by Christians everywhere; the rumor even circulated that Nero would rise from the dead to persecute again. In fact, the famous Beast of the book of Revelation (Rev 13) who bears the number 666 may be a coded reference to Nero, using assigned numerical values to Nero's name for those who knew the "key" to decoding the text.

In the second century, the Roman emperors did not actively persecute Christians, although Christians were occasionally martyred for being atheists (from a Roman perspective, they were called thus because they refused to acknowledge the gods of Rome and the *genius* or protective guardian spirit of the Emperor) and dangerous social radicals (because they worshiped someone the Romans had put to death as a dangerous criminal). The fear of martyrdom must have existed as a reality; what we do not know is how much of a fear it was. It is certainly clear that there were many Christians in the city of Rome, and these groups had many different ideas about what it meant to be Christian. The very diversity of Christian groups in the city suggests that not all Christians stood in direct opposition to Rome; many must have been interested in accommodating or assimilating Christian belief to the realities of Roman civic life.

Rome was also the home of some of our great Christian intellectuals, who conducted study circles there. Some were what people have called Gnostic (e.g., **Valentinus**); some were not Gnostic but other sorts of so-called heretics, such as the famous teacher Marcion, who taught a deeply anti-Jewish and conservative form of Christianity, complete with its own set of scriptures. These teachers were not usually native Romans but immigrants drawn to Rome's unique qualities and financially supported by local Roman elites or sub-elites.

Profile #3: Edessa

The ancient name for the city of **Edessa** was the kingdom of Osrhoene; it was not actually a Roman city at all. Edessa sat between two empires (Roman and Persian) and on one of the major trade routes to the East, so therefore it had a very "Eastern" flavor. There had been Christians in Edessa for a long time, although we know almost nothing about when and how they arrived. The predominant language of Christians there was **Syriac**, a dialect of **Aramaic**, the language of Jesus and his followers. There was also a sizable Jewish community in Edessa, and Jews and Christians appear to have been relatively close and on good terms.

Edessa's favored disciple of Jesus was Thomas, who according to legends had come to evangelize in the city in the first century. Many scholars locate what we call a "Thomasine" school in the city; we can see evidence for this, perhaps, in the Nag Hammadi writings associated with Thomas (*Gospel of Thomas*; *Book of Thomas the Contender*) and two other popular early Christian texts, the *Acts of Thomas* and the *Infancy Gospel of Thomas*. Another set of legends popular in Edessa claim that Jesus had corresponded with Edessa's most famous king, Abgar, in the first century.

Syrian Christianity as we find at Edessa had both a courtly aspect (many of the Christians there were members of the royal court, and even the kings of Edessa themselves were Christian

from an early date) and a more ascetic form. The desert was not far away, and from the fourth century on, Christians from this area rivaled Egyptian monks for their acts of asceticism.

Edessa was another center for Christian book production, along with Alexandria. Famous scholars from the area include Tatian (ca. 120–180 CE) whose learned work called the *Diatessaron* (ca. 170 CE) combined the New Testament gospels of Matthew, Mark, Luke, and John seamlessly into one master narrative, and Bardaisan (154–222 CE), a scholar in the court of Edessa who composed an influential treatment of astrology and fate, the *Book of the Laws of the Countries*. Two other significant Christian texts we think might have been composed in Edessa are the *Odes of Solomon* and the so-called *Hymn of the Pearl*, which many modern scholars have classified as Gnostic literature.

A GLIMPSE FORWARD

By the fourth century, the power and strength of the Roman Empire had diminished considerably, although it had not yet fallen. The biggest change concerned the Empire's religious identity. In 312 CE, the emperor **Constantine I** (306–337 CE) won a decisive battle, the **Battle at Milvian Bridge**, against his rival, Maxentius. Constantine attributed his victory to the Christian god. From this point on, Constantine allowed Christianity to flourish openly, and he financially supported the religion, building major Christian basilicas in Rome, Jerusalem, and Bethlehem.

Constantine also had a hand in creating a new, powerful imperialized Christianity. He convened the first ecumenical (that is, universal) Christian council, the **Council of Nicaea** (325 CE) where bishops from all over the Empire gathered to discuss, among other things, what to do about Christian heresy. By the fourth century, so-called Gnostic groups (now splintered into dozens of smaller sects, each with its own name) were no longer the target of direct persecutions, but they

FIGURE 4.1 The Emperor Constantine's adoption of Christianity as his personal religion changed Christianity's fortunes forever.

still apparently existed. The reign of Constantine was a defining era where, in effect, Christianity turned against itself for the first time, with Christians persecuting other Christians rather than Roman authorities persecuting Christians.

We began this chapter with all the things that Christianity did not have in the second century. By the fourth century, after Constantine, the landscape changed considerably. Christians now had churches and basilicas, creeds that were on their way to being formalized, a clearer sense of oversight and administration, and scriptures that could openly circulate. This did not solve or end debates about how things should be done, but it did mean that Christians began to change their thinking about themselves and their place in the world. The

religion was now public, and it continued to grow, drawing significant numbers of new adherents.

Constantine did not make Christianity the official religion of the Roman Empire; he made it legal and sanctioned it. But at the end of the fourth century, another emperor called **Theodosius I** (375–395 CE) put into place much more strenuous sanctions against anything but official, Roman Christianity. Theodosius was also interested in Roman law; the collection of laws he assembled and which his jurists developed, the **Theodosian Code**, makes it quite clear what was to become of various groups seen as Gnostic or heretical:

> For the rest, who are named with the portentious title Encratites, refuted in judgment together with the Saccophorites and Hydroparastatae, brought forth on an indictment, even when discovered in a small trespass of this crime, we comment [that they] be crushed with the capital punishment and inexpiable penalty (*Cod. Theod.* 16.5.9 issued in 382 CE by the co-emperors Gratian, Valentinian, and Theodosius).

> Absolutely everyone, whomsoever the error of diverse heresites disturbs, that is, Eunomians, Arians, Macedonians, Pneumatomachi, Manichaei, encratitae, Apotactitae, Saccofori, Hydroparastatae, shall not gather in any circles, shall not amass any crown, shall not draw any people to themselves nor display any private walls after the likeness of churches, and shall practice nothing, whether publicly or privately, which could impede Catholic holiness. (*Cod. Theod.* 16.5.11 issued in 383 CE by the co-emperors Gratian, Valentinian, and Theodosius)

In the course of three hundred years, Christianity made its long transformation from the religion of 1 or 2 percent of Romans to the legal religion of the Empire. There were so many differences among Christian groups at this time—and so little real cohesion—that it is fair to speak, as many scholars now do, of Christianities, not Christianity. These Christianities were highly local, very diverse, and without any standard or established ways of doing things or ways of being faithful.

A new way to think about what used to be called Gnosticism or heresy in the Empire is to think of early Christianity instead in terms of its range of relations with Empire. The heresiologists who controlled the picture of what Gnostics thought and did were, in the broader context of the Empire, in effect hard-line traditionalists who actively preached on the importance of keeping Christianity pure of Roman influences. For them, the search for knowledge (*gnosis*) looked too much like **Platonism**, or **Stoicism**, or other pagan philosophies of the day. For others, however, there may have been relief in being able to reconcile ancient wisdom and traditional ways of being religious in the Empire with the freedom to worship a new God.

QUESTIONS TO CONSIDER

1. Think about ways that people convert to a religion today. Do you imagine that things worked similarly in the Roman Empire? Why or why not?

2. How did the phenomenon of Christian martyrdom help or hurt the growth of Christianity?

3. How does place (i.e., geography) shape religion?

KEY TERMS

Aramaic	ascetic	Peter	Stoicism
Syriac	Paul	Constantine I	Battle of the Milvian Bridge
Valentinus	Edessa	Council of Nicaea	
Pax Romana	Theodosius I	Platonism	
Theodosian Code	Alexandria	Rome	

FOR FURTHER READING

Fox, Robin Lane. *Pagans and Christians*. San Francisco: Harper Collins, 1988. A long but well-written study of the rise of Christianity in the Roman Empire.

Pagels, Elaine. *The Gnostic Gospels*. New York: Random House, 1979. The most important book written on the Gnostics and the rise of Christianity in the last thirty years. A must read, although some of the conclusions and perspectives are now becoming out of date.

Stark, Rodney. *The Rise of Christianity. A Sociologist Reconsiders History*. Princeton: Princeton University Press, 1996. A controversial study because it was written by a sociologist of contemporary American religions rather than by a historian of Rome, this book introduces some provocative ideas from sociology to explain the rise of Christianity. For a nonspecialist audience.

Wilken, Robert. *The Christians As the Romans Saw Them*. New Haven: Yale University Press, 2003. An accessible study, which reproduces documents that reveal how Romans thought of early Christians and Christianity.

5

Gnostic Prayer

PRAYER OF THE APOSTLE PAUL (NHC I, 1) AND *PRAYER OF THANKSGIVING* (NHC VI, 7)

The Nag Hammadi Library (NHL) as it is published in English translations begins with a short piece clearly identified by its ancient copyist as a prayer, the *Prayer of the Apostle Paul* (PrApP). We know that this copyist carefully copied this piece into the front flyleaf (i.e., the inside cover) of Codex I (the **Jung Codex**), so although it is a short work, it was meant as an important preface for what is to come in the rest of the codex. It was unknown to us before the discovery of the NHL, and it is a nice little introduction to this early Christian library. Like the rest of the texts in the library, it seems to have been originally written in Greek and, at some point, translated into Coptic.

In terms of genre, the *PrApP* looks much like other prayers that circulated in the ancient world, not all of which were Christian or Jewish. As a matter of fact, some of the closest "sister-texts" to it are found in a collection of **pagan** texts known as the **Corpus Hermeticum**. One of them, a *Prayer of Thanksgiving* (PThanks), is even found in the NHL! So one of the things we will do in this chapter is compare the Christian *Prayer of the Apostle Paul* from Codex I with the pagan *Prayer of Thanksgiving* from Codex VI. Given that they are both contained in a largely Christian library, would people in antiquity have noticed the difference between the two, or did it not particularly matter—a prayer to God was a prayer to God, no matter who used it? Let's see if closer examination can shed some light on the matter. We will also consider other prayers that we find in the NHL, to discern if we can get a better sense of the range and the purpose(s) of ancient prayer.

THE *PRAYER OF THE APOSTLE PAUL*: BACKGROUND

If you are reading through the NHL sequentially, the tractate is the first writing you encounter, and if you're like most readers, you will probably already feel lost on the first page. Remember that for the most part, these texts were written for an "inside" audience that already knew the distinct vocabulary and theology of their community. Only very rarely were these texts written for outsiders. Although some modern readers are put

THE TERM "PAGAN"

In antiquity, the term "pagan" meant something insulting like a "rustic" or a "hick." Many historians of the Roman Empire reject the word, but the problem is that we do not have many better adjectives for a person or writing or practice that was not Christian. "Non-Christian" doesn't work, because Jewish texts are just as "non-Christian" as "pagan" ones. "Roman" or "Graeco-Roman" doesn't work because Christian texts produced in the Roman Empire are also "Roman or "Graeco-Roman" (if they were written in Greek), and many Christians were also Roman. Some NT scholars like the word "gentile" (instead of "pagan") because the apostle Paul used it in his letters, but "gentile" is another ancient Christian word that was also a label, and not necessarily a nice one. So "pagan" ends up being the best adjective we have for people, things, and actions that were neither Christian nor Jewish.

off by the obscurity of these ancient texts, considering them to be elitist (one of the things these readers often feel characterizes Christianity is that it is technically open to everyone who hears and accepts its central message of salvation), we need to be fair: in the second century when these texts were written, Christianity was an underground movement, and Christians were known to be persecuted. Thus "hidden" or "elitist" forms of Christianity helped to protect its members and preserve the movement. Virtually all religious movements have their own vocabularies, set of beliefs, and so on; some of these texts sound strange to us today, not because they set out to exclude others but because they (unlike the writings of the NT) come from sources that were lost and then recovered in the modern period; therefore their distinctive vocabulary did not enter our cultural mainstream. At the time, though, an ancient audience would have been less confused by some of the terms and concepts we encounter here.

As an exercise, it might be helpful to make a list of the unfamiliar words or terms in the *PrApP*. It might look something like this:

- **Pleroma**/Fullness
- the "psychic God" (or "animate God")
- "light soul" (note that the "light soul" is distinct from "spirit"; the author of *PrApP*, like many others, distinguished the human *spirit* from the human *soul*).
- **Repose**
- **Mind**

We will see these terms again. But for now, it is enough to point out that "**Pleroma**," for example, is a fairly common word in the NT letters Colossians and Ephesians (translated in English Bibles as "fullness"). So although we appear to be on strange territory, the author of this piece is in fact drawing *directly* on the writings of the apostle Paul. Other words are not so strange, but are typical technical words that these writers used differently than we use them, like "repose" (Gk *anapausis*) or "mind" (Gk *nous*). Some of these unfamiliar terms derive from Paul's writings; others come from the Gospel of John; still others derive from Greek philosophy. These became common words in second-century Christian writings; their presence here helps us to date the *PrApP* from, at the earliest, the second or third century.

THE PRAYER OF THANKSGIVING: BACKGROUND

Unlike the *PrApP* that begins a codex, the *PThanks* comes as a kind of epilogue to a text called the *Discourse on the Eighth and Ninth* in

WHY PAUL, IN *PRAYER OF THE APOSTLE PAUL*?

Although Paul is well known in contemporary Christianity, what is most remarkable was that in the second century, Paul's importance to Christianity was highly controversial. Not all Christians agreed that he was equally authoritative, and most remarkably of all, Paul was a favorite, not of the proto-Orthodox or proto-Catholic Christians but of those whom they despised: the so-called Gnostics. In fact, so popular was Paul among those the proto-orthodoxy considered **heretical**,

he acquired in the second century the nickname "the Apostle of the Heretics" (Tertullian, *Against Marcion*, 3:5). Consequently, while Paul's letters were certainly circulated in the second century, those who quoted him tended to be those whom the fledgling mainstream Church scorned. But all this changed in later centuries; in fact, the NT contains thirteen Pauline works out of a total of twenty-seven books...quite a turnaround for the "Apostle of the Heretics."

Codex VI, a collection that includes many non-Christian texts (see chap. 16). We knew about the *PThanks* even before the discovery of the NHL: the same text is appended to an ancient Greek magician's spell book now in Paris (called the *Papyrus Mimaut*) and another popular ancient pagan text titled *Asclepius* (a partial Coptic translation of *Asclepius* is also found in Codex VI). This tells us that *PThanks* circulated widely in antiquity and was "repurposed" by various authors in their writings. In fact, in the NH collection, we actually have a short **colophon** or note from the copyist (65:8–14) explaining his rationale for including this prayer:

> I have copied this one of his discourses. A great many have come into my hands, but I have not copied them because I thought they were already in your [pl.] possession. I even hesitate to copy these things for you [pl.], since perhaps you may already have received them and the matter may annoy you, for that person's discourses that have come into my hands are many. (trans. Marvin Meyer, *The Nag Hammadi Scriptures*, San Francisco: HarperOne, 2009: 423)

The scribal note gives us some tantalizing information. First, the copyist has many similar writings at his disposal. Given that all evidence points to this scribe being Christian, it's a bit odd that he has access to so many pagan prayer texts. Second, it remains mysterious who asked this scribe to copy

this prayer and the other pagan texts in Codex VI. If he were a monk, as many scholars assume, what would a Christian monk have wanted with pagan prayers? Or, was it perhaps not a monk at all but an independent Christian copyist? This remains, yet again, another mystery.

WHAT CONSTITUTED "PRAYER" IN THE ANCIENT WORLD?

To answer this question, let's first consider the different types of prayers we find in the ancient world. They are actually much the same as prayers today and cross the boundaries of many religious traditions.

When we read or hear that someone has been praying or has offered up a prayer, we usually have a sense of what that means. Someone has spoken words—silently or out loud—calling on a higher power for some kind of assistance. But a prayer for assistance is really just one type of prayer. Besides *PrApP* and *PThanks*, the NHL actually contains many prayers, of different types, embedded into various documents. Some have words; some were silent, and some even have sounds but no words. Here are just a few of the types we find represented:

- **glossolalia** or "tongue speaking," in the form of strings of vowels
- turning inward, praying silently
- hymns and singing
- repeated chants, like liturgical prayer
- **invocations** or "calling upon" a higher power
- prayers to avoid temptation, sin
- **petitions** or prayers for assistance
- praises to God, Jesus and/or other celestial beings

Prayer can be collective or individual; it can be rehearsed/repeated or spontaneous; it can be accompanied by actions or done in stillness and silence. All prayer, though, is predicated upon a central belief: that humans can communicate with the divine, and that the divine listens.

In the case of the *PrApP* the petitioner asks for a number of things, including redemption, the "gift of the spirit," authority (presumably to lead others), healing, and a direct experience of the Savior ("And the firstborn of the Pleroma of Grace—Reveal him to my mind!" *PrApP* I A, 23–25). Really, this prayer is a petition, asking the divine to grant something or a series of things.

By contrast, the *PThanks* works from the other direction: it thanks the divine for gifts *already* received, in this case, the triple gifts of "mind, word, and *gnosis*." Together, these bring enlightenment: a blissful knowledge of the Father. In both cases, the central goal of the prayer is the direct experience of the divine.

WHY DID THE ANCIENT COPYIST CHOOSE *PRAYER OF THE APOSTLE PAUL* TO BEGIN CODEX I?

In the past decade, scholars have paid closer attention to the logic of the NH codices; that is, we're trying to figure out why certain ancient writings were copied and preserved, and why they were put in the order that they were.

In the case of *PrApP*, it begins a book that contains the following writings: the *Apocryphon* (or "Secret Book") *of James*, the *Gospel of Truth*, *Treatise on the Resurrection*, and the *Tripartite Tractate*. This is kind of an eclectic collection, but the last three all probably come from the same school of thought called **Valentinianism** (see chaps. 6, 7). Key terms in *PrApP* like "rest"

"WHAT NO ANGEL EYE HAS SEEN"

In one line of the *PrApP*, we read, "grant what no angel eye has seen and no archon ear has heard and what has not entered the human heart." Whoever composed this prayer borrowed here from Paul's First Letter to the Corinthians 2:9: "What no eye has seen, nor ear heard, nor the heart of man conceived, what God has prepared for those who love him" (RSV). And Paul in turn borrowed these words from Isaiah 64:4: "From of old no one has heard or perceived by the ear, no eye has seen a God besides thee." When Paul paraphrased these words, he did not change them too much; but whoever wrote *PrApP* added the words "angel" and "archon" to Paul's words as we find them in the New Testament. On one level, these additions help us to date the document and to attribute it to a kind of Christian philosophy because many Gnostic texts of the second century mention **archons** as celestial beings. More striking is what the additions tell us about the way this author thought about the world: one had to guard against malevolent celestial beings who were, at base, less capable of revelation or *gnosis* than the Christians of his circle.

(Gk *anapausis*) and "fullness" (Gk *pleroma*) are very common in Valentinianism, so one hypothesis is that *PrApP* is a specifically Valentinian prayer (i.e., no one other than Valentinians would have used it). In fact, the Canadian scholar of Gnosticism, Michael Kaler, noted that a set of important vocabulary words in this prayer is found in all five of the main tractates in Codex I; these include mind, rest, spirit (Gk *pneuma*), grace, light, and elect. Thus it made good sense to begin this codex with a prayer that suited the general set of beliefs and vocabulary reflected in the volume as a whole.

In addition, a prayer that invokes the authority of the apostle Paul seemed to be a good beginning to Codex I. Of all the NT writers, Paul had the most profound impact on those who composed many of the Christian writings in the NHL. Paul/Saul was not one of Jesus's twelve disciples; in fact, he never once met Jesus. Instead, Paul's knowledge of the resurrected Christ came from a direct mystical experience on the road to Damascus. Consequently, Paul became the figurehead for people receiving a special revelation from the Lord directly, rather than through hearing about Jesus's preaching or actions on earth.

THE VIEW OF JESUS IN *PRAYER OF THE APOSTLE PAUL*

The *PrApP* contains five distinct titles given to Jesus Christ:

- Lord of lords
- King of the ages
- Son of man
- Spirit
- Advocate (or Paraclete) of Truth

All five are common titles for Jesus in the ancient world, and all come from the New Testament or the Hebrew Bible. "Lord of lords," for instance,

is used three times in the NT, in 1 Timothy 6:15 and Revelation 17:14 and 19:16, where it is paired with another title, "King of kings. These appellations do not appear in *PrApP*. Readers familiar with Handel's *Messiah* may remember the "Hallelujah" chorus with its repeated phrases "Lord of lords, and King of kings." "King of the ages" is also found in 1 Timothy (1:17) and Revelation (15:3). You will find that some English translations of *PrApP* prefer to leave the word untranslated (Gk *aeons*), so you will find "King of the aeons." The result is that the prayer ends up sounding a lot stranger than "King of the ages" to Christian readers familiar with the Bible; in antiquity, however, readers would have recognized the shared language and imagery.

"Son of man" is a tremendously important early Christian title for Jesus, occurring eighty-two times in the NT **gospels** as well as in other NT writings. It is also found numerous times in the Hebrew Bible, but in most instances the term does not seem to signify someone of particular importance: it could just be a synonym for any human being. By the time Christians applied the term to Jesus, "Son of man" seems to have been a title connected with Jesus's function as an eternal, powerful being connected to apocalyptic revelation. Some modern scholars do not like the translation "Son of man" and prefer the gender-neutral "Son of humanity," but the original Greek term can reasonably be translated in any of these ways.

By contrast, Jesus as "Spirit" is pretty unusual and the first hint that the *PrApP* is something a bit different from what we might find in most NT writings, or in the perspective of later, proto-orthodox writers. But in the Gospel of John 7:39, Jesus is called "Spirit" without any explanation. The unusual titles "Advocate (NRSV et al.)," "Counselor (RSV et al.)," or "Paraclete (NJB)" for Jesus also come from the Gospel of John (15:26; 14:26, 16:7). We learn from this not that the author of this prayer was a heretic but that he or she evidently read the Gospel of John, the letters of Paul, and probably the book of Revelation.

All this tells us a few things. First, the *PrApP* is definitely a Christian document. This may seem obvious, but it should not be taken for granted, especially because one modern school of thought separates Gnosticism from "Christianity" (see chap. 2). Remember that not all the NH writings are Christian. Second, the source texts for the prayer's imagery (and ideas of Christ's nature, or what we call **Christology**) all derive from writings that are in the NT. This helps us to date the prayer, to see which books of the NT were known at the time this prayer was composed, and finally, to see that this author's "go to" texts were not heretical but perfectly orthodox. Given that this prayer begins a codex of a supposedly heretical library, it is interesting that there is not much here that might have offended a **heresiologist** such as **Irenaeus of Lyons**.

GOD IN THE *PRAYER OF THANKSGIVING*

Since the *PThanks* is a pagan prayer, you may be surprised to see, first of all, that it is directed not toward a minor god but toward one, single God. This is because the particular group of texts from which this thanksgiving prayer emerges, the Corpus Hermeticum, are all pagan **monotheist** texts, in keeping with the monotheistic systems of Graeco-Roman philosophical thought. The next significant title for God, here, is "Father." The Christian scribe who copied out this prayer may not have considered a pagan prayer directed to "God the Father" as anything scandalously heretical.

The only eyebrow-raising image in this prayer is that God, the Father, apparently has a womb from which every creature is born. How could a male God have a womb? This kind of gender-bending is not unusual in ancient texts. God was understood to be beyond gender, possessing both male and female aspects or energies. Even in the Hebrew Bible, God is sometimes described with feminine, maternal metaphors, such as in Hosea 11:3–4 or Isaiah 42:14, where God says, "I will cry out like a woman in labor; I will gasp and pant." God's love for humankind, in these ancient Jewish texts, has sometimes been articulated as a sort of "womb-love"—as all-encompassing, miraculous, and beautiful as the love of each mother for her child as she brings it into the world. In fact, the Hebrew root word from which "compassion" and "mercy" (used to describe God's love for his children in the Jewish scriptures) derive come from the Hebrew *rechem*, which means "womb." Such richness of language and metaphor conveys the Father's encompassing of all elements of creation and procreation.

THE INVISIBLE ASPECTS OF PRAYER

A written prayer, in and of itself, tells us only the *content* that the person praying wishes to convey. What we usually cannot find out about are the *performative* aspects of prayer. Prayer often involves movement—consider Muslims prostrating themselves as they face Mecca, for instance, or Sufi Muslims whirling in ecstatic prayer, or some evangelical Christians raising their hands toward heaven, or orthodox Jews *davening* or rocking back and forth while praying or when in front of the Western (Wailing) Wall in the Old City of Jerusalem. Other small actions associated with Christian prayer include anointing, making the sign of the cross, bowing before the altar, lighting candles, using incense, and kneeling. Written prayers, unless they come with instructions, cannot even tell us what small actions should accompany them: for example, eyes open, closed, or upraised? Hands held up, or pressed together, or at one's sides? In texts such as the *PrApP* and *PThanks*, all we can tell about prayer is what words were used, and that gives us a kind of impoverished picture, overall. We cannot tell where the prayer was performed (inside or outside? facing a specific direction? in a house or in a church?) or when (how many times a day? on what particular times of the year?). Interestingly, however, the *PThanks* as we have it in the NHL does preserve one bit of information about the ritual context of this prayer: it says at the end, "when they prayed and said these things, they embraced and went to eat their sacred bloodless food" (presumably, "bloodless" means "vegetarian," although it might mean "kosher."). Still more interestingly, when we find the *PThanks* at the beginning of the magician's handbook (*Papyrus Mimaut*), immediately before the prayer begins, we read, "when someone wants to entreat God at sunset, he should direct his gaze to that quarter, and likewise at sunrise toward the direction they call east." We do not know if the copyist who copied the *PThanks* knew about these instructions and deliberately left them out, or whether they had been added by whoever copied out *Papyrus Mimaut*. Nevertheless, it is very interesting to have at least a small hint as to how this prayer should be conducted.

OTHER PRAYERS IN THE NAG HAMMADI LIBRARY

One form of prayer that we find sometimes in the NHL (but that are not present in *PrApP* and the *PThanks*) are hymns involving long strings of vowel sounds, such as we find in the *Discourse on the Eighth and Ninth* (55:23–57:25), or this one from the *Gospel of the Egyptians:*

> Yesseus
> ĒŌ O U ĒŌ ŌUA
> Truly, in truth
> Yesseus Mazareus Yessedekeus
> Living water
> Child of the child
> Glorious name
> Truly, in truth
> Everlasting being
> IIII
> ĒĒĒĒ
> EEEE
> OOOO

> UUUU
> ŌŌŌŌ
> AAAA
> Truly, in truth
> ĒI AAAAA OOOOO
> The one who sees the eternal realms. (*GosEg* 66:8)

We do not know if these vowel strings were sung (along with the rest of the prayer) or intoned. It is a bit amusing to imagine a scribe writing out all those vowel strings, but they were thought to be crucial to the efficacy of the prayer itself. On the other hand, many magical papyri contain strings of vowels carefully arranged into specific shapes such as triangles or diamonds, like this (see also fig. 5-2):

> A
> EEEE
> OOOOOOO
> EEEE
> A

In cases such as this, probably the efficacy of these vowels comes not from intoning them for specific lengths of time but from the act of writing them out, or from having them so arranged on the papyrus or whatever amulet contained the letter strings. We do not know if, in their original Greek form, the vowel strings in texts such as *GosEg* were arranged into shapes on the manuscripts on which they were first written; we do know, though, that the Coptic scribes who copied the texts merely wrote them out in a long line (see fig. 5-1: Codex IV, p 54 of *GosEg*).

This might mean that they either did not know the original "magical" written efficacy of the vowels arranged in a shape, or else they did not want to turn their sacred texts into something that looked like a magical text. Either way, it is impossible to say.

The NHL also contains more conventional-looking prayers. For instance, in the heavily damaged *Dialogue of the Savior*, the Savior tells his disciples explicitly how to praise God:

FIGURE 5.1 A very fragmentary page of the *Gospel of the Egyptians* from Codex IV. Note the strings of vowel sounds in the top fragment.

Now when you offer praise, do so in this way:
Hear us, Father,
As you have heard your only Son
And have received him to yourself.
[You have] given him rest from many [labors],
Your power is [invincible],
[because] your armaments are [invincible],
…light…alive…inaccessible…[above].
The [true] word [has brought] repentance for life,
[and this has come] from you.
You are the thought and supreme serenity
Of those who are alone.
Again, hear us
As you have heard your chosen.
Through your sacrifice the chosen will enter.
Through their good works they have freed their souls
From blind bodily limbs,
So that they may come to be forever.

Amen. (*DialSav* 121:3–122:1, trans. Marvin Meyer, *The Nag Hammadi Scriptures* [San Francisco: HarperOne, 2007]: 301–2)

There is nothing really unusual or heretical in this prayer; it is a beautiful petition and song of praise. A similar kind of prayer is spoken by Jesus's brother James just before his martyrdom in the *2nd Apocalypse of James* (62:12–63:29). It is too long to reproduce here in full, but contains similarly inspiring and beautiful words:

[Bring me to where my] salvation is,
and deliver me from this [place of] sojourn.
Let not your grace be squandered on me,
But let your grace be pure.
Save me from an evil death.
Bring me from the tomb alive,
For your grace is alive in me,
The desire to accomplish a work of fullness. (trans. Wolf-Peter Funk, "The Second

Apocalypse of James," in Marvin Meyer, ed., *The Nag Hammadi Scriptures*, San Francisco: HarperOne, 2007: 341)

This prayer is intended to be recited by a martyr shortly before death. But some scholars surmise from its language that it was not originally composed for that purpose, since it seems to presuppose that the person reciting it will not necessarily perish from his or her trials. It may, then, be another example of an ancient prayer, which was repurposed to fit another narrative, but it itself could fit into various contexts. Other prayers in the NHL that are petitions or praises occur in the *Teachings of Silvanus* ("Hymn to Christ," 112:37–113:23), but few prayers are as poignant as this one in *2ndApJas*, since it remains one of our earliest Christian prayers to be recited right before death.

OTHER PRAYERS OUTSIDE THE NAG HAMMADI LIBRARY

There are other early Christian texts outside the NHL from the second and third centuries that also demonstrate how Jesus prayed, sometimes in rather surprising ways. In a passage called the "Round Dance of the Cross" from an apocryphal text called the *Acts of John*, Jesus prays while his disciples sing "amen!" and dance around him in a circle holding hands:

> I will play the flute. Dance, everyone.
> Amen.
> I will mourn. Lament, everyone.
> Amen.
> The Ogdoad sings with us.
> Amen.
> The twelfth dances on high.
> Amen.
> The whole cosmos takes part in dancing.
> Amen
> Whoever does not dance does not know what happens.

> Amen.

In another ancient Gnostic text, the *Books of Jeu*, Jesus performs an elaborate fire baptism with prayers offered in the four directions:

> Hear me, my father, father of all fatherhoods, infinite light. Make my disciples worthy to receive the baptism of fire, and release them from their sins, and purify them from their transgressions: those which they knowingly committed and those which they do not know they committed, those which they have committed from childhood up to this very day, as well as their slanders, their curses, their false oaths, their thefts, their lies, their lying accusations, their whoring, their adulteries, their lusts, their greed, and things which they have committed from childhood up to this very day.

This all sounds fine, until the prayer takes a surprising turn:

> Yea, hear me, my father, as I invoke your imperishable names that are in the treasury of the light:
>
> Azarakaza A … Amathkratitath
>
> Yo Yo Yo
>
> Amen Amen
>
> Yaoth Yaoth Yaoth
>
> Phaoph Phaoph Phaoph
>
> Chioephozpe Chenobinuth
>
> Zarlai Lazarlai Laizai
>
> Amen Amen Amen. (trans. Violet McDermott, *The Books of Jeu*, Leiden: E. J. Brill, 1978: 111)

Here, a prayer in traditional form for forgiveness from sin turns into a magical invocation of God's divine, secret names. If you think about it, the line between prayer and magic can be pretty thin; some people distinguish between the two by saying that in prayer, an individual *asks* a deity for something, whereas in magic, an individual *commands* a deity to do something. Many magic spells invoke the names of deities and petition for something, just as we find in prayers in certain NHL writings such as the *GosEg*.

A GREEK MAGICAL PAPYRUS

We are lucky enough to have hundreds of Greek magical texts, including this one, now in the Kelsey Museum at the University of Michigan. The amulet protected its wearer, a woman named Helena, from fever. The text reads:

[IA]RBATH AGRAMME FIBLO CHNEMEO
[A E]E EEE IIII OOOOO UUUUU OOOOOO[O]
Lord Gods, heal Helena, daughter of [...]
From every illness and every shivering and [fever],
Ephemeral, quotidian, tertian, quar[tan],
IARBATH AGRAMME FIBLO CHNEMEO
AEEIOUOOUOIEEA

EEIOUOOUOIEE
EIOUOOUOIE
IOUOOUOI
OUOOUO
UOOU UUUUU
OO

Note how much in common this magical spell has with a Christian prayer from this same time period: an appeal to the divine, a specific request for protection or healing, and the invocation of vowel strings. Unlike our vowel strings in the NHL, however, this papyrus retains vowels shaped into triangles.

FIGURE 5.2 A papyrus magical spell against fevers (Pmich inv. 6666 = PGM CXXX. Egypt, 3rd cen. CE.)

The Nag Hammadi library, as a collected set of volumes, begins with a prayer text. The *Prayer of the Apostle Paul* is a wonderful introduction to a varied body of writings that, despite holding different perspectives, all agree on the significance of prayer. In fact, the more you look for evidence of ancient prayer in the NH writings, the more you will find. But the *PrApP* is also a gentle lead-in to texts that will soon begin to look quite a bit more unfamiliar to the uninitiated reader. Since there seems to be good evidence that whoever composed this writing appeared to be deeply familiar with Valentinian Christianity, it is to that tradition that we turn in the following chapter.

QUESTIONS TO CONSIDER

1. Consider this ancient Greek magical charm:

   "Take papyrus and write thus: I am CHPHYRIS. I must be successful. MICHAEL RAPHAEL ROUBEL NARIEL KATTEL ROUMBOUTHIEL AZARIEL IOEL EZRIEL SOURIEL NARIEL METMOURIEL AZAEL AZIELSAOUMIELROUBOUTHIELRABIEEL RABIEEL RABCHLOU ENAEZRAEL, angels, protect me from every bad situation that comes upon me." (PGM XXXVI.170–175).

   Is this a magic spell, or a prayer? How do we distinguish one from the other?

2. Do you agree that all the activities listed in the first set of bullet points are kinds of prayer? Or do you see these as different activities?

3. Why do you think the Christian scribe who copied *PThanks* included a pagan prayer in Codex VI? What do you make of the colophon?

KEY TERMS

pagan	invocation	christology
gospel	*aeons*	repose (*anapausis*)
heresiologist	Irenaeus of Lyons	glossolalia
monotheist	Pleroma	Valentinianism
Corpus Hermeticum	colophon	Jung Codex
Mind	petition	

FOR FURTHER READING

Barnstone, Willis, ed. *The Other Bible*. San Francisco: HarperOne, 2005. A good collection of hard-to-find Jewish and Christian texts outside the Bible. Includes a translation of the "Round Dance of the Cross."

Good, Deirdre. "Prayer of the Apostle Paul from the Nag Hammadi Library." In *Prayer from Alexander to Constantine*, edited by Mark Kiley et al., 291–95. London: Routledge, 1997). An excellent readable article on *Prayer of the Apostle Paul*.

Kaler, Michael. "The Prayer of the Apostle Paul in the Context of Nag Hammadi Codex I," *Journal of Early Christian Studies* 16/3 (2008): 319–39. For more advanced readers, an analysis of why the *PrApP* is the first document in Codex I.

Meyer, Marvin, and Richard Smith, eds. *Ancient Christian Magic: Coptic Texts of Ritual Power*. Princeton, NJ: Princeton University Press, 1999. Another great primary source collection, this time of Christian magical texts. There are many examples of Christian prayers here, a few with further details on how these should be performed.

6

Valentinus and the Valentinians

Of all the second-century heretics, the one about whom we know the most may be **Valentinus** (100–175 CE). An Egyptian by birth, Valentinus was born in the town of Phrebonis on the Nile Delta. Educated at nearby Alexandria, he received a classical Greek education. During the time of the emperor Hadrian (117–138 CE), Valentinus embarked upon a teaching career. It is also clear that by this time, he had converted to Christianity, counting among his teachers the Christian Gnostic philosopher **Basilides** and **Theudas**, who had reputedly been a student of the apostle Paul. By the end of Hadrian's reign, sometime around 138–40 CE, Valentinus moved to Rome to continue his teaching. By all accounts, he was a wonderfully successful teacher, a keen philosopher, and a skilled public speaker. Even the heresiologists speak about him with a modicum of respect. One intriguing story is that Valentinus was such an effective Christian leader that he was nearly elected bishop of Rome. It is interesting to contemplate, if Valentinus had become bishop, how Christianity might be different today. (He lost out, so the story goes, to someone who had confessed his faith under fear of persecution—supporting the heresiologists' claim that the Gnostics scorned martyrdom and would do anything to get out of it.)

Valentinus stayed in Rome for fifteen or twenty years, and then he seems to have disappeared. Most probably, he died in the city. We do know that he was neither condemned nor exiled as a heretic. Still, the trail runs cold around the 160s. One heresiologist, **Epiphanius**, claims that Valentinus left Rome, shipwrecked on Cyprus, and went mad, but there is no hard evidence for this story. Some scholars speculate that at the end of his life, Valentinus moved back to Alexandria, which explains why Clement of Alexandria, the great Christian theologian of the third century CE, was evidently familiar with his work. It is entirely possible, however, that Clement could have known Valentinus's work without having learned it from him directly, and Valentinus's later ties with Alexandria remain tenuous at best.

IRENAEUS ON VALENTINUS AND THE VALENTINIANS

One reason we know about Valentinus and the Valentinian school is because they were the focus of **Irenaeus** of Lyons's special scorn. His great five-volume work, *Against Heresies* (*Adv. Haer.*), was above all an attack on Valentinianism. Part of what incensed Irenaeus about the Valentinians is that they closely resembled proto-orthodox Christians, so much so that Irenaeus refers

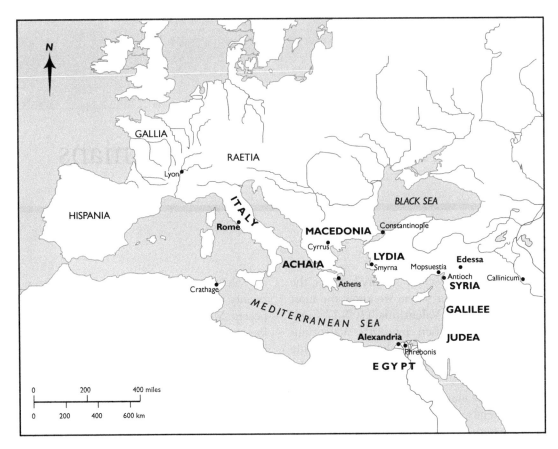

MAP 6.1 Cities with Known Valentinian Churches Across the Roman Empire

to Valentinian teachers as "wolves in sheep's cloth-ing." He notes that they, like their proto-orthodox peers, confess "God the Father" and "our Lord Jesus Christ." They claim an identical doctrine with the proto-orthodox, and deny that they are heretical in any way. Thus Irenaeus saw the Valentinians as a particular danger: they were obviously com-pelling as teachers as well as highly successful in winning converts. In *Adv. Haer.*, Irenaeus paints Valentinianism predictably; his aim was to make it look as unappealing as possible to people who might be interested, and to bring to the forefront what might have been very small or minor distinc-tions between proto-orthodoxy and Valentinian Christianity. The Valentinians were doing un-Christian things, he claimed, and their group(s)

had neither merit nor integrity. Now, with the dis-covery of the NHL, we can read this kind of polemic "between the lines" (or to use a phrase professional scholars of Christianity use, "against the grain"): what it really means is that Irenaeus felt profoundly threatened by the Valentinians's success.

Because the Catholic Church's rejection of Valentinianism in the fourth and fifth centuries was so complete, very few Valentinian texts sur-vived before the discovery of the NHL. What we knew about the movement at that time, there-fore, was limited to what Irenaeus had told us. He begins *Adv. Haer.* with what we call the "**Great Account**," a lengthy presentation of Valentinian theology and cosmology. Irenaeus appears to have drawn this account from various sources. His goal was to pick up on the areas in which Valentinianism evidently taught something quite different from what Irenaeus considered "straight-thinking" Christianity. Two main areas attracted his attention: (1) Valentinian teachings about God, and (2) Valentinian teachings about anthropology, or the nature of human beings.

In Irenaeus's account of Valentinus's cosmology, the cosmos emanates in a system of symmetrical male/female pairs called **syzygies** (sing., **syzygy**). The first principles, the Ineffable (male)

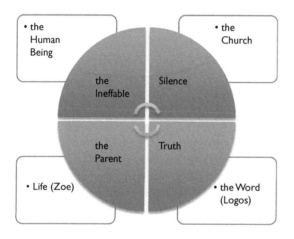

DIAGRAM 6.1 The primary Ogdoad of the Valentinian System.

and Silence (female), generate a second set of syzygies, the Parent (male) and Truth (female). These in turn produce four more paired **aeons** (the Human Being, the Church, Life, and the Word) resulting in a primary **Ogdoad** (see diagram 6–1).

At this point, the Word and Life produce ten more "powers" (the **Decad**) while the Human and the Church produce twelve more "powers" (the **Dodecad**). Altogether, there are thirty aeons dwelling in a divine realm called the **Pleroma** ("Fullness"), which is contained within two boundaries called "Limits": one separating the beings in the Pleroma from the Ineffable, and another separating them from "the Mother" (also called **Achamoth**, one of the last in the set of twelve powers produced from the Human Being and the Church [see diagram 6.2]).

Next, the Mother, alone outside the Pleroma, engenders both the Anointed ("Christ") and Shadow, or matter. But the Anointed strips himself of matter and ascends to the Pleroma, leaving the Mother bereft of her spiritual substance. She then produces the **Demiurge** along with a being called "the ruler on the left" (perhaps a sort of Satan figure).

Since the discovery of Valentinian texts at Nag Hammadi, we are now in a position to compare these texts with Irenaeus's "Great Account."

WHERE DID THE CONCEPT OF AN OGDOAD COME FROM?

It is often thought that Valentinus and the Valentinians drew their systems of **monads, dyads,** and **tetrads** from **Pythagoreanism.** But Valentinus seems to exceed the bounds of Pythagorean number theory by developing a system in which a system of eight, a primary Ogdoad, features as the core set of divine beings. Scholars of Egyptology have pointed out that ancient Egyptian religion also featured an Ogdoad of gods (known by that term) who were worshiped in the city of Hermopolis. The eight deities were headed by either Hathor and Ra, or Hathor and Thoth in later versions, and arranged as male-female pairs. These deities were associated with primordial space: Naunet and Nu represented the primordial waters; Amunet and Amun represented air; Kauket and Kuk represented darkness; and Hauhet and Huh represented infinite space. Although there are no direct connections between the list of Egyptian deities in the Ogdoad and the aeons in Valentinus's system, it is still possible that Valentinus, as a native Egyptian, had learned about the earlier system, or at least its terminology, and adapted the term to suit his own model of the cosmos.

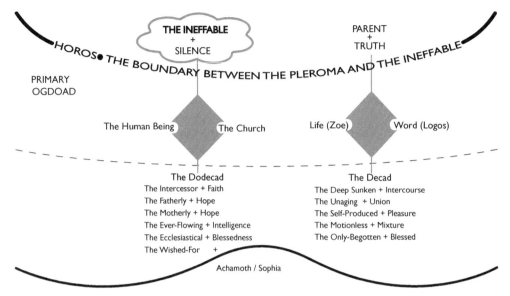

DIAGRAM 6.2 Valentinus's Cosmology According to Irenaeus's "Great Account"

We've discovered that there is not very much overlap or similarity, which of course leads us to wonder about Irenaeus's reliability on this issue. Remember that his goal was to discredit, not to faithfully present, Valentinian cosmology. On the other hand, there are enough similarities with some other Valentinian texts to suggest that Irenaeus did not invent this system but merely adapted or modified it according to his polemical perspective.

WHAT KIND OF A CHRISTIAN WAS VALENTINUS?

One of the hallmarks of Valentinian Christianity is that it is very close to mainstream or proto-orthodox Christianity. Unlike baffling or confusing texts such as the *Gospel of the Egyptians* or *On the Origin of the World*, the surviving works of Valentinus lack elaborate mythic schemes, cosmologies, and casts of characters. Many scholars of Valentinus imagine that he and his followers probably worshiped with other mainstream Christians, but then held additional private meetings in which the hidden or higher meanings of such things as

the sacraments were discussed. In that way, the followers of Valentinus were able to "pass" as non-Valentinians. Time was spent in careful study of the Jewish and Christian scriptures, such that the very first Christian exegeses of scripture that we possess were written by followers and students of Valentinus. Valentinus was therefore recognizably Christian—he taught about the coming of Jesus as the Savior, for instance. But he was probably also an assimilationist, drawing freely on Greek philosophy to fill out his ideas of the world and of Christ.

THE WRITINGS OF VALENTINUS

Valentinus's writings have survived in only about a dozen tiny fragments, none of which were found at Nag Hammadi. They are simply lines quoted by heresiologists, and they do not fit with any of our texts found at Nag Hammadi. Since they are not NH texts, we will look at a representative sample here:

> Valentinus, the leader of a sect, was the first to devise the notion of three subsistent entities (*hypostases*),

in a work that he entitled On the Three Natures. For he devised the notion of three subsistent entities and three persons—Father, Son and Holy Spirit. (Marcellus of Ancyra, *On the Holy Church*, 9)

Here, Valentinus is actually responsible for formulating the same Christian Trinity that later becomes a prominent part of Catholic doctrine. We might—but should not—take for granted that this fragment also clearly pegs Valentinus as a Christian. We find no such explicitly Christian theology in many of the so-called Gnostic texts from Nag Hammadi (compare, for instance, *HypArch* or *Thunder, Perfect Mind*). Thus Valentinus's work as a Christian theologian accords with Irenaeus's words about him: that he, and his followers, look much like other more mainstream Christian teachers.

> However much a portrait is inferior to an actual face, just so is the world worse than the living realm. Now, what is the cause of the portrait? It is the majesty of the face that has furnished to the painter a prototype so that the portrait might be honored by his name. For the form was not reproduced with perfect fidelity, yet the name completed the lack within the act of modeling. And also God's invisible cooperates with what has been modeled to lend it credence (quoted by Clement of Alexandria, *Stromateis* 4.89. 6–4.90.1.).

In this brief passage, we see Valentinus's debt to Platonism. Plato had suggested a division between a Divine Reality and then a world of Forms, which are based on realities as inferior (but wholly good)

replicas. A few of Valentinus's fragments use metaphors related to craftsmanship or art; although it is difficult to know what to make of this, it is a hallmark of his writing.

> He was continent, enduring all things. Jesus digested divinity: he ate and drank in a special way, without excreting his solids. He had such a great capacity for continence that the nourishment within him was not corrupted, for he did not experience corruption. (quoted by Clement of Alexandria, *Stromateis* 3.59.3.)

To a modern audience, it might seem a little strange for Christian theologians to debate whether Jesus ever had a bowel movement. But other biographies of holy men in antiquity also noted that their subjects had mastered this particular biological necessity, indicating their purity and holiness. At the same time, one of the major theological issues in second-century Christianity concerned what sort of body Jesus had. One position, known as **Docetism** (from the Greek verb *dokein*, "to seem"), argued that Jesus had only a sort of phantom body, merely appearing to be human. This position came from contemplating something that many ancient thinkers found impossible to accept: that a divine being might suffer, even die. Thus the idea that Jesus only had a ghostly, spiritual body protected his divinity. Other Christians, however, drew on a source like the Gospel of John's prologue to argue that Jesus had indeed incarnated into human flesh. But if he had done so, he would therefore have to be

THE *GOSPEL OF TRUTH*

In *Adv. Haer.*, Irenaeus mentions that Valentinus wrote an important work titled the *Gospel of Truth*. That work, along with the rest of Valentinus's work, did not survive the Catholic Church's purge of heretical documents. But some scholars maintain that an untitled tractate discovered at Nag Hammadi may be the lost *Gospel of Truth*. The first line of the NH work begins, "The gospel of truth is a joy for those who have received grace from the father of truth, that they might learn to know him through the power of the Logos" (16:31). Because of its opening words, we now call this untitled text the *Gospel of Truth*. The document from NH may well be Valentinus's work, since it is a beautiful sermon full of striking imagery and poetic turns of phrase, much like our surviving fragments of Valentinus's writing. It also fits with what we know about Valentinianism as very much in keeping with mainstream Christianity. For more on the *Gospel of Truth*, see chap. 8.

fully human with all that that entails—including having bodily appetites like hunger or having bowel movements. Thus Valentinus seems to be engaging in an anti-docetic position. He says that Jesus did indeed need food (since he was fully human) yet he did not eliminate waste. But, he argues, this was not because his body was not fully human but because Jesus had mastered the flesh: he had a "great capacity for continence."

> I see in spirit that all are hung
>
> I know in spirit that all are borne
>
> Flesh hanging from soul
>
> Soul clinging to air
>
> Air hanging from upper atmosphere
>
> Crops rushing forth from the deep
>
> A babe rushing forth from the womb. (quoted by Hippolytus of Rome, *Ref.* 6.37.7–8)

This is a lovely poem, something that seems to have come out of the pen of a true Christian mystic. It bears the title "Summer Harvest." In terms of intellectual background, it shows Valentinus's Greek philosophical training; here, we see the influence of **Stoicism**, which posited that all things in the cosmos were linked by a single, all-pervasive, all-good spirit. Although many people have characterized Gnosticism as "world-negating" or at least "dualist," this fragment shows Valentinus to have been a **monist**—someone who sees the world as all essentially linked through one pervading (and wonderful) principle.

An interesting thing about these fragments of Valentinus is that they do not accord with anything Irenaeus writes about Valentinianism in his "Great Account." There is no hint of any elaborate cosmology, no mention of Sophia, no Demiurge, and no reference to the threefold division of human nature. It is as if Valentinus himself were not a Valentinian. In fact, one prominent scholar of Valentinianism, Christoph Markschies, makes this very argument. Markschies maintains that Valentinus's successors did not merely repeat their teacher's doctrines unchanged, but made frequent and significant innovations such that their Valentinianism was very different from the original teachings of Valentinus. Other scholars, however, find Valentinianism a generally unhelpful category in the same way that Gnosticism does not hold as a category. There was no central Valentinian position or proto-orthodoxy, and without a set of definable characteristics it is difficult to speak of Valentinianism as a coherent movement.

VALENTINIAN TEACHERS AND LATER VALENTINIANISM

Remarkably, we have a long list men and women associated with Valentinian Christianity, the most prominent of which are Alexander, Ambrose, Axionicus, Flora, Florinus, Heracleon, Marcus,

---

VALENTINUS'S LOST WRITINGS

We know from various sources that Valentinus wrote a good deal, but hardly anything still survives. Here is a list of some of his known works and what became of them:

- *Gospel of Truth*. We are not sure if this is the same work as the one we have at NH
- *Epistle to Agathopous*. A letter on the topic of Christology, we have only one brief fragment (on Jesus's digestive system, quoted earlier)
- *Epistle on Attachments*. On Jesus's role in salvation. We have only a brief fragment surviving
- *On Friends*. Only a single fragment remains
- *On the Three Natures*. This treatise on the Trinity is lost
- *Sophia*. This work is lost

TABLE 6.1: Known Valentinian Teachers

Name	Location	Time	Source	Significance	Surviving Writings?
Adelphius	Rome	250–280s CE	Porphyry	Along with Aquilinus, Adelphius leads a Valentinian study group in 3rd c. Rome	no
Agathopous	Alexandria?	150s CE		Valentinus wrote him a short instructional letter, surviving in a fragment	yes
Alexander	Libya	210–220s CE	Tertullian, Porphyry	One of the most famous Valentinians of the 3rd c. CE	no
Ambrose	Alexandria	220s CE		A financial supporter of Valentinians	no
Aquilinus	Rome	260s CE	Porphyry, Plotinus	See Alexander	no
Ardesianus	Edessa?	175–200 CE	Hippolytus		no
Axionicus	Antioch	175–200 CE	Tertullian	Some speculate passages of the *GosPhil* were written by Axionicus	maybe
Beron	Rome?	ca. 200 CE	Hippolytus	A dissident Valentinian, associated with Helix	no
Candidus	Athens	220s CE	Origen	Debates Origen publicly in Athens	no
Cleobulus	Alexandria? Syria?	2nd c.?	Ignatius	Associated with Theodotus	no
Demostratus	Lydia (modern Turkey)	3rd c. CE	Porphyry	Associated with Philokomos and Alexander	no
FlaviaSophe	Rome	180s CE	inscription		yes
Flora	Rome	150s CE	Ptolemy through Epiphanius	Recipient of an instructional letter from Ptolemy	no
Florinus	Rome	Late 2nd c.	Irenaeus	An assistant of the bishop of Rome in 200 CE	no
Helix	Rome	220 CE	Hippolytus	See Beron	no
Heracleon	Rome	150–200 CE	Clement of Alexandria	His commentary on the Gospel of John is largely preserved	yes
Julius Cassian	Alexandria	175–220s	Clement of Alexandria	Strongly condemned marriage; we have a few fragments of his work *On Continence*	yes
Leucius	Syria	Late 2nd c. CE		Supposedly gathered material for the *Apocryphal Acts of John*	Yes, but as editor not author

Continued

TABLE 6.1: *Continued*

Name	Location	Time	Source	Significance	Surviving Writings?
Marcus	Alexandria, Gaul (modern-day France)	150s CE	Irenaeus	Portions of his teachings on numerology survive in *Adv.Haer.*	yes
Philokomos	Rome	3rd c. CE	Porphyry	Mentioned in association with Demostratus and Alexander	no
Prodicus	Alexandria	Late 2nd c. CE	Tertullian, Clement of Alexandria		no
Ptolemy	Rome	150–160 CE	Epiphanius	His *Letter to Flora* remains intact	yes
Rheginus	Alexandria?	2nd or 3rd c. CE	*Treatise on Resurrection (Epistle to Rheginus)*	Known only as the recipient of this letter from Nag Hammadi	no
Secundus	Rome	150s CE	Irenaeus		no
Theodotus	Alexandria	150s CE	Clement of Alexandria	Extracts from his writings still exist in substantial amounts	yes
Theotimus	Rome	Late 2nd c. CE	Tertullian	Writes a lost treatise on the Jewish law	Perhaps, in *Adv.Haer.* 1:17:1–18:3
Theudas	Alexandria	Late 1st–early 2nd c. CE	Irenaeus (?)	Valentinus's teacher	no

Known members of the Italic or Western School are in darker gray; known members of the Eastern School are in lighter gray. Source: The data in this table draw extensively from David Brons's helpful material at www.gnosis. org/library/valentinus/Valentinian_Personalities.htm.

Ptolemy, and Theodotus (see table 6.1). Of these, we still have substantial portions of writings from Heracleon (a commentary on the *Gospel of John*), Ptolemy (a letter written to Flora, a female student, to teach her about the nature of God; this is titled *Letter to Flora* and is preserved complete in the writings of Epiphanius), and Theodotus (preserved by Clement of Alexandria and called the *Extracts of Theodotus* or the *Excerpta ex Theodoto*).

Since none of these works was found at Nag Hammadi, we will not discuss them here, except to say that they are quite amazing, for those interested in learning more about Valentinianism.

Often, scholars of Valentinianism divide the school into Italic/Western and Eastern branches. The two schools apparently differed on a relatively minor distinction in their **Christology** (idea of Christ's nature). The

Eastern school had more of a docetic interpretation of Christ's body, maintaining that it was purely spiritual and that Jesus had therefore passed through his mother Mary's body "like water passes through a pipe," without absorbing any material or fleshly nature. Jesus, therefore, only *appeared* to be human but was a fully spiritual being who temporarily hid his divine nature in a human body. Such a view is reflected in, for instance, the *GosPhil*, in which the human Jesus hanging on the cross cries out "My God, why have you forsaken me?" (Mk 15:34; Mt 27:46) to signal the moment that his spiritual component left his body to return to its heavenly origins. Docetism was a serious intellectual position that assumed that it was impossible for Jesus, as a powerful deity, to gestate in a human womb, suffer, and then die, as Jesus appears to do in the NT gospels. By contrast, the Western Valentinians taught that Jesus was born with a **psychic** (ordinary, human) body, but then this body was transformed into a spiritual or **pneumatic** body. Even in the Western Valentinian school, ancient Christians debated when this transformation happened: some said in Mary's womb, and others, at the moment of Jesus's baptism in the Jordan River.

WHAT HAPPENS TO THE VALENTINIANS?

There is no indication that Valentinus ever ran afoul of any of the established Christian teachers or communities in the city of Rome. Most likely his group functioned relatively harmoniously there, and Valentinus lived out his days in the great city without ever having been condemned or exiled for his beliefs. Although he himself did not attain to the position of bishop of Rome, one of the later popes, Victor (189–199 CE) had a Valentinian presbyter named Florinus as his assistant.

As early as the middle of the second century, some Valentinian communities had their own bishops (see timeline 6.1). At some later point, Valentinians ran their own churches. We know from church legislation that in 326 CE during the time of the first Christian emperor, Constantine, Valentinian heretics were not allowed to hold meetings. The next piece of information we hear about them dates from 388 CE. That year, at the instigation of the local bishop, a mob of angry monks burned a synagogue and a Valentinian church in the small Mesopotamian town of Callinicum. These decades at the end of the fourth century saw spasms of violence from Christians against other Christians, Jews, and pagans. A set of rulings known as the **Theodosian Decrees** ensured that no Valentinian church or Valentinian text was likely to survive the fires of persecution. Some scholars speculate that it was probably at this time, if not earlier, that the scribes of Nag Hammadi copied the NHL texts and hid them in the desert. But Valentinianism may have survived this violent persecution; a church council held in 692 CE (the Council of Trullo) composed articles or legal rulings against the Valentinians. But after that point, our trail runs cold.

QUESTIONS TO CONSIDER

1. What do you make of the fact that Irenaeus's account of Valentinus's cosmology does not appear to match anything we have in our extant fragments of Valentinus's writing? What are the range of things this might mean? What are the ways we can explain the disparity?

2. Why do you think the Roman Catholic Church, as it developed, persecuted Valentinian Christianity so violently?

3. Judging from the fragments of writings reproduced in this chapter, would you call Valentinus a Gnostic? Why or why not?

KEY TERMS

Epiphanius	Basilides	Great Account
Irenaeus	Ogdoad	Theodosian Decrees
Theudas	Pleroma	Decad
Dodecad	Demiurge	Pythagoreanism
Syzygy (pl.: syzygies)	Achamoth	Aeons
Monad	Stoicism	Tetrad
Valentinus	Dyad	Christology
Monist	Docetism	

FOR FURTHER READING

Desjardins, Michel. *Sin in Valentinianism*. Society of Biblical Literature Dissertation Series. Atlanta: Scholars Press, 1990. A detailed study that may interest some readers, particularly those with a Christian background.

Dunderberg, Ismo. "The School of Valentinus." In *A Companion to Second-Century Heretics*, ed. Antti Marjanen and Petri Luomanen. Leiden: Brill, 2005. This is a wonderful, lucidly written introduction to Valentinus and Valentinianism from a top scholar of Gnosticism. Recommended for general and upper-level readers.

Layton, Bentley. *The Gnostic Scriptures: A New Translation with Annotations and Introductions*. Yale University Press, 1995. Reproduces excellent translations of all the surviving fragments of Valentinus's writings.

Thomassen, Einar. *The Spiritual Seed: The Church of the Valentinians*. Leiden: Brill, 2008. The most detailed, state-of-the-field study of Valentinianism. For advanced readers.

TIMELINE 6.1: Valentinianism

ca. 90 CE:	Birth of Valentinus in Phrebonis, Egypt
ca. 110 CE:	Valentinus meets Theudas
ca. 120 CE:	Valentinus founds school at Alexandria after having a vision of Christ in the form of a child. Theodotus is among the first of Valentinus's followers.
ca. 139 CE:	Valentinus goes to Rome. His most important pupils there are Ptolemy and Secundus
143 CE:	Valentinus a candidate for bishop of Rome
ca. 150 CE:	Florinus moves from Smyrna (modern day Izmir, Turkey) to Rome where he joins the Valentinian school
ca. 165 CE:	Death of Valentinus

TIMELINE 6.1: *Continued*

ca. 155–175 CE:	Secundus, Herakleon, and Ptolemy active at Rome; Theodotus and Marcus in Alexandria. The Valentinian school spreads throughout the Roman Empire.
ca. 160 CE:	Justin Martyr writes of a Christian named Ptolemy being imprisoned and later martyred; it may be the same man as the Valentinian Ptolemy
ca. 160 CE:	Heracleon moves from Sicily to Rome where he becomes one of the leading figures of the Valentinian school
ca. 165 CE:	Miltiades opposes Valentinians in Smyrna.
ca. 170 CE:	Julius Cassian splits with the Valentinian school at Alexandria over the issue of marriage
ca. 175–225 CE:	The second "Golden Age" of Valentinianism. Alexander active in north Africa; Theotimus and Florinus active at Rome; Axionicus active at Antioch; Marcus active at Lyon and Syria. North African Valentinians translate the writings into Latin. First opponents of the Valentinian school emerge (Irenaeus, Tertullian, Clement of Alexandria)
178 CE:	Irenaeus composes *Against Heresies*.
ca. 180 CE:	Burial inscription of Flavia Sophe
95 CE:	Valentinians in Carthage opposed by Tertullian
200 CE:	Florinus becomes presbyter and assistant to the bishop of Rome. Irenaeus writes the bishop of Rome demanding Florinus's dismissal. The Syrian school under Axionicus rises to prominence. Leucius integrates Valentinian material into *Apocryphal Acts of John*. Tertullian attacks the school in *Against the Valentinians*. Clement of Alexandria opposes the Valentinians at Alexandria
ca. 225–325 CE:	Candidus at Athens. Philokomos, Adelphius, and Aquilinus at Rome. Demostratus active in Lydia
ca. 229 CE:	The famous Valentinian teacher Candidus debates the Christian philosopher Origen at Athens. Their debate circulates as a written text for one hundred years, but eventually all known copies are destroyed.
ca. 230 CE:	Hippolytus composes his *Refutation of All Heresies* against the Valentinians at Rome
ca. 235 CE:	The teachings of Beron and Helix lead to dissent with the Valentinian school at Rome
ca. 350 CE:	Egyptian scribes copy Valentinian writings in Coptic for the Nag Hammadi collection, placing most of them in either Codex I or Codex XI
ca. 326–379 CE:	With imperial support, the Catholic Church begins to expel Valentinian "heretics" from their congregations and prevent them from having meeting places of their own

TIMELINE 6.1: *Continued*

ca. 326–379 CE:	With imperial support, the Catholic Church begins to expel Valentinian "heretics" from their congregations and prevent them from having meeting places of their own
326 CE:	Catholicism becomes the state religion of Roman Empire. Valentinians (among others) forbidden to assemble by Emperor Constantine. No penalty was imposed on those who did
ca. 350 CE:	Arians persecute Valentinians in Edessa
379–395 CE:	Theodosius I is emperor. Christianity, specifically Catholicism, becomes the new state religion; all other religions are banned. Under the "Theodosian Decrees" heresy becomes punishable by death. Numerous books and religious buildings are destroyed. "Heretics," including Valentinians, are forcibly expelled from larger cities and their property confiscated
ca. 380 CE:	Epiphanius composes his *Panarion* against Valentinians and other sectarians
385 CE:	In Spain, Priscillian is accused of having connections with the Valentinians. He and two followers are executed— the first of many executed for heresy.
386 CE:	Valentinians in Antioch opposed by the local bishop John Chrystostom
388 CE:	Burning of the Valentinian chapel at Callinicum (modern Syria). Bishop Ambrose of Milan convinces the emperor (Theodosius I) not to punish the perpetrators of these acts nor to give reparations to the Valentinians
395–500 CE:	Decline of Valentinianism
400 CE:	Valentianians persecuted by Severian at Gabula.
400 CE:	Valentianians persecuted by Theodore at Mopsuestia.
428 CE:	Valentinians forbidden to assemble by Emperor Theodosius II on pain of death.
450 CE:	Valentinians persecuted by a bishop, Theodoret, in Cyrrus.
500–800 CE:	Valentinianism reduced to a small underground movement.
ca. 600 CE:	A small group of Valentinian "Hermetics" active at Constantinople
692 CE:	Suppression of Valentinianism is mentioned by the Council of Trullo.

The data in this table draws extensively from David Brons's helpful material at www.gnosis.org/library/valentinus/Chronology.htm.

7

Some Valentinian Writings from Nag Hammadi

TRIPARTITE TRACTATE (NHC I, 5), *INTERPRETATION OF KNOWLEDGE* (NHC XI, 1), AND *A VALENTINIAN EXPOSITION* (NHC XI, 2)

There can be absolutely no doubt that in the Roman Empire from the second through the fifth centuries, **Valentinian** Christians could be found in virtually every part of the Empire, from Lyons in Gaul (modern France) in the West to the far reaches of Mesopotamia in the East. It is therefore no great surprise that Valentinian writings appear in the NHL, although it is still very exciting to now have complete Valentinian texts. Given how much of Valentinus's own writings were lost (or, more accurately, destroyed) by the Roman Catholic Church, it is wonderful to now have more of what Valentinians wrote. Most scholars of Valentinianism would agree that we have at least five documents from NH that are unquestionably Valentinian: the *Tripartite Tractate*; the *Interpretation of Knowledge*; *A Valentinian Exposition* (plus short fragments that appear to be some sort of appendices to this writing); the

Gospel of Truth, and the *Gospel of Philip*. This chapter focuses on the first three of these; we'll save the two named Valentinian gospels for chapter 8. But first, let's look at each of these three texts separately before we tackle the question of what links them all together and makes them Valentinian.

TRIPARTITE TRACTATE (NHC I, 5): BACKGROUND

The longest complete Valentinian theological treatise that we possess, the *TriTrac* weighs in at an intimidating eighty-eight manuscript pages in a single copy from Nag Hammadi's Codex XI. We do not know who wrote it, although it might have been Valentinus's student Heracleon (see chap. 6). Originally written in Greek, as were all the NH texts, *TriTrac* was poorly translated into Coptic. The title is modern, based on the

- Sophia as a repentant aeon?
- Christian names and features for cosmological beings/aeons, e.g. "Church" or "Anointed Christ" as aeons?

- Is there evidence for a community behind the text that thinks of itself as a Christian group or assembly ("church")?

- Does it make use of NT writings, especially the Gospel of John, the Gospel of Matthew, and the writings of Paul?

- Is there evidence for Christian ritual being performed, such as baptism, chrism and (especially) the **Bridal Chamber** (unique to Valentinianism)?

Modern scholars of Valentinianism apply these criteria to the NH texts to try to discern which ones are truly Valentinian. Table 7.1 gives a more-or-less consensus view of which NH writings are clearly or possibly Valentinian, and why.

Along with the texts that most scholars agree are Valentinian, there is a variety of NH writings that may or may not be Valentinian. In fact, you can get a sense of how likely these texts are to be Valentinian by looking at the table. For instance, *Treatise on the Resurrection* (*TreatRes*) satisfies two of four established criteria. The author draws upon the NT and talks about Jesus's relation to the cosmos in a way that can be reconciled with Irenaeus's "Great Account." However, the text does not mention the sacraments at all, and rather than talking about a church community, the author expresses his thoughts on resurrection in the form of a one-to-one letter from a teacher to a student. This is not to say that the author did not belong to a Valentinian community. It is possible that the limitations of the genre he chose to express his ideas (a letter rather than a sermon) also restricts our way of understanding this document in relation to Valentinianism. It is also likely that although the author of *TreatRes* knew technical Valentinian terms for elements in the cosmos, he does not use

them in this particular letter because it is written for a non-Valentinian who would not have known such specialized Valentinian vocabulary. Again, the genre of the writing makes it hard to know everything the author thought and thus how he fits into the bigger picture of Valentinianism. For this same reason, scholars are more skeptical about calling *TreatRes* Valentinian.

We can see a similar situation with the *First Apocalypse of James* (*1stApocJas*). According to the list of criteria, it doesn't look very Valentinian. On the one hand, we would not necessarily expect Valentinian elements to shine out in this kind of writing: a **revelation discourse** from Jesus to James. On the other hand, some scholars wonder if it is indeed Valentinian because it shares a large amount of material with Irenaeus's account of a Valentinian group called the Marcosians. Because Irenaeus calls this shared material "Valentinian," we have to wonder if it ended up in *1stApocJas* because its author was a Valentinian and had access to this material. Again, it is possible that Irenaeus got things wrong when he attributed that material to the Marcosians; it is also possible that both the Marcosians and the author of the *1stApocJas* used identical material that they had borrowed from another non-Valentinian source. The difficulty in figuring out problems like this explains why, if you consult other scholarship, you may find different lists of which texts from NH are Valentinian.

OTHER SIGNS OF VALENTINIANISM FROM NAG HAMMADI

There are other texts from Nag Hammadi that have strong similarities with Valentinian ideas but are probably not themselves Valentinian. These texts usually do not satisfy any of the criteria listed above, and yet, there is something about them that makes some scholars furrow their brows and think, "hmmm...Valentinian?" These questionable Valentinian texts are:

TABLE 7.1: Valentinian Texts from Nag Hammadi

Certain or very probable Valentinian texts (Valentinian features given in check boxes)	Probable Valentinian texts (Valentinian features given in check boxes)
Tripartite Tractate (NHC I,3) (√) cosmology consistent with Irenaeus? (×) group identity as a church? (?) use of NT scripture? (×) sacraments?	*Treatise on the Resurrection* (NHC I,4) (√) cosmology consistent with Irenaeus? (×) group identity as a church? (√) use of NT scripture? (×) sacraments?
Gospel of Philip (NHC II,3) (×) cosmology consistent with Irenaeus? (√) group identity as a church? (√) use of NT scripture? (√) sacraments?	*First Apocalypse of James* (NHC V,3) (×) cosmology consistent with Irenaeus? (×) group identity as a church? (×) use of NT scripture? (?) sacraments?
Gospel of Truth (NHC I,3) (×) cosmology consistent with Irenaeus? (√) group identity as a church? (√) use of NT scripture? (?) sacraments?	*Prayer of the Apostle Paul* (NHC I,1) (√) cosmology consistent with Irenaeus? (×) group identity as a church? (√) use of NT scripture? (?) sacraments?
Interpretation of Knowledge (NHC XI,1) (×) cosmology consistent with Irenaeus? (√) group identity as a church? (√) use of NT scripture? (×) sacraments?	
A Valentinian Exposition (NHC XI,2) • *On the Anointing* (NHC XI,24.1–29) • *On Baptism A* (NHC XI,2.40.30–41:38) • *On Baptism B* (NHC XI,2.41:1–43:19) • *On the Eucharist A* (NHC XI,2.43:20–38) • *On the Eucharist B* (NHC XI,2.44:1–37) (√) cosmology consistent with Irenaeus? (√) group identity as a church? (?) use of NT scripture? (√) sacraments?	

- *Apocryphon of James*
- *Authoritative Teaching*
- *Apocalypse of Peter*
- *Teachings of Silvanus*
- *Dialogue of the Savior*
- *Thunder: Perfect Mind*

Here again, there is nothing to prove a solid case against them, especially if we consider that Valentinians may have used and enjoyed writings that, although not from their school, were nevertheless found interesting and edifying. In fact, this seems to have been the case for the *Apocryphon of James*, which was the only non-Valentinian writing bundled with clearly Valentinian writings in Codex I. The Valentinians probably also knew and used the *Gospel of Thomas* (although they do not cite it in any of the Valentinian works that survive) because it appears to be very old for a Christian text, and Plato's *Republic*, also present in the NHL, because it was such an esteemed text.

A VALENTINIAN "SCHOOL"?

In his description of Valentinus and his followers, Irenaeus explicitly uses the term "the school of Valentinus," (Lat.: *Valentini schola*); the term is unusual for a Christian group, so he must have meant it in a technical sense: it was apparently modeled on ancient Greek philosophical schools. Interestingly, some of our Valentinian texts at NH actually use the language and imagery of ancient schools; in *Gospel of Truth (GosTruth)*, for example, Christ appears in "schools," and "spoke the word as a teacher" (19:20). In the *InterpKnow*, Christ is the "teacher of immortality" who opposes someone called the "arrogant teacher" (20:18–25). But did Valentinians have special classrooms or formal schools? Unfortunately, we do not know.

The word we find associated most frequently with the Valentinians from their own documents is *ekklesia*, a word often translated as "church" but which means, more properly, an "assembly." Thinking of the Valentinians as an "assembly" prevents us from mistakenly thinking of "church" as a building or a Christian community that meets in a building. Since there were no public, designated church buildings until after the fourth century, Valentinians were meeting in private homes. Yet they thought of themselves as a *community*, and even more striking from their cosmologies, they envisioned their *ekklesia* as one modeled on one of the primary aeons of the Ogdoad, which they called church (Gk: *ekklesia*). Thus just as individuals bore within themselves the image of God, singly and imperfectly reflected, the community, too, was modeled on a divine reality. This language is much more prominent than the school language. Could Irenaeus have used "school" language to downplay the Christianness of the Valentinian church, making it seem more like one of the philosophical schools he disdained? Or was he merely reading a Valentinian document or set of documents that, like the *InterpKnow*, envisioned Jesus as a sort of teacher?

VALENTINIANS ON THE GROUND

While we have a lot of Valentinian writings both at Nag Hammadi and outside of it, it is very hard to develop any kind of a social history for Valentinianism. We have texts, but no archaeological evidence that tells us definitively that people who were called Valentinians lived in a particular place. Recent work has unearthed, literally, some intriguing evidence for real-life Valentinians living in the city of Rome in the middle of the second century—the time that some of the key Valentinian texts from Nag Hammadi were written.

We have two different funerary inscriptions from Rome, carved in stone, both of which seem to have been dedicated to ancient Valentinians. Remarkably, both memorialize women. The most complete is a tombstone commemorating the life of a Roman woman named Flavia Sophe. Her stone—discovered around 1858 and now on display in the Museo Nationale delle Terme in Rome—records the following epitaph:

> You who desires the light of the Father,
> My sister, my bride, my Sophe
> You have been anointed in the baths of Christ
> With imperishable, pure oil;
> You hastened to gaze
> upon the faces of the divine aeons,
> the Angel of the great Council, the True Son

FIGURE 7.2 The Greek funerary inscription of Flavia Sophe. Her name is spelled out as an acrostic if you read the first letter of every other line on the left hand side (Φ Λ A B...or F L A V...).

after you entered the Bridal Chamber and rose incorruptible into the Father's house [inscription breaks off here]

On the other side, there is a curious epigram in a slightly different script:

She had no ordinary end of to life, this woman who died.

She perished but she lives, and sees in reality the incorruptible light.

She lives to those who are alive, she has truly died to those who are dead.

O Earth, why do you marvel at this type of corpse? Or are you frightened?

Unfortunately, we do not know much about Flavia Sophe. Her first name, Flavia, comes from the Flavians, a dynasty of emperors. Because she has two names and not three, Flavia Sophe was not elite, but at some point either she or her

ancestors may have been slaves in the imperial household (freed slaves took the names of their patrons). "Sophe" is from the Greek *sophia* or "wisdom," so we cannot be sure that this was her name from birth, or it might have been a Christian name that she received upon her conversion and baptism into Christianity. Certainly it is a fitting name for a Valentinian. We also think the epitaph is Valentinian because of certain key words and terms: "the light of the Father," the aeons, the Bridal Chamber, and the idea of entering the Bridal Chamber to rise "incorruptible" to the realm of the Father. These were not terms that were conventionally used in second-century Christianity.

The second Valentinian tombstone is known by its museum number, NCE 156 (see Fig. 7.3).

It is fairly securely dated to the Antonine Period, that is, the middle of the second century, the same period when we know Valentinians were active in the city. This one is a bit fragmented but can be reconstructed to read:

The brothers of the Bridal Chamber celebrate with torches the sacred baths with me;

They hunger for the banquets in our dwelling-places;

Praising the Parent and glorifying the Son,

There exists in that place solitary Silence and Truth.

The last line, although it has been reconstructed, seems to suggest that whoever composed this stone had read Valentinian theology; note how the primary tetrad in Irenaeus's "Great Account" consists of four beings: Parent, Son, Silence, and Truth (see p. 65).

Both stones were found in the same area, in the southeast quadrant of Rome's suburbs on a road known as the Via Latina. Does the presence of these two stones from this one area prove to us that Rome's Valentinians had a villa or meeting place of some kind on the Via Latina? If so, this is the closest we have come to pinpointing the precise whereabouts of any Gnostic community.

FIGURE 7.3 The reconstructed inscription known as NCE 156. In Greek, it records what appears to be a Valentinian Bridal Chamber ritual and a return of the deceased woman's soul to the Pleroma.

Something else worth contemplating is that these epitaphs are some of the very earliest extant Christian inscriptions. Given that we do not have more archaeological evidence for Christianity as a whole in this period, the discovery of two separate Valentinian gravestones makes Valentinian Christianity seem more popular and widespread than a small esoteric group of people with some very strange ideas, as Irenaeus portrays them. If they were so rare and secret, why would we have two Valentinian epitaphs that survive but not a single other Christian epitaph from the same period? Still, the presence of these stones give us the sort of concrete evidence for Valentinians that make them come alive for us, and for that, we are very fortunate.

QUESTIONS TO CONSIDER

1. Valentinians didn't all teach or believe the same things. Can you find places in the Nag Hammadi Valentinian literature where these points of difference become clear? What are they, and what do you think might have been at stake in disputing them?

2. What are the distinctive features and characteristics of Valentinian **cosmogonies**? Do they remind you of anything?

3. What evidence can you find in the Nag Hammadi Valentinian writings for the sorts of communities the Valentinians must have had? What might a "church" meeting have looked like (bearing in mind that there were no churches as public buildings before the fourth century)? Which sacraments were performed, and what might they have looked like? What were their functions (hint: although we do not discuss it in this chapter, you might want to turn to the *Gospel of Philip*, a Valentinian text with much to say about the sacraments).

KEY TERMS

Valentinian	Great Account	revelation discourse
Demiurge	Colossians	Monad
Pleroma	*ekklesia*	Monogenes
Sophia	chrism/chrismation	catechumen
Logos	Tetrad	homily
Wisdom Traditions	Nous	Bridal Chamber
cosmogony	1 Corinthians	Dyad

FOR FURTHER READING

Dunderberg, Ismo. *Beyond Gnosticism: Myth, Lifestyle, and Society in the School of Valentinus*. New York: Columbia University Press, 2008. An excellent discussion of Valentinianism in its ancient intellectual context. Indispensible for advanced readers.

Thomassen, Einar. "The Valentinian School of Gnostic Thought," In *The Nag Hammadi Scriptures*, edited by Marvin Meyer, 790–94. San Francisco: HarperOne, 2007. A good clear introductory essay on Valentinianism by one of the world's experts on the topic.

8

Two Valentinian Gospels

THE *GOSPEL OF TRUTH* (NHC I, 3 AND NHC XII, 2) AND THE *GOSPEL OF PHILIP* (NHC II, 3)

The NHL contains a number of gospels: the *Gospel of Truth*; the *Gospel of Thomas*; the *Gospel of Philip*; and the *Gospel of the Egyptians* (there is also the *Gospel of Mary*, which was not found at NH but which modern scholars have included in English editions of the Nag Hammadi library). Even a quick comparison of these documents raises a vexing question: What exactly is a gospel? What ties these otherwise disparate texts together? If you were to consult the *Cambridge History of Early Christian Literature*, you would find an entry, "Gnostic Literature," but no "Gnostic Gospels." And yet, if you check the list of tractates at Nag Hammadi, there they are. Why the confusion?

Many of us think we know what a gospel is: there are, after all, four examples from the New Testament: the Gospels of Matthew, Mark, Luke, and John. These four share certain basic characteristics; they are all biographies of Jesus. But a gospel is different than a biography—at least, judging from the perspective of the four NT gospels. First of all, they do not try to be comprehensive nor historically accurate; they cover only a portion of Jesus's life. Only two of the four (Lk and Mt) record stories of Jesus's birth; only one (Lk) contains a story about Jesus's childhood. All four focus on Jesus's active ministry and the story of his arrest, torture, and execution. All four also include resurrection appearances, when Jesus comes back from the dead to further instruct his disciples (although it is widely believed that the resurrection story in the Gospel of Mark was added slightly later than the original gospel account). So from all this, we can conclude that a gospel is a type of biography that focuses not just on Jesus's life, but on the *message* of that life: salvation for all who believe that Jesus was the awaited Messiah.

The word **gospel** is a modern English rendering of the Old English *godspell*, which means "good news." That, in turn, is a direct translation of the Greek *euanggelion* (or *evangelion*; eu = "good" + *angelion*, "message"). It is the same root word as that for "angel," which literally means "messenger," and from which the English word "evangelist" derives. The word *evangelion* was not originally part of a title, but begins the Gospel of Mark: "The good news (*evangelion*) of Jesus Christ, Son of Man."

Some of the tractates in the NHL that bear the title "gospel" do so because that was what they were called in antiquity. But not all. The *Gospel of Thomas* (GThom), for example, begins not with the title but the announcement, "[T]hese are the secret words that the living Jesus spoke and Didymus Judas Thomas wrote down." So it is clear that in the second and third centuries, Christians understood the title *gospel* as covering something more broad than simply an account of Jesus's death. The *Gospel of Truth* (GosTruth), as another example, is not biography but a sermon; the *Gospel of Philip* (GPhil) is something like a handbook of passages to be used by a preacher to prepare sermons. The *GThom*, as a collection of Jesus's sayings, is the most similar in form and content to one of the NT gospels—although it lacks a narrative and any account of Jesus's death—and the *Gospel of the Egyptians* (GosEg) is completely different from any other kind of gospel writing, as we will see.

Although we must be careful not to confuse the task of assigning a title to a text with assigning that same text a literary genre, all the Nag Hammadi gospels feature their own idea of how Jesus came to bring the "good news" of salvation to humankind. How he did so, however, varies widely in these documents. Two of them—the *GosTruth* and the *GPhil*— are both Valentinian texts and here we need to focus on these two very different kinds of gospels. Because the *GThom* and the *Gos Eg* are important texts but *not* Valentinian, we will reserve them for their own chapter.

THE *GOSPEL OF TRUTH*

The *Gospel of Truth* is preserved in two copies in the NHL: a complete version in Codex I written in **Subakhmimic Coptic** and a very fragmentary copy in Codex XII written in **Sahidic Coptic**. Both were copied just before 350 CE. We do not know when the Greek original from which they were translated was written, but our best guess is somewhere between 140 and 180 CE. Around 185 CE, **Irenaeus of Lyons** refers to a *Gospel of Truth*:

> But the followers of Valentinus, putting away all fear, bring forward their own compositions and boast that they have more gospels than really exist. Indeed their audacity has gone so far that they entitle their recent composition the *Gospel of Truth*, though it agrees in nothing with the gospels of the apostles, and so no Gospel of theirs is free from blasphemy. For if what they produce is the *Gospel of Truth*, and is different from those which the apostles handed down to us, those who care to can learn how it can be show from the Scriptures themselves that [then] what is handed down from the apostles is not the *Gospel of Truth*. (*Adv. Haer.* 3.11.9)

Since it has no title, we are not sure whether the tractate we found at Nag Hammadi is the same text to which Irenaeus refers in this passage. Irenaeus declared the *GosTruth* a heretical document, the product of the **Valentinian** school, and the tractate we find at Nag Hammadi certainly bears the characteristics of Valentinian theology, so it is likely that this (or something very close) was the same document that Irenaeus condemned.

The *GosTruth* starts out proclaiming the "good news" ("The Gospel of Truth is a joy" or, "The Good News of Truth is a joy," depending on how you translate the sentence) and in this sense it *is* a gospel: it preaches the good news of Jesus, who comes to bring knowledge and thus salvation, and to banish ignorance and the state of oblivion that shrouds the world. But strictly speaking, the *GosTruth* is not a gospel but a **homily**—a portion of a sermon that explicates or bases itself upon passages of scripture. It was meant to be read aloud for a community, and it speaks directly to members of its audience in a way that aims to help people to connect personally with the message. Rather than simply looking at the passage from *GosTruth*, try reading it aloud, and as you do so, imagine an audience of Christians listening, trying to absorb its ideas and imagery. You can imagine an eloquent, charismatic preacher holding rapt his audience, as they hang on his words. He speaks to them about the nature of salvation, of Jesus's true role in the world, and how they must behave as the true Children of the Father.

A sermon contains various types of material: a homiletic portion, a doctrinal exposition in which teachings are conveyed, and **paranesis** or moral exhortation, in which a community is encouraged in certain types of behavior.

While all of this might not seem extraordinary by modern standards—what is so amazing about having a Gnostic sermon, after all?—for scholars of Gnosticism, the *GosTruth* offers precious evidence that these texts were not all composed by individuals writing private reflections on the world for their own purposes, but that there existed actual communities of like-minded Christians who would gather together regularly. In other words, the *GosTruth* offers evidence of a Valentinian community that we did not have prior to the discovery of the NHL.

To say that this community was Gnostic, though, is unhelpful. Read through the *GosTruth* again and ask yourself the question: If you were a member of a proto-orthodox community, would you find anything therein doctrinally offensive? Is there anything particularly Gnostic or heretical about the ideas there? Most students are struck by how mainstream the theology of the *GosTruth* is. In fact, this mainstream flavor is in keeping with what we know of second-century Valentinianism; some scholars have suggested that Valentinians worshiped in early prayer meetings and assemblies alongside more mainstream Christians without much problem. They differed from proto-orthodox Christians only on certain points of interpretation, not in practice or in general belief.

Of all the tractates in the NHL, the *GosTruth* is one with which modern readers most often connect. To begin with, there are very few confusing terms and ideas. The text is accessible to most readers without a deep knowledge of second-century Christianity; in fact, some years ago Harold

Attridge, a scholar at Yale University, suggested that the *GosTruth* is a rare example of a document written for outsiders—that is, to introduce readers (or listeners, since it was meant to be read aloud) to the distinct theology of the Valentinians. It was probably meant to be inclusive and thus bring various types of early Christians together into a healthy, functioning community. Note that members of the community are encouraged to be socially responsible: to help "those who have stumbled," to take care of the sick and give rest to the weary; to feed the hungry, and to always endeavor to support others. This, the author explains, is doing "the will of the Father," which is appropriate since those in the community are "from Him."

Language and Imagery in the *Gospel of Truth*

The *Gospel of Truth* is beautifully written; it stands as one of the most well-crafted of early Christian documents. It is clear that whoever wrote it was not only highly educated but also a gifted writer and preacher. It is such a compelling piece that many scholars attribute it to the second-century teacher Valentinus. If so, this would be quite remarkable, because the later Catholic Church destroyed all but a few fragments of the writings of this charismatic and popular teacher who came to be considered a heretic (see chap. 6). Still, the style of the *GosTruth* is reminiscent of our remaining fragments of Valentinus's writings, and it is easy to imagine that this inspired sermon comes from the pen of such a talented theologian.

Notice how the sermon weaves in allusions to various New Testament writings such as the parable of the lost sheep or the Sermon on the Mount; there are anywhere between thirty and sixty scriptural allusions in the *GosTruth*. We know from this that the audience was already familiar with these writings. Although the New Testament did not yet exist as a completed document, the gospels that ended up in the NT did circulate separately, as discrete documents or as a collection of four. But there are many other references to texts now included in the NT, including letters of Paul (Gal, 1 Cor, 2 Cor, Eph, Col) and other writings (1 John, the book of Revelation, and Heb). Of all these writings, perhaps the Gospel of John contributes the most to the distinctive flavor of the *GosTruth*.

The *GosTruth* is full of striking metaphors and similes; for instance, it is not the Roman authorities but "Error" who grew angry with Jesus and persecuted him; Jesus is nailed not to a cross but to a tree, where he became "fruit of the knowledge of the Father" (thereby reversing, in a sense, the fruit of the knowledge of good and evil that led to the downfall of Adam and Eve). The children of the Father are his "fragrance"; knowledge passes from the Father to the Son "like kisses." The Children of God, having gained *gnosis*, have in their hearts "the living book of the living"; Jesus "wraps himself" in this document and "published his Father's edict upon the cross."

The *Gospel of Truth's* Creation Myth

The *GosTruth* opens with a "creation myth," which accounts for the appearance of Error in the world. Here, Error is personified as a female figure. She creates the material world as a type of "fog" or as "oblivion" (16:12). In it, human beings are ignorant, unaware of their spiritual origins and knowledge of the Father. Jesus appears to rectify Error's lack; she responds angrily and "nails him to a tree" (18:24). There, he becomes "fruit of the Father's *gnosis*" (18:25) so that those who eat of it, metaphorically, discover the Father within themselves.

This spiritual myth of origins, very different from Irenaeus's "Great Account," sets the tone for the central theology of the *GosTruth*: people need to receive *gnosis* in order to obliterate ignorance and thereby rescue the cosmos from oblivion. Since oblivion came into existence because the Father was not known, then if the Father comes to be known, oblivion will not exist from that moment on (18:3–11). Here, the *GosTruth* transforms a Christian creation myth into pure allegory; it also transposes the "field of action" or "field of transformation" of individual Christians from the cosmos to the individual. Salvation is not universal; it does not happen as an external event all at once, contained in linear time. It is instead an internal transformation of the consciousness.

The *GosTruth* is unusual in that it imagines not a fiery, apocalyptic end to the world (as did many other early Christian texts) but a reconciliation or rectification of the cosmos. Deficiency will be transformed into completion; multiplicity will join together into a state of unity. The preacher

THE DREAM PASSAGE

One of the most remarkable similes in the *Gospel of Truth* describes living without *gnosis* as like "when one falls sound asleep and finds oneself in the midst of nightmares: running toward somewhere—powerless to get away while being pursued—in hand-to-hand combat—being beaten—falling from a height—being blown upward by the air, but without any wings; sometimes, too, it seems that one is being murdered, though nobody is giving chase—or killing one's neighbors, with whose blood one is smeared: until, having gone through all these dreams, one awakens. Those in the midst of all these troubles see nothing, for such things are (in fact) nothing. Such are those who have cast off lack of *gnosis* from themselves like sleep, considering it to be nothing." (*GosTruth* 29:8–35, trans. Bentley Layton, *The Gnostic Scriptures* [New Haven: Yale University Press, 1995]: 258–59)

This document reveals remarkable insight into the human psyche from nearly 2,000 years ago: how interesting to see that Roman Christians had the same sort of nightmares that we still have two millennia later!

of this text turns this apocalyptic myth into an opportunity for silent prayer and reflection:

> When unity makes the ways complete, it is in unity that all will gather themselves, and it is by *gnosis* that all will purify themselves out of multiplicity into unity, consuming matter within themselves as fire, and darkness by light, and death by life. So since these things have happened to each of us, it is fitting for us to meditate upon the entirety, so that this house might be holy and quietly intent on unity."
> (*GosTruth* 25:8–23, trans. Bentley Layton, *The Gnostic Scriptures*, 257, with some modifications)

Jesus in the *Gospel of Truth*

Here, Jesus is portrayed as a divine, human character whose significance is described in wholly cosmic terms; that is, his adversaries are not the Roman emperor, scribes, or Pharisees but the personified, hypostasized figure of Error. Jesus comes to reverse and nullify—to neutralize—Error's power in the world. Coming to Earth and incarnating in human flesh, Jesus becomes a teacher or *paedagogue* (19:20).

Summary

The *Gospel of Truth* is a significant document. It reverses some of the existing stereotypes for what ancient Gnosticism was. It has no elaborate cosmologies, no Demiurge, no cosmic pessimism, or strong dualism. It is a highly poetic, engaging sermon which was easy for ancient audiences to understand, and like any good sermon, it draws on inspirational imagery, scriptural allusions familiar to the preacher's audience, and experiences with which people can identify. There are points in the *GosTruth* where the ideas it expresses are still strikingly unusual compared to the letters of Paul or the New Testament Gospels (e.g., the assertion that Error created the world rather than the God mentioned in Genesis). But there are also indications that the community that listened to this sermon were not so far removed from what we

think of as mainstream Christians: they revered the New Testament Gospels and the letters of Paul, and their preacher encouraged them, in a good Christian manner, to feed the hungry and minister to the sick. In short, the *GosTruth* gives us precious insight into how one community in the second century thought of itself, thought of Jesus, and understood their mission in the world.

GOSPEL OF PHILIP: BACKGROUND

A somewhat different kind of work from the *GosTruth*—but no more like a traditional New Testament gospel—the *Gospel of Philip* also presents a Valentinian worldview. In terms of genre, scholars see the *GPhil* as more of a collection or anthology of sayings, almost randomly put together. We can identify in it snippets of sermons, letters, treatises, or sayings. Although we have the thirty-two-page text of *GPhil* in only one manuscript version from Codex II (dating from ca. 350 CE), the gospel itself is probably from the second century. We believe it was first composed in Greek, but some puns on (or etymologies of) Syriac words suggest that parts might have been written in Western Mesopotamia, where Christians were bilingual, speaking both Greek and Syriac. Or, the author's use and explanation of foreign terms might simply be a way to impress readers or listeners with the author's learnedness. At any rate, the text is remarkably well preserved.

As in the *GosTruth*, the title "Gospel" here functions more in the original sense of the word as "good news" or "teachings." There are many teachings collected together in the *GPhilip*, which is why scholars often think of this tractate as a kind of preacher's handbook. As he (or she) prepared a sermon for a congregation, a preacher could draw upon phrases and passages from this handbook. Because the passages seem to fall neatly into little chunks, the German scholar Hans-Martin Schenke divided the document into 127 sayings, which the American scholar Bentley Layton used in his excellent edition in *The Gnostic Scriptures*, albeit with modifications. For ease of use, we will refer to Layton's numbered system of passages here, as well as the traditional folio-and-line citation.

Jesus in the *Gospel of Philip*

Intriguingly, Jesus does quite a bit of speaking in *GPhil*, and when he talks, he sometimes says things that are familiar to us from the NT, but other times, they are things we've never heard before. Could the author of the *GPhil* have been drawing on the authentic lost sayings of Jesus? Let's look at the familiar sayings first (Table 8.1), and then the unfamiliar ones (Table 8.2), to see what we can conclude.

We learn some interesting things in Table 8.1. First, we can see that whoever wrote the *GPhil* had access to the Gospel of Matthew, the Gospel of John, and Paul's 1 Corinthians. These are exactly the same Christian sources that other Valentinian texts draw upon, so it confirms the Valentinian nature of *GosPhil* and also which NT writings were known in the second century. Another interesting thing is the way in which this author quotes Jesus—not to give authority to his own words ("do things my way because Jesus says this is the way you do things") but in order to explain the hidden, allegorical meanings behind Jesus's words (look closely at the context for the first two

Jesus-sayings, for example). There is the assumption that someone is needed to interpret scripture, not just to quote it at the right place and time.

Whoever wrote *GPhil* cites the NT sayings of Jesus on nine separate occasions. But he also cites things that Jesus said an additional eight times; in other words, half of all his quotations of Jesus-sayings come from a lost source or sources. Let's look at these lost sayings now.

Although these quotations in Table 8.2 are unfamiliar, they look like the sayings of Jesus we have in the NT Gospels, which tend to be either parables or short statements called *aphorisms*. For example, consider the first saying in Table 8.2 (55:37–56:3): "Take something from every house. Gather (things) into the Father's house, but do not steal and remove (anything) while in the Father's house," or the fourth saying (63:29–30), on Jesus as a dyer. In form, both sayings look as if they might be very old, even authentic sayings of Jesus. But, as in the case of 63:29–30, Jesus says the Son of man has come "like a dyer." It is a bit odd, but it builds upon a wordplay in Greek: *baptein* meant "to dye," where *baptizein* mean "to baptize." Since Jesus spoke Aramaic, not Greek, it is doubtful we could trace this saying back to him.

Some of the other Jesus-sayings use specifically second-century Valentinian jargon, such as 58:10–14, which talks about the "perfect light" and joining with angels as images, or 59:25–27,

WHO WAS PHILIP?

This text bears the ancient title *The Gospel of Philip*, but nowhere does it say that it was actually written by the apostle Philip. Instead, it is probably called that because Philip is the only one of Jesus's disciples in the text actually mentioned by name (73:8). This Philip appears on ancient lists of "the Twelve," Jesus's original disciples (see Lk 6:13–16). The apostle Philip, according to ancient texts such as the fourth-century *Acts of Philip*, had an active mission in the Greek East of the Empire, including Syria. Tradition also tells us that he was put to death either by crucifixion or by beheading in the city of Hierapolis (now the resort town of Pamukkale, Turkey), although many people consider these accounts to be historically unreliable. Philip's body has never been securely identified.

TABLE 8.1: Jesus's Sayings from the NT in the *Gospel of Philip*

Jesus's Saying as Found in *GosPhil* (numbering from Robinson and Meyer editions at left and Layton editions at right)		Corresponding NT Saying (RSV)	
55:33–34	#15	"My Father Who Is In Heaven . . ."	Matt 16:17
57:3–5	#21	"One who does not eat my flesh . . ."	Jn 6:53
68:8–12	#61	"Go into your room, shut the door . . ."	Matt 6:6
68:26–27	#64	"My God, My God, why have you forsaken me?"	Matt 27:46; Mk 15:34
72:33–73:1	#78	"Thus shall we perfect all righteousness . . ."	Matt 3:15
77:18	#93	"Love builds up . . ."	1 Cor 8:1
83:11–13	#104	"Already the axe is laid to the base of the tree . . ."	Matt 3:10; Lk 3:5
84:7–9	#104	"If you know the Truth, the Truth will set you free."	Jn 8:32
85:29–31	#106	"Every plant that my Father in Heaven has not planted . . ."	Matt 15:13

TABLE 8.2: Unknown Jesus-Sayings in the *Gospel of Philip*

Jesus's Saying as Found in *GosPhil* (numbering from Robinson and Meyer editions at left and Layton editions at right)		
55:37–56:3	#16	"Take something from every house . . ."
58:10–14	#24	"You who have united Perfect Light with Holy Spirit . . ."
59:25–27	#30	"Ask your mother, and she will give you . . ."
63:29–30:	#47	"So the Son of Man has come as a dyer . . ."
64:2–9	#48	"Why don't I love you like her?" (parable of the blind person)
64:10–12	#49	"Blessed is the One Who Is before coming . . ."
67:30–35	#61	"I have come to make [the lower] like the upper . . ."
74:25–27	#84	"Some have gone into heaven's kingdom laughing . . ."

which apparently refers to a divine Mother. These two sayings would be out of place in the time that Jesus was teaching. As for 64:10–12 and 67:30–35, they sound a lot like those in the *G Thom*. In fact, 67:30–35 is probably a form of *GThom* #22. And this teaches us that whoever wrote the *GPhil* probably also knew the *GThom*. In the end, however, it is hard to sustain the idea that the *GPhil*

quotes a lost source of Jesus's authentic sayings, although it is tempting to think so.

Ritual and Sacraments in the *Gospel of Philip*

The most intriguing task to scholars working on the *GPhil* has been to uncover the text's reference to five **sacraments** (called here "mysteries"): **baptism**, **chrism** (anointment with holy oil), **Eucharist**, **Redemption**, and the **Bridal Chamber**. While baptism and Eucharist (Communion, the Lord's Supper) are familiar to many modern Protestants, and baptism, Eucharist and chrism are familiar to many modern Anglicans, Roman Catholics, or Eastern Orthodox Christians, the last two sacraments, Redemption and Bridal Chamber, are far more mysterious. They appear to be part of a sacramental system practiced by certain Valentinian Christian communities. Unfortunately, the *GPhil* does not give us enough information on these texts to let us know precisely what happened during these sacraments. We have to do a bit of detective work to put together all the clues we can.

It is notoriously difficult for historians of the ancient world to uncover information about ritual. After all, ritual is what people do rather than what they believe or think, and while people tend to write down what they think or believe in order to pass down that information to others, ritual is taught by performing it and learned by participating and/or watching. For that reason, we have virtually no early Christian text that helps walk us through a ritual or sacrament. We might be able to discern something about what that rite means, but hardly ever can we know what the ritual looked like.

Ritual is also slippery because it can have different meanings or interpretations, depending on who is watching. Let's say you had never been exposed to Catholicism and you walked into a Roman Catholic church where a man at the front of the room was putting little round wafers on people's tongues. What would you imagine they were doing this for? How would you know the inner meaning of the rite: that the man was passing along to the faithful the transubstantiated body of their savior? Even if this were explained to you, you'd probably have a lot more questions: What savior? What does he have to do with little round wafers? Why are they round? Why is it a

man who is handing these out, and why don't people just stop by the altar and pick one out of a bowl? There are explanations for all these details, of course. But the explanation of the priest might be different from that of a congregant or an anthropologist. But most of the time the meaning of the rite is never really made clear because the point of it is to participate in it. Furthermore, if everyone in a group belongs to the same religion or sect or affiliation, chances are that most of the time people would not really spend too much time writing down the exact steps of the sacrament or explaining them. They would not need to, because everyone in that group would have more or less the same understanding; they also would have learned it from having seen it and done it all their lives.

The situation is similar with the *GPhil*. The text does not explain the sacraments because it is not meant for outsiders—it is meant for people who already understand what is meant when the author refers to the Bridal Chamber.

One exercise that can be helpful is to consider each of the *GPhil*'s five sacraments separately. Look up all the sayings you can from the gospel about baptism, about chrism, and so on. Does this help clarify matters? Why or why not? Which sacraments are most fully explicated or most often discussed, and which are the most mysterious?

As Christianity took hold in the Roman Empire, many Christians adopted the term "mystery" to refer to their sacraments. In part, this meant that there was a hidden meaning to rites, such as baptism, that was closely guarded by initiates. Although Christianity was open to all as were the Eleusinian Mysteries (see **Mystery Cults**), one became a full Christian only through being initiated into the community, usually through baptism. The *meaning* of baptism (beyond just dipping a person in water) is the "mystery," although baptism itself, insofar as it is a rite, is likewise a "mystery." In part, therefore, the word "mystery" meant more like "ritual" or "something done" than something secret.

Various Christians disputed the hidden or esoteric meaning of their sacraments, just as they disagreed on how many were necessary, how often they needed to be performed, and who was authorized to perform them.

Let's go over each one of the GPhil's five sacraments. They seem to be arranged in order of importance:

1. **Baptism**. One of the benchmarks of early Christianity was the rite of baptism. This practice likely derived from Judaism as a purification ritual. Certainly, in the NT writings, baptism is central to early Christian theology. There, Jesus does not baptize anyone but is himself baptized by John "the Baptist," who conducts the rite for redemption from sin and preparation for the End of Days. In Paul's letters (which are actually written before the gospels) baptism is a rite of inclusion into a Christian community; it is also a symbolic passage into death and rebirth, thus a way for an individual to identify himself or herself with Christ.

   Baptism in the second century was a rite of initiation, and undertaken only by adults who had spent a great deal of time preparing for the ritual (during this period of instruction, Christians were known as **catechumens**). The practice of infant baptism was not yet widespread in Christianity and was confined to instances where a child was about to die. Baptism was sometimes done at dawn, and if performed in a special baptismal font, the catechumen was immersed naked into the waters. It was therefore a private ritual that could be quite an ordeal and was taken very seriously indeed—particularly because of the belief that one could not sin after receiving the "new birth" of baptism. Baptism "wiped clean" not just the individual's sins, but his or her astrologically ordained destiny. A newly baptized person was therefore called a **neophyte**, literally, a "newborn." He or she received new white robes, a new Christian

name, and for a time was even fed milk, like an infant.

The problem of sin, however, persisted. One of the heated debates in the first Christian centuries concerned whether people could be baptized more than once. Some said yes; others said no. It is not clear what the Valentinians thought, but the GPhil hints that baptism was not the most important rite there was, and that indeed, it was possible for someone to go down into the baptismal waters and come up without having received anything (Layton #51; 64:22–25).

2. **Chrism**. Chrism or chrismation was a rite of anointing with oil, usually olive oil. This could be done in combination with a water baptism, as part of an exorcism, or as a rite directly before death (now called Extreme Unction or Last Rites). The GPhil makes it clear that chrism is a more important rite than baptism, because the word "Christ" means "anointed." According to the GPhil, therefore, baptism does not make you a Christian but chrism does, since this is what the term "Christian" means. Chrism is associated in GPhil with light imagery, perhaps because oil was used in lamps to provide fuel. If baptism (water) was associated with the primordial waters of Genesis 1:2, then chrism (light) was associated with the primordial light of Genesis 1:3. It also seems that chrism was performed because it transformed the soul after death into a light-being, such that it could not be seen or seized by the malevolent powers that might hinder the soul on its ascent to the Father after death.

3. **Eucharist**. The Eucharist is a ritual consumption of bread and wine in commemoration of Jesus's words and actions at the Last Supper (Mt 26:17–30, Mk 14:12–26, Lk 22:7–39 and Jn 13:1–17:26). It is difficult to know where the Eucharist (literally, "thanksgiving") fits in the ritual scheme of GPhil, but it does not seem to have been particularly significant.

This may have had to do with the author's argument that the rite of "eating flesh and drinking blood" Jesus meant entirely symbolically; the "flesh" is the Word and the "blood" is the Holy Spirit (see saying #21).

These three sacraments—baptism, chrism, and Eucharist—all became important in later Catholic Christianity and are still practiced in other Christian denominations as well. But the *GPhil* also discusses two additional sacraments that never became part of later mainstream Christianity: Redemption and the Bridal Chamber.

4. **Redemption**. The mysterious rite known as the Redemption appears to have been unique to Valentinianism. The word for this rite (Gk *Apolytrosis*) is a compound word that means, literally, an "untying." But what is being untied? One hint is that it appears to have been some kind of ritual performed at the point of death, when the soul was being loosened or untied from the body. Therefore, the point of this rite was to facilitate the soul's ascent at death. References in *GPhil* to Redemption are relatively rare and always obscure. In Bentley Layton's translation of *GPhil*, he prefers to translate "redemption" as "ransom."

5. **Bridal Chamber**. Equally mysterious to the Redemption is the Valentinian rite known as the Bridal Chamber. People have spent a lot of time trying to decide if the Valentinians celebrated an actual earthly marriage of a man and a woman, or whether the Bridal Chamber was a sort of ritual of sexual intercourse between husband and wife, or whether the rite refers not to social or sexual practices on earth but was actually some kind of "spiritual marriage" performed in the higher realms between a soul and its spiritual counterpart.

A standard feature of Valentinianism is the importance of male-female pairs called **syzygies** (see chaps. 6, 7). The belief was that all men had a female spiritual counterpart, and all women had a male spiritual counterpart. An important part of salvation or spiritual rectification of the cosmos was the reunification of male-female pairs into a single "one," a kind of undoing of creation or a return to a primordial state of androgynous unity. Therefore, the Bridal Chamber ritual could conceivably have symbolized the reunification of a single (i.e., unmarried) person with his or her spiritual counterpart. But it might also have symbolized the joining of Sophia with her own spiritual counterpart through the act of marriage, and thus a more profound rectification of the "original sin" that rent apart the cosmos in the first place, when Sophia decided to procreate without her divine syzygy. Finally, the Bridal Chamber might have symbolized the soul's reunification with its spiritual syzygy in the cosmos, and thus was part of a death ritual.

Most likely, the five sacraments were performed together in some way, or, at least, their symbolism was essentially linked. In two passages toward the end of the *GPhil*, the sacraments are likened to the Jerusalem Temple. Baptism is like the forecourt of the Temple, which the author calls "Holy." The forecourt encloses the Temple proper, which is like Redemption; the author calls it "the Holy of the Holy." Inside the Temple lies the "Holy of the Holies," which is equated with the Bridal Chamber. By the time the *GPhil* was written, the Jerusalem Temple had long been destroyed, but clearly its memory was still potent for ancient Christians.

The *Gospel of Philip* and the *Gospel of Truth* are very different from the NT gospels, but they give us precious information about what Valentinian Christianity looked like. In both cases, there is an emphasis on building a Christ-centered community and on interpreting some of the writings that would later make it into the New Testament: the letters of Paul, the Gospel of Matthew, and the Gospel of John. Whoever wrote our two Valentinian gospels revered Christian scripture and sought to understand it, not to replace it by

JESUS AND MARY, SITTING IN A TREE

One of the most provocative elements of the *GPhil* is its portrayal of a romantic relationship between Jesus and Mary Magdalene. What is unfortunately not so clear (due to damage or holes in our sole manuscript) is what kind of relationship these two had. The text says,

"And the companion of the [...] Mary Magdalene. The [...loved] her more than [all] the disciples, [and he used to] kiss her on her [...more] often than the rest of the [disciples]" (63:32–64:8/#48, trans. Layton, *The Gnostic Scriptures*, 329)

Of course, the burning question is: where exactly did Jesus kiss Mary Magdalene? The impulse to supply the word "mouth" is strong for those who want to argue that Jesus and Mary had some sort of romantic relationship. But consider how differently the text would read if we filled up the hole with something like "cheek" or "forehead."

On the other hand, even if the missing word were "mouth," we should be cautious not to assume that this indicated a sexual relationship between Jesus and Mary. The *GPhil* talks about kissing as a spiritual act: "for it is through a kiss that the perfect conceive and give birth." To grow in spiritual knowledge, the community also kiss one another: "for this reason [i.e., to share *gnosis*] we too kiss one another: it is by the grace residing in one another that we conceive." To "kiss" Jesus, therefore, is to absorb the *gnosis* in his speech (the Logos, which literally means "word" or "speech"), to be "nourished from [Jesus's] mouth," as *GPhil* puts it.

writing alternate gospels. In the end, the *Gospel of Philip* and the *Gospel of Truth* are perhaps some of the most valuable second-century documents for understanding how one group of Christians, or one type of Christianity, thought about what it meant to be Christian.

QUESTIONS TO CONSIDER

1. All the texts in the NHL that we call "gospels" are really not much like gospels at all. Is our definition of gospel therefore driven by NT examples, or should we broaden our definition to include texts that were evidently called gospels in antiquity just as the NT texts were?

2. "Gospel" really means "good news" or "good message." What are the different "good messages" that we find in the gospels covered in this chapter?

3. Is it possible to have a non-Christian gospel (consider the case of the *Gospel of the Egyptians*, which is only barely Christian)?

KEY TERMS

gospel

Valentinian

paedagogue

catechumen

chrism

baptism

Subakhmimic Coptic

paraenesis

sacrament

neophyte

Bridal Chamber

Redemption

Sahidic Coptic

homily

Irenaeus of Lyons

syzygy (pl.: syzygies)

Eucharist

FOR FURTHER READING

Perkins, Pheme. "What Is a Gnostic Gospel?" *Catholic Biblical Quarterly* 79 (2009): 104–24. A clear exposition of the problem of genre, with useful tables in the appendices. For intermediate readers.

Segelberg, Eric. "The Coptic Gnostic Gospel According to Philip and Its Sacramental System," *Numen* 7 (1985): 189–200. A classic study of GPhil's five sacraments. For advanced students.

Van Unnik, E. C. "'The Gospel of Truth' and the New Testament." In *The Jung Codex*, translated and edited by F. L. Cross, 79–129. London: A. R. Mowbray, 1955. An early but interesting first study of the *Gospel of Truth*'s relation to various writings in the NT. For intermediate readers.

9

The Thomas Literature

THE *GOSPEL OF THOMAS* (NHC II, 2) AND THE *BOOK OF THOMAS THE CONTENDER* (NHC II, 7)

There is a wonderful story that scholars of Gnosticism tell about the discovery of the *Gospel of Thomas*. In 1945 when the Nag Hammadi codices reached the antiquities market in Cairo, no one had any idea what kind of a treasure mine they were. There was, at the time, a moderate interest in discovering new materials and sayings of Jesus. Word of these newly discovered codices spread around the world within academic communities, and scholars of Coptic were dispatched to see whether the ancient books were worth purchasing for museum or university collections. A Dutch scholar by the name of Gilles Quispel traveled to Cairo to examine the manuscripts. He picked up a codex and began to translate from the Sahidic Coptic a text that had not been seen in 1,600 years. His finger trembled as it followed along the neat handwriting on the yellowed papyrus page; clearing his throat, he slowly began to translate:

> These are the secret words that the living Jesus spoke to his disciple, Judas Didymus Thomas. Whoever learns the meaning of these words will not taste death.

Imagine the thrill of excitement for Quispel; he had discovered a lost gospel—a secret document that had lain hidden for nearly two millennia. All in all, the *GThom* presents 114 separate sayings or **logia** of Jesus. Some of these sayings are identical to those we find in the canonical Gospels of the NT. Others closely resemble things that Jesus says in the NT but differ in small or insignificant ways. Finally, some sayings are completely unlike anything we had ever read in the NT before. The *GThom* was to radically shake up our understanding of Jesus's teaching and the formation of early Christianity.

Like many other titles discovered at Nag Hammadi, the *Gospel of Thomas* was mentioned by the early Church fathers (including Hippolytus, Origen, and Cyril of Jerusalem) as a heretical book, so we knew that it existed before we any copies were found. The Roman heresiologist Hippolytus wrote in his *Refutation of All Heresies* (220–235 CE):

> And concerning this (nature) they hand down an explicit passage, occurring in the Gospel inscribed

according to Thomas, expressing themselves thus: He who seeks me, will find me in children from seven years old; for there concealed, I shall in the fourteenth aeon be made manifest (5.7.20). (trans. J. H. MacMahon, "Hippolytus, Refutation of All Heresies." In *A Library of the Ante-Nicene Fathers*, Vol. 5 [Peabody, MA: Hendrickson, 1999], 254, modified)

This exact saying is not in our copy of *GThom* from Nag Hammadi, but it does bear a resemblance to Logion #4:

Jesus said, "The person old in days won't hesitate to ask a little child seven days old about the place of life, and that person will live. For many of the first will be last, and will become a single one."

The gospel appears to have been quite popular; sources from the fifth and sixth century reported its use, particularly within **Manichaean** communities.

Scholars also knew that the *Gospel of Thomas* existed because we had fragments of it before the discovery of the NHL.

These three fragments came from Oxyrhynchus, an ancient city in Egypt:

- *Papyrus Oxyrhynchus 1 (P. Oxy 1)* is now in the Bodleian Library, Oxford. It preserves sayings 26–30, 77, and 30–31.

- *Papyrus Oxyrhynchus 654 (P. Oxy 654)* is in the British Library—it was written on the back of a discarded document and contains sayings 1–7 (see Fig. 9.1).

- *Papyrus Oxyrhynchus 655 (P. Oxy 655)*, is a fragment of a scroll now in the Houghton Library at Harvard University and preserves sayings 36–40.

All three fragments are written in Greek—the gospel's original language of composition (other scholars say it was originally written in Syriac, but the high percentage of Greek loanwords in the Coptic suggest a Greek original). But then, in 1945, we finally had a complete copy of the gospel, in NHC II, this time in Coptic.

FIGURE 9.1 Gospel of Thomas, Oxyrhynchus, Egypt, third century. Preface and Sayings of Jesus. BL Papyrus 1531, verso.

Despite its ancient title, the *Gospel of Thomas* is not really a gospel in the conventional sense; it contains no narrative or story. Instead, it consists purely of sayings, most beginning "Jesus said...." Thus it is more like a compilation of wisdom sayings, akin to the book of Ecclesiastes or Proverbs, two Hellenistic Jewish wisdom collections now in the Hebrew Bible. So the *GThom* is unique, different in form from any other extant early Christian writing.

We do not know who assembled the *GThom*, when it happened, or where. It had to have been complete by 140–200 CE, the approximate date range of our earliest Greek papyrus fragments of the gospel. The core of this tractate may be dated much earlier, but we do not know for sure how much earlier. A substantial number of scholars of early Christianity, including figures such as E. P. Sanders and John P. Meier, believe that the gospel is, on the whole, a second-century production, and thus useless as a source of information about the historical Jesus. On the other hand, there are also many scholars who think that the *GThom* is a very precious source. The earliest date these scholars propose for *GThom* is about 50 CE, earlier than the gospels contained in the NT and

contemporary with the letters of the apostle Paul. Those who favor an early date argue that the *form* of the gospel suggests a first-century composition; presumably, **sayings collections** of Jesus would have circulated shortly after his death, to which narrative filler such as we find in the NT gospels would later be added. All the scholars agree, though, that the earliest form of the gospel is very early indeed, and it is possible that some of Jesus's sayings come from the first generation after his death. This makes the *GThom* as good a source for authentic teachings of the historical Jesus as the gospels of the NT.

At the same time, these "authentic teachings" can be difficult to distinguish from later sayings of Jesus, which are found in the NT. Thus one

THE DISCIPLES IN THE *GOSPEL OF THOMAS*

Gospel tradition tells us that Jesus had twelve main disciples, but the *GThom* does not. One would think that because of the gospel's title, Thomas would be considered the most important disciple. So it is surprising to come to saying #12, where Jesus commands that authority after his death should go to "James the Just," identified in the NT as Jesus's brother but *not* one of the twelve: "No matter where you are you are to go to James the Just, for whose sake heaven and earth came into being." After Jesus's death, James and his fellow disciple Simon Peter established themselves in Jerusalem as the first generation of what scholars call the **Jesus Movement**. There were communities who therefore held James in high regard; this saying appears to have derived from them. But strangely enough, the *Gospel of Thomas* as a whole does not seem to privilege James (note that it is not called the *Gospel of James*). Our best explanation is that the James-saying is probably quite old and got incorporated into the *GThom* by someone collecting sayings of Jesus, even though its "hero" was James, not Thomas. Saying #12 was likely not Jesus's authentic words but a piece of propaganda written by someone in a community that understood James to be the legitimate successor to Jesus. This is perhaps

the best explanation, but it is not the only one, since James was also revered by groups of Christians in the second century and beyond.

Two other disciples mentioned in *GThom*—Matthew and Simon Peter—are included in the twelve and both are important in the canonical tradition. Here, however, they do not come across as stellar disciples; when Jesus asks them what he "resembles" (saying #13) both Matthew and Simon Peter get the answer wrong. Some scholars detect here a veiled attack on other Christian communities of the first or second century that considered Matthew or Peter the most important of the disciples.

Significantly, *GThom* also mentions two women disciples, Mary (Magdalene) and Salome. Although Salome plays no role in the NT gospels, she was evidently known in some Christian communities as a valuable disciple. Mary Magdalene plays a greater role in the NT; because of the part that she plays in the empty tomb and resurrection accounts at the end of the four NT gospels, she gets more attention than do many of the other disciples. But it is clear that in some circles in Christian antiquity, Mary Magdalene was known, even revered, as a woman around Jesus who "understood the All."

of the tasks for scholars of early Christianity is to decide which sayings are likely to date from the first century, and which from the second. How do we do this? Fortunately, we have a lot of material with which to compare. The first task, then, is to compare the sayings of Jesus in the *GThom* with the sayings of Jesus in the four gospels of the NT. The second task is to focus on the distinctive vocabulary and theology that is more characteristic of the second century than the first (note that this, too, is an exercise in comparison, in that we compare the *GThom* to other second-century writings in order to determine what "sounds right" for a second-century document). In the end, we can have a good idea of what is the earliest "Jesus-saying material" here and what is part of later tradition.

WHO WAS THOMAS?

The Thomas named in the title of this gospel is probably the same Thomas mentioned in the NT letter of Jude and at the end of the Gospel of John (Jn 20:24–29); tradition holds that after the death of Jesus, Thomas traveled eastward, converting people to Christianity. His travels took him through Syria, Mesopotamia, and as far east as India. Still today, in India, there lives a small community of so-called Thomas Christians whose center of worship in Chennai (Madras) still includes a cathedral holding Thomas's sacred relics (see fig. 9-2).

A set of legends preserved as the *Apocryphal Acts of Thomas* feature wonderful stories about the apostle Thomas, but these stories were told

FIGURE 9.2 The cathedral of St. Thomas in Chennai, India claims to hold the relics of the apostle Thomas.

largely for entertainment rather than for their veracity. They do tell us that Thomas was also revered in Syria. The bones or relics of St. Thomas were, in the fourth century, on display in the city of Edessa. It is possible, given all of this, that the GThom was written in Edessa or Syria; however, it is important to add that we do not have any Syriac copies or fragments of the gospel.

The GThom does not explicitly associate the disciple Thomas mentioned in the NT with *this* Thomas who gives the gospel its name, although we can speculate that they are one and the same. Of him, we are told very little: only that Jesus spoke these words that were written down by his disciple Judas Didymus Thomas. But the name itself contains a vital clue about who this Thomas is. "Didymus" and "Thomas" both mean "twin," the first in Greek, the second in Aramaic and Syriac. Judas (or Jude) was a very common name in Roman Judaism and meant "a Jewish man" (the female form "Judith" just means "a Jewish woman"). So the name of this disciple is "the Jewish twin twin."

One of the great secrets of this gospel requires the reader or listener of these words to figure out the mystery of Jesus's twin, and how Jesus might have had a twin brother. In what way is Thomas Jesus's twin? We will return to this puzzle presently.

WAS THERE A THOMASINE SCHOOL?

A number of ancient texts focus on the apostle Thomas, leading some to suggest that there was in antiquity such a thing as a "Thomasine school" of Christianity, probably centered in Syria. Besides the *Gospel of Thomas* and the *Apocryphal Acts of Thomas*, we also have an *Infancy Gospel of Thomas* and, from Nag Hammadi, the *Book of Thomas the Contender Writing to the Perfect*. The problem with the "school" hypothesis is that all four texts are very different in their philosophies; all that connects them is their interest in

the disciple Thomas. In the *Apocryphal Acts of Thomas*, *Gospel of Thomas*, and *Book of Thomas the Contender*, Thomas is explicitly presented as Jesus's "twin," but this feature is absent from the *Infancy Gospel of Thomas*.

The Infancy Gospel of Thomas

The *Infancy Gospel of Thomas* is a highly entertaining set of stories about Jesus's childhood. These were apparently very popular in Christian antiquity, because we have this text in a variety of ancient languages, attesting to how widespread it was. Although it does not talk about Thomas specifically, readers will be surprised, maybe even shocked by the text's depiction of Jesus: he often acts like a spoiled child or worse, even striking dead his playmates for no apparently good reason. No doubt the stories made for fun listening, but they do appear to have a serious intent, perhaps to show what happens when God incarnates into human flesh. Thus these stories appear to take seriously a theological position adopted at the Council of Chalcedon in 451 CE: that Jesus was both fully human and fully divine. What might this look like, after all? How would a child who was both fully human (and thus not yet in control of his emotions) and fully divine (thus possessing tremendous power) deal with everyday life?

Book of Thomas the Contender

Like the GThom, the *Book of Thomas the Contender* is a wisdom collection, and Jesus (here, "the savior") is predominantly a wise and authoritative teacher. This text comes to us only in a sole manuscript found at Nag Hammadi, as the last document in Codex II (NHC II, 7). The author identifies himself as the disciple Mattathias (the replacement disciple after the death of Judas Iscariot, to preserve the sacred number of twelve disciples), and claims that he put together the book by editing eyewitness records of conversations between Jesus and his disciple Judas Thomas. We do not know, however, if this Mattathias was Jesus's disciple, or someone else with the same name, or someone adopting the name of Jesus's disciple Mattathias.

It is evident from reading this short text that it falls into two parts, a revelation dialogue followed by an eschatological sermon, which do not seem to fit together very well. But we do not know how these pieces came to be put together, by whom, or when.

BThomas is a bold treatise with a radically **ascetic** or **encratitic** worldview. Here, the author strongly emphasizes the importance of denying physical appetites, particularly sexual desire, which may indicate that the treatise is from a later date, since radical asceticism did not characterize Christianity until around the fourth century and would have been perfectly at home within Egyptian monastic communities at that point. On the other hand, perhaps this text originated in Syria, where asceticism took root early; many scholars have pointed out that Thomas was the favored disciple of early Syriac Christianity. But the *BThomas* could in fact be traced back to a variety of different Christian communities; for example, it is similar to some of Paul's writings, especially chapters 7 and 8 of his letter to the Romans, where Paul speaks in dramatic terms of his body as a sort of prison for his soul. Still, other modern scholars argue that Paul did not invent this negative assessment of the body; it

was widespread in Greek philosophical writings throughout the Mediterranean basin. At any rate, the *BThomas* is one of the texts from Nag Hammadi that challenges the blanket definition of Gnostic, since its theology is in no way out of line with proto-orthodox or monastic Christianity, even if it looks radical, even distasteful, to many of us today.

THE CURIOUS CASE OF THE *GOSPEL OF THOMAS*

Perhaps one of the most curious things about the *GThom* for those reading it for the first time—particularly for many Christian readers—is that this gospel lacks any reference to Jesus's death. There is no arrest, no trial, no crucifixion, and no resurrection. Since these events are central to most modern understandings of what Jesus was about, this absence can puzzling. It is indeed difficult to understand how a Christian gospel could not even mention the crucifixion or the resurrection. Instead, Jesus is portrayed as a teacher of wisdom. His teachings are directed not to crowds of people but to his disciples, or sometimes, apparently to the reader herself (note that Jesus uses the direct form of address, the singular form "you" in some of these sayings. To whom is he speaking but to a solitary person who hears this?)

The *Gospel of Thomas* is, therefore, most like an ancient piece of Jewish Wisdom literature, such as the book of Ecclesiastes or Proverbs. Jesus

---

LITERARY BREAKDOWN OF *BTHOMAS*

I. Anthology of Wise Sayings

II. Revelation dialogue

A. Treatises
   1. the nature of *gnosis*
   2. the fate of souls and bodies
   3. the wise and the fool

B. Eschatological sermon
   1. Description of the underworld
   2. Woes and Blessings
   3. Call to wakefulness

(from Bentley Layton, *The Gnostic Scriptures* [New Haven, CT: Yale University Press, 1995]:401)

often speaks short aphorisms we call "**Wisdom sayings**" (e.g., #26, 31, 32, 33a, 33b, 34, 35, 39b, 45a, 45b, 47a, 47b, 47c, 47d, 67, 92, 93, and 94). The author did not invent these sayings; most of them are also found in Matthew's Sermon on the Mount or in Luke's Sermon on the Plain, but those that are not found there *are* in Mark. Since Thomas does not show any of the editorial peculiarities of Matthew, Mark, or Luke, it seems that his source may have been a very primitive collection of proverbs. Note that Jesus is never the *subject* of these sayings; they are not about him. If they were, we would be able to date them to after Jesus's own time. But they are always about other things, and thus could be very ancient indeed.

When a gospel portrays Jesus as more a human teacher of wisdom than as a divine being, we say that it has a "low **Christology**." This is very different from a document like the Gospel of John, where Jesus is equal to God and is a preexistent being who descends to earth; the Gospel of John therefore has a "high **Christology**." On the face of it, GThom certainly has a low Christology. A careful reader might note that the title "Christ" is never used here for Jesus. Titles such as Lord, Savior, Logos, and Messiah are also missing. One scholar, Stevan Davies, suggests that these terms are absent because GThom was written before these terms were used of Jesus, and thus indicate the gospel's early date. On the other hand, saying #77 infers that Jesus is the source of all things, including the underlying structure of all reality; it is hard to imagine a higher Christological position than that. All things considered, then, it is difficult to conclude that the entire gospel has a low Christology.

One way of tackling the Christological issue is to investigate what titles Jesus has in any given Christian document. In the case of the GThom we find some interesting things. In sayings #52, #59, and also the prologue, Jesus is the "Living One." This is a unique term, and it seems significant. It could be that the title refers to Jesus

after his resurrection. If this is the case, then even though the GThom does not have a passion narrative, it still presupposes Jesus's death and resurrection as key transformative events. Unlike the four NT gospels, this one takes place after Jesus's life on earth as Jesus of Nazareth, beginning with the wisdom that Jesus imparts to his disciples after his triumphant return from death.

IS THE GOSPEL OF THOMAS "GNOSTIC"?

More than most texts from NHL, one of the controversial aspects of the GThom concerns whether it should be considered a Gnostic text. Some of the arguments against it being Gnostic are:

- It may be very early and therefore before the flowering of the movement now called Gnosticism in the second century.
- It does not seem to presuppose a Gnostic myth as featured in other NHL texts such as the HypArch and ApJn. There is no reference to a demiurgical figure, or archons.

Arguments for this being Gnostic include:

- the fact that self-knowledge is mentioned in the text as a form of salvation
- the individual is meant to identify with Jesus, not to "believe in" Jesus. Thus the text is about self-transformation through the salvific knowledge that Jesus brings in a hidden form.

One good way to solve the puzzle is to say that while the GThom *is* Gnostic in that it teaches that self-knowledge is the key to the Kingdom of God, it may not be a product of second-century Gnostic groups, nor of classical Gnosticism as a formal movement. A better solution is simply to note that the GThom provides us with a wonderful example of how the term "Gnostic" is unhelpful, since it depends on shifting opinions on what constitutes Gnostic or Gnosticism in the first place.

THE END OF THE WORLD IN THE *GOSPEL OF THOMAS*

If you read *GThom* carefully, you may note that the document not only lacks a passion narrative but also lacks any sayings where Jesus (or John the Baptist, who is not present here) is an apocalyptic prophet, warning people to repent or to change their ways. Instead, the gospel follows what scholars call a **realized eschatology**; the belief of the author is not that Jesus's Second Coming is on its way but that, in an important sense, the time has already arrived. Thus Jesus tells his disciples,

> #3: "If your leaders say to you, 'Look, the (Father's) kingdom is in the sky,' then the birds of the sky will precede you. If they say to you, 'It is in the sea,' then the fish will precede you. Rather, the kingdom is within you and it is outside you."

also:

> #18: The disciples said to Jesus, "Tell us, how will our end come?" Jesus said, "Have you found the beginning, then, that you are looking for the end? You see, the end will be where the beginning is. Congratulations to the one who stands at the beginning: that one will know the end and will not taste death."

and:

> #51: His disciples said to him, "When will the final repose for the dead happen, and when will the new world come?" He said to them, "What you are looking forward to has already come, but you do not recognize it."

> #113: His disciples said to him, "When is the kingdom going to come?" "It won't come by waiting for it. No one will say, 'Look, here!' or 'Look, there!' Rather, the Father's kingdom is spread out upon the earth, but people do not see it."

The realized eschatology of *GThom* can teach us two things. One, it might be an indication of the relative late date of these sayings. They might have been written at the end of the first century or in the second century, when much of the previous century's apocalyptic speculation had toned down. Or, if these sayings are authentic (that is, that Jesus himself really spoke them) they might

indicate that Jesus himself did not believe that the end of the world was in sight.

There is another possibility, though. The *GThom* shifts the reader's attention away from the *end* of the world and focuses instead on the *beginning*. Note sayings like "Have you found the beginning, then, that you look to the end" (#18) or "Congratulations to the one who stands at the beginning: that one will know the end and will not taste death" (#18) or "Blessed is the one who came into being before he came into being" (#19). The gospel also brings readers "back to the beginning" by invoking images of the primordial light of Genesis 1:2, where God says "let there be light!" and light suddenly shines down into the cosmos. As in the beginning of the Gospel of John, the *Gospel of Thomas* makes it clear that this primordial light is none other than Jesus: "Jesus says, 'I am the light that is before all things. It is I who am all things. From me all things come forth, and from me all things extend" (#77).

THE *GOSPEL OF THOMAS*'S RELATION TO THE NEW TESTAMENT GOSPELS

One of the mysteries concerning *GThom* is determining what sort of relationship exists between this gospel and those found in the NT. In particular, *GThom* shares evident similarities with three of the four NT gospels: Matthew, Mark, and Luke. Since these three gospels share a great deal of source material, scholars call them the **Synoptic Gospels**.

If we look at the Synoptic Gospels without considering *GThom* for a moment, we can see that they share this source material in specific ways. First of all, virtually all of the Gospel of Mark is reproduced in both Matthew and Luke, and kept in the same order. It appears that the Gospel of Mark, presumably the first written, was one of the sources that the authors of Luke and Matthew used, quite independently of each other, as they compiled the source material that went into their gospels. However, Luke and Matthew share a great deal of source material that is not in Mark. Therefore, there must have been a second source that the two writers shared. We do not actually have a copy of this proposed or hypothetical source, but we call it **Q**, from the German word for "source," *Quelle*. This theory about sources is called the **Two-Source Hypothesis**. It can be mapped like this:

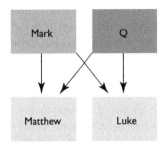

DIAGRAM 9-1 The two-source hypothesis.

New Testament scholars have spent considerable time thinking and writing about Q. Some doubt that it ever existed, but this is a misunderstanding of what Q means. Simply put, Q is the shared material between the gospels of Matthew and Luke that is not already in Mark, so the source itself *does* exist. What does not exist, however, is an actual ancient manuscript of Q. This is not to say that one did not exist at one point, but we have no surviving copies. This is not surprising because we do not have very ancient complete manuscripts of any of the canonical gospels; also, if Q once circulated, it was also quickly replaced with the later canonical gospels, so there was no need to keep manuscript versions of it around after the canonical gospels were put together.

What is really interesting about Q, however, is that it consists of a particular type of source material: the sayings of Jesus. In other words, if you find Jesus saying something in

both Matthew and Luke but not in Mark, you are reading Q. This sayings collection as we can reconstruct it from Matthew and Luke had no narrative, no frame story, no infancy narratives, and no passion narrative. It was entirely made up of Jesus's sayings. But when the Q hypothesis started circulating, many skeptics said that there was no such thing as a Christian "sayings collection," thus the whole idea of Q was moot. But once the *GThom* was discovered, we had, for the first time since antiquity, a complete gospel that consisted solely of Jesus's sayings. The discovery of this gospel thus bolstered the Q hypothesis.

Are the *GThom* and Q the same document? The answer is no, because the sayings of the *GThom* are not the same as Q sayings (although we do not have a manuscript of Q, we know what Q says, because it consists of the sayings material in both Matthew and Luke that are absent from Mark). However—and here's where it gets really interesting—some of the sayings in *GThom* are the same as in Q, so there is an obvious relation between the two sources. Here are some examples of shared sayings from Q and *GThom*, using the Gospel of Luke's versions of the Q sayings (RSV):

> Lk 6:39/#34: Can a blind man lead a blind man? Will they not both fall into a pit?

> Lk 12:2/#6b: Nothing is covered up that will not be revealed, or hidden that will not be known.

> Lk 12:51–53/#16: Do you think that I have come to give peace on earth? No, I tell you, but rather division; for henceforth in one house there will be five divided, three against two and two against three; they will be divided, father against son and son against father, mother against daughter and daughter against her mother, mother-in-law against her daughter-in-law and daughter-in-law against her mother-in-law.

At the same time, *GThom* also uses sayings that are not from Q. For instance, every saying from Mk 3:35–4:34 is found also in Thomas (# 6, 9, 20, 21, 33, 35, 41, 44, 62, 99). Also, there are seven sayings found in Luke but not in Matthew or in Mark (thus not in Q either) but also found in Thomas. What all this points to is that at the heart of the *GThom* we have a very early collection of Jesus's sayings that were in circulation in the middle of the first century, then used by a variety of early Christian writers. And because *GThom* tends to preserve a simpler form of these sayings without elaboration and commentary, some scholars suspect that *GThom*'s words come closer to Jesus's actual words than do the NT gospels. These NT gospels often fill out sayings in characteristic ways. Consider this saying that is shared between *GThom* and Matthew:

(GThom #8)	*(Mt 13:47–50) (RSV)*
And Jesus said, "The person is like a wise fisherman who cast his net into the sea and drew it up from the sea full of little fish. Among them the wise fisherman discovered a fine large fish. He threw all the little fish back into the sea, and easily chose the large fish. Anyone here with two good ears had better listen!"	[Jesus said] "Again, the kingdom of heaven is like a net which was thrown into the sea and gathered fish of every kind; when it was full, men drew it ashore and sat down and sorted the good into vessels but threw away the bad. So it will be at the close of the age. The angels will come out and separate the evil from the righteous, and throw them into the furnace of fire; there men will weep and gnash their teeth."

The sayings are similar, but the author of the Gospel of Matthew chooses to have Jesus interpret his own saying as a metaphor or analogy for the coming apocalypse: "So it will be at the close of the age." There is no indication, meanwhile, from Jesus's saying in *GThom* that he is talking about the end of the world. Matthew also throws in the bit about weeping and gnashing of teeth, which is an expression that Jesus uses often in the Gospel of Matthew. Because of this, we suspect that Jesus himself may not have used that expression, but Matthew inserted it for poetic license.

There are a number of parables in *GThom* that many scholars think may derive ultimately from Jesus: #9, 57, 63, 64, 65, 76, 96, 107, 109 (e.g., box below). These may be authentic even though they differ from those in the Synoptic Gospels: the versions that we have in *GThom* might indeed be closer to what Jesus actually said than those in the Synoptics. Although this might be controversial for some Christian readers who object that the versions in *GThom* just "do not sound right," consider that perhaps the Synoptic versions "sound right" simply because they are the more familiar versions (see item at left).

Which version of the parable do you think Jesus actually told? Which one(s) do you think were changed later, and why might this have been?

Some of the parables in *GThom* are unique, but again, this does not mean that they aren't traceable back to Jesus. To make this determination, scholars rely on a methodological tool known as the **criterion of dissimilarity**. By this criterion, the uniqueness of a saying may indicate that Jesus

---

#107	*Mt 18:12–14 (RSV)*	*Lk 15:3–7 (RSV)*
Jesus said, "The kingdom is like a shepherd who had a hundred sheep. One of them, the largest, went astray. He left the ninety-nine and looked for the one until he found it. After he had toiled, he said to the sheep, 'I love you more than the ninety-nine.'"	[Jesus said]: "What do you think? If a man has a hundred sheep, and one of them has gone astray, does he not leave the ninety-nine on the mountains and go in search of the one that went astray? And if he finds it, truly, I say to you, he rejoices over it more than over the ninety-nine that	"What man of you, having a hundred sheep, if he has lost one of them, does not leave the ninety-nine in the wilderness, and go after the one which is lost, until he finds it? And when he has found it, he lays it on his shoulders, rejoicing. And when he comes home, he calls together his

continued

never went astray. So it is not the will of my Father who is in heaven that one of these little ones should perish."

friends and his neighbors, saying to them, 'Rejoice with me, for I have found my sheep which was lost.' Just so, I tell you, there will be more joy in heaven over one sinner who repents than over ninety-nine righteous persons who need no repentance."

really *did* speak it, since it is not likely to have been invented and transmitted in a collection where it does not fit unless whoever edited the gospel in question felt that the saying had to be recorded as authentic. Put differently, if a saying is dissonant with tradition—it says something radically different than all our other sayings— it might well be authentic, because no one was likely to have made it up. One example of a parable many scholars consider authentic is that of the woman with the jar of meal (#97). Another is the parable of the assassin (#98):

> Jesus said, "The Father's kingdom is like a person who wanted to kill someone powerful. While still at home he drew his sword and thrust it into the wall to find out whether his hand would go in. Then he killed the powerful one."

Why would Jesus compare the kingdom of God to a hired killer, of all things? It is hard to imagine an early Christian who thinks of Jesus as a peace-loving prophet inventing a saying like this. The very idea is therefore dissonant with tradition. Sayings such as these, however, are not only a bit strange to our ears because they are unfamiliar to us, but they also fit with Jesus's style of speaking in parables. So the criterion of dissimilarity combined with their general similarity to Jesus's authentic parables lead many scholars to reconsider these logia as quite possibly authentic too.

It is clear here that the *GThom* has ancient roots, quite possibly older than the gospels of Matthew and Luke, and as ancient as the Gospel of Mark. It shares source material with all three, making it clear that its author used the same

source as Matthew and Luke (Q) and either the Gospel of Mark or the same source that Mark used. From then, the *Gospel of Thomas* developed independently, it seems, picking up or developing other sayings that are more reminiscent of the second century than the first.

WHAT IS SECOND-CENTURY ABOUT THIS GOSPEL?

Even though the *GThom* has very ancient roots, the text as we have it today probably dates from the middle of the second century or later. We know this primarily from characteristic vocabulary. Consider these sayings:

> #28: Jesus said, "I took my stand in the midst of the world, and in flesh I appeared to them. I found them all drunk, and I did not find any of them thirsty. My soul ached for the children of humanity, because they are blind in their hearts and do not see, for they came into the world empty, and they also seek to depart from the world empty. But meanwhile they are drunk. When they shake off their wine, then they will change their ways." (trans. Marvin Meyer, "The Gospel of Thomas," in Marvin Meyer, ed., The Nag Hammadi Scriptures [San Francisco: HarperOne, 2007]: 143)

> #42: Jesus said, "Be passersby."

The emphasis on concepts such as the world being "drunk" or "passersby" are generally out of place for the first century; we do not find them being used until the second century or later. Imagine that you are reading a document in the year 2050 that contains phrases like "global warming" or "blogging"; you would be able to date that document fairly accurately from the use of these expressions that

IF IT IS SO OLD, WHY ISN'T THE *GOSPEL OF THOMAS* RECOGNIZED BY MOST CHURCHES?

The New Testament is the official set of scriptures for Christianity, and if an ancient Christian writing isn't in the canon—the list of approved books that made it into the NT—it does not carry much authority, no matter how old or how great it might be. The process of how the canon came together is actually quite complicated, but one of the factors for choosing books was not, apparently, how old a book was. We have other Christian writings that are as old as some of the NT books. Instead of the antiquity of the writing, one of the determining factors was literary form. The *Gospel of Thomas* looks very different from the four NT gospels, and thus it did not match the accepted style. What probably happened was that whoever wrote the three **Synoptic** Gospels drew

on Q as a collection of sayings, and incorporated these into their writings. At that point, if indeed it was an early gospel, the *GThom* became nothing more than source material; it could not stand up to the narrative format of the other gospels. But there are other reasons, too, including the lack of emphasis on Jesus's death and resurrection, which gives *GThom* a very different "feel" from those in the NT. The *Gospel of Thomas* continued to be a popular text throughout at least the second century when it underwent another set of redactions (edits) to make it look like it does now. This second-century material probably upset heresiologists such as **Irenaeus of Lyons**—it was not simply the case that the *Gospel of Thomas* got rejected because it was heretical.

did not exist in general parlance before the late twentieth or early twenty-first century. Dating ancient documents can work the same way. What this tells us is that at some point in the second century, someone either composed the gospel "from scratch," or else an editor redacted or edited the text of *GThom* that he had in front of him and added additional sayings (he might have written these, or he might have taken them from another contemporary source). Most likely the same thing happened in the fourth century, as scribes in Egypt were copying the manuscript of *GThom*.

THE GOSPEL OF THOMAS AND THE GOSPEL OF JOHN: AN EARLY CHRISTIAN CONFLICT?

A careful reader who knows her New Testament might have detected a similarity between some sayings in the *GThom* and the Gospel of John. A few modern scholars have explored this relationship, beginning with Gregory Riley in his book *Resurrection Reconsidered: Thomas and*

John in Controversy (1995), and most recently Elaine Pagels in *Beyond Belief: The Secret Gospel of Thomas* (2003). Pagels joins Riley and others in claiming that the author of the fourth gospel knew—and disapproved of—the *GThom*, consciously rejecting its theology.

What is nifty about this is that prior to Riley's scholarship, most people assumed that *GThom*, as a Gnostic gospel, was later than the NT gospels. Those who thought it was early found direct connections between Thomas and the three Synoptic Gospels (Mark, Matthew, and Luke) but not with the Gospel of John. By contrast, Pagels argues that the Gospel of John was actually written to directly contradict and correct some of the dangerous ideas in *GThom*. For example, while the *GThom* actively presses the reader to "seek within" to find the kingdom of God, the Gospel of John makes it clear that salvation is found only through believing in Jesus Christ. As Jesus himself states, "I am the way, and the truth, and the life; no one comes to the Father but by me" (Jn 14:6). In what may be

WOMEN ARE NOT WORTHY OF LIFE?

People often like the *GThom* until they reach #114, where the apostle Peter demands that Jesus make Mary Magdalene leave, "for women are not worthy of life." It is an odd saying, a little bit out of keeping with the rest of the gospel. It is the first time we've run into Peter in this particular text, and it is not a very complimentary picture. The fact that Peter says such a strange thing, and that Jesus's response is, in its way, equally strange (what does it mean that he will attract Mary to "make her [more] male?") and that, finally, the **logion** assumes that women cannot get into heaven unless they are "more male," leads some to believe that #114 was not originally part of the original *GThom*. Other scholars, however, try to make sense of the logion as an actual part of the gospel from an early date. Graeco-Roman antiquity was a male-dominated, male-oriented culture in which masculine qualities were esteemed over female qualities, and if we remember this, the logion no longer looks so strange, although it is offensive to modern Western sensibilities. One interesting thing about the logion, however, is that it appears to record a conflict between Mary Magdalene and Peter. This conflict also appears in other ancient sources, namely the *Gospel of Mary*.

an intentional barb, Jesus speaks these famous words to none other than the disciple Thomas, who is a character known in the NT primarily from the Gospel of John. Here's a second example: one of the most prominent themes in both gospels is the origins and nature of light. But where is this light? In *GThom*, it is "within" each of us:

> #50: When they say to you, where are you from, say to them, "we came from the light, the place where the light came into being by itself, and was revealed through their image." If they say to you, "who are you?" say "we are its children, the chosen of the living Father.'"

In the Gospel of John, by contrast, light is embodied only in Jesus, the light who comes into the world or cosmos, "but the world did not recognize it" (Jn 1:4, 6–11).

The Gospel of John is quite adamant: the primordial light of Genesis 1:2 should be understood as identical with Jesus, the light of the world (Jn 8:12; 9:5; 12:46). It therefore contradicts the *GThom*, that there is "light inside a person of light, and it lights up the whole darkness" (see too, #24: "seek the light within"). This connects with the belief, common in Jewish mysticism, that God created a Light Adam or primordial human being in his own image. This Light Adam is not a unique being separate from us but is our spiritual ancestor, since we are all made in the image of God. We see this theology of the Light Adam in some of the creation stories from Nag Hammadi (*ApJn*, *HypArch*, *OrigWld*). It also builds on a pun in ancient Greek, where the word *phōs* means both "light" and "human," depending on how it was accented.

The Gospel of John, by contrast to the *GThom*, has Jesus claim repeatedly that he is a unique being: "You are from below, I am from above" (Jn 8:23). He alone is the "only" (Jn 1:18) Son of the Father, and if you want salvation, only one thing is required: belief in Jesus as God. As Jesus puts it, "you will die in your sins, unless you believe that I am he" (Jn 8:24). Put differently, in order to be a proper Christian according to the Gospel of John, you needed to put your faith in Jesus. And to do that, you needed to go outside yourself to find him. But consider the message of the *GThom*: in order to be a proper Christian according to the *Gospel of Thomas*, you needed to look within. There is, therefore, no need of a church, a community, a clergy, or any kind of institutional structure. All these things are unnecessary for salvation, since salvation is found by turning within. This is an inspirational message, but not one what works well with community or institutionalized Christianity.

THOMAS IN THE GOSPEL OF JOHN

The apostle Thomas is sometimes better known as the "Doubting Thomas," because at the end of the Gospel of John, Thomas is skeptical that the Jesus who appeared to him and his fellow disciples was the same Jesus who had suffered and died on the cross. At a key scene (Jn 20:27) Jesus invites Thomas to put his fingers inside the wound in his side, proving his true identity to him as well as the reality of the resurrection. Thomas responds, proclaiming Jesus as Lord. Is this curious incident (the only occasion of the apostle Thomas having a "speaking role" in this or any other gospel) meant by the author of the Gospel of John as a sort of "jab" at Thomasine Christianity, which de-emphasizes the teaching of the resurrection of the flesh and the need for belief in Jesus?

FIGURE 9.3 Caravaggio, The Incredulity of Saint Thomas (1601–1602)

GNOSIS AND SELF-KNOWLEDGE IN THE GOSPEL OF THOMAS

From its opening logion, the author of *GThom* urges the reader to seek the meaning of Jesus's words. What is the hidden message of this gospel?

To begin with, you may have noticed that the disciples usually seem to be on the wrong track, and often ask Jesus questions about his nature:

#24: "Show us the place you are, for it is necessary for us to seek it."

#37: "On what day will you be revealed to us and on what day will we see you?"

#43: "Who are you to say these things to us?"

#91: "Tell us who you are so that we can believe in you."

The most elaborate of these identity riddles is logion #13. The first part of the saying is:

> Jesus said to his disciples, "Compare me to something and tell me what I am like."
>
> Simon Peter said to him, "You are like a just messenger."
>
> Matthew said to him, "You are like a wise philosopher."
>
> Thomas said to him, "Teacher, my mouth is utterly unable to say what you are like." (trans. Marvin Meyer, "The Gospel of Thomas," in Marvin Meyer, ed., *The Nag Hammadi Scriptures* [San Francisco: HarperOne, 2007]: 141)

The message of this gospel, apparently, is that inquiry into the nature of Jesus is improper; those who think they know (Jesus's chief disciples, in this case) are actually ignorant. They do not know the answer because they are looking in the wrong direction. What is the right direction, then? Obviously Thomas discerns it, so let's consider his answer and what happens next in logion #13. Here, Jesus answers the identity questions by emphasizing that people must look for what is already present. In #24, the true direction is to "seek the light within." In #37, the nature of Jesus is discerned in the meaning of his words, not in his physical nature or person. And in #91, people do not recognize what is right in front of them.

What counts, then, is the discovery of the nature of the present reality, the time or place or person right in front of you:

> #3: Jesus said, "If your leaders say to you, 'Look, the (Father's) kingdom is in the sky,' then the birds of the sky will precede you. If they say to you, 'It is in the sea,' then the fish will precede you. Rather, the kingdom is within you and it is outside you. When you know yourselves, then you will be known, and you will understand that you are children of the living Father. But if you do not know yourselves, then you live in poverty, and you are the poverty.

What does it mean to "know yourselves"? The answer seems to be hidden in the text of G*Thom*. In #50, members of the community are asked directly who they are; they answer that they are "children of the light" and children of the "living Father." In #3, self-knowledge is connected to recognizing that the kingdom of the Father lies within. In #22, self-knowledge is to "make the two into one," in #24, it is to recognize the light within.

Turning and searching within for one's spiritual connection appears to lie behind another interesting saying:

> #6: Jesus's disciples asked him and said to him, "Do you want us to fast? How should we pray? Should we give alms to charity? What diet should we observe?" Jesus said, "Do not lie, and do not do what you hate, because all things are disclosed before heaven. After all, there is nothing hidden that will not be revealed, and there is nothing covered up that will remain undisclosed."

What is remarkable here is that Jesus rejects the standard ways of being religious in an ancient Jewish context: do not fast, do not pray, and do not bother with almsgiving. These are all ways of turning one's faith outward, supporting tradition and community. Typical of this gospel, the correct way of being spiritual, Jesus says, is to turn within and self-examine. After all, only we can discern when we are lying, or what it is we hate. Thus we are the sole mediators of our relationship with the Father, and knowledge of our spiritual origins comes from looking deeply and honestly at ourselves.

UNDERSTANDING THOMAS AS JESUS'S TWIN

The G*Thom* probably started as a very ancient collection of wisdom sayings, perhaps many of them spoken by Jesus himself. What is certain is that the writers of the Synoptic Gospels considered many of Jesus's sayings to be authentic, since they incorporated them into their own writings. As a sayings collection, there is no narrative and little cohesion or organization to the G*Thom*. Sayings were gathered such that the collection grew over time, without being edited to smooth out textual inconsistencies. We are left with a compendium of sayings, some familiar to us from the NT, and some unfamiliar.

Jesus in *GThom* acts as a teacher of wisdom, not so much as someone in whom to believe or place one's faith but as a spiritual guide who can set listeners on the right path: self-knowledge or *gnosis*. Guidance is not openly given; it takes work to discover the meaning of Jesus's words. But properly understood, the *GThom* guides the listener into realizing that the primordial light from Genesis 1:2 shines in the cosmos and in all people. Jesus came to remind people about these celestial origins, to actualize the light within. Those who *do* become "children of the light" participate in the clear, undifferentiated world of eternal beginnings: the kingdom of God lies within them.

So in what sense is Thomas Jesus's twin? Does this gospel mean that Jesus and Thomas shared an actual womb? Or does it mean "twin" in a purely spiritual sense? The text itself gives us a hint; let's go back to logion #13, after Thomas reveals that he cannot actually reveal what Jesus is like. Jesus turns to him and says:

> "I am not your teacher. Because you have drunk, you have become intoxicated from the bubbling spring that I have tended."

> And he took him and withdrew, and spoke three sayings to him. When Thomas came back to his friends, they asked him, "What did Jesus say to you?"

> Thomas said to them, "If I tell you one of the sayings he spoke to me, you will pick up rocks and stone me, and fire will come from the rocks and consume you." (trans. Marvin Meyer, "The Gospel of Thomas," in Marvin Meyer, ed., *The Nag Hammadi Scriptures* [San Francisco: HarperOne, 2007]: 141)

This is a strange and shocking thing for Thomas to say. What might have been the three things that Jesus said? To figure this out, we can put a few clues together. First of all, we know that whatever Jesus told Thomas would, if Thomas repeated it, get him stoned to death. In Jewish law, stoning was a punishment for a number of things, but what seems to fit best with the context

here is the religious crime of blasphemy. To warrant such a punishment, you couldn't just take the Lord's name in vain or curse God, for example. The only truly blasphemous thing one could say was "I am God." (In the trial narratives of the NT gospels, the Jewish religious authorities ask Jesus directly who he is, trying to goad him into committing blasphemy so they can put him to death. Significantly, only in the Gospel of John does Jesus come very close to saying that he is God.) So perhaps the first thing that Jesus said to Thomas might have been "I am God."

What about the second thing? In #13, Jesus speaks of Thomas as having drunk from the "bubbling spring" (or "living water"), which, in Jesus's words, is because Thomas fully understood Jesus's identity. In another saying, #108, Jesus tells us the consequences of drinking from Jesus as the "bubbling spring": "whoever drinks from my mouth will become as I am, and I myself will become that person, and the mysteries will be revealed to him." In other words, Thomas *becomes* Christ. That he does so is revealed in his very name, "twin." So the second thing Jesus said to Thomas might have been something like, "I am you."

That leaves one more secret saying. We do not know this for sure, but a clue might be in the "doubleness" of the word "twin" in the *GThom*. Thomas is twins with Jesus, but he is also twins with someone else, and that would be whoever reads and understands the words of the living Jesus. They who understand these words, in the end, are returned to the primordial light; they understand that they, too, become Christs. And so here *might* be what Jesus said to Thomas:

> I am God

> You are me.

> We are the kingdom of God.

If this is the true meaning of the gospel, it is a pretty radical message. Can we all become Thomases? Can we, too, all become Christs?

THE *GOSPEL OF THOMAS* IN POPULAR CULTURE

The American horror/thriller movie *Stigmata* (dir. R. Wainwright, 1999) tells the story of a young, atheist woman named Frankie (Patricia Arquette) who becomes possessed by the spirit of a dead

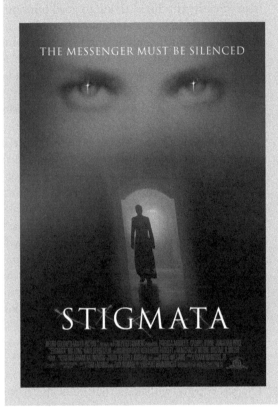

THE MESSENGER MUST BE SILENCED

STIGMATA

priest who wants the existence of a new gospel containing the authentic words of Jesus to be revealed to humankind.

It turns out that this gospel is none other than the *GThom*, which is presented as a dangerous text deliberately hidden from the public by the Roman Catholic Church. Of course, the truth is that the Catholic Church isn't that interested in the *GThom*. Widely available in print, it can also be downloaded or read free online, and you do not have to suffer stigmata as a consequence!

Despite being a Hollywood blockbuster, *Stigmata* actually cites scripture more or less accurately, and it presents an authentic struggle in ancient Christianity recast as a modern dilemma: Where does one find the kingdom of God? The line in the film, repeated at various points, is "The kingdom of God is inside/within you (and all about you), not in buildings/mansions of wood and stone. (When I am gone) Split a piece of wood and I am there, lift the/a stone and you will find me." The line is a combination of Logion 3a from *GThom* ("Jesus said: If your leaders say to you 'Look! The kingdom is in the heavens!' Then the birds will be there before you are. If they say that the kingdom is in the sea, then the fish will be there before you are. Rather, the kingdom is within you and it is outside of you") combined with *GThom* 77b: "Split a piece of wood, I am there. Lift up a rock, you will find me there." There are also echoes of Stephen's words in Acts 7:48: "the Most High does not dwell in houses made with hands."

QUESTIONS TO CONSIDER

1. What do you think might be the points of contact between the *Gospel of Thomas* and the Synoptics? What about *Gospel of Thomas* and the Gospel of John? Do you see similarities or dissimilarities?

2. Do you think that the Jesus of the *Gospel of Thomas* has a "low Christology" (i.e., he is more of a human teacher) or a "high Christology" (i.e., he is the resurrected, "living" Christ)?

3. Why do you think that the *Gospel of Thomas* was buried as a heretical document and the Gospel of Mark was not?

KEY TERMS

realized eschatology	logion/logia	Manichaean
sayings collection	Jesus Movement	ascetic
encratitic	Wisdom sayings	low Christology
high Christology	Q	synoptic gospels
Criterion of Dissimilarity	Two-Source Hypothesis	Irenaeus of Lyons

FOR FURTHER READING

Davies, Stevan L. *The Gospel of Thomas and Christian Wisdom*. Bardic Press, 2004. A groundbreaking study of the *Gospel of Thomas*. For a general educated audience.

DeConick, April D. *Recovering the Original Gospel of Thomas: A History of the Gospel and Its Growth*. T. & T. Clark, 2006. This study by an important American scholar of Gnosticism contains the author's original translation of the text and an important study of how the gospel came to be. For advanced readers.

Kloppenborg, John S., Marvin W. Meyer, and Stephen J. Patterson, eds. *The Q Thomas Reader*. Sonoma, CA: Polebridge Press, 1990. A useful volume for comparing the *GThom* and the NT source we call Q, with translations, commentaries, and introductory essays. For those who want to know more about early Christian gospel material.

Lumpkin, Joseph B. *The Tao of Thomas*. Fifth Estate Books, 2005. This book offers new translations of *GThom* and the important ancient Chinese religious text, the *Tao Te Ching*. The parallels are, at times, quite provocative.

Meier, John. *A Marginal Jew: Rethinking the Historical Jesus*. Vol. 1: *The Roots of the Problem and the Person*. Anchor, 1991. Meier leads the charge of scholars who do not date *GThom* early, providing a helpful bibliographic survey of modern scholarship on the issue.

Pagels, Elaine. *Beyond Belief: The Secret Gospel of Thomas*. New York: Random House, 2003. A highly readable book, *Beyond Belief* contrasts, provocatively, the spiritual teachings of the *Gospel of Thomas* with the Gospel of John. For general readers.

Internet Resources

Gospel of Thomas Bibliography. A good compilation of academic materials for studying the *GThom*. http://agraphos.com/thomas/about/

Gospel of Thomas Homepage. Maintained by Stevan Davies, with an excellent range of resources in English for students of all levels. http://users.misericordia.edu//davies/thomas/Thomas.html

For other Thomas writings, including the Infancy Gospel of Thomas:

Barnstone, Willis, ed. *The Other Bible*. San Francisco: HarperSanFrancisco, 1984. This is a collection of various early Christian writings in an accessible format for nonspecialist readers.

Schneemelcher, W., and Robert McL. Wilson, eds. *The New Testament Apocrypha*. 2 vols. Louisville: Westminster/John Knox, 2006. This is a collection of early Christian writings translated by and for specialists, and is therefore more technical in nature. It is an important starting point for more professional work on early Christian apocrypha.

10

Sethian Gnosticism

THREE STELES OF SETH (NHC VI, 5)

How many children did Adam and Eve have? Most people would quickly answer "two." And most would be able to name these two as Cain and Abel, perhaps even to know that Cain murdered his brother, Abel, uttering afterwards the famous retort, when asked where his brother was, "Am I my brother's keeper?" (Gen 4:9) And yet the right answer—at least, going by the story in Genesis—is three: Cain, Abel, and then their younger brother **Seth** (Gen 4:25). In that story, Eve says that with God's help, she has another

THE DEVELOPMENT OF SETHIANISM

- The first Sethians were not Christians but Jewish. They lived somewhere in the eastern Mediterranean around the turn of the Millennium (1st cen. BCE – 1st cen. CE) and, like many other groups in the area, practiced baptism. This community (or communities) took the biblical figure Seth as their spiritual ancestor and savior (or Revealer). This group believed that Seth had given them hidden wisdom, but would return to save his followers through the power of baptism.
- As Christianity spread through the Mediterranean in the late first century, Sethianism was gradually Christianized; Seth (or sometimes his father Adam) were identified with the pre-existent Christ. This may have happened as Christian baptismal groups met and mingled with the non-Christian baptismal Sethians.
- As Christianity developed toward the end of the second century and beyond, Sethianism became estranged, separated from it once more;
- by the third century as Christian orthodoxy began to develop, it rejected Sethianism. At the same time, Sethians were attracted to third-century Platonism, a pagan intellectual movement with spiritual practices and teachings that could be accommodated to Sethian cosmology and mysticism.
- Platonists rejected Sethianism, sending these communities and individuals into a kind of dispersal and decline.

child to replace Abel: "God hath appointed for me another seed instead of Abel, whom Cain slew" (Gen 4:25, KJV). Why "appoint seed" instead of "given me a child"? It is really very unusual, and just not the usual way of talking about having children. After that, we hear very little about Seth. He becomes a father at the ripe old age of 105, fathering Enosh or Enoch, but then lives another 807 years, fathers other unnamed children, and dies (Gen 5:6–8). In the NT, Seth appears only once: as the father of Enoch and the son of Adam in a genealogy of Jesus (Lk 3:38). Remarkably, however, in the NHL this same Seth is a towering figure, for whom the term **Sethianism** or Sethian Gnosticism is named.

Sethianism is the second major modern sectarian division of Gnosticism; **Valentinianism** is the other. And yet, they are very different from one another for a number of reasons. While Valentinianism was named after a historical teacher, Valentinus, Sethianism is named after the biblical figure Seth. While we have the names and settings for a number of Valentinian teachers, we know of only a few people associated with Sethianism. While **heresiologists** spend a great deal of time outlining Valentinianism, they have much less to say about Sethianism, and in fact our best source, Irenaeus, says nothing about Sethianism at all. Let's look at what we can know about Sethianism and what we cannot know, and how we make those sorts of determinations.

Our job in this chapter is to examine more closely the shared features of writings from NH that scholars have classified as Sethian. Since we will have occasion to look at most of these Sethian texts in more detail in other chapters, we will focus on only one classic Sethian text here—the *Three Steles of Seth*—to see how it holds up against the classic features and characteristics of Sethianism once we have laid them out. We will then be in a better position to determine the usefulness of the category Sethian and understand why scholars make the determinations they do about Sethianism.

HOW THE HERESIOLOGISTS DO NOT HELP

The first heresiologist to mention Sethians by name is a little-known figure we call **Pseudo-Tertullian**, who wrote toward the end of the second century. He probably copied most of his material from Irenaeus and another lost source, **Hippolytus of Rome**'s *Syntagma*. At around the same time, Hippolytus also writes about Sethians in his *Refutation*, but what he has to say about the group there in no way resembles what Pseudo-Tertullian has to say. A century later, **Epiphanius of Salamis** also discusses Sethians, and then their name also shows up in many legal rulings after the fourth century without any description of what they believe.

So did Sethians ever exist? One scholar of Gnosticism, Frederik Wisse, famously likened the search for Sethians to the search for the mythic unicorn. It is unlikely that any group of people in antiquity ran around calling themselves "Sethians." At the same time, it is undeniable that a number of Nag Hammadi texts understand Seth to be a centrally important figure, one who either "stands for" Jesus Christ or replaces him altogether as a Savior. These same NH texts, as well as others that do not necessarily feature Seth, share common and distinctive traits that are very different from what we find in, say, Valentinian texts. Most notably, Sethian texts lack overtly Christian language and imagery such as we find in Valentinianism. They are also more concerned with **cosmology** and cosmological language. Finally, it appears that some people considered themselves to have descended from "another seed," that is, from the direct lineage of Adam and Eve's third child, Seth—those whom Eve commented were "appointed by God." Whether these people banded together as a community is still a matter of dispute. What is clear, however, is that for the most part, the NH Sethian texts have little to do with the Sethians mentioned in our heresiological sources.

HOW TO RECOGNIZE A SETHIAN (TEXT)

Scholars of Gnosticism still actively dispute which treatises from NH are properly called Sethian. The reason for the disagreements has to do with the process of categorization. How many qualities of a classification does something have to have in order to fall under any particular classification? Let's look at an example from the natural sciences to help illuminate the issue. For instance, consider the biological class of mammal. To count as a mammal, an animal needs to be a vertebrate. But then there are other criteria:

- The presence of hair or fur
- The presence of three middle-ear bones
- The presence of mammary glands on the female of the class, used to produce milk to nourish young

Beyond these three criteria that define the classification, there are also subclasses of mammals, where it is possible for one subclass to differ substantially from other subclasses. For example, all mammals give birth, except for the subclass of the monotremes, which lay eggs. Some small mammals, such as marsupials, carry their infants in pouches, but many do not. What this tells us is that at some point when classificatory schemes were being developed in the natural sciences, the presence of all three criteria in vertebrates was necessary for an animal to be considered a mammal, and other criteria such as the ability to give birth rather than lay eggs was common, but not necessary, for the vertebrate to be placed in that classification.

But the process of taxonomy, of building classification, leads to some vexing problems in biology. For example: take the example of a penguin, which looks like a bird, has feathers and a beak, and lays eggs. Unlike a bird, however, a penguin cannot fly and in fact spends a lot of its time in the water rather than in the air. There are many ways in which a penguin seems more like a mammal that lays eggs (like a platypus, a monotreme that is also challenging to classify) than like a bird. Nevertheless, there is a level at which we necessarily create subclasses to account for difference while simultaneously fitting things into broader categories like "bird" or "mammal." When the platypus was first discovered in 1798 (and thought to be a hoax, because it was so strange), naturalists were at a loss as to how to classify it. It had fur but also lay eggs that divided in the manner of reptile eggs, and unlike any other subclass of mammals, it located its prey through electroreception; that is, a series of sensors on its duck-billed snout (also an anomaly) could sense the electrical impulses generated when muscles contract. Nevertheless, the platypus was classed as a mammal because it fit enough of the key qualities to classify as a mammal even if it didn't share much with other mammals.

So what does this have to do with Sethianism? Modern scholars are still in the process of hashing out classifications and taxonomies in Gnosticism and other religious movements in the ancient Mediterranean. Sethianism proves to be a tricky category or classification, because we ourselves have to choose how to classify texts as Sethian—there is no ancient guide to do it for us, and no easy out like naming a movement after a leader (e.g., Valentinianism) or after a theological position (e.g., **docetism**). In the case of Sethianism we have a movement, which was not founded by a single, named, historical figure. And since the heresiologists never clearly outlined Sethian characteristics or theology, we cannot use that as a starting point. We need to develop other criteria first. For something to be Sethian, for example, does it have to merely mention Seth? (The answer here is no. Of the two tractates in the NHL that name Seth in their title—the *Three Steles of Seth* and the *Second Treatise of the Great Seth*—only one of them is classified as a Sethian writing.) Does it have to explicitly name

Seth as a savior? (The answer here is also no. The *Apocryphon of John* is a good example of a NH text that is Sethian but does not feature Seth as a savior, and there are quite a few others in this category). If a text has a cosmology that it shares with other Sethian texts that do name Seth as a savior, but it does not mention Seth, is it still Sethian? (Here, the answer is yes, since cosmology is one of the most consistent features across Sethian texts).

Some scholars have taken a broad approach, and thus the most generous list of Sethian texts from NH includes all of the following:

- *Apocryphon of John*
- *Hypostasis of the Archons*
- *Gospel of the Egyptians*
- *Apocalypse of Adam*
- *Three Steles of Seth*
- *Zostrianos*
- *Melchizedek*
- *Thought of Norea*
- *Marsanes*
- *Allogenes*
- *Trimorphic Protennoia*

This list is based on the work of Hans-Martin Schenke, the prominent German scholar of Gnosticism, who considered a number of features as basic to Sethian Gnosticism (see Table 10.1). You can see from the table that no text classified as Sethian has every single one of the classic Sethian themes present within it. Nevertheless, the entire group shares these themes to varying degrees.

SETHIAN TYPOLOGIES

Scholars of Gnosticism noticed that the creation myths and cosmologies of many texts from Nag Hammadi share a number of features or "types." The American scholar John Turner,

who has devoted the last forty years to studying Sethianism, has identified these features as characteristic to this set of documents:

1. A preoccupation with recounting the sacred history of the offspring of the biblical figure Seth. This history comes from a particular way of reading or interpreting Genesis 1–6 in certain Jewish circles.

2. A Hellenistic Jewish doctrine about a feminine divine figure called **Sophia** (Wisdom), along with allusions to a myth of Sophia's origins, her "fall," and her restoration.

3. References to a baptismal rite, often called the **Five Seals**, which involves departure from the fleshly world and transportation into the realm of light through the invocation of certain divine figures.

4. Certain "**Christological**" speculations that identify Christ with primordial figures such as Adam and Seth.

5. Abundant resonances with Platonist metaphysical concepts of the structure of the divine world, combined with mystical teachings concerning ways to come to experience this world through visionary, ecstatic ascent.

From this set of elements (sometimes called **mytholegoumena**), Turner suggests the following hypothetical "history" of Sethianism (see Box on page 118).

Turner's work is highly speculative, and not every scholar of Gnosticism accepts his reconstruction. However, his reconstruction helps us to make sense of many Sethian texts that have very strong Jewish influence; in addition, a few have Christian features that seem not especially well integrated to the text, as if the Christian elements of the texts were later additions, while another set display strongly pagan **Platonist** language and imagery. We can divide up our Sethian texts like this:

TABLE 10.1: Sethian Characteristics as Found in Classic Sethian Texts from NH

	ApocAdam	GosEg	ApJn	3StelesSeth	Melk.	Zost.	Allog.	Mars.	TriPro	HypArch	Norea
The self-understanding of the Gnostics that they are the pneumatic seed of Seth	√	√	√	√	√	√					
Seth as the heavenly/earthly savior of his seed	√	√					(√)	√			
The four lights of the Autogenes (Harmozel, Oroiael, Daveithai, and Eleleth) constitute the heavenly dwelling places of Adam, Seth, and the seed of Seth		√	√						√		
The heavenly trinity of the Father (Invisible Spirit), Mother (Barbēlō), and Son (the Autogenes or Anthropos)		√	√	√		√	√	?	√		√
The evil demiurge Yaldabaoth who tried to destroy the seed of Seth			√						√	√	
The division of history into three ages and the appearance of the savior in each age	√	√	√						√		
A special prayer				√VII,5: 125,24; 126, 17		√VIII, 1: 51,24–52,8; 86,13–24; 88,9–25	√XI, 3: 54:11–37				

TABLE 10.2: Subdividing Sethian Texts by Intellectual Influence

Predominantly Jewish	Predominantly Christian	Predominantly Platonist
Hypostasis of the Archons	Apocryphon of John	Allogenes
Apocalypse of Adam	Melchizedek	Zostrianos
Trimorphic Protennoia	Gospel of the Egyptians	Marsanes
		Three Steles of Seth

Jewish Sethian Texts (*Hypostasis of the Archons, Apocalypse of Adam, Trimorphic Protennoia*)

The three Sethian texts that show the most Jewish influence are discussed elsewhere in this book (see chapters 11, 12, 13, and 19) and so here we can summarize what is significantly "Jewish" about them:

- None of them includes a prominent role for Jesus nor mentions any explicitly, recognizably Christian doctrine.

- There can be a deliberate reliance on ways of reading the Jewish scriptures that was typical for Jewish scholarship at the beginning of the millennium, using techniques of **midrash** and allegorization.

- They draw on the Jewish genre of **apocalyptic literature.**

- They are familiar with other Jewish scholarly writings and genres, such as **Wisdom literature.**

- They often are based on Genesis 1–6, which they considered a problematic but nevertheless sacred text.

These markers do not make these texts unequivocally Jewish. They might have been composed by Christian authors who drew on traditional Jewish ways of reading scripture or methods of writing. On the other hand, the Jewish elements in these writings are more prominent than any Christian one, so it is difficult to see why, if a

Christian had written them, he or she would not simply have made Jesus the savior rather than Seth. Still, the very focus on Seth derives from Jewish tradition.

Although he does not play much of a role in Genesis, Seth is an important figure in some ancient Jewish writings. He is associated with two things: (1) as a key ancestor for humanity, or (2) as someone possessed of special wisdom or knowledge. In the first category, a number of Jewish texts depict Seth as the ancestor of humankind since, they argue, the offspring of Cain and Abel were destroyed in the flood (Gen 6). A few texts suggest that the "race" of Seth (that is, the descendents of Seth) are superior to others. Jewish sources also record a tradition that Seth was a wise and virtuous man who raised equally wise children.

Christian Sethian Texts

If John Turner's reconstruction is correct, then at some point, Sethian groups joined with Christian groups and accordingly "Christianized" their theology. A classic example is the *Apocryphon of John (ApJn)*, the core of which does not seem very familiarly Christian but which is set in a clearly Christian "frame-story," where Jesus reveals secret knowledge to his disciple, John of Zebedee. As it stands today, it would be impossible not to consider *ApJn* a Christian writing. The *Gospel of the Egyptians (GosEg)* is also Christian; Jesus appears in it as the Christ, although he does not exactly play a starring role. Nevertheless, he is there, and thus the text is "Christian" in some sense.

lines. The most important of these lines was, of course, that of Adam and Eve's third child, Seth. Thus at baptism, one became symbolically "reborn" in full recognition of one's true origins as a child of Seth, part of the "Great Race" or "Great Generation." In the *ApocAdam*, when the initiate reaches the **Thirteenth Kingdom**, he or she is told that they "shall live forever" (83:14).

Another phrase that is often used of the "seed of Seth" in Sethian texts is "the immoveable/unshakeable race." At the flood (Gen 6), the immovable race is divided; the human seed of Seth inhabits the earth, while their heavenly counterparts dwell in the aeons of the Four Luminaries (Daveithai, Eleleth, Oroael and Harmozel). When Seth makes his final appearance on earth in the guise of the **Logos**, he will judge the archons, and the earthly seed of Seth will be reunited with their heavenly counterparts. Until that time, the seed of Seth remains connected with their heavenly counterparts through revelations that Seth left for them. These were written down, either in books, or on wooden tablets, or else on steles (standing stones) of clay and brick, and preserved on a sacred mountain. The Sethians could also be reunited with their counterparts through a ritual of celestial ascent that Seth himself passed down to his spiritual offspring. This celestial ascent ritual appears to have had some affinities with baptism, although it is not clear precisely how.

3. Teachings about Sophia

The important character or hypostasis Sophia (Gk: wisdom) derives from Hellenistic Jewish speculative philosophy. In this strand of philosophy, Sophia is God's active feminine principle, at once part of God but also separate from God (Prov 8, Job 28, Sir 24).

In Sethian texts, Sophia is identical with Barbelo, the Mother-figure in the Sethian Trinity. She functions as Divine Thought, and as such, helps to create the highest, spiritual parts of human beings. But Sophia also has a "lower" function in which she acts less like a divine principle and more like a willful, independent agent. Sophia's decision to create a child for herself with neither the consent nor the cooperation of the Father produces the monstrous Ialdabaoth. This creation is sometimes described as Sophia's "fall," and her subsequent sorrow and repentance becomes a potent narrative for why evil entered into the world.

4. Baptism and Ritual Practice

Most Sethian texts allude to baptismal ritual, so we can be fairly certain that the people who used these texts practiced baptism. However, it appears that Sethian baptism must have looked very different from modern-day baptism. In contemporary liturgical Christianity (Roman Catholic, Anglican or Episcopal, Lutheran), for example, baptism is a rite of initiation in which individuals joining the church—usually newborn babies—are brought into the community by being sprinkled with holy water on their foreheads (called **aspersion**); sometimes a small amount of water is poured on the head instead (called **affusion**). The priest performs this baptism in full view of the parents and the congregation. Other denominations(Eastern Orthodox and some Protestant denominations, most notably Baptists) practice immersion or submersion of the initiate into baptismal water, either in a small pool or font designed for this purpose, or occasionally outdoors in a body of water.

Early Christians practiced a variety of different types of baptism: immersion, submersion, affusion, and aspersion. However, some Sethian texts betray a deep suspicion of water baptism. For them, water was a dangerous, even impure element created by Sophia and ruled over by archons or even demons (see, for example, the

ApocAdam), but these Sethian texts do not reject baptism as a rite. Quite the opposite: Sethian texts take for granted, even emphasize, the importance of baptism. What was different, in their opinions, was both the way baptisms should be performed and what they signified. In the *GosEg*, baptism is described as "holy" and is said to have been established by the Great Seth in order to rescue the "generations" from the devil.

Many Sethian texts—and only Sethian texts—allude to a mysterious rite known as the **Five Seals** (see *TriPro*; *GosEg*; *Zost*; *ApJn*). It is not clear exactly what this rite involved, but we have some clues that we can piece together. First, unlike Christian baptism, this rite apparently took place only in the celestial realm. Three beings oversee the baptism. Interestingly, the people who performed the Five Seals rite appeared to find the "regular" baptism of the Christian church as defiled or polluted.

THE *THREE STELES OF SETH*

This is a classic Sethian work, found in a single Coptic copy in Codex VII. It is difficult to date, because it does not give us too many "markers." To return to John Turner's proposed reconstruction of Sethianism, The *Three Steles of Seth (3 StelesSeth)* cannot be dated as early as, say, *HypArch* because it does not seem to have any overtly Jewish elements or markers. The same can be said about Christianity. There are, however, Platonist elements in the tractate, which suggest that it comes from the third stage in Sethian development, when Sethianism broke from Christianity and developed links with Platonism. At the same time, *3StelesSeth* is a bit different from Platonizing Sethian texts *Allogenes*, *Zostrianos*, and *Marsanes*, which were probably written somewhat later. It has a simpler cosmic architecture and consists largely of hymns of praise, most of which are offered in the first-person plural ("we rejoice!") rather than in the first-person singular, like all the other Sethian apocalyptic writings.

The *3StelesSeth* is a revelation supposedly copied down by Dositheos, who in a vision sees the writing that Seth copied down on three steles by Seth for his offspring. We do not know anything else about Dositheos, although someone by the same name (perhaps the same person) is mentioned in various ancient texts as a Gnostic teacher from Samaria in the first century who leads a group of people who practiced baptism and considered themselves the children of Seth.

The tractate's title refers to large, engraved standing stones (steles, sometimes pluralized as *stelae*) that Dositheos sees in his vision. These steles are engraved with Seth's revelation to his spiritual offspring. Since Seth knew from his father, Adam, that the world would be destroyed, he ordered his knowledge to be copied down on two steles. The first stele would be made of stone (to survive the flood) and the second, of brick to survive the next destruction of the world, which tradition held would be by fire. Of course, these steles never actually existed; rather, the story is a fairly common literary "conceit" to give esoteric knowledge a special pedigree (compare *Zost.* 130; *GosEg* III, 68). In fact, even in the NHL we find a very similar story recounted in three very different writings: *Zostrianos*, *Gospel of the Egyptians*, and the *Discourse on the Eighth and Ninth*.

The steles contain discrete prayers to the heavenly beings:

First Stele:
1. Seth's hymn to his father, Pigeradamas (118:25–119:15)
2. Seth's hymn to Autogenes (119:15–120:17)
3. A prayer from a Sethian community to Barbēlō (120:17–121:16)

Second Stele:
1. A prayer from a Sethian community to the Barbēlō Aeon
2. A prayer from a Sethian community for eternal life and unification

Third Stele:
1. A hymn of praise from a Sethian community to the Supreme One Pre-existent One
2. A prayer to the Supreme One

3. A hymn of praise to the Supreme One

The text ends with instructions on how to use the steles for a ritual of mystical ascent and descent. A **colophon** after the end of the text adds a brief prayer from the monk who copied the text.

The *3StelesSeth* has a tripartite form and a relatively streamlined cast of characters, based largely on Platonist jargon:

Other names invoked to the Supreme Pre-existent One include: Senaon the Self-Generated, Asineus, Mephneus, Optaon, Elemaon, Emouniar, Nibareus, Kandephoros, Aphredon, Deiphaneus, Armedon (cf. *Zost.* 51, 86, 88; *Allogenes* 54). It is not clear, however, if these names are separate beings, or epithets associated with the Supreme Pre-existent One.

One of the most remarkable aspects of *Three Steles of Seth* is the use of first-person plural in some of its prayers and hymns. Note passages such as this one: "We have blessed you, for we are able. We have been saved, for you have willed always that we all do this" (126:29–32). Who is "we," here? Is this evidence for a Sethian community? Most scholars of Sethianism seem to agree that it is. What is more, this community appears to have been engaged in some sort of "ascent ritual." Notice the following passage that seems to give instructions on this ritual:

> For they all bless these individually and together. And afterwards they shall be silent. And just as they were ordained, they ascend. After the silence, they descend from the third. They bless the second; after these the first (*Three Steles of Seth*, 126:29–32)

The passage concludes, "The way of ascent is the way of descent" (127:11–12). This short sentence is not original to *Three Steles of Seth*; it is a quotation from a famous sixth-century BCE philosopher, Heraclitus. How it got here remains a bit of a mystery; nevertheless, what we can know is that for this community, their active prayer life was somehow connected with an ecstatic or mystical ritual. Unfortunately, we can only guess what this must have looked like.

TABLE 10.3: Cast of Characters/Cosmic Architecture

Name	Relationship	Alternate Names and Epithets
Emmacha Seth	Son of Pigeradamas	
Pigeradamas	Father of Emmacha Seth	• Mirotheid (i.e., son of **Mirothea**) • Adamas • Heavenly Adam
Autogenes	Lowest subaeon in the Barbēlō aeon	• Mirotheid
Barbēlō	Parent of Pigeradamas	• Triple Male (as in *ApJn*, *TriProt*) • Male virgin • First shadow
Kalyptos	The uppermost subaeon in the Barbēlō aeon	• Name means "Hidden One"
Protophanes	The middle subaeon in the Barbēlō aeon	• Name means "first-appearing" • Fatherly god • Divine child • Logos • Sophia • Gnosis (Knowledge) • Truth • Mind

FINDING THOSE ELUSIVE SETHIANS

Sethianism remains a problematic category. On the one hand, it seems unlikely that a group of people ran around 1,800 years ago calling themselves "Sethians" although they may have understood themselves to be the offspring or "seed" of Seth. On the other hand, there are such evident similarities between the texts we call Sethian that it is hard to imagine that they weren't all connected in some way with an independent school of thought. And the tractate *3StelesSeth* offers a persuasive argument for community, although we have no idea whether the people who practiced the ritual it described called themselves Sethian, or how many of them there were. Recently, the American scholar David Brakke, following the argument of Bentley Layton, argued that this group called themselves not *Sethians* but *Gnostics*. Thus when the heresiologists refer to the Gnostics as a group and describe their systems of belief, they are describing the same group that modern scholars have, up to this point, been calling Sethian.

What seems clear, however, was that at some point in the third century, our extant Sethian texts make a radical and decisive shift in the direction toward Platonism, and away from Christianity as we would recognize it. These Sethian texts have their own set of shared characteristics, and we study them in chapter 19.

QUESTIONS TO CONSIDER

1. If we cannot find any evidence of an ancient group calling themselves Sethians but yet we have a series of texts that seem to venerate Seth, do you think we can accurately speak of Sethians or Sethianism? How do we define a religious group or social category?

2. How does Sethianism differ from Valentinianism?

3. What might the communities who circulated and read these Sethian texts have thought? Believed? Practiced as a religion? What kind of an education did they have: did they think of themselves as Christian, Jewish, pagan, or none of the above? What did they think of the Roman Empire? What did they think of Jesus?

KEY TERMS

Seth	*praxis*	colophon
Pseudo-Tertullian	Barbēlō	Valentinianism
Docetism	Adamas/Ger-Adamas	cosmology
midrash	Sakla	emanationist
soteriology	Five Seals	cosmos
Invisible Spirit	hypostasized	First Principle
Mirothea	heresiologists	Ennoia
Ialdabaoth	Epiphanius of Salamis	Pronoia
affusion	Platonist	Protennoia
Refutation	Wisdom literature	Epinoia
Christological	Syzygy (pl.: syzygies)	monads

Sethianism	Autogenes	Micheu, Michar, Mnesinous
Hippolytus of Rome	Angels of the Entirety	Thirteenth Kingdom
mytholegoumena	aspersion	Logos
apocalyptic literature	Syntagma	

FOR FURTHER READING

Brakke, David. *The Gnostics*. Cambridge, MA: Harvard University Press, 2011. This outstanding scholar of Gnosticism argues that Sethians did indeed exist as a community and that they identified themselves as Gnostics. A provocative and well-argued book that has the potential to change the way we think about Gnosticism.

Scott, Alan B. "Churches or Books? Sethian Social Organization." *Journal of Early Christian Studies* 3.2 (1995): 109–22. This academic article argues that Sethians had only very weak social networks and thus were not organized into churches and communities as were Valentinians.

Turner, John. "Sethian Gnosticism: A Literary History" available online at: http://jdt.unl.edu/ lithist.html. This is a challenging read but easily accessible. Professor Turner outlines his understanding of how Sethianism developed in the first four centuries CE.

———. "The Sethian School of Gnostic Thought." In *The Nag Hammadi Scriptures*, edited by Marvin Meyer, 784–89. This is a fairly accessible overview to Sethianism, as one of the closing essays provided by top scholars at the end of Marvin Meyer's new edition of the Nag Hammadi Library.

Wisse, F. "Stalking Those Elusive Sethians." In *The Rediscovery of Gnosticism*. Vol. 2: *Sethian Gnosticism*, edited by Bentley Layton, 563–76. Studies in the History of Religions (Supplements to Numen). Leiden: E. J. Brill, 1981. A landmark article, for advanced readers.

In the Beginning: Two Creation Myths

HYPOSTASIS OF THE ARCHONS (NHC II, 86.20–97.23)
AND *ON THE ORIGIN OF THE WORLD*
(NHC II, 5 AND XIII, 2)

If you were an ancient Christian or a Hellenized Jew with a scientific mind, you might have had a question: How did the world begin? Christians and Jews had a precious ancient text, the book of Genesis, which told the story of creation, what we call a **cosmogony** or cosmogonic narrative. Had you been raised as an educated person, you already knew stories about creation during the course of your education. Some of these might have been in the form of mythology, like the Greek writer Hesiod's archaic work *Theogony* (ca. 700 BCE). Others might have read philosophical treatises such as the Greek philosopher Plato's dialogue, *Timaeus* (ca. 360 BCE). As a Roman citizen, though, you would have had a variety of scientific theories at your disposal about how the world came to be, just as most people nowadays have at least a passing knowledge of theories like the Big Bang or Creationism.

Christians and Jews alike turned to Genesis as a "foundational myth," but for Roman converts to Christianity or for Hellenized Jews, Genesis was hardly satisfactory as a scientific text. To begin with, it left out a whole lot of detail. Where did the planets come from, for example? What about a cosmic principle like fate or destiny? When did God create the angels and other celestial beings? Do angels have souls like human souls? Did God create souls at the same time that he created human bodies? Why aren't these things mentioned in Genesis?

These issues came about from the encounter of Jewish and Christian tradition with Greek and Roman ideas on the nature and structure of the world; in response, second-century writers composed remarkable mythological narratives about the origins of life and the cosmos. Nothing like these texts had been seen before in the ancient world, and their composition stopped within a hundred years. The **heresiologist Irenaeus** had written about such texts and ridiculed their complexity and obscurity, but it was not until the Nag Hammadi discovery that we were able to see these documents for ourselves. In this chapter, we'll discuss two of the three cosmogonies from Nag Hammadi: *Hypostasis of the Archons* and *On the Origin of the World*. The third, and most

THE STRUCTURE OF THE COSMOS IN SECOND-CENTURY SCIENCE

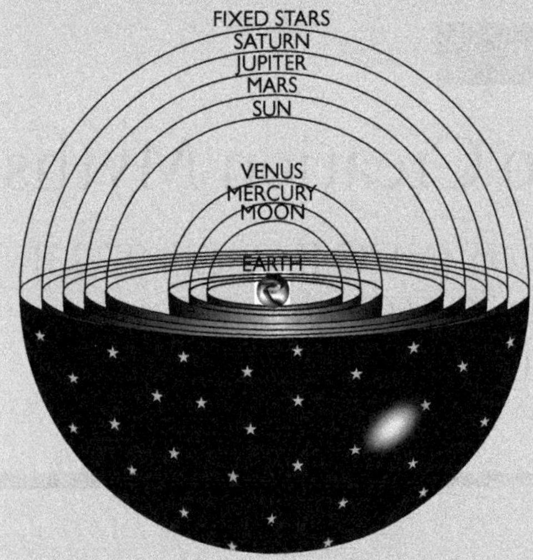

FIXED STARS
SATURN
JUPITER
MARS
SUN

VENUS
MERCURY
MOON

EARTH

The most prevalent model of the cosmos in Graeco-Roman antiquity was in the process of being established by the famous astronomer Claudius Ptolemy (90–168 CE). Ptolemy proposed a **geocentric** model, where the earth is at the center of the cosmos. Seven planets (Sun, Moon, Mercury, Mars, Venus, Jupiter, and Saturn) orbit the earth, each confined to its own planetary sphere. Beyond these lay the twelve constellations of the Zodiac, and beyond this, the realm of the fixed stars.

DIAGRAM 11.1 The Graeco-Roman Cosmos

important, of the cosmogonic myths—a treatise called The *Apocryphon of John*—is significant enough to warrant its own chapter. Nevertheless, all three texts share many things: a preoccupation with **protology** or the study of the origin of things; literary genre (they are all cosmogonies); an unusual cast of characters; and a fascination with the book of Genesis. All three texts interpret Genesis by using Greek and Roman philosophical ideas concerning the nature and structure of the cosmos. All three, remarkably, connect the knowledge of the origins of the cosmos with spiritual salvation.

HYPOSTASIS OF THE ARCHONS: HISTORY OF THE TEXT

The mythological narrative we call *Hypostasis of the Archons* (or, in some translations, *The Reality*

of the Rulers) is extant only in one manuscript version, although it is well preserved. It is the fourth text in Codex II, a collection of "greatest hits" that includes the *Gospel of Thomas*, the *Gospel of Philip*, and the *Apocryphon of John*.

The *HypArch* was originally written in Greek, but we are not sure where or when, although our best guesses are in either Alexandria (because of the text's eclectic use of traditions, particularly Jewish traditions) or Syria (because of some puns and wordplays that make sense only in Syriac). Most probably it was composed toward the end of the second century. There are clues, however, that the text has been compiled from earlier sources. The opening invocation of the apostle Paul and the closing apocalyptic passages do not fit well with the tractate as a whole; since they are the only explicitly Christian parts of *HypArch*, they are probably later Christian additions to what was originally Jewish commentary on Genesis 1–6. This commentary seems relatively cohesive until the arrival of the angel **Eleleth**. This section may have been a separate **revelation dialogue** since it essentially repeats some of the earlier cosmological portions of the narrative and gives the backstory to the narrative that precedes it.

If you read carefully, you might notice that *HypArch* seems to start *in media res*, that is, in the middle of a story (compare it, for instance, with *ApJn*). It begins with an account of the chief archon, whom we learn is called **Samael**, "god of the blind," making an ignorant and blasphemous assertion: "It is I who am God, and There is none other apart from me," paraphrasing Isaiah 46:9. It is a curious place to begin a story. What's the setting? Who is this Samael? What is he doing, wherever he is, and why? We learn, here at the outset, only that he boasts that he is the chief deity, but is ignorant of a higher force. We don't learn Samael's backstory until the great revealing angel Eleleth tells us—at the *end* of the narrative.

ON *THE ORIGIN OF THE WORLD*: HISTORY OF THE TEXT

On the Origin of the World can be found in two separate **redactions** or versions in the Nag Hammadi Codices, the first in Codex II (II, 5) and the second in Codex XIII (XIII, 2), although the version in XIII is extremely fragmentary and contains only the first page of the tractate. A few fragments of it also exist from a Coptic manuscript preserved in the British Library. Since the copy in Codex II is in very good shape, we have a very well-preserved text. The original title is lost, so scholars have generally agreed on its modern title, which is really shorthand for *An Untitled Treatise on the Origin of the World*. Scholars have debated whether this text is Christian. Note that Jesus is completely absent. While this does not necessarily discount the text as being Christian, it is also clear that the author was not preoccupied

with creating an explicitly Christian narrative of creation. But many of the tractate's points of reference are actually Jewish, making Judaism the most important "ground" for *OrigWld*.

A likely date of composition for *OrigWld* ranges from the second to the fourth century. The later date is based upon the dizzying range of materials and allusions we find here: Greek philosophy, Egyptian, Christian, and Jewish ideas; figures from Greek mythology; and bits of magical traditions all mixed together, evidently coming from a fairly eclectic social environment. Alexandria, a rather cosmopolitan city, is therefore a good guess for where it might have been written, although the emphasis on Greek philosophical and mythological traditions might also suggest Athens. But it is hard to ignore the almost "nationalist" references to Egypt, which this author considers "God's Paradise."

The fact that we have two redactions from Nag Hammadi plus papyrus fragments of the texts in a separate manuscript strongly suggests that *OrigWld* was an important and popular text. It also might be that *OrigWld* was meant as more of an accessible treatise than its sisters, *ApJn* and *HypArch*, even a missionizing tractate to draw in curious readers/listeners to its particular religious worldview.

THE QUESTION OF LITERARY RELATIONSHIP BETWEEN *HYPOSTASIS OF THE ARCHONS* AND *ON THE ORIGIN OF THE WORLD*

These two tractates bear an obvious similarity, but scholars of Nag Hammadi have been unable to discern the precise nature of their relationship. Since, however, the differences in worldviews between these texts is actually quite substantial, it may be that they look similar because they work with the same source material (for instance, the book of Genesis) using similar techniques, but that there was no direct relationship between them. Imagine two different writers, working in the Empire at around the same time, using similar reading techniques to work with Genesis but without reading each other's material. Whoever wrote the *HypArch* and *OrigWld* were evidently up to the same thing.

OrigWld presents a somewhat special case, in that it also has significant points of contact with two other Nag Hammadi writings, *Eugnostos the Blessed* and *Thunder: Perfect Mind*. Beyond these, however, it is difficult to know which way the relationship runs. When Eve begins her song at *OrigWld* 114:2, does the author of this tractate borrow her words from the *Thunder* 13:19? Or did the literary borrowing work the other way? Or did both *Thunder* and *OrigWld* take Eve's song from a different source altogether? Unfortunately, without more ancient texts and information coming to light, we cannot know.

OrigWld is the most eclectic and confusing of the three Nag Hammadi mythological cosmogonies. Many scholars have noted that unlike *HypArch* and *ApJn*, it does not fully cohere or come together as a text. Some passages do not make much sense, to the point that scholars speculate that something must have been lost in translation when the text was translated from Greek to Coptic, or perhaps the versions we have from

Nag Hammadi were later editions of a translation not yet finished. Although the original version of *OrigWld* was meant to be accessible to a nonspecialist audience, it is no longer that way from the manuscript versions that remain.

THE NATURE OF THE ARCHONS IN *HYPOSTASIS OF THE ARCHONS* AND *ON THE ORIGIN OF THE WORLD*

The *HypArch* starts with a reference to the "great apostle," that is to say, **Paul** of Tarsus, and a direct quotation from one of his letters: "For we are not contending against flesh and blood, but against the principalities, against the powers, against the world rulers of this present darkness, against the spiritual hosts of wickedness in the heavenly places" (Eph, 6:12 [RSV]; compare Col 1:13). "I have sent this (to you)," writes the author of *HypArch* to an unknown recipient, "because you [sing.] inquire about the reality of the authorities." The word "reality" is the same word as in the title, "**hypostasis.**" A hypostasis is a Greek technical term that can be translated as "nature" (as in the "nature of" something) or "reality," but here it really means something more like the making real of something that had been

---

OTHER SCRIPTURES IN *ON THE ORIGIN OF THE WORLD*

This work is unusual in that it refers the reader, tantalizingly, to a number of other treatises:

- *First Book of Noraia*
- *First Discourse of Oraia*
- *Archangelic Book of Moses the Prophet*
- *Book of Solomon*
- *Configurations of the Fate of Heaven Beneath the Twelve*
- *The Holy Book*

- *The Seventh Cosmos of Hieralias the Prophet*

Unfortunately, none of these books has survived. We do have a *Testament of Solomon*, and a Nag Hammadi tractate called the *Thought of Norea* (NHC IX, 2). Another collection, the Greek Magical Papyri, also refers to the *Angelic Book of Moses the Prophet*. But these references remind us of how little we actually have of ancient sacred literature.

purely conceptual. For instance, a concept like Truth becomes hypostasized when it becomes transformed into the goddess Truth.

The author of this introduction seems to respond to the unwritten question: Are the **archons** or evil celestial beings real? There is another question buried inside this one: Where does evil come from? What do we fight against, when we struggle? In the ancient world that provides a context to this writing, "evil" is often connected to the human body. It was not precisely that bodies or flesh were evil (although sometimes, most radically, they were considered that way), but that people wondered where our physical drives—including the impulse to do bad things—came from. More specifically, many people (and this author is certainly one of them) had a profound mistrust toward bodily urges and considered them as produced by external forces. While we generally think of ourselves as autonomous or self-driven, a more common ancient conception of "self" was that we are constantly acted upon by external forces, some of which are clearly malevolent. The author of *HypArch* draws on Paul to assert that our great struggle is not against ourselves, our own appetites and drives, but against those who plant those drives in us and continue to control us unwittingly.

The archons are interesting creatures. The *HypArch* describes them being both male and female—hermaphrodites. They also have "bestial" faces. Thus the archons are hybrid beings: neither clearly male nor clearly female; neither clearly human nor clearly animal; neither clearly divine nor clearly demonic. They transcend category, which in the thought-world of antiquity, was not a good thing. In the hierarchy of beings that governed the way that people of the second century envisioned, the closer that particular being was to being Divine, the less differentiated ("mixed up" or "hybridized") that being was. God was indivisible, and thus the

opposite of the hybrid, mixed-up archons, who represented the farthest that a created being could be from God.

Another interesting thing about the archons concerns the nature of gender and emotions. Although they are technically "male-female," in *HypArch* they behave like males. They are sexually obsessed with the female divine power and apparently have no spiritual impulse or discernment. When they get a glimpse of a spiritual being from a higher celestial realm—the "image" of incorruptibility reflected in the waters—their response is to want to rape and sexually defile it, not pray to it or be inspired by it. They exercise power only in order to dominate and defile other beings, particularly female beings.

What is particularly interesting about these writings—and we see this clearly in *HypArch*—is that the language used to describe those who oppress us through enslaving our minds and hijacking our appetites is *political*. The word "archon" is the Greek word for a political ruler. Thus texts such as *HypArch* and *OrigWld* convey a deeply political message: our enemies are "those in high places." They are demons; their powers are real; their power to oppress is real. But at the same time, their power is limited. They can harm us, oppress us, violate us, imprison, and enslave us—but they do this because they are themselves envious of what they lack that they dimly recognize in us. Brutalized by the archons, the readers recognize their own enslavement as contingent. The archons enact their violence only on our bodies; they cannot harm our spirit. This is the deeply political, positive message behind *HypArch*.

ARE THESE TEXTS "RETAKES" OF GENESIS OR ARE THEY ANTI-GENESIS?

Both *OrigWld* and *HypArch* are heavily dependent on the book of Genesis, particularly the first six chapters. In fact, the text is really an exercise in reading and commenting on scripture, a practice we call **exegesis** (from the Greek "to draw out" meaning). At some point around the second century, an author had the text of Genesis in front of him and chose to write a commentary on it to help explicate its meaning (see table 11.1). Rather than a standard line-by-line commentary, the author chose to write a story. This kind of combination storytelling/commentary intertwined with scripture in Judaism is called a *targum*, and its literary form suggests that the authors of these texts were Jewish or were schooled in Jewish traditions of reading, explicating, and commentating on scripture.

But what kind of Jews were these authors? Notice what they do with the stories from Genesis. While Genesis understands the created world to be "good," in the *HypArch* and *OrigWld* tractates the world is only a twisted shadow. The creator of the world is not omnipotent or omniscient or even good; he is a lesser, monstrous being who can never fully understand the Divine. The tree in the garden of Eden brings salvation, not death; the snake is a positive figure who brings salvific knowledge to humankind. At every turn,

TABLE 11.1: Genesis Parallels in *Hypostasis of the Archons*

The *HypArch* follows events as they unfold in Genesis, dipping into various moments in the texts:

Narrative element	Genesis parallel
"Come, let us create a human being that will be soil of the earth."	1:26; 2:7
The chief archon breathes into the first man's face and the human being came to be animate	2:7
The human being is named Adam, "since he was found moving on the ground."	2:7
The animals and birds are gathered and named by Adam	2:18–19
Adam is installed in the Garden	2:15
"From every tree in the garden shall you (sing.) eat, but from the tree of knowledge of good and evil you must not eat, nor even touch. For the day you (pl.) eat from it, with death you (pl.) will die."	3:3
Adam sleeps, and the archons open his side	2:21
Adam names Eve, who has been taken from his side: "It is you who have given me life, and you will be called 'mother of the living.'"	3:20
The snake speaks to Adam and Eve	3:1–5; 2:16
Eve eats from the tree and gives some to Adam	3:6ff.
The chief ruler calls "Adam, where are you?"	3:9ff.
The chief ruler curses Eve for her disobedience	3:13ff.
Adam and Eve are expelled from the Garden	3:24
Eve bears Cain	4:1ff
Cain pursues his brother Abel	4:8
Eve bears Seth, a replacement for Abel	4:25; 4:1
Humankind multiplies and improves	6:1
Noah receives instruction to build an ark	6:13ff.

the Genesis story is set on its head; perhaps the most blatant example that stands out to even those readers not familiar with Genesis is what it says about the world just before the flood: "then humankind began to multiply and *improve*" (*HypArch* 2:3). Most readers know that in Genesis 6, God sends the flood because humankind began to multiply and people became wicked.

WHO IS THE CHIEF RULER?

The chief creator god of *HypArch* and *OrgWld* is **Ialdabaoth**, a demonized and degraded form of Yahweh, the chief creator god of Judaism. But where does this characterization come from? This is one of the many mysteries in the writings from Nag Hammadi. The name "Ialdabaoth" doesn't really mean anything. It is possible that it derives from the Aramaic for "child of chaos." Only once in ancient sources do we get an etymology, in the *OrigWld* 100:12–14, where the name supposedly means, "Youth, move over here." But the problem is that it doesn't mean that in any of the ancient languages of the Mediterranean.

Ialdabaoth has other names, too: "Saklas," which is related to the Aramaic word for "Fool" and "Samael," which is Aramaic for "Blind God" or "God of the Blind." (In *HypArch* that's the only name by which the chief ruler is known.)

We know from the *HypArch* that Ialdabaoth has a monstrous form; he is "molded out of a shadow" and cast out by his mother, Sophia. The imagery here is very striking: Ialdabaoth is like an aborted or miscarried malformed fetus. But why? He's probably malformed because Sophia commits the sin of creating on her own initiative. In the ancient world, it was believed that both parents contributed something at the point of conception: one parent contributes form and the other, essence. In the *HypArch*—as in some other ancient texts—the woman appears to contribute spirit, and the man, form. So in one sense, since Sophia conceives without the permission or participation of her consort, she can only contribute one portion, and the child is doomed to be malformed.

Why does the chief ruler have the head of a lion? The name for a creature who is partly animal-shaped is **theriomorphic**; specifically, Ialdabaoth is **leontomorphic**, lion-formed. Some scholars have

FIGURE 11.1 In this funerary statue from Rome, a devotee of the god Mithras depicts himself as a man transformed into a lion-headed God, Aion. He holds the symbols of initiation into that particular level. Could it be that whoever developed the idea of Ialdabaoth, the lion-headed monster with a serpentine body, had seen images like this one?

noted that the lion in ancient Greek philosophy represented the irrational passions. Thus Ialdabaoth, who cannot control his arrogance, anger, and lust, is in the form of a lion.

It is interesting to speculate as to what sort of impact this text must have had on an ancient audience. It is likely that many Jews were deeply offended, even outraged, by this characterization of God and by the inversion of their scriptures. Some have suggested that a text of this sort counts as "**protest exegesis,**" meaning that it was written by those who had recently broken away from Judaism as a form of political or religious rebellion or protest, and their redaction of Genesis reflects that spirit. If this is so, then *HypArch* allows us to see a key "turning point" in the creation of a separate Jewish or Christian "protest movement" in the second century. Others, however, reject the idea that these texts constitute "protest exegesis," since we do not know for certain that Jews composed the texts. These scholars view the texts as having been written by Christians, or perhaps by Jews with a different understanding of God than we imagine most Jews to have had; Judaism took many different forms in antiquity, and it is very possible that there was room within Judaism to account for the particular theology and treatment of the Jewish scriptures that we find here in these texts. Still, let's take a look first of all at the theory that these two writings are predominantly anti-Jewish.

In one way of reading them, *HypArch* and *OrigWld* are disturbingly anti-Jewish texts stating that the God of the Jews, Yahweh, is boastful, ignorant, and blind. And those are his better qualities. He is also a liar, a thug, and a rapist. All on his own, he manages to violate most of the Ten Commandments that he himself, later in the Hebrew Scriptures (Exod 20), establishes. In fact, in one interesting way of reading it, his boast "I am the only god" in fact echoes the Ten Commandments, "You shall have no other gods before me." And then he proceeds to break the rest of the commandments. He makes an image of the divine (Adam the mud man, "after the image of god that had been shown forth to them"). He lies ("on the day you eat of the tree, you'll die.") He dishonors his mother and father by failing to

recognize them. He "commits adultery," that is, has illicit sex by raping **Eve**, whom he most definitely covets.

Is this text unrelentingly anti-Jewish? That is certainly one way of reading it. But there is another way.

GENESIS: QUESTIONS AND QUALMS

If we want to move past the simplistic notion that *HypArch* and *OrigWld* were simply anti-Jewish, satirical texts, we need what we call a new hermeneutic or "reading strategy," Some people have been taught that the scriptures are not to be questioned but accepted at face value. Certain modern Christian denominations, in fact, teach biblical inerrancy—the Bible is never wrong and contains no mistakes and must be read as literal truth. Rather differently, Judaism teaches that scriptural study is a necessary and responsible duty. Not only is the scripture there to be read, it is there to be examined and questioned. There is the idea that scripture contains at least two levels of meanings: one manifest (Christians might say "literal"; in Hebrew this is called *peshat*) and one hidden (in Jewish scholarship, one level of hidden meaning is called *remez*: the symbolic or allegorical meaning of the text; another is *derash*, the metaphorical meaning; a third is *sod*, the mystical meaning of the text derived through revelation). Often, there are multiple hidden meanings. The goal of study is to comment on and explore all possible levels of meaning.

Let's go back, not to *HypArch* or *OrigWld* but to the text on which they are based: Genesis 1–6. Pretend, for the sake of argument, that we are ancient Jewish scholars reading through Genesis. We will agree that it is perfectly acceptable—in fact, it is our solemn religious duty—to read carefully and thoughtfully, without shrinking away from some of the issues that arise from our reading.

Like most creation stories, Genesis's function is *etiological*: it aims to explain the origins of things that exist. Think back, for example, to Rudyard Kipling's *Just So Stories* such as "How the Leopard Got Its Spots" and "How the Giraffe Got Its Long Neck." Genesis does much the same thing. It aims to answer a lot of "why" questions about the world:

- Why is there day and night?
- Why is time divided into days and weeks?
- Why do people till the soil?
- Why do we wear clothes?
- Why do snakes crawl on the ground?
- Why does childbirth hurt?
- Why do we die?

This is only a small sampling of the questions that Genesis answers in the course of its narrative. Start reading the book of Genesis, and make your own list.

But there are also a number of tougher "why" questions that Genesis fails to answer. Some of these questions have to do with the text itself. Try raising some of these *unanswered* questions:

- Why is the order of creation confused? In Gen 1 the order is as follows:
    - Heaven and earth (1:1–2)
    - Light and darkness (1:3–5)
    - The sky or firmament (1:6–7)
    - Earth (1:9)
    - Vegetation (1:11–12)
    - Sun, moon, stars (1:14–18)
    - Sea creatures and birds (1:20–21)
    - Land animals (1:24–25)
    - Humankind, male and female (1:26–27)
- But in Gen 2:4 and following, there is a different order:
    - Earth and heaven (2:5)
    - A man (2:7)
    - A garden (2:8)

- Trees, rivers (2:9–14)
- Land animals, birds, (2:19)
- A woman (2:21–22)

- Why does the creation of humankind appear to happen twice, in two different ways? In Gen 1:27 God creates man and woman together, simultaneously, "man and woman he created them." In Gen 2:7 and following, God first creates Adam from mud, then causes him to fall into a deep sleep, and creates Eve from his rib. Not only is woman here created after man, she is not his equal but his subordinate. Why are there two stories?

Then there are a number of questions about God's behavior (remember, as ancient Jewish scholars we can call even this into question without it being inappropriate or blasphemous). For instance:

- Why does God use the plural in 1:26, when he says, "let *us* create [humankind] in *our* own image"? Isn't he alone?
- Why does God lie? He says (according to the report of Eve and the snake) that if Adam and Eve eat of the tree of the knowledge of good and evil, that they will die (3:3). They do eat of the tree, and they don't die. Is he lying? Or is he wrong? How could God be wrong?
- Why does God not want Adam and Eve to have knowledge, specifically the knowledge of good and evil (and thus the ability to make a discerning, free choice)? Isn't knowledge a *good* thing? So what if Adam and Eve would therefore become "like gods"? Is God threatened by this? Why?
- If God is omniscient, doing things like creating everything, how come he has to ask Adam where he is (Gen 3:9)? Wouldn't he know?

These are just a few of the tough questions, and it can be quite freeing to ask them. Being unsettled by Genesis is not such a bad thing, because it is an unsettling book.

These tough questions are natural ones for any thoughtful person to ask about Genesis; many ancient readers also asked them. In fact, *HypArch* and *OrigWld* are proof that they asked them. Both narratives move sequentially through Genesis 1–6, asking these same questions implicitly, and then trying to come up with rational explanations.

ANSWERING QUESTIONS, ADDRESSING QUALMS

Before answering these tough questions, the authors of *HypArch* and *OrigWld* had a couple of ground rules or basic principles:

1. As sacred scripture, the text of Genesis cannot have mistakes in it, so any logical problems with flow or sequence need to be reconciled or explained without saying "maybe the author of Genesis made a mistake." If there are two stories of Adam and Eve's creation, for instance, then Adam and Eve were actually created twice, not once. (This, by the way, is an example of *pshat*: a literal reading of the text which reveals a surprising, hidden meaning).

2. Genesis is an important sacred text, but there are also other important sacred texts with which Genesis needed to be reconciled. The most significant of these were the letters of Paul and Plato's dialogue on the creation of the world, the *Timaeus*.

3. There is a manifest meaning to scripture but also hidden or esoteric meanings on a variety of levels (like *remez*, *derash*, and *sod*). This meaning is revealed, for instance, through allegory or double meanings. Read properly, scripture reveals the path to salvation.

4. God is identical with the Good. Any other characterization of God cannot be correct but must be a sign of some hidden meaning to the narrative.

Let's return to the present and start investigating the ancient texts as we have them today, starting with the last principle, (4) God is identical with the Good. In the first and second centuries, Judaism had been influenced by **Hellenization,** Greek ideas and ideals. This process changed the ways that Jews understood God. God was understood to be abstract, a kind of cosmic force or entity that was the ideal primordial Source. God did not have gender, or personality, or body. Given this change in the way of thinking about God, imagine how some Jewish textual critics must have read Genesis. There was but one way to understand God's behavior in Genesis—his apparent disingenuousness, his inability to find Adam in the garden, even the mention of his "footsteps." Whoever this being *was* in Genesis, it could not have been God. It must have been a lesser being, someone still powerful enough to create human beings, but with a body (and thus footsteps) and complex emotions: a celestial being that certain authors of this era called an **archon**. He only masqueraded as God, but he did a pretty good job, as it turns out, convincing many human beings that he was indeed God.

Working with principle (2), a learned Jewish interpreter of Genesis at this time would likely also turn to another revered text, Plato's *Symposium*. We find there a God who is identical with the Good, but also a being who creates the cosmos, called a **Demiurge**. This lesser god creates the first human beings together (actually, literally joined together, in this case, as a hermaphroditic being). He does so, not alone but with the assistance of other celestial beings. Thus Hellenistic Jewish readers of Genesis borrowed from one revered creation text—Plato's *Timaeus*—to explain human creation in another sacred text. Along the way, they added details to their understanding of how the big picture worked. Yahweh was not the highest god but a lesser creator god: a Demiurge. He created humankind "male and female," as Genesis and the *Timaeus* record. And he worked with others: the *Timaeus* makes this explicit and helps explain the puzzling detail of God's use of the plural in Gen 1:26 "let *us* create…in *our* image" when, previously, it had appeared that God was all alone. Put simply, the *Timaeus* helped to solve some of Genesis's problems without readers resorting to the conclusion that it was full of errors.

This is not to say that the person who wrote *HypArch* or the *OrigWld* thought that God was a demon. Rather, the author knew that God was no such thing. To imagine that Yahweh was a demon was not blasphemy; it was in fact to protect the *real* God from blasphemy: to prevent people from mistaking this character in Genesis with the real God and honoring him with honors due only to the True God. It was to also to believe, implicitly, that a portion of Jews (and later, Christians) who read Genesis simplistically, were fools. This is not exactly anti-Jewish. The authors of these texts may even have been pious Hellenized Jews; they just did not buy that Yahweh, as we find him in Genesis, was the True God. But this did not mean that Genesis had no value; rather, read with full understanding, it revealed the truth of the human situation, which included a recognition of the goodness of the True God and God's path to human salvation. It also explained some of those nagging questions: why "God" would lie, or be ignorant, or work with others while boasting that he was really alone, or not be able to see Adam in the garden. Only a lesser, deeply flawed deity would do such things. God, therefore, was identical with the Good.

READING GENESIS LIKE AN ANCIENT READER

Here is a passage from *HypArch*. Let's read this as if we were the same clever reader of Genesis or, more precisely, as if it were written by the same clever reader:

> The rulers took counsel with one another and said, "Come let us cause a deep sleep to fall upon Adam." And he slept. Now, the deep sleep that they "caused

to fall upon him and he slept" is lack of gnosis. They opened his side like a living woman. And they built up his side with some flesh in place of her, and Adam came to be merely animate. And the spirit-endowed woman came to him and spoke with him, saying "Arise, Adam." And when he saw her, he said, "it is you who has given me life; you will be called mother of the living." (*HypArch* 89:3–15; trans. Bentley Layton, *The Gnostic Scriptures*, New Haven, CT: Yale University Press, 1987: 70, with slight modification)

We have already established that the Chief Ruler does not create alone (since he uses the plural "we" in Genesis) but with other beings. Genesis tells us that Yahweh casts a "deep sleep" (Gen 2:21) on Adam. The author uses *refez*, determining that the story is allegorical; what is actually meant is not physical sleep but sleep in Adam's spiritual perception. Adam now lacks the ability to recognize his spiritual origins. The archons open his side "like a living woman"; there is an allusion here to the spiritual component, the "living" or immortal part that is gendered female. The *gloss* (the name for a textual addition by way of explanation) also draws an association with the opening of Adam's side as a sort of childbirth; in a paradoxical image, Eve will be born of her father/husband, of Adam her "mother." But the consequences of Eve's birth mean something rather sinister for Adam, here: "Adam came to be merely animate." Adam had no female earthly component; his earthly body is male while his spiritual body was female—but the archons, in birthing Eve from him, have removed his female component, his **pneuma**. Without this, Adam is left as an animated mud-body without spirit. This body is called **choic** ("of the soil") or **hylic** ("of matter") or sometimes **sarkic** ("of the flesh").

Next, Eve (here described as the "spirit-endowed woman" because she has the spirit that was in Adam) approaches Adam and wakes him up from his spiritual or perceptual sleep. He recognizes her immediately, not as his subordinate drawn from his rib (as some might read Genesis) but as his superior: the one who has given him life. Here, the interpreter of Genesis "inverts" the creation narrative but does so by reading through to its deeper, spiritual significance. Eve wakes Adam because it is the higher part of us that wakens us to our spiritual origins. Adam instinctively recognizes his lack; he sees the paradox ("it is you who has given me life") because, now woken from his perceptual sleep, he recognizes that it was the spirit that gave him life in the first place. The punchline of the story, "It is you who has given me life; you will be called Mother of the Living" paraphrases Genesis (3:20). It makes sense of a curious passage ("why, given that Eve is derivative from Adam and comes from his body, does Adam say that she is Mother of the Living?") and also reveals the author/reader's knowledge of an Aramaic pun: the name Eve in Aramaic, *Hawwāh*, is closely related to the word for "life," *hayyayā*, and the participle *hawe*, "the one who teaches."

GENDER AND POWER: THE RAPE OF EVE

Eve is the clear heroine in these narratives, but her story in *HypArch* is harrowing. One of the most disturbing elements of *HypArch* is undoubtedly the behavior of the archons, who collectively conspire and then gang-rape Eve. This is a story of shocking violence: not just male violence against women but also divine violence against human. There is a precedent to this behavior in Greek myths, where the gods (Zeus being the worst offender) desire human women and have sex with them, often impregnating them. The women are sometimes brutalized; they are often deceived, believing themselves to actually be having sexual relations with their husbands. The story is also present in ancient Jewish documents, including the third-century BCE "Book of the Watchers" (1 Enoch 1–36), and remains, as a mere mention, in the story of the Nephilim in Genesis 6:4.

In the case of *HypArch*, the spiritual Eve escapes from the archons' clutches by turning into a tree. It is likely that the tree in question is the tree of life (Gen 2:9), building on an Aramaic pun: the name Eve is *Hawwāh*; the word for "life" is *hayyayā*. In the OT book of Proverbs, the female character Wisdom is "a tree of life to those who lay hold of her" (Prov 3:18; see also 4:13: "Do not let her go; guard her, for she is your life.") But the story also has precedents outside the Bible. One Graeco-Roman myth, in which the god Pan lusts for a tree nymph known as a *hamadryad* (from the Greek meaning "together with a tree"), has strong parallels with *HypArch*. A first-century floor mosaic from Pompeii depicts Pan, his erect phallus exposed, standing leering at a hamadryad (see fig. 11.2).

Another popular Greek myth—the seduction of Daphne—also has parallels here. The god Apollo, compelled by the jealousy of the god Eros, became enamored with the nymph Daphne, a virgin who scorned male attention and wished to remain unmarried all her life, like the goddess Artemis. Apollo pursues Daphne,

FIGURE 11.2 In this floor mosaic from Pompeii, the god Pan, his phallus erect, approaches a hamadryad or tree nymph as she turns into a tree to escape his advances.

but she runs from him, calling on her father, the river god Peneus, to preserve her virtue. Peneus transforms her into a laurel tree, thus presumably thwarting Apollo. Both these myths recall the curious incident in *HypArch* in which Eve "becomes a tree" to escape the archons' clutches. The similarities between the stories are evident: (1) The women are sexually pure, (2) the women are pursued against their will by divine male aggressors, and (3) both Daphne and Eve are "rescued" by being transformed into a tree.

Could the Romans be behind this theme? The Romans were famously proud of their way of conquering peoples by invading and raping their

FIGURE 11.3 The story of Rome's origins is full of brutal accounts of women trying to escape the clutches of men who use their physical strength to dominate them. This Renaissance sculpture from Florence depicts the Rape of the Sabine Women.

women. Such is the story of the "Rape of the Sabine Women," recounted by Roman authors such as Livy and Pliny (see fig. 11.3). In this ancient story of Rome's founding, the Romans wish to intermarry with the Sabine tribe. The Sabines refuse, so the Romans arrange for a celebration, a sort of sinister picnic. At the party, the Romans (understood to be all men) launch a surprise attack and carry off the Sabine women, forcing them into wedlock.

Modern translators often translate the Latin *raptio* (here, translated as "rape") as "abduction," thus downplaying the sexual violence of the English word "rape." In fact, the ancient Roman author Pliny insists that the women were not sexually assaulted but given substantial rights, such as the ability to own property. In reality, not only did the Romans not shy away from sexually violent narrative, they were fond of depicting it in a wide variety of triumphal art. A broken, violated woman stood as a graphic symbol of Roman power and triumph over its enemies, and the Rape of the Sabine women was just one of a number of triumphant images used to showcase the founding of the Roman peoples.

RAPE AND ANCESTRY: FOUNDING A PEOPLE

As shocking and horrific as the *HypArch*'s rape account is to our modern sensibilities, ancient readers may simply have more or less shrugged it off; raping women (and sometimes men) was merely part of the brutal way that oppressors exercised their power over the oppressed. The point of the narrative here is not merely to highlight the brutishness of the archons. Rather, it is to account for the appearance of a new "race" of peoples. In the ancient world, "race" was not yet a term for differences in skin tone or other features. One's "race" was one's ancestry—real or symbolic—and it was something with which the writers of *HypArch* and *OrigWld* were preoccupied. Just as the point of the Sabine story was not to make a statement on Roman violence against women—it was to showcase the emergence of a new "race" of people born from Romulus's men and the Sabine women—the point of the Eve narrative is to highlight the consequences of the archons' actions: Eve becomes pregnant after Ialdabaoth rapes her, and she gives birth to her first child, Cain. Cain is thus not fully human: he is half human and half archontic. Likewise, his progeny will evermore bear the hidden stigma of being the illegitimate, monstrous offspring of a monstrous act. Even worse, since Ialdabaoth is devoid of the spiritual element and the spiritual element flees from Eve's "tree" body before it is raped, Cain and his progeny lack any spiritual element. Thus, Cain is the ancestor of people who are what these

communities called *sarkic* ("fleshly," from the Gk *sarx*, meaning "flesh"), *hylic* ("earthly," from the Gk *hylos*, meaning "matter") or *choic* (earthy, from the Gk *choikos*). Cain himself is, in Genesis, a negative figure, whose sole act is to murder his brother (Gen 4:8). In a sense, then, *HypArch* provides the backstory that accounts for Cain's murderousness. He is monstrous because he is the son of a monster.

In *HypArch*, Eve's second son, Abel, is the product of the sexual union between Eve and the first man, Adam. Adam is in this narrative a kind of composite being; he is *sarkic* but also has a spiritual element to him—what many so-called Gnostics called "**psychic**" (Gk *psyche*), which means something like "soul." Thus their

WHO IS NOREA?

Before the discovery of the Nag Hammadi Library, the figure of Norea was an obscure one, mentioned by the fourth-century heresiologist Epiphanius. In his *Panarion* (26.1.3–9) Epiphanius recounts the contents of a lost scripture known as *Norea* or *Noria*. He says this text was used by Sethians and tells the story of a figure identified with the figure Pyrrha from Greek myth. In this myth, Pyrrha is the wife of Deucalion, a sort of Noah-like figure who survives a great deluge. In the book *Norea*, Epiphanius says, God sends the flood down and Noah tries to escape. A divine figure called Norea breathes fire on the ark, however, incinerating it not once but three times.

Scholars were pleased to discover a text called *The Thought of Norea* at Nag Hammadi; however, it does not appear to be the same text that Epiphanius knew, for his summary of it is very different from the document itself. Perhaps the book in Epiphanius's possession was the same as one of the lost scriptures mentioned in *On the Origin of the World*: the *Account of Oraia*, and the *First Book of Noraia*.

With the discovery of the NHL, we learn much more about the figure of Norea. In *HypArch*, Norea

is the fourth child of Eve. When Ialdabaoth tries to send down a deluge and Noah builds an ark to escape, a figure called Orea tries to board it. When Noah prevents her, she breathes fire on the ark and destroys it. This account is remarkably similar to the one that Epiphanius tells, so the two narratives appear to have drawn from the same source. But ultimately, Norea/Orea is the heroine of *HypArch*; unlike her brothers, she is composed of pure spirit and is destined in this text (and this text only) to be the ancestor of the Great Immovable Race.

The name Norea may be related to the Syriac word for light or fire, *nur*. Or it may reflect the Hebrew *na'amah*, "pleasant" ("sister of Tubal-Cain...Na'amah," Gen 4:22); it may also be related to the Greek word for "beautiful," *oraia*, which is how the **Septuagint** translates *na'amah*. Perhaps, then, to form the name Norea whoever came up with the character took the N from *na'amah* and added it to the same word in Greek: *noraia*. Our extant manuscript of *HypArch*, in giving us both the names Norea and Orea, indicates only that there has been some scribal confusion, and the figure of Norea was on her way to being forgotten by the fourth century.

son, Abel, is the prototype for a second type of human, the psychic or "ensouled."

In Genesis, we read about three children born to Adam and Eve; after Cain kills Abel, Eve bears a third son, Seth, as a replacement (Gen 4:25) for Abel. Interestingly, the *HypArch* lacks a developed narrative about Seth. Like Abel, Seth is the offspring of Eve and Adam. But *HypArch* goes on to tell a "secret" story, not from Genesis but one known in older Jewish tradition. In this secret story, Eve gives birth to a fourth child, a daughter named **Norea**. Significantly—and unlike Eve's other offspring—Norea's father is not explicitly named but is indicated by the ambiguous pronoun "he":

> Again Eve became pregnant, and she bore Norea. And she said, "He has begotten on [me a] virgin as an assistance [for] many generations of humankind." She is the virgin whom the forces did not defile. (*HypArch* 91:34–92:3, trans. Layton, *Gnostic Scriptures* 1987:72)

Like her mother before she was defiled by the archons, Norea is pure. But more significantly, she is pure *spirit*. Thus she becomes the prototype of a third type or "race" of human, the spiritual or pneumatic (Gk *pneuma*, which means "breath," "wind," and "spirit"). She is wise enough to recognize that she is superior to the archons and refuses to be intimidated by them:

> The rulers went to meet her, intending to lead her astray. Their supreme chief said to her, "Your mother Eve came to us." But Norea turned to them and said to them, "It is you who are the rulers of the darkness; you are accursed. And you did not know my mother; instead it was your female counterpart that you knew. For I am not your descendant; rather it is from the world above that I am come." (*HypArch* 92:20–26, trans. Layton, *Gnostic Scriptures* 1987:73)

Again, Ialdabaoth bears down upon her threateningly, his face becoming black with anger. He demands that she service him sexually as her mother had. Norea lifts up her voice in supplication, praying to be rescued. The great **angel of the Entirety, Eleleth,** then appears at the climax of the narrative, which switches to a first-person account spoken by Norea. Eleleth comes, he explains, to tell Norea about her "root," that is, her spiritual origin. He begins with a recounting of creation before creation and ends with Norea's own experience of the archons. She then asks the key question of the tractate: "Sir, am I also from their matter?" Eleleth's answer is a beautiful statement of origins:

> You, together with your offspring, are from the primeval father; from above, out of the imperishable light, their souls are come. Thus the authorities cannot approach them, because of the spirit of truth present within them; and all who have become acquainted with this way exist deathless in the midst of dying humankind. (*HypArch* 96:18–28, trans. Layton, *Gnostic Scriptures* 1987:75)

We can imagine these moving words spoken aloud as a kind of creed, or by a bishop to a community.

WHERE DOES THE TRIPARTITE DIVISION OF HUMANKIND IN THESE TEXTS COME FROM?

Years ago, Elaine Pagels noted that this "tripartite anthropology" (the division of humankind into *hylic*, *psychic*, and *pneumatic*) appeared to have an unexpected source: the apostle Paul's **First Letter to the Corinthians (1 Corinthians)**. There, Paul does some Genesis interpretation of his own. In a curious passage, he writes,

> Thus it is written, "The first man Adam became a living being" [Greek = "*psyche*"]; the last Adam became a life-giving spirit [Greek = "*pneuma*"]. But it is not the spiritual which is first but the physical, and then the spiritual. The first man was from the earth, a man of dust; the second man is from heaven. As was the man of dust, so are those who are of the dust; and as is the man of heaven, so are those who are of heaven. (1 Cor 15:45–48)

The context of this passage is a discussion of bodily resurrection; people in Paul's community worried that they might die before Christ's

Second Coming, while others in Corinth insisted that no resurrection was coming at all. Paul reassures those in his community by letting them know that everyone would be resurrected at the end of time, and that there was such a thing as a "resurrection body" that had a unique makeup.

In this passage, oddly, Paul seems to misquote Genesis. Although Paul is apparently quoting Gen 2:7, that text says, "and man became a living being." It says nothing about a "first Adam" and a "last Adam." Where do these multiple Adams come from? Presumably by the "last Adam" Paul meant, metaphorically, Jesus, but not all ancient readers might not have agreed with this reading. The important point is that Paul contrasts a first "man of dust" (the Greek original actually reads "the *choic* man") with an Adam who is a "spiritual" being (the Greek original says "pneumatic"). He even introduces a third category, the "physical" (Greek: *psyche*) being. Apparently one ancient way for Christian readers to interpret Paul's words here is to think that he was referring to either a multiple creation of Adam hidden in Genesis, or to a theory of human beings based on the ancestor and prototype of all human beings, Adam.

It is worth pointing out that *HypArch* actually begins with a quotation from one of Paul's letters in the NT, his Letter to the Ephesians: "For we are not contending against flesh and blood, but against the principalities, against the powers, against the world rulers of this present darkness, against the spiritual hosts of wickedness in the heavenly places" (Eph 6:12). There is also a portion in Colossians 1:13, where the archons are referred to in "the dominion of darkness." Paul was a dynamic, influential leader of the fledgling Christian movement in the middle of the first century. Whoever wrote the *HypArch* considered him "the great apostle"—high praise indeed! One way of looking at *HypArch*, then, is as an exegesis not of Genesis but of Paul's writings, starting with that quotation from Ephesians. Here *HypArch* focuses on explicating the hidden meaning of two

sacred authorities: Genesis from the OT, and Paul, whose letters would come two hundred years later to comprise a large portion of the NT.

THE ENTHRONEMENT OF SABAOTH

One of the remarkable elements to both these creation myths is the installation of the so-called repentant archon **Sabaoth** onto a throne. That name is Hebrew for "powers" or "armies" but was also an ancient and traditional name for God. The image of God sitting on a heavenly chariot-throne is also ancient, and derives from the book of Ezekiel. In other words, it is Sabaoth and not Ialdabaoth, who corresponds in this text to the God of the Jews.

Sabaoth is a fascinating figure, because unlike his father Ialdabaoth/Saklas/Samael who is unremittingly bad, Sabaoth "repents," recognizes his father's ignorance, and praises his mother Sophia. This act of repentance prompts Sophia to "save" him; in fact, she installs him as the ruler of the seventh heaven. The image of Sabaoth enthroned on a throne chariot, surrounded by fiery angels, is drawn from ancient Jewish **merkavah** literature ("*merkavah*" is Hebrew for "chariot"), the earliest of which is seen in Ezekiel 1:4–26. There, it is the God of the Jews who sits upon the throne, surrounded by four cherubim (four-winged angels) who guard the throne. A very similar vision takes place in the book of Revelation 4:8 (here the author of Revelation speaks of seraphim, or six-winged angels). Whoever wrote *Hypostasis of the Archons* and *On the Origin of the World* appears to know of this tradition, understanding the God who sits on the heavenly throne to be merely an archon, installed on a throne to rule the cosmos but forever hidden in a luminous cloud to disguise his monstrousness.

THE END OF THE STORY

Both *HypArch* and *OrigWld* end with a **hierophany**, a manifestation of the divine. But their

FIGURE 11.4 This figure depicts a sketch of an ancient Graeco-Egyptian amulet, bearing the name "Sabao[th]." Here, as in most depictions of him on magical amulets, Sabaoth wears the dress of a Roman Emperor ready for battle, and rides a *quadrigens*, a four-horse chariot. There is no direct correlation between this imagery of Sabaoth here and the Sabaoth we meet in *HypArch* and *OrigWld*, yet the name—and his status as an archon—is consistent in both written and visual sources.

hierophanies are quite different from one another. At the end of *HypArch*, the heroine of the narrative, Norea, prays that she may be saved from the malevolent archons, whose true nature the great angel Eleleth then reveals to her. Norea fears is that she will learn that somehow, in the scale of creation, she and the archons share a basic genealogy—that she and they are made of the same substance. Eleleth reveals to Norea that she derives from a higher source and a higher spiritual essence. Chaos and domination is all around, but in the end, Eleleth reveals, she (and her "people," those readers who identify with her) will emerge victorious.

Those who listened to this story being read aloud to them were comforted; they learned that however distressing things appeared to be at that moment, it was happening according to divine plan: "All these things came to be by the will of the Father of the All" (*HypArch* 96:11). In the

WHO IS ELELETH?

When at the end of *HypArch* Norea calls out to the higher celestial powers to rescue her from the archons' clutches, she receives an intervention from a rather curious source: the great angel Eleleth. We might have expected Jesus to have made an appearance instead (compare, for instance, the *ApJn*, where "the Savior" appears at the climax of the story), or perhaps the same spiritual female principle that earlier in *HypArch* had entered the snake in the garden. We know Eleleth from other Sethian narratives at Nag Hammadi, but nowhere else does he play such a key role as here.

end, Norea's people would be vindicated, because they will become spiritually immortal: "All who know this way of truth are deathless among dying humanity" (*HypArch* 96:26). The final lines are a poem or, more probably, a hymn. It concludes,

> The Father's truth is just;
>
> the Son is over the Entirety and with everyone, forever and ever.
>
> Holy, Holy, Holy! Amen. (*HypArch 97:17–21*)

The three-time repetition of the word "holy" is called in Greek the **trisagion** (from *tri-* "three," and "*hagion*," holy). An ancient prayer, it is first found in the Hebrew Bible (Isa 6:3) and then in the New Testament book of Revelation 4:8. It is still used in Christian prayer today, particularly in liturgical churches and in Eastern Orthodox Christianity.

The end of the *OrigWld* is a full-blown apocalypse; it describes the destruction of the cosmos:

> Before the end [of the age], this whole region will shake with loud thunder. The archons will lament because of their [fear of] death, the angels will grieve for their human beings, the demons will weep over their times and seasons, and their people will mourn and cry on account of their death.
>
> Then the age will come, and they will be disturbed. Their kings will be drunk from the flaming sword and will wage war on one another, so that their earth will be drunk from the blood poured upon it. The seas will be troubled by war. The sun will darken and the moon will lose its light. (*OrigWld* 125:32–126:10, trans. Marvin Meyer, in *The Nag Hammadi Scriptures* [San Francisco: HarperOne, 2007]:220)

The passage continues in this vein for some time, and it is quite horrifying and frightening. But notice that interestingly (and unlike the book of Revelation), this passage does not really concentrate on people being killed or punished for being sinful, or for not believing in Christ; rather, this apocalypse is a complete collapse of the cosmic forces that control human destiny: the stars in their circuits, and the gods of chaos, and the abyss itself. And then, remarkably, at that point the "light will [overcome the] darkness and banish it. The darkness will be like something that never was" (126:35, trans. Meyer, NHS: 221). There is salvation for all people and not just the righteous (here, called the "perfect").

In both the *Hypostasis of the Archons* and *On the Origin of the World* we notice that there is really a "positive" outcome to the apocalypse, which is typical of Jewish and Christian apocalypses in general. Although the view of the world is somewhat pessimistic in both treatises, the authors assure their readers/listeners that God and the higher powers are still in control; to quote the American writer Max Ehrmann's famous *Desiderata*, "the universe is unfolding as it should." Although the situation seems bad, the people who considered these texts believed that if they had faith and held on, things would get better. This belief seems to correct Hans Jonas's characterization of Gnosticism as nihilistic and pessimistic. Help was on the way.

QUESTIONS TO CONSIDER

1. Get out your Bibles and compare Gen 1–3 with the story as told in *HypArch*. How does this later text "read" Genesis? What points in the Genesis narrative seem to have been problematic to the author of *HypArch*, and how does the narrative resolve these problems?

2. Does Samael strike you as a demonic or a tragic figure? Some say that it is not Samael's fault that he is born a monster but the fault of his mother. But nothing happens to redeem him—he cannot recognize the spiritual because it is not part of his essential makeup. Does this strike you as fair or

unfair? What do you think the ancient author of this text meant to convey?

3. How do depictions of women and femininity in *HypArch* and *OrigWld* differ from those in Genesis? Why do you think the authors of these two texts rewrote the passages from Genesis with different interpretations of its female characters?

KEY TERMS

cosmogony	sarkic	psychic	Hellenization
psyche	redaction	leontomorphic	exegesis
hylic	Paul	theriomorphic	protology
revelation dialogue	hypostasis	geocentric	Demiurge
Eleleth	archon	Septuagint	pneuma
Ialdabaoth	Sabaoth	protest exegesis	Norea
trisagion	Samael	choic	
Corinthians, First Letter to the	merkavah (or merkabah)		

FOR FURTHER READING

King, Karen L. "Ridicule and Rape, Rule and Rebellion: The *Hypostasis of the Archons*." In *Gnosticism and the Early Christian World: In Honor of James M. Robinson*, edited by James E. Goehring et al., 3–24. Sonoma, CA: Polebridge, 1990. This is a challenging read for upper-level students; it offers a critique of the *HypArch* based on an understanding of ideas of masculinity and femininity in the ancient world.

McGuire, Anne. "Virginity and Subversion: Norea Against the Powers in the *Hypostasis of the Archons*." In *Images of the Feminine in Gnosticism*, edited by Karen King, 239–58. Philadelphia: Fortress Press, 1988. A top scholar offers a feminist interpretation of Norea. For intermediate students.

Pagels, Elaine. "Pursuing the Spiritual Eve: Imagery and Hermeneutics in the *Hypostasis of the Archons*." In *Images of the Feminine in Gnosticism*, edited by Karen King, 187–206. Philadelphia: Fortress Press, 1988. An important article for upper-level students but requires some knowledge of the New Testament and ancient Greek.

In Popular Culture

The group Secret Chiefs 3 have a song titled "Hypostasis of the Archons."

12

A Classic Text

THE *APOCRYPHON OF JOHN* (NHC II, 1; III, 1; IV, 1; BG, 2)

The tractate known as the *Apocryphon* ("Secret Book") *of John* is one of the few Gnostic sources that scholars knew about even before the discovery at Nag Hammadi.

In the second century, the *ApJn* appears to have been both popular and influential. We know this because, unusually, we have four separate versions (**recensions**) of this text: three from the Nag Hammadi Library (NHC III,1; II, 1 and IV, 1) and one from another manuscript in Berlin, p. Berol. 8502, known as the Berlin Gnostic Codex (Berolinensis Gnosticus) or BG, 2. **Heresiologists** such as **Irenaeus of Lyons** were apparently familiar with the *ApJn*, because they allude to various aspects of the myth that it contains. From this we can date it tentatively to sometime before 180 CE when Irenaeus was writing. We also know that at least one group, the Audians, were still using the *ApJn* as their scripture in Mesopotamia as late as the eighth century. All the different versions also suggest that the text was frequently changed to fit the situation and theology of different groups in antiquity.

The *ApJn* is predicated on a simple question: How did evil and deceit come into the world? To answer this question, the text as we have it today weaves together Genesis interpretation, fragments of popular Stoic and Platonist philosophy, resonances of Pauline and Johannine theology, and other material gleaned from less easily identifiable sources into a complex, mythological account of creation. These new mythological cosmologies became part of an intellectual effort that the Israeli scholar of Gnosticism Gedaliahu Stroumsa elegantly termed "the last significant outburst of mythical thought in Antiquity" (G. Stroumsa, *Another Seed: Studies in Gnostic Mythology*, Nag Hamadi Studies [Leiden: Brill, 1984], 1), as authors from these circles deftly transformed abstract philosophical principles into agents and characters in a huge cosmic drama. Ultimately, the *ApJn* covers a huge sweep of world history, from the beginnings of the cosmos to the individual salvation of the believer and the end of time itself.

RELATIONSHIP BETWEEN THE MANUSCRIPTS OF THE APOCRYPHON OF JOHN

At some point in antiquity, two scribes, working separately, translated a single Greek version of

TABLE 12.1: Comparing the *Apocryphon of John*'s Four Recensions

NHC II, 1 (LONG)	NHC III, 1 (SHORT)	NHC IV, 1 (LONG)	BG 8502, 2 (SHORT)
First treatise of seven in the codex	First treatise of five in the codex	First treatise of two in the codex	Second treatise of four in the codex
Well preserved	Poorly preserved	Very poorly preserved	Well preserved
A regular, upright script	Unique scribal hand with elegant, easy-to-read script	Almost identical script to that found in other NHC codices	Irregular but skilled script
	Copied from a prior Coptic text		Copied from a prior Coptic text
In Subachmimic and Sahidic	In Sahidic	In Sahidic	In Sahidic

ApJn into Coptic. This Greek version was short; it omitted a lot of the technical names and lists that were present in another version of the Greek *ApJn*. Of the two copies made in Coptic, one was included in the NHL (*ApJn* III, 1); the other (BG, 2) was preserved in a manuscript now in Berlin. Next (or perhaps before, we cannot be sure!), an unknown scribe translated another Greek version into Coptic, from which additional Coptic scribes then copied. This second Greek version was much longer. Two of *these* copies, now translated into Coptic, were included in the NHL: II, 1 and IV, 1. So what we have in the end is rather confusing: four different texts of *ApJn* in three different versions, and of two different recensions (short and long) (see table 12.1). What this means is that when you read translations of *ApJn* in English or any other modern language, what you are actually reading is a synthesized version of all four texts harmonized into one. While this is in some ways troubling—if you read any one of the Coptic texts in isolation it would differ slightly from what you read in English—the process is actually very similar to what we do when we read the New Testament in English translation. Any English translation—be it King James, the New International Version (NIV), the Revised Standard Version (RSV), the New Revised Standard Version (NRSV) or what have

you—is based on scholars reading multiple manuscripts of the Greek New Testament, no single manuscript of which is completely identical with another, and then synthesizing all the manuscript evidence into one, single, "best possible" text.

Understandably, the task of working through all four versions of the *ApJn* has taken scholars a while. It wasn't until 1995, fifty years after the discovery of the NHL, that a modern English critical edition of the treatise was published. Now one can now read all the versions in parallel texts. This kind of careful work of comparing versions is called **redaction criticism**, and scholars of the New Testament are very familiar with it. It can teach us a great deal about the function of a text, its transmission over time, and sometimes, about the scribe or community who copied the text. To get a sense of how this works, look at table 12.2. If you compare a single passage in each of the *ApJn*'s four redactions, you'll find that the narrative of **Adam** and **Eve's** expulsion from paradise is found in three of our four remaining recensions of the *ApJn*. Arranging them as we have done here allows the similarities and differences between the different versions to become apparent. When you are reading this, note that the angle brackets mean the original letter (Y in this case) was missing from the manuscript and has been added by a modern editor. The square brackets mean that

do we make of this? It is likely that the author of this passage was trying to convey different things. First, he was making the point that the Savior (he is not called Jesus in this text) is fully transcendent; although he always has a human appearance, he is not human but something else. There are other texts from the second century, which also depict a shape-shifting Jesus: In the *Gospel of Judas*, for example, Jesus also appears as a child. As strange as a shape-shifting savior seems to us, in the ancient context this may simply be the way to express Jesus's transcendent nature. But there are other possible associations. In some more mystical forms of Judaism, there emerged the idea that there were two powers in heaven: God, plus a powerful angel sometimes called Metatron. One of Metatron's forms was that of a youth. God, as the chief power in heaven, is sometimes featured in Jewish apocalyptic literature as an old man on a throne (see for instance the throne vision of Ezek 1). As Christianity developed, one of the questions people asked was whether God and Jesus were identical, or whether Jesus was this "second power in the heaven" known from Jewish sources. One tactic in the *ApJn*, then, might be to show that the Savior was in fact two separate forms of the one God: he is both God (the old man) and Jesus (the youth). In the second century, these ideas were still very much in flux, and it wasn't until the fifth century that the dominant dogma of Catholic **christology** developed: that Jesus was both fully human and fully divine, and that the Son is identical with (and of the same substance and nature as) the Father.

Jesus as only one aspect of the Father brings us to the other surprising depiction of the Savior in the *ApJn*: he is Father, Son, and Mother. This lets us know that when the *ApJn* was written, many Christians considered that the Trinity was really a sort of nuclear family; the later concept of the Trinity as Father, Son, and Holy Spirit had not yet taken hold. In an important sense, the Trinity we find here is more akin to Jewish

thought, in that the Mother was associated with God the Father's creative spirit and breath (in Hebrew, the word for breath, *Ruach*, is grammatically feminine). The Son's creation is described as the "only-begotten child of the Mother-Father which had come forth; it is the only offspring, the only-begotten one of the Father, the pure Light" (trans. Frederik Wisse, *The Nag Hammadi Library in English* [San Francisco: Harper & Row, 1988]: 108). The language echoes the **Johannine Prologue**, but *ApJn*, by contrast, includes a feminine power in the primordial divine source.

APOPHATIC THEOLOGY AND THE PROBLEM OF CREATION

Toward the beginning of *ApJn*'s frame story, the Savior reveals to John the nature of the "Great Invisible Spirit." The language to describe God comes not from Jewish scriptures but from Greek philosophy. The Great Invisible Spirit is a **Monad,** a single abstract principle, not a personality or a being. What is this Monad like? The Savior offers a variety of adjectives. It is:

- Eternal
- Illimitable
- Unsearchable
- Immeasurable
- Invisible
- Ineffable
- Unnameable

This way of talking about the Divine is called **apophatic theology**: characterizing the Divine by what it (or he, though the use of gender is misleading here) is not. Apophatic theology is sometimes called the *via negationis*, the path [to a knowledge of God] through negatives or negation. The point of apophatic theology is to get past the limitations of human language and human thinking, to point to something even more profound than our ability to describe or conceptualize.

WHO IS BARBĒLŌ?

Like many names in the NHL, the name Barbēlō does not actually mean anything. But we know it is not a Greek word. One guess is that it is related to the Coptic verb *berber*, "to overflow, boil over." If that is so, it is a fitting name for Barbēlō, who comes into existence as the overflow of the Monad's creative energies. Barbēlō, as the most significant active being in the **Pleroma**, also has lots of other names in the *ApJn*:

- the Virginal Spirit
- the Mother-Father (Gk *Metropator*)
- the Triple Male
- the Triple-Named

The problem with thinking of God this way—as complete perfection and the absence of lack—is that it is hard to explain (a) creation; and (b) difference and differentiation. Why would a complete, perfect "being" need to create anything? Is it not it complete in and of itself? Also, what accounts for difference in the cosmos? There are obviously things that are not perfect, so how did they come to exist as distinct from complete perfection? Thus much of the force in this cosmogony, as in *HypArch* and *OrgWld*, is to explain how evil or even imperfect things came to be, given the existence of a perfect First Principle. The author of *ApJn* borrows a number of metaphors and images from **Middle Platonism.** Here are two:

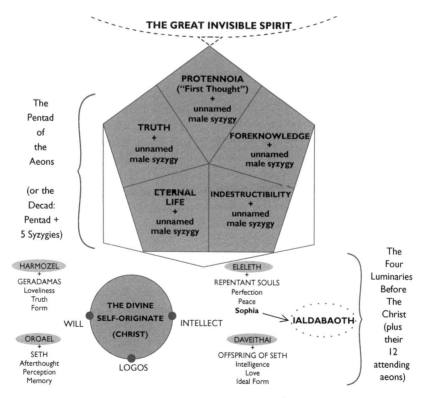

DIAGRAM 12.1 The structure of the upper cosmos or Pleromatic Realms according to the Apocryphon of John.

FIGURE 12.1 A sketch of a Graeco-Egyptian amulet featuring a powerful creature known as Chnoubis. Notice his serpentine body and leonine head—a similar body to that of Yaltabaoth/Ialdabaoth in the *ApJn*.

1. Imagine the original force in the cosmos as a giant eye that can look. All it does, in fact, is look. When it looks, it sees only itself reflected in the primordial waters. This reflection or image is not the *First Principle* but a natural reproduction of it: a *Second Principle*. It is therefore a form of differentiated creation; not the original thing but its reflection. This is one way that an original First Principle can and does "create" asexually, thus producing difference. The reflection is also inferior to the original, because it is derivative. Thus the farther one gets in reflected or refracted derivation from an original, the more difference or defect that it has from an original.

2. Imagine the original force in the cosmos as a big giant brain. In the *ApJn*, as in other texts from Nag Hammadi, the Great Invisible Spirit is like a limitless, eternal, incorporeal mind. This mind does what minds do: it thinks. Here, it *thinks* out the cosmos; all higher creation comes from the act of thinking (rather than

from procreation, which needs bodies and the distinction of gender, neither of which the Great Invisible Spirit has or needs).

Middle Platonism thus stands as a major intellectual influence behind the *ApJn*, as with many other texts from Nag Hammadi. In some cases, Greek philosophical ideas provided the best material to think with in Christian antiquity.

THE STRUCTURE OF THE COSMOS

The Upper Regions

The Great Invisible Spirit (also called **Barbēlō** here, because Barbēlō is the creative aspect or energy of the Great Invisible Spirit) thinks its first thought, which is in the *ApJn* actually called First Thought (Gk **Protennoia**). First Thought is joined by Foreknowledge, and then by three other principles: Indestructibility, Life, and Truth.

Together, we are told, these are the "Pentad of the Aeons"—the primary set of entities present in the highest cosmic realm. Each of these elements in the Pentad has a corresponding masculine partner, because First Thought (*Protennoia*), Foreknowledge (*Pronoia*), Indestructability (*Aphtharsia*), Life (*Zoe*), and Truth (*Aletheia*) are all feminine abstract nouns in Greek. These partner pairs are **syzygies** (sing: syzygos), and together they form the basic components of the upper heavens. The Pentad of five hypostases plus their five masculine counterparts make ten aeons called the **Decad**.

Notice that they are all abstract concepts drawn from Greek philosophy, but here they are more than just concepts; they are beings or divinities. We call this process of transforming a concept into a being **hypostasization**. The presence of hypostasized beings or characters appears to have been very common in second-century philosophical writings. So far, the picture of the cosmos in *ApJn* reflects the idea of divine harmony and unity, built upon male-female pairs. But things are about to change.

PLATO'S *TIMAEUS*

There was no text more studied in Graeco-Roman antiquity than the Greek philosopher Plato's famous dialogue, the *Timaeus*. It begins with a group of friends convening on the feast of Athena to entertain their guest, Socrates. One of the friends, Timaeus, is selected to give a discourse on the nature and structure of the world. He begins with outlining three principles: (1) the **Demiurge** or World Creator, (2) the Ideas, and (3) Matter. The Demiurge is also called God or the Monad; he is wholly good and creates a world that is also wholly good and reflective of the order of the upper realms. The Ideas are the patterns on which the world is created, and Matter is the substance and the principle of Multiplicity.

The *Timaeus* distinguishes between Being and Becoming, with Being far superior to Becoming: "As Being is to Becoming, so Truth is to Opinion"

(*Tim.* 29C). Still, even the world of Becoming is based on goodness and order, if only reflective of the divine realms. The Demiurge therefore creates the best possible world, suffused with order and harmony. Humans are created threefold, possessing a mortal, immortal, and animal soul. Furthermore, human beings are microcosms to the macrocosm of the divine realm, created in the best possible way and with direct links to God through mind, soul, and reason. All in all, the picture of the cosmos—and humans' place in it—is one of harmony and practicality.

While the *ApJn* picks up on many elements of the *Timaeus*, it seems to view the cosmos very differently. No longer a reflection of goodness, the cosmos in *ApJn* is fractured, with its lower regions full of beings bent on the enslavement of humankind.

The Creation of the Lower Regions

One archon, the "**Sophia** of the Epinoia," does the thinking rather than the Great Invisible Spirit. Acting without her consort and without the consent of her Mother-Father, she creates a being with a form dissimilar from its mother. The monster **Ialdabaoth** has the form of a lion-faced serpent; repelled and ashamed by her own creation, Sophia casts her child out of the highest aeon, surrounds it with a luminous cloud, and places it on a throne in the middle of the cloud so no one but the holy spirit can see it.

Ialdabaoth, in turn, creates twelve **archons**:

- Athoth
- Harmas
- Kalila-Oumbri
- Yabel
- Adonaiou, or Sabaoth
- Cain, or the Sun
- Abel

- Abrisene
- Yobel
- Armoupieel
- Melceir-Adonein
- Belias, "he who is over the depths of Hades"

These twelve are evidently related to the signs of the Zodiac; in fact, at least one of them, Yobel, is Hebrew for "ram" or the zodiacal sign Aries. Seven of these archons are placed over the seven heavens, and five over the depths of the abyss; this is a traditional division in antiquity. Each archon then creates seven powers, and each of the seven powers creates six angels until there are 365 angels. Although the math does not quite work, the point was that both time and space was fully under demonic control.

At this point, the narrative of the creation of the cosmos continues, but here it begins to interpret (exegete, literally, "draw out the meaning of") Genesis 1–4.

THE CREATION OF IALDABAOTH AND THE REPENTANCE OF SOPHIA

The drama of **Sophia** occupies a great portion of the narrative and warrants some attention. Since the aim of this text is to illustrate how evil came to be in the world, the moment at which evil first appears is significant. Until we get to the story of Sophia, the universe has "emanated" or differentiated in a harmonious manner. In fact, the entire cosmos is harmonious, based on balanced male-female pairs, until Sophia diverges by deciding, without permission and without a male partner, to create an offspring for herself. The result, her child

Ialdabaoth, initiates a profound rupturing throughout the balanced cosmic hierarchy.

Although many Christians nowadays consider the origin of evil to be linked to Adam and Eve's behavior in the garden of Eden (or to the snake's intent), here it is not human fault or frailty that introduces evil in the world. This text says that evil started much earlier, and it was a divine being, not a human one, who created the problem in the first place.

A significant, though short, part of the narrative of the *ApJn* concerns Sophia's repentance. The story tells us that when Sophia recognizes that the child she created was both monstrous and arrogant, calling himself the sole god, she weeps and repents. Her sorrow is heard within

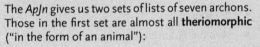

THE SEVEN ARCHONS AND THE PLANETS IN THE *APOCRYPHON OF JOHN*

The *ApJn* gives us two sets of lists of seven archons. Those in the first set are almost all **theriomorphic** ("in the form of an animal"):

Athoth (sheep-faced)
Eloaiou (donkey-faced)
Astaphaios (hyena-faced)
Yao (serpent-faced with seven heads)
Sabaoth (dragon-faced)
Adonin (monkey-faced)
Sabbede (fire-faced)

In the second set, each archon is affiliated with a specific quality:

Athoth (goodness)
Eloaio (foreknowledge)
Astraphaio (divinity)
Yao (lordship)
Sabaoth (kingdom)
Adonein (envy)
Sabbateon (understanding)

Some scholars have worked to understand to what, if anything, these archons correspond. We do know

a few things, though. First of all, these names and lists of seven are not unique to *ApJn*—they show up in a number of other sources ranging from other NHL writings (*GosEg*; *OrigWld*) to Roman tombstones and amulets. Second, the lists are confused across the four versions of *ApJn*, so whoever wrote them down did the best he could to make sense of something that likely did not make sense to him. Third, they appear to be connected to either the zodiac or the planets, but it is not clear precisely how. One clue, however, comes from the last archon, Sabbede/Sabbateon, which is related to the Hebrew word for the Sabbath and thus, to the week. From this clue, we might infer that the seven archons may not be directly related to the planetary spheres in the cosmos but to the days of the week (which were themselves thought to be "ruled over" by specific planets; in fact, our modern English names like Sun-day and Mon(Moon)-day preserve traces of this teaching). The point of these lists here, then, may not be to say that the entire cosmos is saturated with demonic archons, but that time itself is ruled by archontic beings.

TABLE 12.3: The Seven Archons and Their Cosmic Correspondences

Archons	Powers	Planets	Corresponding bodily substances
Iaoth	Pronoia	Moon	Marrow
Eloaios	Divinity	Mercury	Bones
Astaphaios	Goodness	Venus	Sinews
Iao	Fire	Sun	Flesh
Sabaoth	Kingship	Mars	Blood
Adoni	Comprehension	Jupiter	Skin
Sabbataios	Wisdom	Saturn	Hair

the **Pleroma** or divine realm, and the Holy Spirit pours over her to "correct her deficiency." She is then caught up to a higher aeon than her son's, until she has fully repented. The scene is important because Sophia represents the repentance and conversion of individual Christians. Sophia's repentance also sets the stage for the great teaching and revelation of the First Man in human form (presumably—although the text does not say for sure—this First Man is both Jesus and Adam).

THE CREATION OF HUMANKIND

The *ApJn* interprets Genesis 1:26 as it picks up on the words of Yahweh: "Come, let us create a human according to the image of God and according to our own likeness." Astonishingly, the speaker here is revealed to be not Yahweh, the benevolent God of Judaism, but the monstrously arrogant Ialdabaoth speaking to his archon minions. The seven archons then begin

ADAM'S BODY IN *APJN*

Only the long recension of *ApJn* contains an extensive list of demons along with the human body parts that they govern. The list may seem a bit overwhelming—indeed, slightly comical—to most modern readers. As well as demons for the anatomical parts of the body, there are also demons assigned to particular emotions, including pleasure, desire, grief, and fear. These lists seem to derive from two sources: (1) Stoic philosophy and teachings on the nature of human emotions; (2) Greek and Egyptian magical papyri and funerary texts; in fact, most of the demon names derive from Egyptian roots.

Medically, these lists probably served a very practical function: to help to diagnose disease and cure ailments through magico-medicinal rites and practices. One interesting detail to notice is that this primordial human body has male, not female, genitalia but also apparently possesses a uterus. Does this author therefore think of the first human being as androgynous, both male and female? If so, this is very much in line with Platonic views of the first human being.

WHAT IS THE *BOOK OF ZOROASTER?*

The *ApJn* at 17:63 notes that the configuration of the stars can be found in the *Book of Zoroaster*. Is there such a book? If there is, we haven't found it yet. It is one of two books mentioned in the *ApJn*; the other is the *Book of the Configuration of the Twelve Beneath the Heavens*. In fact, the Nag Hammadi writings, along with the heresiologists, mention a variety of books lost to us today. Maybe these titles were simply invented in order to give the tractate a kind of mystical pedigree. Or perhaps it is just a matter of time until we find these texts. For instance, before its discovery in the 1970s, the *Gospel of Judas* was also on the list of lost, quasi-mythical books.

to form Adam, beginning from the inside and proceeding to the outside, giving him seven souls:

- A bone-soul from Goodness
- A sinew-soul from Foreknowledge
- A flesh-soul from Divinity
- A marrow-soul from Lordship
- A blood-soul from Kingdom
- A skin-soul from Envy
- A hair-soul from Understanding

Although this looks curious to us, to an educated citizen of the second century, it wasn't that strange. Plato, in the *Timaeus*, writes of the creation of the primordial human being by a Demiurge working with seven minor gods associated with the planets, each of whom contribute a type of soul to the human.

In the *ApJn*, accordingly, we can chart the correspondences something like we see in table 12.3.

Note that the powers are generally beneficent, and yet it is not clear that they should be, given their demonic correspondences. It may be that the author of this list was revealing the false names behind which the malevolent archons disguised themselves. What the author of the *ApJn* is doing here, apparently, is reconciling one revered text (Gen 1:26, "let *us* create man in our image") with another (*Timaeus* 73B–76E). He apparently

saw no theological conflicts in doing so. Another thing he does that is significant and unexpected, is to take the positive characterization of the Demiurge in *Timaeus*, the positive characterization of Yahweh as a creator god as in Genesis, and then turn the tables completely so that the Chief Archon is an evil and inferior being.

The entire passage ends with a bit of a pun: "thus they ordered the whole man." The verb "ordered" here, *kosmein*, is related to the Greek word for "world" or "universe," *kosmos*, which itself means "ordered" or "adorned" (in fact, the English word "cosmetics" comes from the same root; they are things which "order" or "adorn" the face). Thus in the *ApJn*, Adam is ordered and "made cosmic" at the same time. In forms of ancient thought— including medicine—it was believed that humans reflected the same form as the cosmos; in other words, humans were the microcosms (the "little heavens") to the macrocosm that is the universe.

When Yaltabaoth blows his mother's animating spirit into Adam, not only does Adam come alive he also shines with a divine light. His superiority makes the archons so jealous that they throw their creation into the lowest region of all matter, that is, to earth. The Mother-Father takes pity on Adam and sends him a "helper," the luminous aeon **Epinoia**, to teach him.

Remarkably, at this point, Adam is created for a second time: when the archons see that Adam is still superior in the lowest region (they

THE COUNTERFEIT SPIRIT

One distinctive element of the *ApJn* is its description of a "counterfeit spirit" that acts to lead humans astray. According to the text, it "weighs down the soul, and lures it into the works of wickedness, and throws it into a state of forgetfulness" (II 26:39). When John asks where the counterfeit spirit has come from, the revealer gives a condensed version of a creation myth. Ialdabaoth, jealous of the children of the perfect generation, copulated with Wisdom to create Fate. Fate made "all creation blind." But this was only part one of Ialdabaoth's dastardly plan; he sends his angels to earth, where they disguise themselves as women's spouses and then rape the women, filling them with the counterfeit spirit. Then they "begot children out of the darkness, after the image of their spirit. And their hearts became closed and hardened with the hardness of the counterfeit spirit, down to the present time" (ApJn 30:7–11.).

The story about angels coming to earth and mating with human women is a very ancient one, first expressed in a third century BCE Jewish text known as the "Book of the Watchers" in a scripture called *1 Enoch*. You can still detect traces of this legend in Genesis 6:1, where the sons of God come down to the "daughters of men" and human iniquity increases, provoking God to send the great flood. By the second century CE, this story of angels taking human wives was well known and used to explain the origin of various types of corrupting knowledge; here in the *ApJn* the angels bring "gold, silver, gifts, comer, iron, metal, and all kinds of raw materials." By extension, then, the author condemned elements of human civilization and materialism as having sinister origins.

cannot perceive the Epinoia in him, since they themselves lack the spiritual capacity for recognizing what they themselves lack), they bring him "into the shadow of death," then re-form their man out of matter, darkness, desire, and the "counterfeit spirit." This new creature is the earthly Adam, the main character in Genesis. Why are there two creations of Adam? Because in Genesis, there are two creations: one at 1:26 where God creates humankind "male and female" (apparently with some help, since God uses the plural), and another at 2:7, where God creates Adam out of dust and mud. Thus this "double" creation of Adam reflects the way that the *ApJn* dealt with a tricky problem in the Genesis account.

BIBLICAL EXEGESIS IN THE APOCRYPHON OF JOHN

The *ApJn* is particularly important because it is our earliest complete Christian exegesis of a piece of scripture. Here, the book being interpreted is Genesis. In fact, the *ApJn* begins with an account of what happened before Genesis. The *ApJn* provides us with an esoteric or hidden "spiritual" reading of Genesis against a more literal one; it gives listeners the "true history" of the world and how it came to be. For instance, God casting a deep sleep over Adam in Genesis 2:21 before he draws Eve from his side is in *ApJn* interpreted as Ialdabaoth making Adam spiritually asleep—that is to say, Adam forgets his spiritual origins. The author supports this spiritual reading with a line from Isaiah 6:10: "I will make their hearts heavy that they may not pay attention and they may not see" (*ApJn* 22:26). His revealed knowledge explains the book's title: it is a hidden history of the way things are, expressed in this "secret book."

In other ways, the author teaches the reader how to interpret scripture beyond the face value of the text. In essence, this act itself depends on the reader *thinking*, that is what the Great Invisible Spirit does. To think properly, the reader has to use tools that the Great Invisible Spirit has provided: knowledge, perception, and memory.

The very act of scriptural interpretation, therefore, is in a sense "salvific": it allows us to connect to higher truths contained in the scriptures—truths that the lower archons who control human beings are themselves not able to connect to because they, unlike us, are spiritually undiscerning.

THE PRONOIA HYMN

The long recension of the *ApJn* ends with a poem that sounds similar to another tractate from NHL, the *Thunder: Perfect Mind*. In this poem, the Great Angel Eleleth reveals the call and descent of **Pronoia**. It picks up on Jewish conceptualizations of Wisdom as a salvific figure. For example, Roman Catholics and Othodox Christians preserve in their Bibles an apocryphal book called the Wisdom (of Solomon), which has ancient Jewish roots. A passage in this book reads, "Send her [Wisdom] forth from the holy heavens, and from the throne of your glory send her, that she may labor at my side, and that I may learn what is pleasing to you" (Wis 9:10–11). In another ancient Jewish book, Sirach (Ecclesiasticus), Wisdom speaks as a character: "Come to me, you who desire me, and eat your fill of my fruits. The memory of me is sweeter than honey, and the possession of me sweeter than the honeycomb. . . . Those who work with me will not sin" (Sir 24:19–20, 22b) (NRSV).

Jewish Wisdom texts such as Sirach and the Wisdom of Solomon are fairly unknown to many people, but they are important witnesses for the way in which Jews of the ancient world thought about Wisdom as a female character with a unique relationship to God. But scholars working on *ApJn*'s Pronoia hymn have noted that it bears a striking relationship to another, more familiar text that draws on Jewish **Wisdom Traditions**: the Prologue of the Gospel of John. The two texts seem to be related, although it is not clear how. Both were likely early Christian hymns that drew on Jewish thought in similar ways, later coming to be incorporated into the Gospel of John and the *ApJn* respectively. The Johannine prologue was added to the beginning of the gospel and sets the tone for what was to follow; the Pronoia hymn was added to the end of the *ApJn*, at which point an editor went back over the *ApJn* and introduced changes to the main body of the text to bring it more in line with the new, added ending.

WAYS OUT (OF ENSLAVEMENT)

One central message of the *ApJn* is that all human beings are in a sense dual in nature. We have bodily or lower components that originate in archontic matter and substance. But we also have finer, divine substance deep within us, thanks to Sophia and the higher aeons who implanted this substance in all people. On the face of it, then, the *ApJn* text shows the human condition as tragically differentiated, and the human self deeply divided against itself. We are mastered by the existential sleep imposed upon us, and the archons control us through implanting in us human emotions that we mistake as our own appetites and drives. They also control us through our desire for sex, which supplants or masks a higher desire to join with our celestial origins. Sexuality is the antithesis or opposite of spirituality. We are so caught up with our own sexuality that we are distracted from a more sublime form of spiritual union.

Although the German scholar Hans Jonas once suggested that "*the* Gnostic myth" was essentially pessimistic, it must be said that the *ApJn* gives a number of ways for readers to become awakened to the divine spark within them. This is especially clear from the long recension of *ApJn* with its Pronoia hymn. The hymn, which we think might have been used for ritual or sacramental purposes, rounds out an account of at least six ways to awaken to the deceit of the archons and to find one's true spiritual origins:

1. The sacrament of baptism, here called the Five Seals. We know very little about what this ritual looked like, but it is mentioned in a variety of Gnostic documents (*GosEg*; *TriProt*, and the *Untitled Tractate* from the **Bruce Codex**). "Sealing" was a fairly common term in Christian antiquity for a water baptism, but it could also refer to anointing a Christian with oil. It is important to note that the author of *ApJn* alludes to a Christian sacrament as conferring salvation.

2. The descent of the Savior to earth as a redeemer figure. Although this Savior is never directly named as Jesus, this is a Christian text and therefore it is a safe enough assumption that the Savior is indeed Jesus. Here, as in the Prologue of the Gospel of John, he descends from above to bring salvation to his children.

3. Ethical behavior and restraint of the emotions. The detailing of the origin of types of negative emotion in the cosmos was commonplace in second-century philosophy. The idea that a life "properly lived" included trying to control one's emotions was well known at this time, and was predominantly associated with the Greek philosophers known as **Stoics**. (For this reason, we still call someone who holds back emotions as being "stoic"). Stoics aimed to cultivate *apatheia* ("apathy"), which literally means, "the absence of the passions/emotions). Similarly the long recension of the *ApJn* recommends cultivating *apatheia*, considering all emotions or passions to be merely demonic influences that pollute the soul.

4. Sexual continence or abstinence. The author of this text makes it abundantly clear that sexual desire is the consequence of a fallen and sinful cosmos. In his grotesque mimicry of asexual creation by emanation that characterizes the upper heavens, Ialdabaoth copulates with Aponoia ("Madness") to produce the angels. The archons rape **Eve**, and the angels and archons introduce sexual intercourse in order to enslave human beings. At the same time, there is at least a hint in *ApJn* that all sexual behavior is not necessarily sinful. Note that the archons come upon Eve "preparing herself for her husband"—the guess has been for a long time that this was something like a pre-intercourse purification ritual. On the other hand, the text states that the legitimate (sexual) union of Adam and Eve is a mystery that can lead to salvation. In other words, all sexual activity might not be sinful, but only that outside the confines of marriage. If this is the case, then the sexual ethics of this author was not radical abstinence, but more in line with proto-orthodox Christian teachings on sex as permissible only within marriage.

5. Knowledge of the nature and structure of the cosmos, including knowledge of specific demons. Although it is not clear that this type of knowledge led directly to salvation, certainly knowing what type of demons imposed what type of sin or affliction was useful for helping the soul navigate the cosmos and return to its source in the upper realms.

6. Listening to the story itself and hearing Sophia's call. This text is a revelation text, meant to be read aloud. The long recension's Pronoia hymn, in particular, must have been powerfully and emotionally moving. There is a real sense in which listening to Sophia's call must have been intended to "wake" listeners from their spiritual sleep.

All these paths to salvation could, in fact, be combined. Thus the *ApJn* provides a comprehensive handbook of everything that listeners need to know in order to help them to recognize the nature of evil and enslavement, and to turn toward God.

WHO WROTE, AND READ, THIS TEXT?

An old set of debates in scholarship have concerned whether the *ApJn* was originally a Christian text. The presence of a clearly Christian **frame**

THE *APOCRYPHON OF JOHN* IN POPULAR CULTURE

The popular American singer/songwriter Tori Amos features an *Apocryphon of John* song in her eighth album, *The Beekeeper* (2005). Shades of *ApJn* also appear in the American film *Vanilla Sky* (dir. Cameron Crowe, 2001), which was based on a 1997 Spanish-language film *Abre Los Ojos* (*Open Your Eyes*, dir. A. Amenábar). In this movie, the female revealer/redeemer figure is named Sophia. We hear her voice repeating, insistently, "Open your eyes!" as she urges the movie's hero to become aware of his own cognitive sleep and the unreality of his world.

story raises the possibility that Gnostic Christians, at some point, took an essentially non-Christian story and adopted it by adding patently Christian surrounding material. Scholars who argued this also argued that the older non-Christian story of *ApJn* was probably Jewish, since it concerned the proper interpretation of the Jewish scriptures. Further, these same scholars suggested that the Jewish author(s) of the *ApJn*'s main narrative were probably Jews who had become disaffected from mainstream Judaism and thus introduced writings like this one, which suggests that the God of the Jews was really an evil, ignorant archon.

A new wave of scholarship—perhaps best represented by the work of the Dutch scholar Gerard Luittikhuizen—argues instead that the *ApJn* was from the beginning a Christian work. Luittikhuizen notes that Christians of the second century often debated the value of Jewish scriptures. Some thought they were valuable because they revealed or foreshadowed the truth about Jesus. Some thought they were *not* valuable because Jesus's presence on the earth made all other, earlier sources of law and revelation no longer valid. According to Luittikhuizen's theory, the *ApJn* was written by Christians who considered Genesis to be an important source of salvation, but who also believed that it needed to be read and interpreted correctly for it to be valuable.

There are several points where the narrator of *ApJn* says, "It is not as Moses wrote…" Luittikhuizen argues that we should not think of these as moments where we can see Jews rejecting their scripture (since Moses was the traditional author of Genesis) but as one group of Gnostic

Christians arguing against another group of Christians who chose to interpret Genesis literally. Imagine one of these Christians teaching, for instance, that God put Adam into a deep sleep in order to create Eve. The author of *ApJn* rejects a literal reading in place of an allegorical or metaphorical reading: actually, the archons put Adam into a state of metaphorical sleep, where he lost sight of his true spiritual origins. In other words, what was being contested in the second century was different ways of using the Jewish scriptures to arrive at a Christian meaning.

Compared to another mythological creation story from NH, the *HypArch*, the *ApJn* is a little less puzzling. For instance:

- The archons are less malevolent, functioning more like creator gods and less like ignorant bullies
- The snake is not a positive figure but leads Adam and Eve astray
- Jesus appears as the Savior, as opposed to a figure like Eleleth or Pronoia
- Adam and Eve are wrong to eat from the tree of knowledge of good and evil
- Ialdabaoth does not commit blasphemy by claiming to be God
- Adam and Eve's nakedness is connected to the concept of shame, not interpreted metaphorically and spiritually

These points indicate that the *ApJn* was less radical in its interpretation than other Christian texts; it is therefore possible that this accounts for its popularity.

KEY TERMS

Barbēlō	Wisdom Tradition	apophatic theology
revelation dialogue	christology	Stoics
hypostasization	frame story	Demiurge
hierophany	redaction criticism	Middle Platonism
recension	heresiologist	Irenaeus of Lyons
Autogenes	Johannine Prologue	Monad
Protennoia	syzygy (pl.: syzygies)	Decad
theriomorphic	Sophia	archons

QUESTIONS TO CONSIDER

1. Do you think that sexuality is truly evil in this text or only sexual intercourse driven by lust?

2. What do you make of the character of Sophia, here? Is she a positive or negative character (note that she is always positive in Hellenistic Jewish Wisdom literature)?

3. Is the Christianity of *ApJn* familiar or unfamiliar to you? Consider what the text does with its image of the Savior, with the nature of sin and salvation from sin, and the place of the sacraments.

FOR FURTHER READING

Davies, Stevan. *Secret Book of John: The Gnostic Gospel, Annotated and Explained.* Woodstock, VT: Skylight Paths Publishing, 2005. A modern translation for a non-academic audience.

King, Karen L. *The Secret Revelation of John.* Cambridge, MA: Harvard University Press, 2006. Harvard professor Karen King offers her own translation and analysis of the *ApJn*, offering a distinctly political read. Highly recommended.

Luittikhuizen, Gerard. *Gnostic Revisions of Genesis Stories and Early Jesus Traditions.* Leiden: Brill, 2006. An interesting book on how early Christian groups read and interpreted Jewish scriptures. For advanced students.

13

A Classic Liturgical Text

GOSPEL OF THE EGYPTIANS (BOOK OF THE GREAT INVISIBLE SPIRIT) (NHC III, 2 AND NHC IV, 2)

The rather intimidating treatise usually known as the *Gospel of the Egyptians* is present in two versions in the NHL: one in Codex III, and a more fragmentary one in Codex IV. Both versions found at Nag Hammadi are independent Coptic translations of at least two Greek originals; they are two slightly different texts rather than copies of one another, or of a single Coptic translation, or of a single Greek original. It is possible to understand something of the mechanics of translation by comparing the two versions. It is also useful to compare the two so as to be able to fill in the gaps of the narrative; when one version is corrupted, the other version is sometimes complete. Combined, they allow us to restore about 90 percent of the original writing.

Like the *Gospel of Truth* and the *Gospel of Philip*, the *Gospel of the Egyptians* (*GosEg*) looks nothing like a New Testament gospel. In fact, the title is not even its ancient one; it is unrelated to a text of the same name cited by a Church Father, **Clement of Alexandria.** Codex III gives the treatise's name as *The Holy Book of the Great Invisible Spirit*, although it also calls it *The Egyptian Gospel* in a scribal **colophon** at the end (NHC III 69:16–17), but the *Holy Book of the Great Invisible Spirit* is most probably the correct name for this treatise. For simplicity's sake, we will stick with the custom of calling it *GosEg*, but recent scholarship (and translations) prefer *Holy Book of the Great Invisible Spirit*.

If you have been reading the NHL in English sequentially, the *GosEg* may be the first time when you feel really at sea. The text is confusing, with a complicated **cosmology,** and scores of unfamiliar names. It is hard to make sense of it without a basic understanding of **Sethian Gnosticism** or **Sethianism,** which take as their hero not Jesus but a transcendent, celestial figure called **Seth** who is the savior of the so-called incorruptible race. In *GosEg*, it is said to be Seth himself who composed this document over the course of a hundred and thirty years, then placed it high upon a mythical mountain, Charaxio, "on which the sun has not risen and cannot rise" (68:1). The *GosEg* is a Christian Sethian text, because Jesus appears in the text and is associated with Seth. But it is quite different from other Christian Sethian texts such as the *ApJn*. Its cosmology is more complex, and there are key differences in the way the text presents salvation.

WHAT IS **DOMEDON DOXOMEDON?**

In this text, Domedon Doxomedon is the name of a great celestial realm (**aeon**), which contains a throne where the **Thrice-Male Child** sits surrounded by the celestial host. The name may mean something like, "Lord of Glory" or "Lord of the House." The language draws from ancient Jewish mystical traditions, especially what grew to be, much later, an esoteric school of thought called **Merkavah** or **Merkabah** ("chariot-throne") mysticism. Those who espoused Merkavah believed that texts such

as Ezekiel contained secret knowledge about the nature of God, if it were read properly with expert guidance and only by those specially prepared. There are many elements that look like Merkavah mysticism in the *GosEg*. What this means is that whoever wrote this text had inside knowledge of esoteric Jewish traditions, and an interest in envisioning the true nature of God for others in his community (Merkavah was restricted to male sages) who would have understood the allusions.

BACKGROUND AND STRUCTURE OF THE TEXT

The *GosEg* contains three different sections, including a **cosmogony** in the first section, a narrative about Seth's activities in the world in the second section, and finally a liturgical handbook, which contains the names of beings who preside

over baptism. The book concludes with a hymn of praise for the newly baptized initiate. The entire *Holy Book* was therefore meant to be read but not *studied* as much as *consulted* by those preparing to baptize others. It may be useful to think of it as a handbook for a Sethian Christian service or Mass. In essence, the baptism ritual of the **Five Seals** at the end of the book is justified or explained

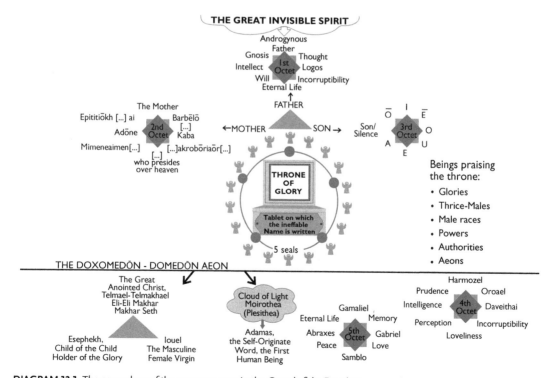

DIAGRAM 13.1 The cosmology of the upper cosmos in the *Gospel of the Egyptians*

TABLE 13.1: The Four Luminaries in the *Gospel of the Egyptians* and Their Celestial Attendants

Luminary	Quality associated with the luminary	Attending angel	Quality associated with the angel	Residents of the Luminary's realm
Harmozel	Loveliness	Gamaliel	Memory	Adamas
Oroiael	Perception	Gabriel	Love	Seth, Son of Man
Daveithai	Intelligence	Samblo	Peace	Offspring of Seth
Eleleth	Prudence	Abrasaks	Eternal life	Souls of the offspring

indirectly in the first part of the book, which gives details about the cosmic architecture and beings that are invoked during the ritual itself.

COSMOLOGY OF THE GOSPEL OF THE EGYPTIANS

In the first part of the treatise, we encounter a bewildering **cosmogony**. The *GosEg* portrays a very lively cosmos, full of swirling action and numerous celestial beings. You might envision it as colorful and filled with sound. The important thing to know, though, is that this is a cosmos that *emanates*; if many people nowadays imagine the cosmos coming about in a "Big Bang," the cosmos here is seen to be a series of emanations, a spilling over from an original source of being, the Great Invisible Spirit. This is a cosmos that grows outward or downward, each cosmic realm being full (the higher realm or **Pleroma** means, literally, the fullness) of beings and power.

In the ancient world, there were different ways of conceptualizing the universe. The most familiar to us was a model in which the heavenly bodies (planets, constellations of the zodiac, and the fixed stars) were encased in concentric spheres. This model derived from Greek astronomy and formed the basis for our current way of structuring the universe. But there were also other ancient models, including one where the universe was thought to be organized as a sort of heavenly court, with palaces and temples. Palaces and temples on earth, therefore, were the terrestrial correlates of a divine order or plan. This model

from the ancient Near East is present in Egyptian, Babylonian, and ancient Jewish sources.

In the *GosEg*, we find a model of the cosmos that is like a giant heavenly court, complete with a palace, celestial thrones, and scores of attendants and courtiers. This is reliant on earlier Jewish modes for thinking about the heavens; witness the book of Ezekiel 1:4–26, and even the New Testament's book of Revelation. At the focal point of this heavenly court is the **Domedon Doxomedon** aeon, where, seated on a huge throne, we find Seth, called here "the Thrice-Male Child." In this throne room we find litanies and hymns chanted by celestial beings, some of which are reproduced in the text.

If we consider the dramatis personae of the *GosEg*, we meet some familiar and unfamiliar characters. The primary being in this universe is the Great Invisible Spirit. He is accompanied by two other aspects of his creative energy, **Barbēlō** (also called Silence and **Pronoia**) and the **Thrice-Male Child.** While in many **Sethian** texts, these beings (or three aspects of one being) form the Primary Triad from which all things emanate, in *GosEg* there are actually *six* primary triads that emanate from the primary triad (see diagram 13.1).

This set of triads (very similar to the named beings in *Zostrianos*) produces, in turn, a set of important beings: Seth, **Adamas**, the self-begotten Son, and finally, the seed of Seth.

In a separate set of emanations, Prophania (Greek: "revelation") gives birth to the **Four Luminaries** plus their four partners and other divine beings (see table 13.1):

These beings along with their attendants constitute the whole of the upper cosmos, and they are all powerful, positive beings.

THE LOWER COSMOS AND ITS BEINGS

Unusually, it is the angel Eleleth who calls for beings to be created to rule over the lower cosmic realms (compare this with *HypArch*, where Eleleth is the Savior). In fact, the *GosEg* gives a very different account of the creation of these beings than other Sethian sources. Rather than the story of Sophia's creation as an aeon whose willful act of producing a child results in the monstrous Ialdabaoth (*ApJn*, *HypArch*), in *GosEg* Sophia appears only briefly, from a luminous cloud, and Ialdabaoth does not appear at all.

The angels Gamaliel and Gabriel literally speak into creation a male-female pair, **Sakla** and **Nebruel**, who sexually reproduce their own angelic assistants, whom Sakla dispatches to rule the lower realms. Their names are:

- Athoth
- Harmas
- Kalila
- Iobel
- Adonaios [also called Sabaoth]
- Cain, the Sun
- Abel
- Akiressina
- Ioubel
- Harmoupiael
- Archeir-Adonein
- Belias

This list is also found in other NH sources, such as the *ApJn* and *OrigWld*. Obviously the twelve angels listed have astral significance, associated with the twelve signs of the Zodiac and the planets (note that Cain is called "the Sun") (for more on these **archons**, see chap. 12).

At this point, the stage is set for **Seth**'s appearance and his act of sowing his seed through the cosmos and appointing four hundred angels to watch over them.

RECOUNTING SACRED HISTORY: A SETHIAN MASS

It can be useful to think of the *GosEg* as a holy book that a bishop or some other person of authority might have held in his hands during a service or **liturgy** of some sort. If the *GosEg* were a liturgy, here is how it might have worked. We can divide the text into sections that correspond to particular moments and actions in a hypothetical Sethian Christian mass:

1. Opening **doxology** or words describing and praising the Great Invisible Spirit (40:12–41:7)
2. Reading: Story of how three powers (Father, Mother, and Child) came forth from the Great Invisible Spirit (41:7–42:4)
3. Recitation of a list of the beings issuing forth from the first **Ogdoad** (Thought, Word, Incorruptibility, Eternal Life, Will, Mind, Foreknowledge, and the androgynous Father) and the second Ogdoad (includes the Mother, Barbl, Epititiokh […], Memeneaimen, Adonai, and the ineffable Mother, but the list is corrupt) of the Domedon Doxomedon aeon (42:5–21)
4. Observation of silence in honor of the ineffable Mother's appearance and the pleasure She took in the "silent silence" (42:21)
5. Recitation of the beings in the third Ogdoad (the Child, the Crown, the Glory of the Father, and the Virtue of the Mother)
6. Hymn or intonation of the seven voices (i.e., vowels) (43:8)
7. Recitation of the description of the Doxomedon aeon, with observed silences and intonations of vowel sounds (44:13)

RACE LANGUAGE IN *GOSPEL OF THE EGYPTIANS*

Certain documents from NH talk about something called the "incorruptible race" or the "heavenly race." It is easy to be thrown by such language, since we tend to understand "race" in a certain way in the modern world. However, the translation "race" is a bit misleading. The word in Greek (and in Coptic) is actually, literally, "generation" (*genea*). It has nothing to do with modern categories of what we call race, but it stems from the same root word that gives us other words like "progeny." In fact, "progeny" is not a bad translation for what many English translators have chosen to translate as "race."

In the ancient Christian context, different communities traced their spiritual ancestry to different figures from biblical history. As Christians, they believed, as did the Jews, that all people had descended from Adam and Eve, the first humans. But in Sethian mythology, Adam and Eve's stories were understood to be more complicated than we

find them in Genesis. For instance, in *HypArch*, Eve is raped by the evil, ignorant rulers, and from that rape Cain is born. By contrast, Abel is Eve's offspring by Adam. And a third child, a daughter called Norea, is Eve's "spiritual" offspring, whom she conceives without a human father (this is similar to stories of Mary's "virgin birth" of Jesus). Various communities therefore traced their ancestry—what they would call their "race"—back to Norea, their spiritual ancestor. In the case of the *GosEg*, the spiritual ancestor of their community or "generation" is also the third child of Adam and Eve, but here that child is not Norea but Seth, who is named in the book of Genesis (Gen 4:25). Just to make things even more complicated, all these earthly figures had heavenly twins or doubles: Sethian texts mention a heavenly Adam (**Adamas**) and a heavenly Seth. It is this divine Seth who is the true spiritual ancestor of the "immortal race."

8. Hymns of praise or doxologies to the Great Invisible Spirit and the male virgin Youel at the generation of the great Christ and the heavenly rite of the Five Seals (44:13)

9. Recitation of the next set of emanations (angels, powers, and glories) (IV 58:23–59:29)

10. Hymns of praise and glory to the divine beings, singing along with the celestial angels (IV 58:23–59:29)

11. Reading on the appearance of the Word, along with a sacred utterance ("…AIA…THATHSTH…Child of the [great] Christ, Child of the ineffable silence…") (IV 59:29)

12. Observation of Silence (IV 60:30)

13. Recitation of the Appearance of Adamas and the utterance of praise ("You are One; You are One; You are One, EA EA EA") (IV 60:30)

14. Hymn of Praise to the Heavenly Beings (III 50:17)

15. Darkening of the assembly room ("the world resembles the night") in preparation for the revelation of the Four Great Luminaries (51:1–5)

16. Lights appear in the assembly room to celebrate the birth of Harmozel, Oroiael, Daveithai, and Eleleth along with their angels (50:17–55:16)

17. Recitation: A narrative about the creation of matter and the "Fall," with the recitation of the twelve angels set over Hades and Chaos (56:22–60:2)

18. Reading: A narrative about the creation of humankind in the image (58:23–60:2)

19. Homily about the End of the Age, ending with Seth's prayer to the Invisible Spirit and a hymn of praise to Seth (61:1–62:12)

20. Reading of Seth's institution of the holy sacrament of baptism, followed by an angelic litany (63:23–66:8)

21. Baptism of initiates, culminating in a baptismal hymn (66:8–68:1).

This list is of course hypothetical, but it moves us in the right direction of thinking of this text as something that was not merely read by individuals in their rooms but was used for a community. That cannot be said of every text found at Nag Hammadi, or even of every Sethian text, but the emphasis in the *GosEg* on hymns and doxologies strongly suggests that it was produced for liturgical use.

WHAT ARE THOSE STRINGS OF VOWELS?

In chapter 44 of *GosEg*, we come across something strange: a series of vowels written out. Was it an ancient chant? Was it sung? Are the number of letters in each vowel series intentional? If you have been reading this textbook sequentially, you will already have come across a similar thing in chapter 1. Actually, strings of vowel sounds like this are quite common in magical spells from Greco-Roman antiquity, where they are called **voces magicae** or *voces mysticae*. The way that they were written was part of their efficacy, and if you look carefully you'll notice that each vowel is written twenty-two times. Thus we can rearrange them as follows:

```
IIIIIIIIIIIIIIIIIIIIII
EEEEEEEEEEEEEEEEEEEEEE
OOOOOOOOOOOOOOOOOOOOOO
UUUUUUUUUUUUUUUUUUUUUU
ĒĒĒĒĒĒĒĒĒĒĒĒĒĒĒĒĒĒĒĒĒĒ
AAAAAAAAAAAAAAAAAAAAAA
ŌŌŌŌŌŌŌŌŌŌŌŌŌŌŌŌŌŌŌŌŌŌ
```

The Yale scholar Bentley Layton noted a few things about this arrangement. First, he noted that this string of vowels was said to have been written on a tablet on the throne of the Thrice-Male Child, almost like a label. Second, he noticed that if you read the tablet as an acrostic—if you read the first line down vertically—it spells out IEOU Ē A (alpha) Ō (omega). The word IEOU is actually a name for God in some third-century sources (such as the *Books of Jeu*, where the name Jeu = Ieou). The letter E (epsilon) may stand here for the number five (epsilon, the fifth letter of the Greek alphabet and used to represent numbers). Five, in turn, was a symbol of wholeness and may represent the original Pentad of beings in the highest aeon. Finally, the letters A (alpha) and Ō (omega) are the first and last

letters of the Greek alphabet and also symbolize the wholeness of God; in the New Testament's book of Revelation, Jesus states that he is the "Alpha and the Omega, the first and the last, the beginning and the end" (Rev 22:13). To put this all together, the string of vowels represent not a meaningless chant, but a condensed symbol for God, or God's ineffable name.

There is a second string of vowel sounds later in the tractate: *uaeieisaeieioeieiosei*. Although this sounds like nonsense to our ears, the vowels can be partitioned to read (in Greek): *u aei eis aei ei o ei ei os ei*. Roughly translated, this means: "[You] who exists as Son for ever and ever. You are what you are, you are who you are."

What all this seems to suggest is that, however nonsensical the strings of vowels may sound to us and our modern ears, ancient hearers would have responded to them quite differently. The sounds were "spiritual sounds," which related to the sounds of the cosmos or the higher beings, and most of all, these sounds could be (and were) interpreted. For example, in another Gnostic text, the **Pistis Sophia**, Jesus speaks in *voces magicae* that are interpreted and explained for the readers or listeners to the text:

> And Jesus cried out as he faced the four corners of the world with his disciples . . . and he said IAO IAO IAO. This is its interpretation: iota, because the All came forth; alpha, because it will return again; omega, because the completion of all completions will happen" (chap. 136, trans. Violet MacDermot, in Carl Schmidt and Violet MacDermot, editors and translators, *Pistis Sophia* [Leiden: E. J. Brill, 1978]: 707).

Not much of a helpful interpretation, really! Nevertheless, the sense is that Jesus's mystical sounds actually mean something to those who have ears to listen.

THE THREE DESCENTS OF SETH

In the second part of *GosEg*, Seth descends to earth three separate times. His first descent takes place at the great flood (Gen 6). Seth comes again when the towns of Sodom and Gomorrah burn

the Christ of this text (and of Christianity) best understood as a form of Seth? Or is Seth different from, and superior to, Christ or Jesus? The text does not tell us, unfortunately. What we do know is that the scribe who copied the manuscript in Codex III was Christian and evidently considered this a Christian text. He gives his name as Concessus, and then includes an acrostic spelling out the letters *IXTHUS*, the first letters of the Greek phrase "Jesus Christ, Son of God, Savior" (III 69:6–17). More intriguingly, however, Concessus also gives us another name,

his "spiritual name": Eugnostos. *Eugnostos* is a Greek word that means, literally, "well-known." Ironically, this name isn't very common, but it is curious that it is also the name of another possibly non-Christian writing from Nag Hammadi: *Eugnostos* (sometimes called *Eugnostos the Blessed*). At any rate, Congessus/Eugnostos is quite clear: the work he is doing copying the text is holy, for he salutes his fellow spiritual brothers, and notes, in words that seem to convey a sense of awe and pride, that God himself wrote *The Holy Book of the Great Invisible Spirit*.

QUESTIONS TO CONSIDER

1. Do you agree with most scholars that the *Gospel of the Egyptians* is Christian? Why or why not?

2. What are some of the key differences you can detect between the *GosEg* and another important Sethian text, the *ApJn*? Can you use these differences to get a sense of what sorts of things might have been a matter of dispute or discussion in Sethian circles?

3. Did the person who wrote *GosEg* think of the heavens and its workings as malevolent or beneficent?

KEY TERMS

colophon	*voces magicae* (or *voces mysticae*)	Clement of Alexandria
Five Seals	Seed of Seth	cosmology
Domedon Doxomedon	Ogdoad	Sakla
Pronoia	Barbēlō	Nebruel
liturgy	Pleroma	archon
doxology	Thrice-Male Child	Pistis Sophia
Sethian Gnosticism	Four Luminaries	Logos
cosmogony	Adamas	
Merkavah (or Merkabah)	Johannine Prologue	

FOR FURTHER READING

Forman, Werner, and Stephen Quirke. *Hieroglyphs and the Afterlife in Ancient Egypt*. Norman: University of Oklahoma Press, 1996. A fascinating read on the *Amduat* by two top Egyptologists.

14

Dealing with Death

THE FIRST APOCALYPSE OF JAMES (NHC V, 3), THE SECOND APOCALYPSE OF JAMES (NHC V, 4), THE APOCRYPHON OF JAMES (NHC I, 2), AND TREATISE ON THE RESURRECTION (NHC I, 4)

People die. Mortality is perhaps the single most poignant existential reality that faces us. Death—the reality of it, or even just the thought of our own mortality and the mortality of those we love—evokes some of our strongest emotions: fear, dread, sorrow. But many of us rarely confront death. Most deaths take place in hospitals, and the bodies of our loved ones are whisked away by professionals who prepare their bodies away from our view. Many people have no personal experience of death, nor have they ever seen a corpse, let alone watched someone die.

But let's transport ourselves back to the second century, when most of our Nag Hammadi texts were being written. There, in the world of the Roman Empire, death was less hidden, and arguably less controlled. The average life expectancy hovered around twenty-four years—a bit more for men, a bit less for women (compare this with the average life expectancy in the United States in 2006: 77.7 years). Such a low life expectancy

did not mean people only lived to the age of twenty-five. The number is low in part because infant mortality rates were so high. For example, in third-century Rome, one-third of live-born children were dead by age one; one-half by age five, two-thirds by age thirty-one, 80 percent by forty-nine and 92 percent by age sixty-two. Those lucky (or hardy) enough to make it to adulthood stood a fairly good chance of living a respectably long life.

Certain geographic, social, and economic factors determined mortality rates. A city like Alexandria on the Mediterranean provided a healthier environment than Rome, which lay along the murky Tiber River that provided breeding ground for malaria and typhoid. Rome's emphasis on economic and military expansion brought back previously unknown diseases from the East that decimated the population. Under the emperor Marcus Aurelius, a period that coincided with the authorship of many of our Nag Hammadi writings, Roman legions brought back plagues from the eastern areas of the Empire that devastated populations, which had no natural immunities. Men died in battle; women died in childbirth. Slaves probably lived shorter, more brutal lives than their masters; the very rich, however, suffered from their own diseases brought about through excessive lifestyles. Some diseases simply did not discriminate. In short, there were many ways to die a horrible death in the Roman Empire, and most people had deep and personal experiences of loss.

AFTERLIFE CONCEPTIONS IN THE ROMAN EMPIRE

People in the Roman Empire had differing opinions on what happened after death. Did one cease to exist? Did one become one of the "restless shades" of a Homeric-like afterlife? Was there such a thing as reincarnation, or does the soul live eternally among the stars? Was there even a soul? Generally speaking, second-century Romans did not believe that any part of us continued on after death. Thus literally hundreds, if not thousands, of Roman pagan tombstones bear mournful epitaphs expressing the sense that death was final. One epitaph sums up a laconic attitude; it reads "*Sum, non sum, fui, non fui, non curo*" ("I am, I am not. I was, I was not. I don't care"). This sentiment was expressed frequently enough that sometimes Romans just used the abbreviation *SNSFNFNC*!

But ideas about the afterlife were in flux in this era. Christianity, although still in the process of formation, offered its adherents a promise of some sort of enduring existence after death, and that appears to be one feature that actively drew new followers. Considering that life in the Empire was "solitary, poor, nasty, brutish, and short," to quote the philosopher Thomas Hobbes, it is little wonder that the Christian promise of life in paradise inspired so many.

Varying religious groups in Rome offered adherents the promise of an eternal blessed afterlife, but no one did so with greater force and clarity of vision and hope than Christians. Beyond the common conviction that Christians need not fear death and would live in eternal repose (the term at the time was **refrigerium**, "refreshment"), Christians themselves still debated what that afterlife looked like, and what needed to be done before death in order to secure that afterlife. Was it enough to be a good person? Or did one need sacraments such as baptism and chrism (anointment with oil) to be safe? Was resurrection literal and physical (the flesh itself would be restored) or was it metaphorical or spiritual? Where did the soul go on its ascent? To paradise? To some other physical realm (e.g., the area around the moon, or to another planetary sphere)? Was there such a thing as reincarnation, or was the ascent of the soul a one-way trip to a new, permanent celestial abode?

THE PROBLEM OF DEATH IN NAG HAMMADI TEXTS

We have considered different ways to divide up or "cluster" Nag Hammadi writings in order to better understand what concerns drove the composition of those texts. We might look at a cluster of texts that share a doctrinal affiliation, such as **Valentinianism** or **Sethianism** (chaps. 6–8 and chaps. 10–12). Or, we might consider grouping texts by literary genre, such as apocalyptic (chap. 18 and chap. 19). But certain widespread concerns cut across virtually all categories, affiliations, and literary genres; death was the greatest of these concerns. Since the "problem of death" was inescapable in the era in which the NH texts were written, it can be helpful to think about the way in which certain of these writings directly or indirectly express anxieties about death. We can identify three different sets of problems that raised anxieties:

1. The Problem of Resurrection
2. The Problem of Martyrdom
3. The Problem of the Afterlife

While one can consider virtually any of the NH writings from the perspective of what they reveal about concerns about death, a few of them are particularly interesting to consider because they directly engage these three issues. Let's take these issues in turn, then, and consider how they play out in a small cross-section of NH literature: the *First Apocalypse of James* and *Second Apocalypse of James*, the *Apocryphon of James*, and the *Treatise on the Resurrection*.

THE PROBLEM OF RESURRECTION

Christianity differed quite radically from any other religion in the ancient world because it taught that Jesus had returned or "resurrected" from the dead. In fact, an early faith statement was that Jesus had suffered and died, but then been literally brought back to life. To believe that this was possible became a key element of what it meant to be a Christian. From there, however, problems began to emerge. What kind of a resurrection was this, anyway? Was Jesus an animated corpse, like a modern-day zombie? Apparently not, but if not, how can dead flesh reanimate? Or, was this resurrection not a literal resurrection of the flesh, but something more paranormal, almost like the appearance of a ghost or, to use more ancient language, a shade?

And then there were the implications of such a doctrine as resurrection for ordinary Christians. Did everyone resurrect, or just Jesus? If everyone did, then what about people who had been cremated (cremation was the standard way to dispose of the dead in the second century)? What if someone died at sea, or was eaten by fish or animals? How could that person resurrect in the flesh? And did the resurrected Christian look just the same as when she or he died, or was the resurrection body perfect: if someone had lost a limb, for instance, would the resurrected body have that limb restored? And if the resurrected body was a sort of angelic body rather than a zombie body, did people still need teeth, since they would not have to eat, or genitals, since they would not procreate? All these points were actively disputed in the second century, and we find them discussed explicitly in a number of early Christian writings, the most famous of which is Athenagoras of Athens's *Treatise on the Resurrection* (ca. 180 CE). But the problem had started with the writings of the New Testament itself, which had sometimes inscrutable things to say about Jesus's own death and resurrection, let alone whether all Christ-followers would also resurrect. Let's look at some of those issues and passages in the NT.

Jesus's Resurrection

One of the earliest Christian **creeds**—a condensation of beliefs to be memorized and recited—comes from Paul's First Letter to the Corinthians chapter 15, and can be dated to around the middle of the first century, perhaps only twenty years after Jesus's death. The creed summarizes the orthodox Christian position:

- Christ died for our sins, as Hebrew scripture had predicted (1 Cor 15:3, 4).
- He was buried, and then was raised on the third day, again as the scripture had predicted (15:4)
- He appeared to Cephas (Simon Peter) then to the twelve disciples (1 Cor 15:5).

The "death event" of Jesus, then, was central to Christian belief, just as it remains today. But it came to be developed even further. Here is a portion of the **Nicene Creed**, which is still used by liturgical Christians today. It condenses a series of convictions concerning the death and resurrection of Jesus Christ:

For us and for our salvation he came down from heaven: by the power of the Holy Spirit he became incarnate from the Virgin Mary, and was made man. For our sake he was crucified under Pontius Pilate; he suffered death and was buried. On the third day he rose again in accordance with the Scriptures; he ascended into heaven and is seated at the right hand of the Father. He will come again in glory to judge the living and the dead, and his kingdom will have no end.

So from the first through the fourth centuries Christians developed the idea of Christ's ascension to heaven, the Second Coming, and the Judgment of the Dead. The details of these beliefs were still a matter of controversy.

What exactly resurrects? The NT gospels provide no clear picture. In the Gospel of John for example, we find a number of post-resurrection appearances of Jesus. In one narrative, Mary Magdalene goes to visit Jesus's tomb but finds it empty (Jn 20). She sees a man standing nearby and thinks it is the custodian of the cemetery. Only when he speaks to her does she realize it is Jesus. Why couldn't she recognize him? Is it just that she wasn't expecting to see Jesus again, or is there something else going on here? Does he look physically different in his resurrection body? There seems to be a hint that the latter interpretation is meant to be correct; when Mary reaches out to grasp her teacher, he moves away from her with a strong admonition: "Do not hold me, for I have not yet ascended to the Father" (Jn 20:17). No one has a clear sense of what Jesus meant. Why couldn't Mary touch him? What would have happened if she had? Would she have somehow defiled him so that he would be unable to "ascend to his Father"? Why had he not already ascended to his Father, given that he was already dead? Where had he been in the interim? Or, if she had grabbed him, would he have been a mere wraith in her arms, insubstantial, a ghost?

A second post-resurrection episode in the Gospel of John is no clearer. When his disciple Thomas cannot believe that Jesus has resurrected from the dead, Jesus tells the "doubting" Thomas to put his fingers in the wound in his side, so that he might believe (Jn 20:24–29).

There can be no more visceral way of proving to an audience that Jesus's resurrection body is both physical and the same body he had during his life. He is no ghost. And yet in the same gospel, Jesus suddenly appears to his disciples in a locked room (Jn 20:19). If his body was physical, how did he suddenly appear in a locked room without walking in the door? Here, in this passage, Jesus seems more like an apparition, a miracle appearance of someone whose body is spiritual, not fleshly.

The post-resurrection appearances of Jesus in the gospels proves that even very early on, Christians hotly disputed what seemed to be a crazy, impossible idea: that Jesus Christ rose *bodily* from the dead. People in the Roman Empire were no more gullible than we are today, and to assert such a thing struck most people as absurd, even grotesque. The doctrine of the resurrection, then, stood as a major stumbling block in getting people to believe. It needed to be sorted out in a sensible, thoughtful way.

The Resurrection of the (Ordinary) Dead

As a rule, those Christians we call Gnostic had a substantial education, particularly in Greek philosophy, and while few disputed the idea of an eternal soul, most took issue with what came to be a central tenet of mainstream Christianity: that the flesh would rise again, and that the resurrection was a literal event. The idea defied reason, and Christians asserting the idea could not even cite scriptures to support their position. Thus some held that resurrection had already happened as a spiritual event. By "spiritual" event, these Christians appear to have meant something like "metaphorical," since literal resurrection was an absurd idea. This interpretation is an ancient one, because Paul, the author of the NT letter known as 2 Timothy, rails against it as an offensive idea (2 Tim 2:18: those "who have swerved from the truth by holding that the resurrection is past already" are "upsetting the faith of some").

But we find it actively discussed in one writing from the NHL, the *Treatise on the Resurrection* (*TreatRes*).

Treatise on the Resurrection (NHC 1,4)

This brief, undated letter of instruction offers one particular interpretation of Christian resurrection. Its anonymous author believed that Christ himself had given him the answers to common concerns about the nature of resurrection (49:41–50:2). Evidently, an ordinary Christian by the name of Rheginus, curious about what he had heard about Valentinian teachings on the resurrection, approached our letterwriter to learn more. The *TreatRes* provides an exposition, drawing upon technical Valentinian vocabulary, which the author then offers to explain in the "next installment" of teachings. The author of the *TreatRes* seems to have been a Valentinian, insofar as he appears to agree with Tertullian's characterization of Valentinus: that he taught that the resurrection already happened (*De praes. Haer.* 33.7; *De res. Mort.* 19, 2–7).

The author makes the following arguments:

1. To be resurrected, one must have faith in Jesus's resurrection and the fact that Jesus overcame death.

2. The resurrection is not the resurrection of a spiritual body at Christ's Second Coming. Instead, it is a form of *gnosis* or spiritual awakening to the unreality of the world, which this author sees as an illusion (48:19).

The *TreatRes* is an interesting text, in that besides the teaching that the "resurrection has already happened"—one of **Irenaeus**'s "benchmarks" of Christian heresy (*Adv. Haer.* 2.31.2)—the letter itself at first glance appears to be full of ideas that are fairly uncontroversial from the perspective of later orthodox Christianity. Consider these excerpts:

> The Son of God, Rheginos, was the Son of Man. He embraced both, having both humanity and divinity, that he might vanquish death. (44:22–27)

> The Savior swallowed up death...then, indeed, as the Apostle said, "we suffered with him; we rose with him, we went to heaven with him."(45:15–29, paraphrasing Paul's 1 Cor 15:54; 2 Cor. 5:4)

> If there is someone who does not believe, he cannot be persuaded. For this belongs to faith, my son; it is not a matter of persuasion: the dead shall arise!...We have known the Son of Man, and we have believed that he rose from the dead....Great are those who believe! (46:3–21)

In the first quotation, Jesus has both human and divine natures. And yet, what this author has to say about Jesus's incarnation—that he came to "vanquish death"—means something a bit different than we might expect; he goes on to associate death not with sin but with the corruptible world. As in the later orthodox position, the *TreatRes* calls for people to have faith, that the dead shall arise, and that Jesus himself rose from the dead. But here again, the author likely meant something a bit unusual. Using Pauline language—that Jesus "swallowed up" death—the author infers that Jesus revealed the entire visible world to be merely illusory. Only spiritual existence is real, he argues, and the recognition of this important fact is what "the resurrection" really means. Thus the *TreatRes* picks up on the controversial "talking points" concerning the nature of the resurrection in second-century debates, expressing them in ways that reflect an esoteric teaching, which replaces a literal understanding of Jesus "resurrecting in the flesh" with a metaphorical one. To "rise again" is really a spiritual awakening, when a Christian recognizes the world to be essentially illusory; it does not involve actually dying at all but fundamentally changing one's understanding of the world.

That the dead will resurrect was a challenging idea. It defied logic, and Christians argued that it could be understood only through faith. In fact, the classic juxtaposition of "faith" with "reason" that defines the ongoing Christian theological debates probably started around this time, as Christians of the first and second centuries tried to figure out what the doctrine of resurrection might be. The most pressing "live" issue by the second century was whether "the resurrection" was literal or metaphorical, and by extension, whether it had already happened (as a metaphor for spiritual awakening or gnosis) or was still to come, as a metaphorical event. The classic view of **Gnosticism** constructed by its opponents is that Gnostics rejected the reality of Jesus rising again from the dead, considering it only as something that "already happened." The NHL's *TreatRes* shows us that the issue was substantially more complicated than that.

THE PROBLEM OF MARTYRDOM

Christianity began as a unique event, with the voluntary death of Jesus at the hands of the Roman authorities. As such, Christianity was in a sense adversarial from the start; many Christians viewed Rome as a demonic power that had tortured and killed God's son. And as Christianity began to grow and develop a public face, some Christians (particularly those who spoke out against Rome as a political entity) were, like Jesus, rounded up and put to death. One question that emerged, therefore, was whether martyrdom was more or less a requirement to be a "good" faithful Christian. Was it a faithful act of imitating Jesus? Or did his self-sacrifice make subsequent sacrifices unnecessary? Martyrdom is an extreme act, and most Christians were more moderate in their beliefs, choosing not to be put to death if they could avoid it. Whether you thought martyrdom were necessary was also connected to your belief about the nature of Jesus's body and incarnation. For instance, those who espoused **docetism** (teaching that Jesus was not really human, but more of a spiritual being who only seemed human) did not believe that Jesus really had suffered and died, since it was impossible for a god to die. We can see this same idea reflected in a number of texts from NH, the *Paraphrase of Shem*, the *Second Treatise of the Great Seth*, the *Apocalypse of Peter*, and (to a lesser extent), the *Gospel of Philip*.

One issue concerning martyrdom was how to behave if and when you had been arrested, tortured, and were facing death. Christians, knowing the agony that they would face, circulated these teachings, some of which advocated practical management in things like pain control, through a sort of self-hypnotization (for example, one early Christian writer called Cyprian advocated meditating on the torture instruments rather than the pain). Other pieces of advice included the reassuring words that the pain would not actually hurt, or that the rewards in heaven would be so great that martyrdom of the flesh was but a small price to pay. Finally, some literature circulated that gave those facing martyrdom prayers or a script to memorize, in order to be properly prepared.

One of the traditional—and oversimplified—perspectives on Gnosticism is that the Gnostics rejected the call to martyrdom. The idea was first put forth in a famous article by an esteemed historian of early Christianity, W. H. C. Frend, in an article "The Gnostic Sects and the Roman Empire" in 1954. Frend assembled evidence from standard early Christian sources, which suggested that most Gnostics refused the call to martyrdom. The evidence seems, at first, quite convincing:

- Justin Martyr (103–165 CE) claimed that the Gnostics were "neither persecuted nor put to death"
- Irenaeus claimed that the Valentinians made fun of Christian martyrs (*Adv. Haer.* 3.18.5) and that the followers of another Gnostic teacher, **Basilides**, denied Christ so as to avoid being tortured (*Adv. Haer.* 1.24.6)
- Tertullian called Gnostics the "opponents of martyrdom" and complained that, in the middle of horrific persecutions of Christians, they "went about as usual."

Frend concluded, on the basis of this information, that only "true" Christians bravely faced the beasts, and that Gnostics argued their way out of the ultimate sacrifice. This view implied that one way we might distinguish "true" Christians from hypocritical ones (or true Christianity from false or heretical Christianity) is by examining their views on martyrdom.

And then came Nag Hammadi. For the first time, we had the texts that were quickly classified as Gnostic, which did not reject martyrdom outright; by contrast, a few even gave instructions for what to do if one were in the position of facing the Roman authorities and their killing beasts. Since this kind of advice would have been dangerous to dispense in the charged political atmosphere of the Roman Empire, the writings usually focused on accounts of the martyrdom of early disciples facing opposition from the Jewish authorities; by removing blame from the Romans in power to the Jews, the subversive or revolutionary elements of these writings could be lessened. For this reason, the three NHL tractates that discuss martyrdom directly all focus not on their contemporary situation but on James, Jesus's brother.

The first NH writing to present a surprising acceptance of martyrdom and a willingness to accept that Jesus suffered, died, and was resurrected is a brief tractate in Codex One, the *Apocryphon of James*.

The *Apocryphon of James* (NHC I, 2)

The *Apocryphon of James* (*ApJas*) appears in a single version, quite well preserved, in Codex I. Sixteen pages long, it was at some unknown point translated from its original Greek into Coptic. As we have it now, it is in the form of a letter that the apostle James sent to an unknown recipient (unfortunately, there's a **lacuna** in the manuscript right where the name should be). It purports to contain secret revelations that Jesus wished to be revealed only to a few special disciples. The setting for the letter is 550 days (one and a half years) after Jesus's crucifixion, where his remaining disciples gather to write down what they remember of the Lord's words (2:7–15).

This "secret book" (1:10) (Gk, *apokryphon*) presents an image of Jesus that for readers of the New Testament does not seem quite so unfamiliar. After all, there is much here that resembles the gospels: we have familiar characters (Jesus, his brother James, and the disciple Simon Peter, plus the mention of twelve disciples); a Jesus who speaks in parables (and alludes to parables in our NT gospels); and post-resurrection appearances. The language and style of the apocryphon is also strongly reminiscent of the so-called farewell discourses of the Gospel of John 13:31–17:26, in which Jesus speaks to his disciples about the nature of his Father's kingdom before his crucifixion. Yet there are also things that are unfamiliar. Jesus's teachings—things such as the need to "become full" or the confusing distinctions between soul and spirit—have no real parallels with NT materials.

One of the most distinctive passages of the *ApocJas* concerns Jesus's teachings on martyrdom. Here, he makes it quite clear that to follow him faithfully, one must "scorn death" and "become seekers of death." The disciples are troubled by his words, but Jesus insists that salvation must be found through martyrdom:

> The Lord answered and said, "Truly I say to you, none will be saved unless they believe in my cross, for God's kingdom belongs to those who have believed in my cross. Be seekers of death, like the dead who seek life, for what they seek becomes apparent to them. And what is there to cause them concern? As for you, when you search out death, it will teach you about being chosen. I tell you the truth, no one afraid of death will be saved, for the kingdom of death belongs to those who put themselves to death. (6:1–19)

These troubling teachings were nonetheless pragmatic in an age where the persecution of Christians was, although not common, a tragic reality. The *ApocJas*, then, proves that at least some Gnostics were as likely to teach that facing death bravely was following the teachings of the Lord.

The *ApocJas* stops short of giving an account of James's martyrdom; instead, the setting is close to the NT gospels' account of Jesus's Transfiguration,

WHY JAMES?

James is the hero of a number of Nag Hammadi texts. He is often known by his title, "James the Just" (the word for "just" can also be translated as "righteous"), in the sense that he had taken ascetic vows. His name is the anglicized version of the Hebrew name "Jacob." We find him in the *ApocJas*, the *1stApocJas*, and the *2ndApocJas*. He also pops up in strange places, including saying #12 from the *GThom* where he is, curiously, named as Jesus's designated successor: ("No matter where you come [from] it is to James the Just that you shall go, for whose sake heaven and earth have come

to exist") and in **Codex Tchacos** (which contains a second complete copy of the *1st ApocJas*). To complicate matters, there are three different Jameses preserved in early Christian literature: James, Jesus's half brother (Gal 1:19); James, the son of Alphaeus, and James, the son of Zebedee, one of the disciples (see Mt 10:1–4). It is far from clear, however, that early Christians always kept these Jameses distinct in their minds. It seems, however, that the James of this literature is James the Just, the brother of Jesus, and not the other disciples named James.

---

a miraculous event where the disciples James, Peter, and John witness Jesus's ascension upon a mountain where he is transformed ("transfigured") into a luminous being and speaks with the prophets Elijah and Moses (Mt 17:1–9; Mk 9:2–8; Lk 9:28–36). At the end of the *ApocJas* tractate, James and Peter make their own visionary ascent to the heavens where they see and hear angelic hosts, but they return to lead their own disciples in Jerusalem. However, the other two NH tractates that bear the name of James in their title do, in fact, provide very explicit guides to early Christians facing martyrdom. The first of these, the *(Second) Apocalypse of James*, we discuss briefly in this part of the chapter. Its sister text, the *(First) Apocalypse of James*, we save for our examination of views on the afterlife, since it offers explicit information there that is both unusual and remarkable.

The *(Second) Apocalypse of James* (NHC V, 4)

This fragmentary text from Codex V is not a martyr text nor, as the title seems to suggest, an apocalypse, but a **revelation discourse,** a genre where Jesus makes pronouncements about the nature of the kingdom; in fact, there is very little

about *2ndApJas* as it now stands that identifies it as an apocalypse.

This tractate contains a fairly detailed account of James's martyrdom by stoning. We know from other ancient sources that the stoning of James was a historical event in the year 62 CE. Stoning was the capital punishment that first-century Jewish law stipulated for, among other crimes, the crime of blasphemy. Unlike Jesus's crucifixion, which was a strictly Roman punishment—usually for the crime of treason against Rome—James's death tells us that he caught the eyes of Jerusalem's high priests and a ruling judicial body known as the Sanhedrin. According to ancient sources, James's activity as a "missionary" for Jesus's message (to say "Christianity" would be anachronistic; James and Jesus were both Jewish) raised the ire of the Sanhedrin. Here, the prayer that James offers up as he is being stoned presents an example for later Christians of how one should behave under similar conditions, thus providing comfort and instruction to the persecuted. The inclusion of this prayer indicates an important thing: the Gnostics reading this text were not likely to have believed, as their ancient enemies claimed, that martyrdom was best avoided as an act of stupidity. Rather, the

2ndApJas provides practical guidance for those who faced the beasts.

The *2ndApJas* explores the relationship between James and Jesus, and this text gives us more information on the relation between the two than any other early Christian text. They are clearly named as stepbrothers, sharing the same mother but different fathers. There is an intimacy to that relationship; Jesus's mother tells James not to fear Jesus, since they were nourished with the same milk; later, Jesus, as brother to brother, kisses James on the mouth. Indeed, the *2ndApJas* says more about family relationships than any other treatise from Nag Hammadi; notice how often words for family members are used: father, brother, mother, and son appear often in this writing.

Throughout the text Jesus is consistently portrayed as a powerful, pre-existent being, not as a human son as James is. In essence, this writing had to do an important job: it had to articulate a relationship between brothers in such a way as to assert Jesus's heavenly nature at the same time as asserting James's earthly nature. Jesus is therefore someone who comes directly from the **Pleroma**; he "stripped himself" and became "perishable," mortal. Like its sister text, the *1stApJas*, the *2ndApJas* contains a number of hymnic fragments, which we surmise were older than the text and added to it. These fragments are about the incarnation, the descent of Jesus into the flesh, and most use the language of Jesus being "stripped" or wearing a "garment,"—conventional language in the ancient world for the soul coming to inhabit a body, then shedding that body at death. In fact, the earliest of these hymnic fragments we can find embedded in the NT, particularly the **Johannine Prologue** of the Gospel of John (1:1–14) and the lovely "kenosis hymn" of Philippians 2:6–11.

Jesus, as a heavenly being, can come and go through the lower cosmos freely. He makes, in fact, a sort of parabolic arc: he comes down from the Pleroma, puts on a human body; that body is put to death, and then the divine nature of Jesus returns to its source. But James, too, faces martyrdom, and seeks Jesus's help with surviving the ordeal. As a human, he does not make the same round-trip journey as Jesus did during his incarnation. But this is where James becomes an important example for ordinary Christians: those facing an early, ugly death were more likely to identify (and be able to be comforted by) James's fate than by Jesus's fate.

THE PROBLEM OF THE AFTERLIFE

Christians of the second century were not necessarily inclined to spend a lot of time thinking about what the afterlife looked like as a physical place or space; the important thing was that one's loved ones lived in repose in this place until the general resurrection of the dead. Early Christian art never shows anything that looks like many later views of "heaven" but sometimes shows their deceased beloved in a pastoral or garden setting. Still, there was a fair amount of interest in the soul's voyage through physical space after it left the body, before it came to rest eternally with God, in our written sources.

One theme that remains consistent in second-century Christian writings is that the soul faces dangers after death and that it is drawn back to its source in the upper cosmos. These dangers were manifold, but in many of our Gnostic sources they took the form of monstrous archontic beings who might seize the soul and trap it in an intermediary zone, which the *Gospel of Philip* refers to as the "Middle," that is, somewhere between Earth and the Pleroma. The idea that the soul would face trials on its ascent to heaven has a rich tradition in antiquity; it is possible that Egyptian traditions, which feature accounts of the soul's encounter with hostile beings in its journey through the underworld, may have had some influence here. Prominent Christian theologians of the late third and fourth centuries, such as **Athanasius**, Origen, and Cyril of Alexandria, all attest to the belief that malevolent beings threaten the soul. In these fourth-century writings, the hostile beings usually took the form of lions and snakes. A fourth-century tombstone of a Christian named Beratius Nikatoras from Rome depicts Jesus as the Good Shepherd with a lamb on shoulders; to his left faces him a lion with threatening jaws, to his right, a monster with a man dangling in his jaws. And Augustine, writing from North Africa, offered up a prayer for his mother, Monica, after her death: "let no one snatch her from Thy protection. Let neither the lion nor the dragon interpose himself by force or deceit. For she will not answer that she owes nothing, lest she be proved wrong and snatched by the cunning accuser" (*Confessions*, 9.13.36).

In our second-century texts, sometimes the malevolent beings that threaten the soul take the form of certain malevolent qualities, such as fear or envy, since their authors believed that negative emotions come from the cosmos (our bodies do not generate them; they are placed in us as the soul incarnates in the body) where they are associated with certain planets (see chap. 20). Although this sounds strange, consider that we use words in English connected to the planets to describe people's personalities: quiet and surly people are saturnine (like Saturn), happy people can be jovial (like Jupiter), people with changeable natures and tempers are mercurial (like Mercury), and the insane are lunatics (influenced by the moon). Some have suggested that the later nonbiblical but Catholic list of Seven Deadly Sins (wrath, greed, sloth, pride, lust, envy, and gluttony) may have been developed from qualities originally associated with the planets, such as lust from Venus and wrath from Mars.

According to ancient logic, as the soul travels upward through the planetary spheres, it sheds these negative emotions, leaving them at their source. How successful the soul is at shedding negative emotion, however, appears to be related to how good a person was during his or her lifetime. Certain concepts of Christian morality, therefore, developed not because it was thought to be important to be good "for goodness' sake," or because one should emulate Jesus, or because one would be directly rewarded for it in heaven, but because one would not successfully reach "heaven" before malevolent vice demons or planetary influences claimed the badly behaved soul back to their realm.

HOW DID THE SACRAMENTS HELP?

Interestingly, many Christians of the second century insisted that it was not enough to simply be a good person in order to successfully complete the soul's voyage after death back to eternal repose.

THE FATE OF SOULS IN GRAECO-ROMAN THOUGHT

The belief in the continued existence of souls after death had already had a long history in second-century Rome, as the great Roman statesman Cicero had written a century earlier in his *Tusculan Disputations* (1.12.27). Platonism was one significant source of these ideas. There were debates among Graeco-Roman philosophers on where souls went after death. Some claimed that souls went to the moon; some, to the region below the moon. Others believed that souls went up to the region of fixed stars, or actually became stars. Some taught that souls went into a celestial holding area, before being reincarnated into new bodies. Even in Christianity, the concepts of heaven and hell were not fully developed and instead reflect these Platonist debates.

Learning to restrain or repress negative emotions such as envy or lust might help, some claimed, but others insisted that some other sort of ritual intervention was necessary to completely protect the soul.

One of the key functions of the sacraments of baptism and **chrism** was to protect the soul from malevolent demons that hindered its ascent. Both sacraments had the ability to transform the soul into a "light being" so that it could not be seen by the celestial demons. Besides this practical, protective ("apotropaic") element to these sacraments, performing such a rite on earth during a person's lifetime enabled whoever performed these sacraments to speak certain words or formulae that could act either as celestial passwords (allowing the soul to pass by a demon) or as a sort of spell that would actively repel or cancel the evil influence of those demons. This kind of practical knowledge of passwords or "ascent formulae" constitute another category of *gnosis*, and we find an all-consuming interest in it in the NHL as well as virtually all our other Gnostic manuscripts outside the NHL. In fact, some of our longest, most elaborate Gnostic writings, the **Pistis Sophia** and the **Books of Jeu**, are actually compilations of passwords, symbols, maps, ascent formulae, and other bits of practical knowledge for the souls after death. Because they all seem to have been composed in Egypt, it is fair to think of them as Christian "Books of the Dead," which took over a very ancient Egyptian tradition of providing explicit, detailed instructions to the deceased in order to be prepared for the afterlife.

One text from NH that pulls together these various teachings on the afterlife ascent of the soul is the (*First*) *Apocalypse of James*.

The (First) Apocalypse of James (NHC V, 3)

Codex V contains two different texts, one right after the other, each titled *Apocalypse of James*. We differentiate them by calling them the *First Apocalypse of James* and the *Second Apocalypse of James* respectively. The two texts are unrelated,

sharing only the motif of a revelation given by Jesus to his half-brother James, and an account of James's martyrdom.

Although the *1stApocJas* was discovered in 1945 at Nag Hammadi, scholars recently discovered a second copy of it in the **Codex Tchacos** (the same codex that contains the *Gospel of Judas*). Since the Nag Hammadi copy is at times frustratingly fragmentary, this more complete second copy has helped us to restore the missing end of the Nag Hammadi copy. We now know, for instance, that it ends with an account of the martyrdom of James. It is quite amazing for scholars who have worked with the Nag Hammadi version to now find out what was there in the original manuscript before it was damaged.

The core of the *1stApocJas* consists of a series of formulae: secret passwords that Jesus teaches James to say to the celestial "toll-collectors" he will encounter as his soul ascends through the spheres after death to its source in the "Pre-Existent One." When this text was first discovered, scholars were surprised to see these formulae there, because we had seen them before; Irenaeus reports that a Valentinian group known as the Marcosians used these identical formulae as part of their death rituals (Irenaeus, *Adv. Haer.* 1.21.5). When a member of the community died, the Valentinian bishop would recite these words directly into the ears of the dying to prepare him or her for an inevitable encounter with hostile celestial beings.

In the *1stApJas*, Jesus prepares James for his impending martyrdom by letting him know what faces him in his post-death ascent. James expresses considerable anxiety that the celestial **archons** will be armed against him; Jesus corrects him, letting him know that the celestial hosts are actually locked in a battle against one another and also directly against Jesus. James then launches into a hymnic passage that the author of *1stApJas* likely borrowed from some lost, earlier source.

What is interesting about this account of James's martyrdom is that we find the idea that a Christian might be prepared in advance for what she or he was about to face. Rather than focusing on how James can bear the tortures from his earthly adversaries, Jesus gives his most esoteric teachings on how to survive the post-mortem journey of the soul. Jesus claims that the archons or "toll collectors" will interrogate the soul, and prepares James for the answers:

Archon: "Who are you? Where are you from?

James: "I am a son and I am from the Father."

Archon: "What sort of a son are you, and to what father do you belong?"

James: "I am from the Pre-existent Father, and a son in the Pre-existent One." (33:16–25)

The dialogue breaks down at this point because of a **lacuna** in the manuscript, then resumes with a long speech (34:1–19). Defenses for the soul to speak before celestial interrogators were more than mere literary dialogue, though. Since the same defense as this one here shows up in Irenaeus's account of a Valentinian community (*Adv.Haer.* 1.30), it seems that these dialogue defenses were once part of a lost liturgy, a prepared text or speech that accompanied a prescribed ritual action, such as baptism or chrism. These sorts of ritual, liturgical passages are quite common in ancient Christian sources. Compare with the *Gospel of Thomas*, Logion 50, which we can break down into a dialogue form:

Archon: "Where did you come from?"

Initiate: "We came from the light, the place where the light came into being on its own accord and established itself and became manifest through their image."

Archon: "Is it you?"

Initiate: "We are its children, and we are the elect of the living Father."

Archon: "What is the sign of your Father in you?"

Initiate: "It is movement and repose." (GThom, logion 50)

When we read these **ascent formulae**, we usually do not have any sense of how they were used. It is interesting that in this text, these formulae are set into the particular narrative framework of preparing James for martyrdom. Their placement suggests two things: first, that whoever read or heard this text probably had heard about martyrdom and likely knew Christians who suffered death at the hands of the Romans, and second, the important thing to understand about martyrdom was not the pain and suffering that one faced from earthly

---

"YOU ARE TO REVEAL THEM TO ADDAI"

In the *1stApJas*, Jesus tells James certain secrets about how to escape the evil celestial archons, and advises James to keep these secrets, even from the apostles. Only one person is permitted to receive the knowledge: someone called Addai. The name is distinctively Syrian, thus linking this text (written in Greek and preserved in Coptic) with the traditional founder of **Syriac Christianity**. Possibly the community that used this text, or the editor who put it together from his own writings and collections of earlier material (witness the hymnic fragment and the liturgical dialogues that parallel those found in other writings), traced themselves back to a scribal scholar named Addai who is otherwise lost to us, but who was himself Syrian and who, perhaps, introduced this material to the Greek East.

adversaries, but the real danger that one's soul might not make it to heaven without some sort of active preparation.

WHAT HAPPENED IN ROME WHEN SOMEONE DIED?

Ideally, the close family of the dying person would be present for the final moments of life; at the actual moment of death, a relative would try to capture the last breath or to kiss the dying individual. The deceased would be laid naked on the ground, head facing the door. This action was the symbolic inverse of birth rites, when the naked newborn was placed on the ground before its father. The corpse was then prepared by closing the mouth and eyes, and the deceased called on by name in a ritual called "*conclamatio mortis,*" to ensure that death had taken hold. Interestingly, this Roman rite is still preserved in the death rituals that are performed whenever a pope dies: a close attendant calls out the pope's birth name three times to the corpse. In ancient Rome, the body of the deceased was then washed, anointed with aromatic oils, then crowned with a wreath of laurel leaves. Funeral ceremonies followed, with the body lying in state from one to seven days, depending on the social status of the departed, then carried on a special litter to a burial site outside the city walls.

Jews and pagans of the second century considered contact with the dead ritually polluting, thus presumably limited the amount of contact with the dying. Although the pagan and Jewish horror of death pollution was strongly condemned in early Christian texts, Christians of the late second century and beyond apparently held different notions of the inherent holiness of the body, which allowed them to ignore ancient purity laws and attend to the corpse. At the same time, the Christians' insinuation that they alone held the corpse as worthy of respect was perhaps only polemical; although contact with a corpse was ritually polluting, a pagan family nonetheless

participated in the mortuary process, returning home to undergo a rite of purification by water and fire called the *suffitio*, then a more general period of cleansing (the *feriae denicales*) and the first commemorative funerary feast, the *silicernium*. In the case of Jewish practice, contact with a corpse could also have been ritually annulled through the appropriate combination of prayer and ritual cleansing.

Christian funerary rites at this period were virtually identical to pagan rites. The only difference was that Christians did not crown their dead with laurel leaves, but otherwise the same processes were followed. And while some pagans followed the ancient Greek practice of placing a coin in the mouth of the deceased to pay the way for the boatman Charon to ferry the soul across the Styx, many Christians adapted this practice to place in the mouth of the deceased a piece of Eucharistic bread. In fact, the Latin name for this ritual is the *Viaticum*, from *viaticus*, something for a journey. Thus one literal translation of Viaticum is "one for the road."

But there is substantial evidence that even if their funerary processes looked similar to their pagan contemporaries, Christians often drew upon their sacraments to sanctify death and to help the souls of their loved ones have a blessed afterlife. To this end, Christians performed baptisms up to the moment of death. Countless funerary inscriptions from the period record the practice. For instance, one Roman Christian inscription to little Tyche, who lived one year, ten months, and fifteen days, tells us that she died on the very day on which she received baptism. Another Roman epitaph makes the connection between final baptism and death more opaque: "Now that I have received divine grace, I shall be welcomed in peace as newly baptized."

Christians also anointed their dead with oil (a practice called unction). Both Graeco-Roman and Jewish traditions demanded a ritual anointment of the corpse. But unction before death was also not uncommon (see the epitaph on the tombstone of Flavia Sophe in chap. 7). Anointing was also called "sealing," and was a rite of protection for the ascending soul, perhaps by symbolically transforming the soul into a light being that could not be recognized by the wicked archons. To escape the celestial interrogators, the *Gospel of Philip* teaches that individuals needed to "put on" light through being ritually anointed (70:6–10). In a third-century Christian romance called the *Acts of Xanthippe and Polyxena*, the heroine Xanthippe, dying, begs the apostle Paul, "Master, why do you leave me all alone? Even now, quickly anoint me so that even though death is overtaking me, I may go to Him who is merciful and kind."

DID GNOSTICS HAVE THEIR OWN DEATH RITES?

When we consider how many ascent formulae are revealed in Nag Hammadi writings (as well as other Christian writings not in Nag Hammadi, such as the *Pistis Sophia* and the *Books of Jeu*), it makes sense to wonder if they might have had a particular life-setting of some sort. Did the people or communities that are often referred to as Gnostic—such as the Valentinians—have their own death rites, in which these formulae were spoken?

The specific, traditional rituals performed in Christian churches are known as **sacraments**, and they function to make the individual feel closer to Jesus Christ and to God. How these sacraments developed is a long and complicated issue. There is much we do not know about sacramental systems in second-century Christianity, but there are strong indications that some communities practiced their own rituals to prepare for the soul's passage from the body through the celestial spheres and back to the Pleroma. These might be performed well before death, immediately before death, or even after death—Irenaeus tells us that one Valentinian group, the Marcosians, whispered certain prayers into the ear of someone at

the point of death and anointed the body (*Adv. Haer.* 1.21.5). Some of these rites—baptism and chrism—were common to Christianity. Two other rites—**Redemption** (Gk *apolytrosis*) and the **Bridal Chamber**—seemed to have special **eschatological** significance and were performed only by Valentinian Christians on certain occasions. Since very little is written about these rites, we can only guess what they involved.

On the sacrament of Redemption we encounter the term for this rite, *apolytrosis*, fairly rarely in the Nag Hammadi writings, almost exclusively within a series of texts identified as Valentinian. The bulk of our references to Redemption are clustered within two Valentinian treatises from Nag Hammadi, the *Gospel of Philip* (GPhil) and the *Tripartite Tractate* (TriTrac). Apart from these texts, the word is used in two other Valentinian texts: once in the *Gospel of Truth* (GosTruth, 16:39) and once in the *Treatise on the Resurrection* (TreatRes, 46:26). The sole non-Valentinian text within the Nag Hammadi corpus to mention *apolytrosis*—which it does no fewer than six times—is the *First Apocalypse of James*. This tractate has a great deal to tell us about Christian responses to death.

Significantly, a number of statements in the *GPhil* also mention either death or the soul's trial after death. Indeed, the gospel itself quickly broaches the topic of death: "Those who are heirs to the dead are themselves dead; they inherit the dead" (51:6–7). The focus on death continues for several more lines, during which the author expresses a characteristic inversion: the term "death" is as misleading as the term "alive"; it is possible to be (spiritually) dead while alive, just as it is possible to be (spiritually) alive after death (52:10). The language here strongly suggests that "the dead" should be taken as a metaphorical expression for those who are spiritually asleep. Yet enough allusions are made to not merely death or "the dead" as a metaphorical category, but to what happens *after* death to raise the possibility that the language in this text is not merely metaphorical.

The passage quoted above concludes: "those who are lifted up above the cosmos are indissoluble, eternal" (53:20–23). Perhaps what was being alluded to here was the ontological superiority of those who, perhaps through receiving the sacraments, had become spiritually alive. But it is equally easy to imagine these words, spoken to a community, as offering comfort for the bereaved, in a funerary setting. The message is that death is not to be understood as either final or limiting; although the dead may be "dead" in an earthly sense, they are even more alive than we are, seen from the perspective of Valentinian salvation history.

In a passage on the nature of salvation, the author of the *Tripartite Tractate* refers to Redemption as a consequence of instruction, after which those given the promise will return to their source and origin in the Father. *Apolytrosis* is "the release from captivity and the acceptance of freedom" (117:23–25). Although here it is not clear that this release was accomplished through the use of ritual sacraments, the author later associates Redemption with baptism (127:30–128.19). In this text, *gnosis* signifies the union of the Christian with God. The Redemption makes that union possible.

Strikingly, the author of the *TriTrac* uses spatial language to discuss Redemption as in the following passage:

> [Redemption] was not only release from the domination of the left ones, nor was it only [escape] from the power of those of the right, to each of which we thought that we were slaves and sons, from whom none escapes without quickly becoming theirs again, but the redemption is also an ascent [to] the degrees which are in the Pleroma and [to] those who have named themselves and who conceive of themselves according to the power of each of the aeons, and (it is) an entrance into what is silent, where there is no need for voice nor for knowing nor for forming a concept nor for illumination, but (where) all things are light, while they do not need to be illumined. (124:3–25)

It is difficult to guess whether Redemption was performed as a rite among those who composed and read the *TriTrac*. The extended discussion on who warranted redemption (did the Savior? did the angels?) and when it was to occur (now, or at the end of days?) backs up Irenaeus's claim that different Valentinian groups disagreed considerably on what "redemption" meant and what event or series of events marked it. Nevertheless, it is clear that the Redemption sacrament involved the ascent of the soul after death and its return to the Father.

Many second-century Christians figured that if one wanted to learn about what life after death was like, there was one person in Christian history who had died and then been resurrected: Jesus Christ. Thus a fairly natural question that Jesus's disciples might ask, had they the chance, is "what is it like out there? What happens after death?" And many of these **revelation discourses** were developed from these traditions and questions; in these discourses, Jesus tells his favored disciples the secrets or "mysteries" of the cosmos, to help prepare them for death.

QUESTIONS TO CONSIDER

1. Look at the resurrection appearances at the ends of each of the NT Gospels. What sort of resurrection body does Jesus have? Is it physical? Spiritual? What comes back from the dead? The same physical body, or a new kind of a body?

2. Consider what Paul has to say about resurrection in 1 Corinthians 15. What sort of resurrection body will we have? Is it the same as Jesus's body, or is it different? Is it the same as our physical bodies, or is it a new kind? Now imagine you're a Valentinian reader in the second century. How might you understand Paul's teachings?

KEY TERMS

refrigerium	Codex Tchacos	Syriac Christianity
Nicene Creed	creed	Valentianism
revelation discourse	docetism	Sethianism
chrism/chrismation	ascent formula(e)	lacuna
Books of Jeu	sacraments	Johannine Prologue
Redemption	Pleroma	Athanasius
Pistis Sophia	eschatological	Bridal Chamber

FOR FURTHER READING

Hope, Valerie. *Death in Ancient Rome: A Sourcebook*. London: Routledge, 2006. An excellent compilation of Roman texts on various aspects of death and dying, in English translation. For beginning and intermediate students.

Segal, Alan. *Life After Death: A History of the Afterlife in Western Religion*. New York: Doubleday, 2003. Contains a great deal of information about afterlife beliefs in the West, particularly focusing on Egypt, the Ancient Near East, ancient Judaism, and Christianity. For intermediate students.

Toynbee, J. M. C. *Death and Burial in the Roman World*. Baltimore: Johns Hopkins University Press, 1996. This is a comprehensive study of Roman death, including Roman and later Christian burial spaces. For readers curious to know more about the social context of death in the ancient world.

Pistis Sophia *and the* Books of Jeu *(English editions)*

Schmidt, Carl, and Violet MacDermot. *The Books of Jeu and the Untitled Text in the Bruce Codex*. Leiden: Brill, 1978.

———. *Pistis Sophia*. Leiden: Brill, 1978. Please note that the editions of this text by G. S. Mead are not reliable at all, and the Schmidt/MacDermot edition is the only responsible version of this ancient text.

Deconstructing the Divine Feminine

THUNDER: PERFECT MIND (NHC VI 13, 1–21, 32) AND *TRIMORPHIC PROTENNOIA* (NHC XIII 35, 1–50, 24)

The two brief texts from Nag Hammadi, *Thunder: Perfect Mind* and *Trimorphic Protennoia*, are among the most remarkable works of ancient Christianity that we possess. Each comes to us in only one **redaction** or version; both were completely unknown before 1945. The manuscript of *Thunder* was quite well preserved; the text appears to have been translated from Greek to Coptic as a single-authored writing comprised of three different types of material: I-sayings, hortatory addresses, and warnings or cautions. The only manuscript of *TriProt*, by contrast, was more fragmentary and had to be partially reconstructed by modern scholars; it is still missing some crucial lines and shows evidence of having been cobbled together. Textual critics suspect that even the original Greek text had been added to by a series of authors, editors, and redactors. This sort of textual patchwork, while a great deal of fun for textual scholars, can produce a bewildering effect on modern readers. Before you read this chapter, be sure to read through both texts carefully, so that you can have a sense of how remarkable they

truly are. While you are reading, be sensitive to the "narrative seams" of both writings, where one section of text by one author is joined to another. If you are like many readers, you may find the *Thunder* easier to understand than *TriProt*, but both are related texts and reading them together can help begin to unravel their mysteries. In this chapter, we sometimes consider these texts together, and sometimes separately.

Let's start with the issue of genre. Although many people describe the *Thunder* as a poem, it is important to remember that the ancient world was predominantly an oral culture. Texts were written to be read aloud, and so we are talking about listeners rather than readers. A poem is a form of literature, and it is not entirely clear that the *Thunder* qualified as a poem. It might equally have been a song or hymn, or else some form of revelatory speech common in the ancient world, such as an oracle. If we imagine the text as spoken or sung, furthermore, we can allow ourselves to wonder who might have spoken such a text, under what sort of circumstances, and how this powerful monologue might have inspired an audience.

FIGURE 15.1 Manuscript page of the *Thunder: Perfect Mind*. Notice the torn page, which fortunately doesn't affect our ability to read most of the text itself.

The *TriProt* is also revelatory, but it combines a first-person address with a treatise on creation and salvation. The title gives us a clue as to what is going on in the treatise; it means "the Triple-formed First Thought." This First Thought (**Protennoia**) was a concept drawn from Greek philosophy; in this text, it manifests itself through the cosmos in different sets of three different forms, such as Father, Mother, and Son (37:22) and Voice, Speech, and Word. Part of what the text seeks to do is to remind the enlightened reader what sorts of triple forms that Protennoia had already assumed (and would continue to assume) in the cosmos. With each manifestation, the message of the Divine becomes more clearly articulated. The text ends with an epiphanic **apocalypse**, an appearance of the Divine revealing itself through the cosmos.

The cosmos is shaken by Protennoia's Voice, and this shaking is reminiscent of the Voice of the unnamed speaker in the *Thunder*, which resonates through the cosmos like thunder. Indeed, the "Perfect Mind" of the rest of the *Thunder*'s title is **Ennoia**, a form of Protennoia.

Both texts, therefore, share a great deal. Both feature a speaker that is a form of a primordial Divine Mind or Thought. Both are revelatory: they reveal divine knowledge. Both use similar speech-forms for divine monologue. And both texts have narratives that take place in the timeless silence of the cosmos. There in the stillness and darkness of the heavens, the Divine reveals itself in the form of light and sound. In the *TriProt*, the revelation is so powerful that it shakes the stars and planets off their courses. Since it was widely believed in antiquity that the stars and planets governed the fate of individuals through astrology, the arrival of the Divine Mind in the cosmos effectively destroys the cosmic bonds of fate. It is a salvific event of colossal importance! And perhaps most remarkably, the heavenly Redeemer in both texts is not a male divine being—although the *TriProt* refers at one point to "Christ" and a number of times to a "perfect being" who is called the "Son"—but a *feminine* divine entity.

Did the Christians who wrote, circulated, and listened to these texts being read believe that God was female, or that Christ was a woman? Not exactly. Rather, they believed that the highest God in the cosmos had divine feminine, as well as masculine, aspects. And since God encompasses the Entirety, God has a feminine "person." This way of thinking about God first emerged in Jewish communities of the Hellenistic era (ca. 330 BCE), where Greek concepts of a perfect, abstract, all-encompassing God-beyond-God began to prevail over earlier Jewish concepts of Yahweh as a male warrior god, as he appears in many books of the Hebrew Bible. Indeed, the *TriProt* retains an early form of the Christian Trinity that most likely comes from Jewish influence: here, we find a Father, Mother, and Son (in place of the Trinity of Father, Son, and Holy Spirit). This is a configuration that we know from other **Sethian** texts, which is partly why *TriProt* is classified, formally, as Sethian.

THE NARRATIVE STRUCTURE OF *THUNDER: PERFECT MIND*

If you look carefully, you'll see that the *Thunder* is composed of four different types of materials: (a) I-sayings; (b) reproaches or exhortations (where the speaker asks questions or tells her listeners to do something); (c) prose statements; and (d) cautions or warnings. These four types of materials are arranged in blocks. A portion of the first line of each section marks the beginning of each section (see box).

This structure is unique among Nag Hammadi literature, but its regularity suggests a hymnic structure and that it might have been sung or chanted.

LITERARY BREAKDOWN OF *THUNDER: PERFECT MIND*

1. Introduction

2. a: I-sayings ("For I am the first and the last")

3. b: questions ("Why, you who hate me, do you love me? . . .").

4. a^1: I-sayings ("For I am knowledge and ignorance")

5. b^1: exhortations ("give heed to my poverty and my wealth")

6. d: cautions ("Be on your guard!..."). This section also has exhortations and I-sayings

7. b^2: questions ("Why have you hated me in your counsels?")

8. a^2: I-sayings "For I am the wisdom of the Greeks")

9. b^3: exhortations ("But whenever you hide yourselves")

10. b^4: questions ("Why do you curse me and honor me?")

11. a^3: I-sayings ("But I am the mind of [...] and the rest of [...]")

12. c: prose statements ("Those who are without association with me")

13. a^4: I-sayings (["I am...] within.")

14. b^6: exhortation ("Hear me in gentleness")

15. a^5: I-sayings ("I am she who cries out")

16. b^7: exhortations ("You honor me [...] and you whisper")

17. c^1: prose statements ("for what is inside of you")

18. b^8: exhortations ("hear me, you hearers")

19. a^6: I-sayings ("I am the hearing that is attainable")

20. b^9: exhortations ("Look then at his words")

21. d^1: cautions ("Give heed then, you hearers")

22. a^7: I-sayings ("For I am the one who alone exists")

23. c^2: prose statements ("For many are the pleasant forms"

THE TRIMORPHIC PROTENNOIA

The structure of the *TriProt* is more detailed than the *Thunder*, and it bears more evidence of having been compiled from different sources. John Turner, the scholar who translated the text for the NHLE, proposes that the present text came together in various stages (see boxed item below).

Thinking about different compositional stages helps us to make sense of the complex and sometimes contradictory nature of *TriProt* as a treatise. Most difficult to figure out is the tractate's view on Christ: is he the only-begotten Son, or part of Sophia, or the evil product of ignorant **archons**? What do you think the text is trying to say?

WISDOM SAYINGS AND "I-SAYINGS"

Although many people think that Judaism has no goddess figure, this is not precisely true. The book of Proverbs, for example, contains references to a female figure who accompanied God when he created the cosmos. In this passage she speaks to us:

> The LORD created me at the beginning of his work, the first of his acts of old. Ages ago I was set up, at the first, before the beginning of the earth. When there were no depths I was brought forth, when there were no springs abounding with water. Before the mountains had been shaped, before the hills, I was brought forth; before he had made the earth with its fields, or the first of the dust of the world. When he established the heavens, I was there, when he drew a circle on the face of the deep, when he made firm the skies above, when he established the fountains of the deep, when he assigned to the sea its limit, so that the waters might not transgress his command, when he marked out the foundations of the earth, then I was beside him, like a master workman; and I was daily his delight, rejoicing before him always, rejoicing in his inhabited world and delighting in the sons of men. (Prov 8:22–31, RSV)

Grammatically, the original Hebrew of this passage makes it clear that the speaker is female. The name traditionally given to this speaker is Wisdom (in some translations, "Lady Wisdom"). The Hebrew noun for Wisdom, *Hokma*, is feminine, as is the Greek noun *Sophia*. By the Hellenistic period Jewish Wisdom traditions had proliferated and, as Nag Hammadi texts demonstrate, enjoyed popularity within certain Christian communities well into the Roman Empire. During this period, too, the concept of a feminine divine Wisdom becomes **hypostasized**,

---

TURNER'S COMPOSITIONAL STAGES OF THE *TRIMORPHIC PROTENNOIA*

First stage of composition:

A triad of I-sayings of Protennoia as Voice, Speech, and Word:

- derived from Jewish Wisdom traditions
- related to the "Pronoia Hymn" that ends the longer version of the *Apocryphon of John*
- possibly not yet a Christian document

Second stage of composition:

An unknown Christian "Barbeloite," a Christian whose theology centered around the myth of Sophia as a supreme being also known as **Barbēlō**, added narrative doctrinal passages on the creation of the world and on the primary trinity of Father-Mother-Son.

Third stage of composition:

Christian **docetists** added passages explaining **Christology**, using language drawn from the Prologue of John's Gospel, apparently in a polemical fashion. At this point, terms like *Christ*, *Beloved*, and *Son of man* are added.

meaning that a concept becomes personified as a being: the idea or *concept* of Wisdom becomes the *character* Wisdom.

Most **Wisdom literature** is not merely a collection of wise sayings as the term seems to suggest, but there are actually bits of monologue where the character Wisdom speaks:

> Hear instruction and be wise, and do not neglect it. Happy is the one who listens to me, watching daily at my gates, waiting beside my doors. For whoever finds me finds life and obtains favor from the LORD, but who ever misses me injures himself; all who hate me love death. (Prov 8.33–36, RSV)

As we find in the *TriProt* and the *Thunder*, Wisdom traditions are characterized by first-person declarations made by a divine feminine being:

> I am Protennoia, the Thought that dwells in the Light.
>
> I am the movement that dwells in the All, she in whom the All takes its stand, the first-born among those who came to be, she who exists before the All....
>
> I am invisible within the Thought of the Invisible One.
>
> I am revealed in the immeasurable, ineffable [things].
>
> I am incomprehensible, dwelling in the incomprehensible. (*TriProt* 35:1–12, trans. John Turner, "Trimorphic Protennoia," in James Robinson, editor, *The Nag Hammadi Library in English* [San Francisco: Harper & Row, 1988]: 461–62).
>
> For I am knowledge and ignorance. I am shame and boldness. I am shameless; I am ashamed. I am strength and I am fear. I am war and peace. (*Thunder*, 14:26–34, trans. George MacRae, in James Robinson, editor, *The Nag Hammadi Library in English* [San Francisco: Harper & Row, 1988]: 272–73)

Scholars note that in antiquity, these first-person proclamations or "I-sayings" formed a characteristic part of what we call **aretalogies**, lists of virtuous attributes ascribed to ancient figures. In ancient Greek, pronouns are ordinarily omitted in everyday speech. One would say, for instance, "am hungry" rather than "I am hungry." The only reason to include the "I" would be for special emphasis, as in "I [alone] am hungry" or "[you may not be, but] *I* am hungry." Thus an aretalogical statement carries particular and unusual emphasis. Simply put, in the ancient world, people didn't speak this way; only gods did. There is no coincidence that in the Gospel of John, for instance, Jesus often uses "I am" proclamations, such as "I am the Way, the Truth, and the Life" (Jn 14:6). Ancient Jewish and Christian listeners would have understood these statements to be especially authoritative—partly because they were associated with Wisdom's speech but also because they were the perceived way that God himself spoke:

> Then Moses said to God, "If I come to the people of Israel and say to them, 'The God of your fathers has sent me to you,' and they ask me, 'What is his name?' what shall I say to them?" God said to Moses, "I AM WHO I AM." And he said, "Say this to the people of Israel, 'I AM has sent me to you.'" (Exod. 3:13–14, RSV)

In the Greek version of the Hebrew Bible called the **Septuagint** (LXX) that the broad majority of Jews and Christians used in the Roman Empire, Yahweh says "I AM" (Gk *ego eimi.*) Jesus, in the Gospel of John, also says "*ego eimi,*" as does the speaker in both the *Thunder* and *TriProt* (although the force is lost somewhat in the translation into Coptic).

But it is not just within Judaism and Christianity that "I am" statements signified divine speech. A series of oracular statements attributed to the goddess **Isis** reveal the goddess' power (see box). Not only in Egypt but throughout the Roman Empire Isis was particularly revered as a savior figure; many scholars speculate that ancient images of Isis suckling her son Horus inspired later Christian icons of Mary suckling the infant Jesus (see fig. 15.2).

Would ancient listeners of the *Thunder* first think of Isis, of Wisdom, or of Yahweh? It is difficult to say for sure. Perhaps in the rich religious environment that was the Roman Empire, the anonymous speaker of the *Thunder* could have been Isis and Wisdom at once. This

THE GODDESS ISIS SPEAKS

I gave and ordained laws for men, which no one is able to change.

I am eldest daughter of Kronos.

I am wife and sister of King Osiris.

I am she who findeth fruit for men.

I am mother of King Horus.

I am she that riseth in the Dog Star.

I am she that is called goddess by women.

For me was the city of Bubastis built.

I divided the earth from the heaven.

I showed the paths of the stars.

I ordered the course of the sun and the moon.

I devised business in the sea.

I made strong the right.

I brought together woman and man.

I appointed to women to bring their infants to birth in the tenth month.

I ordained that parents should be loved by children.

I laid punishment on those disposed without natural affection toward their parents.

I made with my brother Osiris an end to the eating of men.

I revealed mysteries unto men.

Excerpt from the second-century Isis Aretalogy from Cyme, Greece (trans. F. C. Grant, *Hellenistic Religions: The Age of Syncretism* [Indianapolis: Bobbs-Merrill Publishing, 1953]: 131–33).

FIGURE 15.2 This statue of Isis is Coptic art from fourth-century Egypt – could those who copied and read the Nag Hammadi texts have seen it?

would have been especially true if the *Thunder* were written in Egypt, as we suspect it might have been.

One of the most remarkable (and unusual, even in the ancient world) features of the *Thunder*'s aretalogies is that they are posed as *antitheses*, or paradoxical dichotomies. The speaker is at once shameless and ashamed; she shows knowledge and ignorance, strength and fear, and so on. We are left with the sense that the Divine encompasses everything, the totality of existence, with each quality held in balance with its opposite. This

balance of opposites is not is specifically a feature of what it means to be female, yet as a vision of the inherent wholeness of womanhood the *Thunder*'s paradoxes have inspired modern audiences, especially women. The modern African American filmmaker Julie Dash begins her *Daughters of the Dust* (1991) with words from the *Thunder*; more recently (2005), a television commercial directed by Jordan Scott for the design house Prada features a young, beautiful woman quoting from the *Thunder* as she goes about her day. Scott seized upon the writing because she felt it summed up the complexity and totality of what it means to be a woman. Women's nature, some people suggest, is complex enough to encompass opposites, even extreme opposites.

It is not at all clear that whoever wrote the *Thunder* and *TriProt* thought that human females embodied opposite qualities in any positive sense; in fact, it is more likely that the point of the *Thunder*'s paradoxes is that only the Divine is big enough to contain everything and its opposite. Humans, by contrast, are limited, insignificant beings in relation to the Divine Totality. In this way of thinking about human limits, the *Thunder*'s paradoxes function a little like Zen Buddhist *ko'ans*, short statements that paralyze human reason such as "What is the sound of one hand clapping?" and "Without thinking of good or evil, show me your original face before your mother and father were born." *Ko'ans* are used as meditative devices, where the point is not to solve the paradoxes but to paralyze the human mind's capacity for discursive reason—a capacity that can effectively hinder our ability to reach a full understanding of the transcendence of the Buddha nature. The *ko'an* also leaves room for intuition, a form of knowing that can get us closer to divine truths. The paradoxical statements of the *Thunder* may do the same—they leave the hearer to know through intuitive knowledge, not through logic—the truth of the Divine nature. This intuitive knowledge is itself one way of defining the term *gnosis*.

But it is important to note that the statements in the *Thunder* are not just about balancing out opposing qualities or natures. The *Thunder*'s paradoxical statements often seem more like puzzles or riddles that tease the reader, begging to be solved:

> I am she whose wedding is great, and I have not taken a husband. I am the midwife and she who does not bear. I am the solace of my labor pains. I am the bride and the bridegroom, and it is my husband who begot me. I am the mother of my father and the sister of my

husband and he is my offspring. (*Thunder* 13: 23–32, trans. George MacRae, in James Robinson, editor, *The Nag Hammadi Library in English* [San Francisco: Harper & Row, 1988]: 272)

Rather than letting these paradoxes simply ignite our intuitive knowledge, a more active approach would be to try to figure them out. Was anyone, in Jewish or Christian sacred history, both married and unmarried at once? Did anyone suffer labor pains without having given birth? Was anyone at once a bride, bridegroom, and child of her husband? In a wonderful article, the leading American scholar of Gnosticism at Yale, Bentley Layton, took seriously the task of solving the *Thunder*'s identity riddles. If we could figure out who was the offspring of her husband, the mother of her father, sister of her husband, and her husband's mother, we might be in a position to guess the *Thunder*'s real identity. Can *you* solve the riddle of the *Thunder*?

WHO IS PROTENNOIA/ENNOIA?

Let's start with what we know. In the *TriProt*, Protennoia gives herself a variety of names, including the Image of the Invisible Spirit (38:11), **Meirothea** (38:15; the name may mean something like "goddess of fate"), the Incomprehensible Womb (38:15), the Mother (38:13), the Virgin (38:14), **Barbēlō** (38:9), and the Perfect Glory (38:9). This piling on of names is not uncommon for Nag Hammadi texts. In the *Thunder*, the speaker has fewer names or titles, but these include Truth (20:6), the "name of the sound" and the "sound of the name" (20:32–33).

One answer to the riddle of the *Thunder* is that the speaker is Wisdom herself, who in many writings of the NHL appears as a divine female character Sophia. Creation narratives such as *Hypostasis of the Archons* (NHC II, 4) and *On the Origin of the World* (NHC II, 5 and NHC XIII, 2) recount the story of Sophia's "fall." Although this myth takes many forms, the thrust of it is that Sophia, the last offspring (**aeon**) of the highest divine being in the cosmos, introduces materiality into the cosmos through her longing, desire, and sorrow. She is also the mother of **Ialdabaoth**, an evil creator god modeled on Yahweh in the book of Genesis. Sophia is paired on the human level by **Eve**, the first woman who initiates the "fall" of humankind. If we think of Sophia/Eve as two aspects of one character, the riddle of the *Thunder* begins to make sense. Sophia is the mother of Eve's father, Ialdabaoth/Yahweh ("I am the mother of my father"); Eve is the "sister" of **Adam** since they are created by the same father ("I am the sister of my husband"), yet Adam is also Sophia's "offspring," since in some Sethian cosmologies, Sophia is the holy Mother who animates Adam with her breath/spirit. The *Thunder*, therefore, alludes in paradoxical language to a myth that must have been well known to many ancient audiences: a myth where Sophia and Eve are the human and divine aspects of one feminine being.

Sophia is also closely related to another character well known to us from ancient Christianity: the **Logos** or Word. The Logos, however, is always male, whereas Sophia is usually characterized as female (though she can take on the male form of the Logos, as she does in the *TriProt* 47:15–28). In some Gnostic theologies, Sophia is paired with her **syzygy** or male counterpart Jesus; in other theologies, Sophia is identical with the Holy Spirit, or even to the Mother of the Father-Mother-Son trinity that we find alluded to in *TriProt* 37:22. That Sophia = Christ would not have been the answer to the riddle of the *Thunder*, yet for those who had ears to hear, the pairing of the Word with Sophia in *TriProt* would have offered certain Christians a different way of understanding stories of Christ's incarnation ("descent into the flesh") that were gaining in popularity and sophistication in the late first and early second century. As Christians such as

the author of John's Gospel insisted that Christ was preexistent and God's only-begotten, this idea challenged earlier Jewish Wisdom traditions adopted by some Christian groups in which Wisdom had been God's only divine child before the creation of the world.

Early Christians were faced with a number of choices:

1) They could accept Johannine theology and believe that it was Christ, not Wisdom, who was with God at the beginning of creation.

2) They could insist that it was not Christ but Wisdom who accompanied God at creation (although this may sound absurd to some modern readers, note that the **Johannine Prologue** never explicitly identifies God's only-begotten as Christ and so there was room for such interpretations in antiquity).

3) They could find ways to somehow reconcile Christ with Wisdom.

All three options were viable, and we have evidence that Chistians did in fact choose from among them.

The author of the *TriProt* appears to have favored the third option, because the text makes it clear that Christ or the Son was a manifestation of Wisdom/Protennoia, as one of her triple forms. In a sense, this choice dealt effectively with the issue of Christ's maleness in Christian theologies. It was clearly hard for the *TriProt*'s author to conceive of a Redeemer who was entirely male (as in the Johannine Prologue)—not because the author thought women were superior but because the true nature of Divinity had to either transcend or incorporate all difference (including the difference of gender). The author also probably understood God's only active creative agent to be Sophia, who had already been conceived of as a divine female emanative power for around five hundred years by the time the *TriProt* was composed.

THE ENDING OF THE TRIMORPHIC PROTENNOIA

TriProt ends with a puzzling short passage:

> As for me, I put on Jesus. I bore him from the cursed wood, and established him in the dwelling places of his Father. And those who watch over their dwelling places did not recognize me. For I, I am unrestrainable, together with my seed; and my seed, which is mine, I shall place into the holy Light within an incomprehensible Silence. Amen. (TriProt 50:12–20, trans. John Turner, in James Robinson, editor, *The Nag Hammadi Library* in English [San Francisco: Harper & Row, 1988]: 470)

Scholars suspect that this passage may be an *interpolation*, an addition to the original text. One clue is the use of the name Jesus, which appears nowhere else in the text. The passage also does not seem to fit with the overall flow of the text. The **Christology** (the description of Jesus's nature) is also unusual; the idea that Protennoia "put on" Jesus as one might "put on" a costume or a cloak troubled many early Christian interpreters. Not only does Protennoia put on Jesus, she carries him away from the crucifixion (the "cursed wood") so that he does not suffer and die, as many Christians believed. This particular type of belief is called **docetism**, from the Greek verb *dokein*, to "seem or appear." Docetists believed that Jesus only *seemed* to be human but was not actually incarnated into human flesh; he was really a sort of spirit. Accordingly, he only *seemed* to suffer at the crucifixion, but since he was not flesh, he could not be tortured or die. **Heresiologists** such as **Irenaeus** and **Epiphanius** considered docetism a pernicious **heresy**, because it denied the reality of the incarnation and the theology of Jesus's redemptive suffering. Did the author of the *TriProt*—or the community that produced the text—espouse docetism? It does not appear so, but the addition to the text proves that at least some Christians once did, and they read this text in such a way that it seemed to agree with their own understanding of Jesus's nature.

THE TRIMORPHIC PROTENNOIA AND THE GOSPEL OF JOHN

Recently, scholars of early Christianity have been reading texts like the *Thunder* and the *TriProt* as direct responses to—or perhaps even precursors to—Christian theologies that emerged triumphant from debates concerning the nature of Christ. Let's see how that might have worked.

In the 1970s and 1980s, scholars of the ancient world pointed out that the *TriProt* actually bears remarkable similarities to the Prologue from the Gospel of John (Jn 1:1–14; see box on the next page). The Prologue features a divine, preexistent being identified as the Word who descends into a cosmos where it is unknown and unrecognized.

In the *TriProt*, a being called the Son likewise descends as the Word.

> The third time I revealed myself to them in their tents as Word, and I revealed myself in the likeness of their shape. And I wore everyone's garment, and I hid myself within them, and they did not know the one who empowers me. For I dwell within all the Sovereignties and Powers, and within the angels, and in every movement that exists in all matter. And I hid myself within them until I revealed myself to my brethren. And none of them (the Powers) knew me, although it is I who work in them. Rather, they thought that the All was created by them, since they are ignorant, not knowing their root, the place in which they grew. (47:13–28, trans. John Turner, in James Robinson, editor, *The Nag Hammadi Library in English* [San Francisco: Harper & Row, 1988]: 469)

John's **Prologue**, itself a Christian **midrash** of Genesis 1:1, indicates that what existed at the beginning was a divine Word. In the *TriProt*, something actually exists before the Word: Protennoia, the First Thought. But why? Think of it this way: before any being can speak a word, that word must first exist as a thought, because no word can exist without being thought of first. Think of what usually happens when you first come up with something to say—it exists first as

GOSPEL OF JOHN 1:1–14

[1]In the beginning was the Word, and the Word was with God, and the Word was God. [2]He was in the beginning with God; [3]all things were made through him, and without him was not anything made that was made. [4]In him was life, and the life was the light of men. [5]The light shines in the darkness, and the darkness has not overcome it. [6]There was a man sent from God, whose name was John. [7]He came for testimony, to bear witness to the light, that all might believe through him. [8]He was not the light, but came to bear witness to the light. [9]The true light that enlightens every man was coming into the world. [10]He was in the world, and the world was made through him, yet the world knew him not. [11]He came to his own home, and his own people received him not. [12]But to all who received him, who believed in his name, he gave power to become children of God; [13]who were born, not of blood nor of the will of the flesh nor of the will of man, but of God. [14]And the Word became flesh and dwelt among us, full of grace and truth; we have beheld his glory, glory as of the only Son from the Father. (RSV)

an idea, which you proceed to articulate. There can be no speech, no word, without thought.

If we go back to the book of Genesis, we can actually look up the first word, the very first thing that God says: "Let there be light" (Gen 1:3). It stands to reason, therefore, that God *thought* "light" before speaking it. And thus God's first created idea, God's first thought (remember Protennoia actually means "first thought") was itself essentially also "light." And note all the light imagery in the *TriProt*. Light is always connected in this text with revelation and with speech, because the allusion is to Genesis 1:3.

Of course, light has more than one connotation. There is physical light (at creation) but there is also spiritual or metaphorical light that happens when humans receive divine revelation (enlightenment.) The *TriProt* plays on this double quality of light; it happens at the beginning, at the creation in Genesis, but it also happens any time people have a spiritual experience and suddenly "see the light" of their own salvation. And so, by extension, every act of enlightenment recalls creation and connects us with God, our own beginnings, and our own spiritual origins.

In the Johannine Prologue, light also comes into the cosmos, but here it comes *after* the Word,

not before it (1:4). It shines into the darkness, but rather than suddenly filling the cosmos with light, something else happens. In Greek, the verb used in 1:5 is *katalambanein*, which has two different senses: to "to grasp or perceive," or to "seize upon or take possession of." (The English verbs "to grasp" or "to get" function similarly; when we understand something we "get it.") Translators of the text into English therefore face a difficult choice with this verse; it could be "the light shines in the darkness but the darkness did not perceive it" or "the light shines in the darkness and the darkness did not take possession of it." Each carries a slightly different nuance and even different theological implications. Was the light so strong that it vanquished darkness? Or was it that the darkness failed to comprehend it? This second choice of translation seems odd, unless we understand "darkness" metaphorically just as we understand "light" metaphorically. This translation—that the darkness did not comprehend the light—is also supported in 1:10: "He was in the world, and the world was made through him, yet the world knew him not." Given the reduplication, it seems clear that the author of this passage is playing on the double meaning of *katalambanein*, and indicating that we should perceive this event both literally (at creation) and spiritually (as still happening now). Some people, it seems, were enlightened by the arrival of the Word—those who became children of God (1:12)—while others remained in spiritual darkness and ignorance. This sets up what is known in Christian theological circles as "the problem of election": were all people born with equal possibilities for enlightenment, or were the dice loaded, so to speak, from the start?

Let's return to the *TriProt*, since it may have been composed in response to the Johannine Prologue's doctrine of election. In the *TriProt*, Protennoia suffuses the cosmos:

> I am the life…that dwells within every Power and every eternal movement, and (in) invisible Lights and within the Archons and Angels and Demons, and every soul dwelling in Tartaros, and (in) every material soul. I dwell in those who came to be. I move in everyone and I delve into them all. I walk uprightly, and those who sleep, I awaken. And I am the sight of those who dwell in sleep. (35:12–23, trans. John Turner, in James Robinson, editor, *The Nag Hammadi Library in English* [San Francisco: Harper & Row, 1988]: 462)

This kind of divine power we call "immanence," and it is central to the theology of the *TriProt*. Repeatedly, we read that Protennoia indwells every single sentient being in the cosmos, including all human beings (35:12). We ourselves *contain* Protennoia, the divine First Thought. The Johannine Prologue, by contrast, conveys a very different idea: the Word comes into the cosmos, but it/he acts to further divide the cosmos: dark from light, those who understand the Word from those who do not; "his own" from "others," and so on. The message to be learned from the Johannine Prologue is that the Word is a unique entity: it/he is the "only-begotten" (the original Greek actually says "only-becoming"), who comes into the cosmos but "his own did not receive him" (1:10). In this **cosmology**, darkness remains dark even though light shines in that darkness; in the cosmology of *TriProt*, Protennoia comes into the cosmos and dwells in "everyone" and "all": "I am

the real Voice. I cry out in everyone, and they recognize it (the voice), since a seed indwells them" (36:14–16).

Although Gnosticism is widely mischaracterized as an elitist movement, the theology of the *TriProt* is far from elite; it makes clear that everyone has a "seed" of the divine within, and that the divine voice can call out from within *all* people. Furthermore, this indwelling of the light explains why people are drawn to God in the first place: we all recognize, instinctively, that we carry the seed of divinity that enables our enlightenment. In fact, one could make a provocative argument that the Johannine Prologue is far more "elitist," because it speaks of a dramatically divided cosmos where the light/Word comes into his own people and yet not even his own people recognize him. Some may protest that revelation in the *TriProt* comes only to a group known as the "Sons of the Light," but if you read the Johannine Prologue carefully, you will see that those who recognized and accepted the Word became "children of God," a very similar title. No other people seem to comprehend the Word, and the cosmos remains a radically divided place.

THUNDER: PERFECT MIND AND SOCIAL VIOLENCE

You will notice that *Thunder* is not merely a beautiful poem. It is truly haunting, with many lines that convey a brutality and despair. The speaker is violated sexually, humiliated, and displaced. Its imagery bespeaks a social world of violence, inequity, and injustice. In this world, to be female is to endure almost unspeakable pain. Unfortunately, the social world behind the text was indeed violent and misogynistic. Although the text does not name those who savage the speaker, it is pretty clear that they are none other than the Romans. Indeed, in Jewish and Christian apocalyptic literature composed in the world of the Roman Empire, the perpetrators of violence are usually Roman, though it takes a clever reader "in the know" to interpret the coded references. To give a famous example, the great "beast" who bears the number 666 of the New Testament's book of Revelation (13:18) is likely a coded reference to the Emperor Nero, whose name—when the Greek letters of his name transliterated into Hebrew were assigned a standard numerical value in Jewish esoteric teachings—added up to the number 666. Although the *Thunder* contains no such number code, it is clear that the Romans' military might, their unmitigated violence in pursuing and maintaining rule, and their willingness to utterly crush dissenting peoples made them the source of oppression or worse to the author of the *Thunder*. The scholar Davina Lopez has recently pointed out images from Roman triumphal monuments in which the victorious Romans physically trample, humiliate, and subjugate foreign peoples—who, as it happens, are usually depicted as women—sometimes women in military gear. In figure 15.3 (from the forum of the second-century Roman Emperor Trajan at Rome) the subjugated people of Dacia (now part of the modern country of Romania) are represented by a woman bent in grief.

FIGURE 15.3 This carved marble frieze features the Roman victory over the Dacians; the Dacians are represented by a female figure in mourning. From the Forum of Trajan, Rome, now in the Capitoline Museums.

THE QUESTION OF AUDIENCE

We do not know who might have written the *Thunder* and the *TriProt*, but we suspect that both texts date to the middle of the second century, and it is possible that they might have been written in a cosmopolitan city like Alexandria where people encountered a variety of different languages, religions, and cultural traditions. They would already have been acquainted with Judaism, with Isis worship, and with Christianity, and they almost certainly would have known the Johannine Prologue. Beyond that, it is difficult to say much about them. They spoke Greek and had a very solid grasp of the fundamentals of Greek philosophy. The *Thunder* and *TriProt* betray a real sophistication, and they require prior study in order to understood fully.

The very centrality of female revealers in these texts raise the question of whether women played active roles in the communities that made use of them. Women certainly acted as leaders, teachers, and even prophets within some Christian communities of the second century. There is even a hint within the *TriProt* that Protennoia had been "incarnated" into a woman:

> Now I have come the second time in the likeness of a female, and have spoken with them. And I shall tell them of the coming end of the Aeon and teach them of the beginning of the Aeon to come, the one without change, the one in which our appearance

will be changed. We shall be purified within those Aeons from which I revealed myself in the Thought of the likeness of my masculinity. I settled among those who are worthy in the Thought of my changeless Aeon. (*TriProt* 42: 17–27, trans. John Turner, in James Robinson, editor, *The Nag Hammadi Library in English* [San Francisco: Harper & Row, 1988]: 466)

We may have here a reference to a woman prophet who preached to her community an apocalyptic message and who also exhorted members to stay strong and prepare for the final age (*aeon*). Since the text says that this "likeness of a female" was the second appearance of Protennoia and that the first appearance was that in which she revealed herself in "the likeness of my masculinity," this may be an allusion to the initial descent of the Word or the Son— Jesus Christ as the Redeemer: Christ established the revelation, and then a woman prophet continued it. Furthermore, Protennoia also came a third time as a sort of immanent presence who "settled among" the community, similar to the descent of the Holy Spirit at Pentecost that marks the next phase of Christian discipleship after the death of Jesus in the book of Acts (Acts 2:1–41). If the *TriProt* gives us hints that there was known to its author a female prophet, the *Thunder* gives us no such hints. At the same time, it is difficult to imagine a male prophet or teacher standing before a community and reciting this text.

There is one ancient Christian community about which we have a bit of information that might be useful in pondering whether they might have used texts such as *TriProt* and the *Thunder*. The Montanists were groups of committed and apocalyptically minded Christians active in the second century. They originated in a place called Phrygia (now part of modern Turkey) and followed the revelation of a man called Montanus and two women teachers, Priscilla (sometimes called Prisca) and Maximilla. Before long, Montanists had spread beyond Phrygia and were establishing communities across the Mediterranean

basin. Apparently, they allowed women to serve as priests and prophets, and they drew upon a wide variety of ancient scripture. Most authoritative in these groups were collections of oracular statements attributed to Montanus, Priscilla, and Maximilla. These were later destroyed by the Catholic Church, but a few fragments still survive. They offer an intriguing glimpse into the nature of Christian oracles and the role of women in ancient Christianity. In one remarkable oracle, Maximilla reports that Christ visited her *in the likeness of a woman*. Needless to say, many Christians at the time (and today!) found such a statement outrageous. Yet her words seem not dissimilar to the *TriProt*'s claim that Protennoia had come to earth "in the likeness of a female." Certainly, it is easy to imagine that a Montanist female prophet might have been very pleased to read aloud a text like the *Thunder* to her community. When Maximilla was said to have proclaimed, "I am Word and Spirit and Power," it is possible that she had in mind one of our two Nag Hammadi texts where Protennoia speaks in the same words.

The only other thing we can discern about the community behind the *TriProt* is that they appeared to have rituals and some sort of sacrament or communal prayer. There is a reference to a baptismal ritual known as the **Five Seals**, which also comes up in other texts from Nag Hammadi. We're not sure what happened at this rite, but it may have involved ritual anointing with water or oil, either five times or in five different places on the body of **catechumens** (people preparing for baptism and acceptance into a Christian community). The *TriProt* names the angelic figures who stand guard at such a ritual. And at one point, the words of the heavenly aeons sound as if they might be a kind of script or liturgy for a community:

They blessed the Perfect Son, the Christ, the only-begotten God. And they gave glory, saying, "He is! He is! The Son of God! The Son of God! It is he who is! The Aeon of Aeons, beholding the Aeons which he begot. For thou hast begotten by thine own desire! Therefore we glorify thee: ma mo o o o eia ei on ei! The Aeon of Aeons! The Aeon which he gave!" (38:22–30, trans. John Turner, in James Robinson, editor, *The Nag Hammadi Library in English* [San Francisco: Harper & Row, 1988]: 463–64)

The strange string of vowel sounds *ma mo o o o eia ei on ei* are very common in so-called Gnostic texts, but we find them also in magical spells and amulets from the ancient world, from which they receive the name **voces magicae** or "magical voices" (see chaps. 5, 13). All we know about them is that they were intended to be intoned or perhaps sung. They may have been invocations, or their sounds may have corresponded in some way to the perceived sounds of the cosmos. At any rate, they were sacred words and sacred sounds intended to be efficacious in invoking divine powers.

Given that both the *Thunder* and *Trimorphic Protennoia* focus on the importance of revelation through sound—and sound as a sacred medium of salvation—it is extraordinary that each text relies on distinctive uses of sound, as language or poetry, to create an experience for a listener. It is clear that both texts were intended to be performed, therefore, not merely studied in silence.

LAST THOUGHTS

These two texts from Nag Hammadi give us insight into second-century Christian revelatory traditions, particularly in the way that some people conceived of a feminine divine Redeemer. This figure—styled variously as Sophia, Ennoia, Protennoia, Barbēlō, the Mother, and the like—is connected to Hellenistic Jewish Wisdom traditions but also likely evoked elements of Isis worship in the Roman Empire.

Both *Thunder: Perfect Mind* and *Trimorphic Protennoia* take place in the cosmos as the feminine divine principle speaks out to all people.

This revelation has cosmic implications and is connected, particularly in the *TriProt*, with the story of creation in Genesis. Still, the emphasis is not on **protology** (the study of sacred origins) but on Sophia's ability to awaken through her divine call those who are spiritually asleep. In both tractates there is a marked emphasis on light and sound imagery, signifying the call to enlightenment.

Both texts may have reflected early Christian attempts to come to terms with the notion of Jesus's preexistence and incarnation. This theology could not be easily reconciled with Jewish understandings of a preexistent Wisdom figure, who had the power to inspire and enlighten but who did not incarnate into human flesh. Both texts, but especially the *TriProt*, maintain that Protennoia or Ennoia is immanent and dwells hidden within all people until it she activated by a call to awaken. That Sophia is indwelling in all people stands in contrast to some early Christian theologies in which emphasis is placed on believing in or having faith in Jesus Christ, who alone bears within himself both human and divine natures.

And finally, both texts were intended for listeners already well versed in the ideas to which they allude, because nowhere do they lay out or systematically explain their theologies. We can infer that they were used by Greek-speaking communities familiar with Judaism, Christianity, and Roman religious practices. These communities were apocalyptic, in that they believed that they were living at the cusp of a new age or Aeon where they would find new divine favor. In the meantime, they prepared themselves with prayer, listening to teaching and exhortations (including the reading of these texts), and baptism of some kind. It is entirely possible that some communities who used *TriProt* and the *Thunder* might have afforded privileged positions to women prophets and teachers. Whoever they were, they disappeared with barely a trace.

THE THUNDER IN CONTEMPORARY CULTURE

Few ancient nonbiblical Christian texts have inspired as many people as the *Thunder*. Here are just a few examples of the *Thunder* appearing in popular culture:

Umberto Eco's novel *Foucault's Pendulum* quotes a portion of it in chapter 50; the Nobel Prize–winning novelist Toni Morrison uses excerpts from the *Thunder* in her novels *Paradise* (1999) and *Jazz* (1992). Larry Lawson and Levi Lee use about a dozen lines in their play, *Some Things You Need to Know Before the World Ends (A Final Evening with the Illuminati)* (1981). The Native American author Leslie Marmon Silko includes lines from the *Thunder* in her novel, *Gardens in the Dunes* (1999).

A 2005 television commercial directed by Jordan Scott (the daughter of director Ridley Scott) depicts a woman moving through various urban scenes (such as the back of a taxi and a nightclub) while a voiceover female narrator reads selections of the *Thunder*.

An April 17, 1998 episode titled "Anamnesis" from the second season of the *Millennium* TV series dealt with Mary Magdalene and quoted some lines from the *Thunder*.

The poem has been used as inspiration for an album by the apocalyptic folk band Current 93 and industrial music band Nurse With Wound. Excerpts from the text are spoken in the song "I Am" by the band Tulku on the album *A Universe to Come*.

The Twin Cities' Opera Millennium staged *Thunder, Perfect Mind* in Fall 1997 by the award-winning composer Christopher Preissing. The opera featured six female singers/dancer, a soprano soloist, and percussionists performing on large resonators made especially for the performance. Two years earlier, the Finnish composer Ari Vakkilainen also composed music for a staging of his opera, *The Thunder–Perfect Mind* (1983–94). Most recently, the American a cappella group, Anonymous Four, sang *Thunder, Perfect Mind* in Coptic.

QUESTIONS TO CONSIDER

1. The *Thunder: Perfect Mind* is just one of the remarkable documents that emerged from the Nag Hammadi writings. A number of years ago, Yale professor Bentley Layton wrote a wonderful essay in which he treated the text like a riddle. Try out his approach. Who is the Thunder?

2. What sort of people do you think were writing *Thunder: Perfect Mind* and the *Trimorphic Protennoia*? What social class? What kind of education had they received? Did they think of themselves as Christian, Jewish, pagan, or none of the above? What did they think of the Roman Empire? What did they think of Jesus?

3. What sorts of social roles do you think women might have played in the communities that used *Thunder: Perfect Mind* and *Trimorphic Protennoia*?

KEY TERMS

Adam	Sethian	hypostasize
Eve	Ennoia	aretalogy
redaction	Wisdom literature	Meirothea
docetist	Isis	Ialdabaoth
Septuagint	aeon	Prologue (Johannine Prologue)
Barbēlō	syzygy (pl.: syzygies)	Christology
Logos	voces magicae	catechumen
Five Seals	Protennoia	

FOR FURTHER READING

Layton, Bentley. "The Riddle of the Thunder (NHC VI, 2): The Function of Paradox in a Gnostic Text from *Nag Hammadi*." In *Nag Hammadi, Gnosticism, and Early Christianity*, edited by C. W. Hedrick and R. Hodgson, 37–54. Peabody, MA: Hendrickson, 1986. A wonderful article that challenged scholars to look at the *Thunder* in a new way. For advanced students.

Thunder, Perfect Mind. A new translation and edition by Hal Taussig et al. Salem, OR: Polebridge, 2008. This new translation offers a provocative new reading of the *Thunder*. Various chapters and articles included with the translation can be very technical and theoretical, and are designed only for advanced readers.

Jordan Scott's short film for Prada is online at: http://www.youtube.com/watch?v=7hgQ7dOCeeY

16

What Are Pagan Texts Doing in a Christian Library?

DISCOURSE ON THE EIGHTH AND NINTH (NHC VI, 6), *ASCLEPIUS* (NHC VI, 8), AND PLATO'S *REPUBLIC* (NHC VI, 5)

You might think that ancient books gathered, copied, and preserved in an ancient Christian monastery would be Christian. The NHL contains explicitly Christian texts and less obviously Christian texts (those that we cannot tell if they are Christian or not), plus other texts that we are quite certain were not Christian texts at all (see table 16.1). The most famous example of this is the brief fragment of Plato's *Republic*, which we have from Codex VI in a very poor copy. By the time this tractate was copied, that text was already many hundreds of years old, so it is hardly surprising that a fourth-century scribe did not get a very good master document to copy.

Table 16-1 lays out all the Nag Hammadi writings and arranges them according to whether they were Christian, inasmuch as scholars can discern.

As you can see, the NHL is, for the most part, a Christian library, with more than half its documents being either explicitly Christian or probably Christian. Those that we call "probably Christian" do not have an obvious "smoking gun," that is, they do not feature Jesus or any of his disciples, but they might have **Christ** appear as **Seth**, or they might strongly resemble other Christian documents because of their interest in shared themes or language. Those that are "possibly Christian" likewise share affinities in themes and language with our obviously Christian texts, but otherwise give no explicit or implicit hint that their authors thought that Jesus was the Savior. Those that we consider "non-Christian" clearly draw upon other traditions in Graeco-Roman literature and philosophy, and are sometimes attested in other non-Christian collections such as the **Corpus Hermeticum**.

Interestingly, the explicitly non-Christian texts found in the NHL are not there by accident, nor are they scattered in the NHL randomly. Besides Plato's *Republic*, we have three treatises: (1) an untitled tractate we've named

TABLE 16.1: Nag Hammadi Writings by Religious Tradition

Christian	Probably Christian	Possibly Christian	Non-Christian
Prayer of the Apostle Paul	Hypostasis of the Archons	Apocalypse of Adam	Plato's Republic
Apocryphon of James	On the Origin of the World	Thunder: Perfect Mind	Discourse on the Eighth and Ninth
Gospel of Truth	Exegesis on the Soul	Authoritative Teaching	Prayer of Thanksgiving
Treatise on the Resurrection	Gospel of the Egyptians	Paraphrase of Shem	Asclepius
Tripartite Tractate	Concept of Our Great Power	Zostrianos	Three Steles of Seth
Apocryphon of John		Marsanes	Sentences of Sextus
Gospel of Thomas		Allogenes	Eugnostos
Gospel of Philip		Hypsiphrone	
Book of Thomas the Contender		Trimorphic Protennoia	
Sophia of Jesus Christ		Thought of Norea	
Dialogue of the Savior			
Apocalypse of Paul			
1st Apocalypse of James			
2nd Apocalypse of James			
2nd Treatise of the Great Seth			
Acts of Peter and the Twelve Disciples			
Apocalypse of Peter			
Letter of Peter to Philip			
Interpretation of Knowledge			
Valentinian Exposition			
Melchizedek			
Testimony of Truth			

Discourse on the Eighth and Ninth (NHC VI, 6); (2) a short excerpt of a longer piece called *Asclepius* (NHC VI, 8) (also known as the *Perfect Discourse*); and (3) a short prayer, the *Prayer of Thanksgiving* (NHC VI, 7). All three texts are found in the same codex as the fragment of Plato, in Codex VI. All three also derive from a corpus of ancient **pagan** writings called **Hermetica**. What's particularly interesting is that the person who collected these non-Christian writings chose to sequester them together in a single codex.

Why would a Christian scribe collect, copy, and transmit pagan writings in the fourth century?

In this case, the copyist himself gives us some tantalizing information. After copying one text in the codex, he includes a **colophon** at the end:

> I have copied this one discourse of his. Indeed, very many have come to me. I have not copied them because I thought that they had come to you [pl]. Also, I hesitate to copy these for you because, perhaps they have [already] come to you, and the matter may burden you. Since the discourses of that one, which have come to me, are numerous. (NHC VI 65:8–14, trans. Brashler/Dirkse, in James Robinson, editor, *The Nag Hammadi Library in English* [San Francisco: Harper & Row, 1988]: 299)

Who was this copyist? Here, the mystery thickens. There are two possibilities: first, that copyists worked for private patrons who hired them to compile books for them. This scenario would look something like this: A wealthy Roman Egyptian, male or female (let us assume female here, just to shake up our assumptions), would be particularly interested in acquiring a book of sacred writings. She might be a follower of **Hermetic** doctrine, or she might want a collection of texts that might help her get information on what happens after death, for example. If she wanted a book, the place to go would be to a specialist: a scribe, someone who had access to a lot of different writings. She would therefore hire a copyist to produce this custom-order work for her. These books would have cost a fortune, but those few with money in the fourth century often had a great deal of money, and books were very precious luxury objects indeed. In this scenario, the scribe may have had no particular investment in choosing the texts to go in the volume, nor would he have to believe in the doctrine they contained. In the case of Codex VI, the scribe actually leaves us a note intended for his customers, explaining his rationale for including the texts he did. His main aim was to please his customers.

There is at least one other scenario. In this one, the scribe in question is a monk, who produces a volume of non-Christian texts for others within his monastery or others within the Christian monastic world. This would mean something fairly profound: that fourth-century monastic Christianity was elastic enough to find value in pagan texts. In a way, though, this becomes less surprising when you read these documents. Although they are definitely not Christian, they have many ideas and teachings, which they shared with unambiguously Christian texts. Although these pagan texts were pagan, monks understood them not as foreign, forbidden, alien pagan texts but as crypto-Christian texts, or texts that could be interpreted in such a way as to bring them into line with fourth-century monastic Christianity.

While either hypothetical scenario is possible, both lead us to an interesting observation: apparently the lines between Christian and pagan were no more fixed in the fourth century than were the lines between Christian and Jewish in the first century. And although *we* may feel more comfortable assigning a text to one or another religious tradition, this sort of classification suits modern sensibilities, not ancient ones. In the first scenario I suggested, a private non-Christian citizen would have to do business with a Christian scriptorium, and that Christian scriptorium would have to be willing to procure, copy, and keep (for the purpose of making further copies) pagan texts. Since traditionally scholars of antiquity have seen Christians and pagans as habitually locking heads or shedding blood, this scenario forces us to rethink what social relations in the ancient world really looked like. In the second scenario, although a Christian monk would be corresponding only with other Christians, at some point the clearly pagan NHL texts had to come from pagans. If they were truly adversaries, those monks would have burned them or at least, refused to have collected them. Instead, monks collected pagan texts and considered them, too, to be sacred. One thing this tells us is that the line between Christian and non-Christian was probably more fluid than we might expect. In fact, we know the names of at least two Egyptian priests who joined Christian monastic communities and presumably would have brought with them a great source of knowledge. It is very likely that these priests would have brought their own books with them into the monasteries. So what might be in these particular pagan texts copied into the NHL that drew the attention and respect of Christian monks?

THE HERMETICA

The three clearly pagan texts in Codex VI—*Discourse on the Eighth and Ninth*, *Prayer of Thanksgiving*, and *Asclepius*—belong to an ancient spiritual tradition known as **Hermetism/ Hermeticism**. All these texts are called, collectively, the Hermetica. They take their name from their legendary author, an ancient sage by the name of **Hermes Trismegistus** ("Thrice-Great Hermes").

Hermes did not actually exist; the writings ascribed to him were composed by various unknown ghost writers who wrote anonymously for a few hundred years. What did exist, however, is the spiritual path that the Hermetica lays out.

The Hermetica were originally written in Greek but were a quintessentially Egyptian body of literature. Their ties with the past were not authentic—that is to say, when citizens of the Roman Empire read the Hermetic texts, they believed them to be old, whereas in reality they were ancient forgeries. They were inspired, no doubt, by the vast richness of pharaonic Egypt, the remains of which (as still today) filled people with awe and curiosity.

The Hermetica is extraordinarily diverse, incorporating all manner of different ideas and

FIGURE 16.1 In the Renaissance, Hermes Trismegistus was revered as a virtuous pagan who had predicted the birth of Christ. This image of Hermes Trismegistus can still be found on the marble inlaid floor of the cathedral in Siena, Italy.

WHO WAS HERMES TRISMEGISTUS?

In the Hermetic literature, Hermes Trismegistus is primarily a spiritual teacher who delivers lectures and engages in dialogues with his students on the nature of the cosmos. Identified with both the ancient Egyptian ibis-headed god Thoth (who was associated with writing) and with the Greek god Hermes (who served as a messenger between gods and men, and is therefore the god of interpretation of words), Hermes Trismegistus was also what scholars call a **psychopomp**: an otherworldly figure who could lead souls to the afterlife.

traditions. Think of them as sort of ancient pop-culture New Age documents: they contained astrological, astronomical, botanical, medical, alchemical, and magical writings as well as more traditional essays on Platonism and Stoicism. We also find Jewish and ancient Egyptian elements in the mix, making the Hermetica the most eclectic corpus of ancient writings that exist.

The Hermetica, as a corpus of ancient writings, has been woefully ignored in modern scholarship. The problem is not accessibility; unlike the Nag Hammadi texts, the Hermetica were never lost and were actively studied during the Renaissance. In the early twentieth century the texts were favored by mainly British transcendentalists and mystics such as Helena Blavatsky and Aleister Crowley. Their popularity among certain modern Western mystics reflects their nature as ancient esoteric texts, which taught people ways to unite in ecstatic vision with God. Unfortunately, scholars of ancient Christianity have largely ignored these texts; because they are not Christian, there is the idea that they have little to teach us about Christianity, but in fact there are some significant points of overlap between certain Christian texts and the Hermetica, as we will see in this chapter.

As far as pagan texts go, the Hermetica tend to be monotheistic. They assert the superiority of a single God, and this God is characterized by impersonal or abstract qualities (the Good, the Divine). In their theology, the Hermetica drew on traditions of Greek philosophical thought, particularly **Platonism** and **Stoicism**. Some people often make the mistake of thinking that Christianity (and its mother religion Judaism) were monotheisms that grew in an environment of pagan polytheism, but this is a misconception. Many of the ways that Christians conceptualize God actually originated within Greek philosophical circles. To put it differently, in terms of theology, Christians of the second or even fourth century were not likely to have seen much significant difference between the way that they, as Christians, conceptualized God and the way that pagan followers of Hermetic doctrine conceptualized God. Although they do not mention Jesus as a savior, the way they visualize the cosmos and its working, and the way that they think of God, are perfectly in keeping with a Christian worldview. Later Christians—from Saint Augustine to prominent Renaissance thinkers—considered Hermes Trismegistus as one of the pagan "prophets" of Christianity, a figure who attested to the truth of the Christian message by teaching it, in an inchoate form, even before the birth of Jesus.

The Hermetica, however, are not just interesting theological writings; they are based on the conviction that humans have within them a divine spark that connects them to God. Hermes Trismegistus emerges as the wise teacher who will help the student to reconnect to that divine spark (one text counsels, "Who knows oneself knows the All" [DH 9,4]). In order to reconnect, various techniques were assumed, rather than laid out in the ancient documents as clearly as we would like, but they appear to have included meditation, visualization, turning one's attention inward and quieting the mind, chanting or singing, and praying.

The environments from which many of our NH texts emerged and from which the Hermetica stemmed were probably, in some cases, identical. This is why they share so much in common. Both drew from spiritual disciplines alive in their day; both were active schools of thought in Alexandria, Egypt, in the second and third centuries; both were premised upon the assumption that people needed to reconnect with their Divine Source through a process of interiority, turning one's examination within, as in certain meditative techniques. Finally, both probably also issued from the same social class: not from highly educated elites but from moderately to well-educated middle-class intellectuals interested in ancient knowledge.

The three Hermetic writings from Nag Hammadi all qualify as "philosophical Hermetica," in that they are more interested in metaphysics than, for example, botany or astronomy. Two (the *Prayer of Thanksgiving*, and the *Discourse on the Eighth and Ninth*) record specific prayers. (The *PThanks* is such a classic example of ancient prayer that you will find it discussed in chapter 5.) Both texts were unknown to modern readers before the discovery of Nag Hammadi. The third, *Asclepius*, was in a Latin copy, which surfaced in the Renaissance; we were able to recognize the Nag Hammadi version as *Asclepius* even though it is only a fragmentary copy preserved in Codex VI. We will consider *Disc8th9th* and *Asclepius* separately before we look at some of the themes that they share with other, non-Hermetic writings from Nag Hammadi. At that point, we will be in a better position to determine what these particular texts might have been doing in a largely Christian collection of texts.

DISCOURSE ON THE EIGHTH AND NINTH: BACKGROUND

This writing is an initiatory text leading readers toward a mystical union with the All, or the One, the principal source or force in the cosmos. It is of particular interest to scholars because although it is clearly a Hermetic document, it was unknown to us before the discovery of the NHL.

An anonymous student opens the tractate by reminding his teacher Hermes Trismegistus of his promise to lead him into the **Ogdoad**, the eighth cosmic sphere, and then the **Ennead** or the ninth cosmic sphere. Having done all the preliminary work of preparation, the student is now ready for his initiation into the deeper (or higher) mysteries of the cosmos. After a dialogue about spiritual rebirth, Hermes and his disciple pray to the Invisible God and are granted two visions, one of the eighth realm, and one of the eighth and ninth realms. At this point, the initiate is "born again," having received a spiritual kiss (57:27) that symbolizes divine love. The tractate ends with various warnings to preserve the book from misuse.

Cosmology of the *Discourse on the Eighth and Ninth*

Hermes promises to lead his student to the Ogdoad or eighth realm, which tells us a few things. First, it tells us indirectly that the student has just symbolically passed through the lower seven planetary realms. The order of these realms differed in antiquity but included the sun, moon, Mercury, Venus, Mars, Saturn and Jupiter (remember this was a pre-Galilean, geocentric model). The lower realms were under the powers of lesser gods or beings (here called **Ousiarchs** and could often be associated with bodily emotions or appetites; these same Ousiarchs also controlled astrological fate. The Ogdoad was therefore the lowest of the upper cosmic realms that were directed by higher deities; the Begotten One controls this lower realm where also dwell the angels and the immortal human souls of those who had died. In the ninth realm lives the Self-Begotten One, also known as the **Nous** or Divine Mind. Whoever wrote this text probably also imagined a tenth realm where the First Principle or Unbegotten God dwelled, but there is no reference to it in the text. That is not surprising: the realm of the Unbegotten God is completely unreachable to humans, souls, angels, or any other sort of being; it contains only itself. Nevertheless, the soul experiences true bliss by reaching the Ennead and has reached as far as an individual soul could journey and return.

Concepts of God in the *Discourse on the Eighth and Ninth*

The highest God is ineffable and takes three forms: The Unbegotten, the Self-Begotten, and the Begotten. These forms are located spatially but also arranged in terms of hierarchy. Only in the lower of the three forms (the Self-Begotten and the Begotten) does the highest God become visible or knowable to an initiate. Salvation consists of the soul of the initiate (before or after death) rushing up through the lower seven realms to the Ogdoad and Ennead, to participate in the hymns of praise that the celestial inhabitants offer up to the Ineffable God. The goal of this praise and prayer, however, is not merely to praise God but to participate in God's being through the soul's transformation into a higher form, that of Divine Mind itself.

ASCLEPIUS (NHC VI, 8)

Another text that preserves the teaching of Hermes Trismegistus to his disciples Tat, Asclepius, and Ammon, *Asclepius* (*Asclep.*) is

the eighth tractate of Codex VI. Also known as the *Perfect Discourse* (its original title in Greek), scholars have had fragments of the Greek original of this writing for a long time, plus there is a very good Latin manuscript of the entire work, which is fortunate, because the Coptic translation we have in Codex VI is quite fragmentary. Like most Hermetica, *Asclep.* is a dialogue between Hermes and his students. If you've read any of Plato's dialogues, you'll see that these are similar in style: students ask stupid but leading questions; Hermes tells them off and sets them on the right path. *Asclep.* dips into a very ancient genre.

The NH portion of *Asclep.* begins abruptly, with a commentary on the nature of sexual intercourse as a wonderful "mystery" between a male and female. It is a bit strange to find this positive assessment of sex in the NHL, considering it was copied by Christians and came out of a variety of ancient Mediterranean cultures that tended to see sexual intercourse and sexual desire as wayward or even demonic impulses. Why the excerpt begins here is indeed mysterious, but then, we do find similarly positive assessments of sex in, for instance, the *Gospel of Philip*, where sex between a married couple is also considered a mystery that in some way reflects the higher functions of the cosmos.

The main focus of *Asclep.* is worship, specifically, the question of how gods ought to be

---

"OPPOSING THE ACTS OF FATE" (*DISC8TH9TH* 62:41)

We find a curious line at the conclusion of the *Discourse on the Eighth and Ninth*: "And write an oath in the book, so that those who read the book cannot misuse its language, nor (use it) to oppose fate" (62:41). What does it mean to "oppose fate"? In Roman Egypt, we often find this kind of warning on ancient documents; the idea apparently was that unscrupulous magicians might improperly use the invocations and prayers in this text in order to gain freedom from the planetary gods who control human destiny. Compare this ancient magic spell, which provides instructions on how to rid yourself

from your fate. The blank spaces are for the user to fill in her or his name:

An angel will come in, and you say to the angel, "Greetings, lord. Both initiate me by these rites I am performing and present me [to the god] and let the fate determined by my birth be revealed to me." And if he says anything bad, say, "Wash off from me the evils of fate. Do not hold back, but reveal to me everything, by night and day and in every hour on the month, to me, _____, son of _____."

(PGM 13.608–17, trans. Betz [1992], 187)

worshiped. The problem was probably a pressing one at the time that the text was written (probably in the second century) for a couple of reasons. First, pagan monotheists from philosophical traditions such as Hermeticism probably struggled with how to reconcile their monotheistic or **monadic** philosophy with traditional pagan polytheism. Most pagans worshiped a variety of gods, and part of being a good citizen involved participating in temple practices. Egyptians in particular were proud of the antiquity of their temples and their gods. So in *Asclep.*, Hermes explains the nature of the relationship between humans and gods: gods are immortal, but humans are superior because they are *both* mortal and immortal. Second, as the Empire Christianized, Egyptian temples were abandoned, desecrated, or destroyed. Egyptian Hermetists must have faced this situation with deep ambivalence: on the one hand, temple worship and temple religion was only a preliminary step on the path toward knowing God through mystical contemplation and philosophy. On the other hand, the abandonment of the gods and their earthly homes was a horrifying sign of the end of a very ancient culture. In fact, Hermes speaks in apocalyptic terms of this having already happened:

> …but when the gods have left the land of Egypt and have flown up to heaven, all the Egyptians will die, and Egypt will be deserted by the gods and the Egyptians. For you, O river, the day will come when you will flow more with blood than with water. Dead bodies will be piled higher than the dams, and the dead will not be mourned as much as the living. (*Asclepius* 71:12–24, trans. Marvin Meyer, in Marvin Meyer, editor, *The Nag Hammadi Scriptures* [San Francisco: HarperOne, 2007]: 433)

It is tempting to think that the author of *Asclepius* composed these words at a time of social crisis; just as many scholars think that Jewish apocalyptic literature is "crisis literature" (see chap. 18) produced by a disaffected remnant just waiting for their moment of vindication when God would punish the mighty and exalt the meek. For the author of *Asclep.*, however, this moment never arrived.

The Cosmology of *Asclepius*

At the lowest cosmic level, the earthly gods live in temples (69:26). Beyond this, the star-gods dwell in their own abode; at the highest, immaterial level of being exists the Invisible Unbegotten God (75:9–14). This **cosmology** is relatively streamlined, and it also isn't too heavily **Platonized** as we find in other Hermetica, including the *Disc8th9th*. In fact, *Asclepius* is different from many of the NH texts in that it isn't essentially a cosmological treatise; it is about how to honor the gods, or God, properly (and what happens if you do not). More cosmological details come at the final passages on the nature of punishments awaiting wicked souls; the structure of the cosmos and its inhabitants seems to have Greek, Jewish, and Egyptian elements. The afterlife judgment of souls is an ancient Egyptian motif, but the entity doing this is not the Egyptian God of the Dead, Osiris, but a "great demon" that the Supreme God has appointed. The Coptic word for "demon" here is the Greek loan word **daimōn**, which didn't have a negative connotation in the first and second centuries but by the fourth century, at least in Christian writings, had become a designation for an evil being. Here, the *daimōn* is not just a judge but a punisher of wicked souls, as in the *Apocalypse of Paul* and *Book of Thomas the Contender*. These souls are trapped in an area *Asclepius* calls "the open sea of the air," where there is "blazing fire, freezing water, streams of fire, and massive turbulence" (77:12; trans. Marvin Meyer, in Marvin Meyer, editor, *The Nag Hammadi Scriptures* [San Francisco: HarperOne, 2007]: 436). In this otherworldly zone, demons called "stranglers" torment souls into eternity. In this unforgiving portrait of the afterlife, *Asclepius* shares much with later, Christian medieval portraits of hell.

The Concept of God in *Asclepius*

Although *Asclepius* is a pagan document, note that it speaks about God as a single, divine force in the cosmos who looks out for humankind and acts only beneficently. God sends "*gnosis* and learning" to people (66:26); God is the sole creator, and although gods exist, they are neither malevolent like archons nor superior to human beings; God wills good things and creates a good world: "and the good world is an image of the good." God is, finally, omnipresent and omniscient: he is everywhere and sees everything. In this theology, *Asclep.* stands closer to Platonic and Stoic monotheism than to the more radical NH documents such as *HypArch* and *OrigWld*, where the cosmos is not made all good by the Supreme God, and where evil and deficiency percolate through most levels of being.

A FEW HERMETIC THEMES

Hermetic writings from NH share with other Hermetica not included in the NH a series of seminal characteristics. Curiously, though, many of these characteristics are also found in non-Hermetic NH documents. Consider these themes, for example:

1. Mind

    A keen reader will notice the use of the term "mind" quite often in the NH Hermetica. "Mind" (Greek: **Nous**) in these documents encompasses much more than we think of when we use the word. "Mind" connects us with God; it comes from the very essence of God. In the Hermetic worldview, humans are "mortal gods," and our minds are what connect us with the Divine Mind. But Hermetic teaching says that we must cultivate and use our minds properly in order to see or contemplate the Divine. Through contemplation, prayer, and praise, a Hermetist could recognize that she could see through God's eyes, in a sense, and become Mind itself. In *Disc8th9th*, Hermes makes it clear that when he ascends to the Ogdoad, he becomes the Mind: "I am Mind and I see another Mind, the one that moves the soul" (58:5) and "I have said, my son, that I am Mind. I have seen" (58:15).

2. Mystical Ascent

    When Mind goes up to the Ogdoad, it shares in the nature of things in the Ogdoad. But the goal of mystical contemplation is for the individual Mind to join with Universal Mind, at which point it can sail upward to the Ennead or Ninth. While the eighth realm is cosmic (i.e., part of this world) the Ninth is actually hypercosmic, outside the known cosmos or world, where nothing else exists except Mind/God. A mind at this level transcends everything: difference (including gender difference), even sound. For this reason, prayers will not work to get into the Ninth, because there is no sound (sound requires two things: something to make the sound and something to hear it). There is no language ("language is not able to reveal") (58:16–17); note the silent hymn of the souls and angels to the Ennead (58:20). Notice, too, the shift from the pronunciation of sacred vowels and words (useful at the Eighth level) to Silence in the Ennead. To get into the Ninth, Mind must descend and draw one up like iron bits to a magnet; it cannot be achieved through human effort. Other texts that focus on ascent include the Sethian apocalypses (*Zostrianos*, *Allogenes*, *Marsanes*, and *Melchizedek*) (see chap. 19) but the best analogue to *Disc8th9th* is the *Three Steles of Seth* (see chap. 10). The two texts share a number of similarities, particularly the idea of an ecstatic ascent through the upper cosmos to gain a vision of the Father.

3. Knowledge as a Path to Salvation

    The very fact that the Hermetica consistently feature a teacher instructing a student is witness to the fact that those who read the Hermetica were convinced of the importance of knowledge passed down through a human teacher, the acquisition of this knowledge in its fullest form, and the deployment of this knowledge as a form of salvation. In other words, salvation in the Hermetica is not about putting faith in someone or believing in someone; neither was it about grace, a kind of gift from the divine that elevates a faithful person nor was salvation necessarily about ethical behavior (although many Hermetic texts are indeed concerned about the need to be a good person). The most important thing to bring salvation is acquiring knowledge, especially concerning how the cosmos works and how it mirrors God's goodness.

4. Secrecy

The Hermetica are **esoteric** documents, meaning that they were not meant to be read by outsiders. The teachings they contain are sacred, and therefore they sometimes contain admonitions not to reveal their content to outsiders. It is possible that there might have been a small degree of historicity in this claim; in the fourth century, particularly zealous Christians began to systematically destroy pagan sites (particularly in Egypt, the home of the Hermetica) and to persecute non-Christians. It is possible, on the one hand, that in the environment of persecution, Hermetists had to be careful about what they were up to. On the other hand, most Hermetica was probably written somewhat earlier than this and was part of a broad tradition of "secret" writings that one group kept hidden from an audience they considered unworthy. Consider, for instance, the opening lines of the GThom: "these are the secret words that the living Jesus spoke to Judas Didymus Thomas." The Disc8th9th ends with an oath that the content of the book be kept secret, actually cursing anyone who dares to violate the writing's secrecy.

5. The Spiritual Superiority of Egypt

The Hermetica all derive from Egypt, and reflect ancient Egyptian religious traditions or reinterpretations of those traditions; in most cases the religion of the pharaohs had been long lost, along with knowledge of how to read hieroglyphics. As Egyptian "nationalist"

documents, the writings often share a pride in their country and its traditions. In the Disc8th9th, for instance, the anonymous student is instructed to write down his vision on turquoise steles to be placed on the shrine dedicated to Hermes in a place called Diospolis, which is probably known to Egyptian archaeologists as the temple to Thoth in Diospolis Magna, a city once known as Thebes (Luxor), and now known as Kasr al-Agouz.

The *Asclepius* contains a long lamentation on the fallen state of Egypt (70:3–71:9), which it calls "the image of heaven," the "dwelling place of heaven," and "dwelling place of the gods." Although the passage is apocalyptic in tone, it draws its language not from Jewish apocalyptic literature (compare the texts we discuss in chap. 18) but from ancient Egyptian lamentations such as the *Lamentations of Ipou-our* (ca. 2190–2070 BCE) and the *Oracle of the Potter* (ca. 130 BCE). These texts express a profound contempt, even horror, for the foreign invasions of Egypt, the loss of moral values, and the abandonment of the gods. Like the *Oracle of the Potter*, *Asclep.* ends with a full-blown apocalyptic destruction of the world, followed by God's judgment and "setting right" of the now-purified world. The focus on Egypt as an image of heaven is not confined to Hermetic texts; in the NHL, the author of *OrigWld* refers to Egypt as "paradise."

There are many reasons why the people responsible for including non-Christian writings in the Nag Hammadi codices might not have been troubled about what they were copying. It is entirely possible that they were not quite as concerned about drawing the line between Christian and non-Christian writings as we might expect them to have been. Instead, whoever copied and commissioned these non-Christian writings in Codex VI were probably mindful that they contained many points of contact with

Christian texts, including a similar focus on God the Father, and the belief that through prayer, one could become a holy enough person to be granted a vision of God.

QUESTIONS TO CONSIDER

1. What similarities do you detect between the NH Hermetica and Christian writings, especially the NH Christian writings? If you had come to them without knowing better, would you have assumed they were Christian? Or not?

2. Do you think that fourth-century Christians would also have found the similarities between the NH Hermetica and Christian texts suggestive enough that they might have considered them "crypto-Christian"?

3. What kind of practices or social community do you imagine for someone who read and used the Hermetica? Did they pray together, for instance? Practice strange meditation techniques? Were there many of them, or was it just a single teacher and a student or two meeting in a house? What do you think?

KEY TERMS

Hermeticism/Hermetism	Hermes Trismegistus	*Corpus Hermeticum*
Hermetica	colophon	psychopomp
Platonism	Stoicism	Ogdoad
Ennead	Ousiarchs	daimōn
Nous	esoteric	Christ
Seth	pagan	cosmology

FOR FURTHER READING

Copenhaver, Brian. *Hermetica: The Greek Corpus Hermeticum and the Latin Aesclepius in a New Translation*. New York: Cambridge University Press, 1992. This is the best and clearest English-language translation of the original Hermetic texts of the *Corpus Hermeticum*, with helpful notes.

Fowden, Garth. *The Egyptian Hermes. A Historical Approach to the Late Pagan Mind*. Princeton: Princeton University Press, 1988. For intermediate readers interested in learning more about who wrote and used the Hermetica in Roman Egypt.

Van Den Broek, Roelof. "Gnosticism and Hermetism in Antiquity: Two Roads to Salvation." In *Gnosis and Hermeticism From Antiquity to Modern Times*, edited by Roelof Van Den Broek and Wouter J. Hanegraaff. Albany: State University of New York Press, 1998. A somewhat technical essay that paints both traditions with broad strokes, but which illustrates much of the shared conceptual material between some Gnostic documents and the Hermetica. For more advanced readers.

Additional resources

A Dutch private library founded by Joost Ritman, Bibliotheca Philosophica Hermetica in Amsterdam, contains more than 20,000 books on esotericism, including a 1471 edition of the *Corpus Hermeticum*. Find information about it online at: http://www.ritmanlibrary.nl/.

Trismegistos is an Internet portal with significant but hard-to-find ancient documents archived for professional scholars: http://www.trismegistos.org.

17

CHAPTER

Apostolic Traditions in Conflict

LETTER OF PETER TO PHILIP (NHC VIII, 2), *ACTS OF PETER AND THE TWELVE DISCIPLES* (NHC VI, 1), AND THE *APOCALYPSE OF PETER* (NHC VII, 3)

H ere's a quick quiz: What do the *Gospel of Thomas*, the *Letter of Peter to Philip*, the *Apocryphon of James*, the *Apocryphon of John*, and the *Gospel of Philip* all have in common? Besides the obvious (that they are all texts found in the NHL) you have probably had no difficulty answering the question: they are all texts named after Jesus's apostles.

Why would a text be named after an apostle? The short answer is to draw upon the authority of that apostle. Most of these texts purport to have been written by eyewitnesses to Jesus and to record special or privileged knowledge that Jesus passed directly to that person. After Jesus's crucifixion (somewhere around 30 CE), his students gathered to decide how to move forward in a way that was most faithful to what they had learned from their spiritual leader. Inevitably, there must have been clashes as to who remembered traditions best, who really understood the way to move forward, and how these differences should be resolved in Jesus's absence. There was, after all, a great deal at stake.

In this chapter, we consider some Nag Hammadi texts associated with one of Jesus's disciples, Peter. Peter is an interesting character in early Christian tradition. On the one hand, in the Roman Catholic Church he becomes perhaps Jesus's most important disciple. The heart of the Roman Catholic Church is the cathedral known as St. Peter's in Rome, and if you have ever been there, you might have noticed in the center of the church, you find Jesus's words to Peter in Latin: *tu es Petrus, et super hanc petram ædificabo ecclesiam meam:* "You are Peter, and on this rock, I will build my church" (Mt 16:18). In black letters more than five feet high, the phrase circles the inside of the cathedral's massive dome. Many Christians believe that Peter's bones lie under the altar, and each pope claims his own right to be pope from being in a direct line of **apostolic succession** tracing back to Peter, whom they see as the first pope, the person Jesus handpicked to succeed him.

Conversely, if you consider the New Testament, there are very few documents in it that are said

218

to derive from Peter. There is a bit written about him in the book of Acts, but of actual writings ascribed to Peter, we have only two short letters near the end of the Bible, 1 Peter and 2 Peter. Compared to the thirteen much longer letters attributed to Paul, that is not very many. Even more complicated and confusing is the way that Peter is portrayed as the leading apostle in all of the NT gospels. However, that does not mean that he is always portrayed in glowing terms. Sometimes he reveals glimpses of insight. But he can also be quite slow to catch on to Jesus's meaning at many points. In the Gospel of Mark, for example—where all the disciples misunderstand Jesus's purpose on earth—Peter leads in that misunderstanding, at one point even being rebuked as "Satan" for refusing to accept Jesus's journey to the cross (Mk 8:33). Peter is also known in Christian tradition for denying three times that he knew Jesus when confronted by Roman soldiers after Jesus's arrest (Mt 26:71–75; Mk 14:66–72; Lk 22:54–61; Jn 18:15–27). In the NT overall, Peter is hardly the chief hero, the undisputed successor to Jesus. What all these early Christian documents—some pro-Peter, but others apparently anti-Peter—seem to bear witness to, then, is that there was some debate in early Christian communities concerning whether Jesus really favored Peter and chose him over the other disciples to lead the movement forward. The three NH documents that bear Peter's name—the *Acts of Peter and the Twelve Apostles*, the *Letter of Peter to Philip*, and the *Apocalypse of Peter*—all derive from communities where Peter was held in esteem. Ironically, perhaps, they offer more emphasis on this perspective than does our modern New Testament; ironic, too, is that the Roman Catholic Church, with its celebration of Peter as the "rock" upon which the Church was built, considered these three texts to be heretical and ordered them to be destroyed. Why would this be the case? In this chapter, we look at this hidden or esoteric **Petrine** tradition that evidently flourished in some communities, as they vied for authority in the growing Christian movement.

THE LETTER OF PETER TO PHILIP: BACKGROUND

The *Letter of Peter to Philip* (*LPP*) is one of only two letters in the Nag Hammadi collection (*TreatRes* is the other), but in Christian antiquity, there appear to have been a number of similar letters ascribed to Peter; two of them remain at the end of the NT (1 Pet and 2 Pet). Collectively, these documents are known as the Petrine epistles. The *LPP* is similar to some other Petrine letters but dissimilar enough to be considered a new writing when it was discovered at NH. In the 1980s, another copy of the letter was found in the **Codex Tchacos**, which was published in 2006. The NH *LPP* is in good shape, with only very few bits missing, and appears, like all the other NH writings, to have been translated into Coptic from a Greek original at some point in the late second century or perhaps a bit later.

The *LPP* starts with Peter asking Philip to join him and the other disciples for reunion after Jesus's death. Peter gathers the other disciples together at the Mount of Olives in Jerusalem, hoping that Jesus will appear to them still again, as he appeared to them before in that place. The disciples do not yet have wisdom or *gnosis*; when Jesus does appear, they ask him a variety of anxious questions about the nature of the **archons**. Jesus gently chastises them, saying that he had already answered the same questions "when he was in the body" (133:17; 138:3; 139:11), yet the disciples do not seem to have been capable of fully understanding what he had been telling them. You may notice, then, that despite its title, this nine-page-long "letter" is really mostly a **revelation discourse,** a genre where Jesus reveals secret knowledge to his chosen disciples.

Peter, in the *LPP*, comes across as a trusted authority. He is clearly the leader of the remaining

WRITING IN THE APOSTLES' NAMES: PSEUDEPIGRAPHA AND APOCRYPHA

Two strange words you might come across while reading about ancient documents are **pseudepigrapha** (sing.: pseudepigraphon) and **apocrypha** (sing.: apocryphon). Both are Greek technical words for a genre of sacred literature. An **apocryphon** means a secret or hidden writing thought to contain obscure and sacred knowledge. In the NHL, we find an *Apocryphon of James* and an *Apocryphon of John*. These are probably the titles by which they were known in antiquity, but some modern scholars choose to translate apocryphon as "secret book," thus the alternative titles the *Secret Book of James* and the *Secret Book of John*. Both texts purport to be teachings that Jesus Christ revealed to his brother James and his disciple John of Zebedee, respectively. There are actually many works of early Christian apocrypha beyond those in the NHL. Not all of them are what could be called **Gnostic** in nature (in fact most are not); they cover a variety of topics and viewpoints, such as the *Protevangelium of James* (an influential and popular account of Jesus's birth) or the *Apocryphal Acts of the Apostles*, a collection of miracle stories about Jesus's disciples.

A **pseudepigraphon** is a writing composed in the name of someone else, a pseudonym. It was common in antiquity for someone to act as a ghostwriter, composing a text in the name of a biblical figure. It is likely that this was not seen as dishonest but as a tribute to the authority and wisdom of that figure. The *LPP* is a pseudepigraphon, purported to be Peter's composition. We can tell from the style and vocabulary that it was actually written much later. The two gospels in NHL attributed to disciples (*GosThom* and *GosPhil*) are also pseudepigrapha, as are the apocalypses of Paul, James, Adam and Peter, although only the *GosThom* purports to have been written by Thomas; the *GosPhil* is not said to have been written by Philip.

disciples, and it may be that he even has his own disciples (139:10). Filled with the Holy Spirit, he delivers an inspired sermon (compare Acts 2:14–42), after which the disciples go out to perform healings on their missionary journeys.

PETER AND THE TRADITION OF THE TWELVE APOSTLES

According to tradition, Jesus had twelve disciples (Mk 3:13–19; Mt 10:1–4; Lk 6:12–16):

- Peter (also known as Simon Peter)
- Andrew, brother of Peter
- James of Zebedee, the brother of John
- James, son of Alphaeus
- John, also known as John of Zebedee
- Philip
- Bartholomew
- Matthew (perhaps known as Levi)

- Thomas (also known as Judas Didymus Thomas)
- Thaddeus
- Simon (also known as Simon the Zealot)
- Judas Iscariot (replaced by Mattathias after Jesus's death)

The names on this list were likely traditional rather than historical; we think this because the list given in the Gospel of Luke differs in some respects from the lists in Mark and Matthew, and because twelve disciples are not named in the Gospel of John (and the named disciples there also differ slightly from the lists in Matthew, Mark, and John). In fact, Jesus had far more than twelve disciples (for instance, the Gospel of John names as disciples Nicodemus and Joseph of Arimathea). There were also women disciples around Jesus (Salome, Mary Magdalene, and the sisters Martha and Mary are all named in early

Christian tradition). In his important Letter to the Romans 16:7, written before the NT gospels (and therefore our earliest evidence), Paul names a married couple, Andronicus and Junia, as being "of note among the apostles." In another important letter, 1 Thessalonians, Paul also names two other apostles: Timothy and Silas (1:1 and 2:6). In Acts 14:14, Barnabas is called an apostle. So although Jesus clearly had more than twelve disciples, twelve was a significant number for early Christians, probably because it corresponded to the twelve tribes of Israel. The tribes descended from the Jewish patriarch Jacob's twelve sons; each settled in different territories (except for Levi, whose descendants, the Levites, became priests at the Jerusalem Temple) and according to tradition, became the founder of a "tribe" of Jews. Thus as Christianity grew and separated itself from Judaism, a Christian twelve, each with their own area of mission, came to replace the Jewish tribal ancestors.

The number twelve was also significant in the second century because it corresponded to another famous twelve: the signs of the zodiac. This, however, was not a particularly good association, since the constellations of the zodiac were believed to be responsible for astrological fate. Astrological fate was a kind of determinism that suggested that, for example, if you were born under the sign of Aries, the Ram, you were bound to be stubborn. Your personality, and also your fate, was determined by your specific horoscope. The *Gospel of Judas* is one second-century text that seems particularly concerned with the astrological symbolism of the twelve disciples, who are never individually named in that text, but who are clearly associated with the stars and fate. In the *GosJud*, the disciples are negative, even demonic characters (see chap. 20). There are also shades of this belief in the NH *Apocalypse of Paul*, where Paul travels through the heavens and meets all the disciples in the **Ogdoad**, one of the cosmic spheres.

PETER (AND PAUL) IN ACTS

The longest book in the New Testament, the book of Acts of the Apostles (usually just called Acts), begins where the four canonical gospels end: after the death and resurrection of Jesus. In fact, it is the second part of a two-volume work, the first being the Gospel of Luke. Acts is the first work of Christian history, and for this, it is tremendously significant.

According to Acts 1–2, Jesus's disciples gather together fifty days after Jesus's death, and here they experience a joint theophany or manifestation of God, here of Jesus in the form of the descent of the Holy Spirit. Their faith renewed, the disciples receive Christ's commission to go

APOSTLE OR DISCIPLE?

The terms "apostle" and "disciple" are often used interchangeably, but actually mean something slightly different. An "apostle" is from the Greek *apostellein*, "to send forth," that is, disciples whom Jesus sent out as missionaries. A "disciple" is from the Latin *discere*, "to learn." Jesus's disciples were his students who learned directly under him during his lifetime. All the disciples were also apostles, but not all the apostles were disciples; some came afterwards. The apostle Paul, for instance, never met Jesus but became his apostle following an experience of the risen Christ. In other words, while the time of being a disciple of Christ was limited to Jesus's lifetime, others who committed themselves to Christ after the crucifixion could be given the title "apostle" if they engaged in spreading their new beliefs that Jesus was the awaited Messiah and Savior.

out, preach, heal, perform miracles, and draw others into their new religious movement. Acts makes it seem as if this process worked smoothly; other sources, however, let us know that the actual process of first-generation growth of what would become known as Christianity was not quite so easy. Different leaders, some of whom were not present during Jesus's lifetime, vied for authority, each with a slightly different idea of what it meant to "follow Christ."

At the center of this crisis of leadership lay two important figures. The first was the apostle **Paul**, a Jew from Asia Minor who had, so he tells us, been a persecutor of Jesus's first followers until a profound religious experience on the road to Damascus forever changed him and he became an "apostle of Christ Jesus." Paul had never met Jesus, but his experience of the risen Christ compelled him to believe that he, too, could take his place among those whom Jesus had sent out as apostles, missionaries to the new religion. This news apparently came as a surprise to Peter, also known as Simon Peter or Cephas, who along with James was one of the leaders of the Jerusalem Assembly, Jesus's chief successors. Paul and Peter had somewhat different ideas about what it meant to follow faithfully in the direction that Jesus had established. Peter missionized predominantly among the Jews of Roman Judea, as had Jesus; Paul, by contrast, believed that the risen Christ had given him permission to bring the "good news" of Christ risen to the Gentiles, that is, those in the Empire who were not Jewish. Although Acts was written in such a way that the conflict between Peter and Paul is downplayed (claiming that Peter also preached among Gentiles, and Paul also preached in synagogues), it was probably a significant disagreement; aside from Acts, no early Christian text reconciles the two figures. In fact, Paul's own letters (particularly his letter to the Galatians, chap. 2) reveals the tensions between the two followers of Jesus.

Some early Christian texts feature Peter as the most important of the apostles; other texts

TABLE 17.1: NH Texts Associated with Jesus's Apostles

James	Apocryphon of James
	1st Apocalypse of James
	2nd Apocalypse of James
Peter	Acts of Peter and the Twelve Apostles
	Apocalypse of Peter
	Letter of Peter to Philip
	Acts of Peter (BG)
Paul	Prayer of the Apostle Paul
	Apocalypse of Paul
Thomas	Gospel of Thomas
	Book of Thomas the Contender
John	Apocryphon of John
Philip	Gospel of Philip

feature Paul. Other writings favor James, Jesus's brother, as the most significant disciple; others favor Philip, or Thomas, or Mary Magdalene. In the NHL, we find a number of writings that draw on the authority of one or another of their favorite disciples (see table 17.1).

The first half of Acts —1 through 12—is very Petrine; it focuses on Peter as the chief disciple and paints an unambiguously positive picture of him. Whoever wrote the *Letter of Peter to Philip* must have known this writing and agreed with Acts' depiction of Peter, because the two ancient works have many points of similarity. It is interesting to note that in these Petrine works like the *LPP*, Paul does not appear at all. In fact, there is some evidence to point to their anti-Paulism in what it is that they teach.

ACTS OF PETER AND THE TWELVE DISCIPLES AND APOCRYPHAL ACTS

Although the most famous and earliest of them all is the NT book of Acts of the Apostles, in antiquity, more than a few books circulated, which were known as "Acts" of certain apostles. So far as we know, all of these books were written after the book of Acts, and they can be quite a bit more colorful. Christians clamored to know more about Jesus's disciples, and literature about them started to circulate in the second and third centuries. It is possible that these originated as oral literature: stories, anecdotes, and legends told about one or more of their favorite disciples. At some point, these legends were written down. Or, it is equally possible that these books were literary productions from the start, but they were stories designed to delight as well as to build people's faith. Partly because these were popular stories and not specifically the kinds of writings that **heresiologists** bothered to classify as heretical, we actually have lots of apocryphal acts that survived, including:

- *Acts of Peter*
- *Acts of Paul* (which contains the *Acts of Paul and Thecla*)
- *Acts of Andrew*
- *Acts of Philip*
- *Acts of John*
- *Acts of Thomas*

Some of these *Apocryphal Acts* survive in Greek, Latin, or Coptic, but they are also preserved in a host of ancient languages including Syriac, Ethiopic, and Old Church Slavonic, proving how popular they were in antiquity. It is easy to find older English translations of these books on the Internet, and if you read them you will probably be charmed by them. Unlike the book of Acts, they read a little like ancient novels, full of delightfully implausible details. In the *Acts of John*, the disciple stays at an inn so infested with bedbugs that he curses them and tells them all to leave his room; in the morning, John's companions find the apostle has had a restful sleep because the bedbugs are all congregating outside his door, waiting patiently for him to leave so that they may

bite the next guest and not trouble a "servant of God." Other apocryphal acts feature talking dogs and roosters, fish that resurrect from plates to jump into water and swim away, and even a flying contest in the Roman forum between Peter and his archenemy, the wicked magician Simon Magus. The NHL *Acts of Peter and the Twelve Disciples* (*ActsP12*) has none of these charming details, but it nonetheless reads as a fanciful enough tale with almost folkloric qualities to be classified with the other apocryphal acts. It is the only one of its kind at Nag Hammadi, and thus a little bit of an outlier from the other writings in that collection, but nevertheless it represents a very popular literary genre that would have been well known in the ancient Christian world.

ACTS OF PETER AND THE TWELVE APOSTLES: BACKGROUND

The *ActsP12* is found in Codex VI, an eclectic collection that also contains many **pagan** documents (see chap. 16). This text is decidedly Christian and very different from the other writings in that codex. Based on a Greek original, this tractate is different from another ancient document, also called the *Acts of Peter*, which we had not seen before the discovery of the NHL. The NH *Acts of Peter* is a well preserved, twelve-page-long text in the codex, with only minor damage to its first two lines. It is hard to know how to date the original writing, but it contains similarities to another Roman Christian document, the *Shepherd of Hermas*, which dates to the first or second quarter of the second century. By that measure, the *ActsP12* probably derives from the middle of the second century to the third century.

The *Acts of Peter and the Twelve Apostles* is a kind of "romance," an ancient genre, which did not necessarily involve romantic love but tells an engaging story and builds on stock characters (here, the apostle Peter) and stock situations (a sea voyage to a new place, and an encounter with the people living there). It is also an *allegory*, that is, behind the obvious meaning of the text, it really tells a story in veiled terms, a Christian story in this case. Is it Gnostic, though? Scholars are divided on the question, but the majority would say no. The stories that the writing contains are fanciful, but there is nothing overtly heretical about the ideas or the view of Christ or salvation in the text. There is no real emphasis on knowledge, no elaborate **cosmology** featuring, let's say, an ignorant **demiurge**, nor any of the other characteristics that some people use to define a Gnostic text.

ACTS OF PETER AND THE TWELVE APOSTLES AND ALLEGORY

If *ActsP12* is not a Gnostic text, what is it? One thing it clearly is is an allegory. The first clue that this is an allegory comes in the name of the fictional city that Peter reaches, which is called "Habitation" or "Abide-in-endurance." This may mean something like "the inhabited world."

An allegory is much like an extended parable, a speech-form that is very common in the NT. In fact, Jesus speaks a parable in the Gospel of Matthew that may have provided the inspiration for the *ActsP12*:

> Again, the kingdom of heaven is like a merchant in search of fine pearls, who, on finding one pearl of great value, went and sold all that he had and bought it. (Mt 13:45–46, RSV)

Allegories were very common in the ancient world, particularly in philosophical writings, and by the second century they had become a popular literary form. The *ActsP12* is not the only apocryphal act to contain an allegory; there is another very famous one called the *Hymn of the Pearl* in the *Acts of Thomas*. In the *Hymn of the Pearl*, the speaker is the son of a king; traveling to Egypt to capture a pearl from a serpent who guards it, he slowly forgets who he is and what he had been sent to accomplish. A letter from his father, the king, reminds him of his quest; he snatches the pearl, and returns to his kingdom. In a sense, the *Hymn* is a deeply Gnostic allegory: the son represents the soul, sent from the Father in the **Pleroma** and incarnated into a body; the soul then forgets its true spiritual origins and becomes caught up in matter and the material. It requires a "call" or spiritual awakening from above in order to awaken the soul to remember its task: reclaiming the "pearl"—the inner divine spark— and returning to its source. This is the same story we find expressed in the *ApJn*; it is also the same story as expressed a bit differently in another NH text, the *Exegesis on the Soul*. We even find it in

WHY A PEARL?

In the *ActsP12*, Peter comes across a pearl merchant, whose name is Lithargoel (meaning "light-bright stone," from Gk *lithos*, "stone," and *argos*, "shining." The "el" suffix refers to God and often appears in names of angels). Everyone clamors around Lithargoel, wishing to get a glimpse of the precious object. And indeed, pearls were precious objects, carefully harvested during the second century CE by specialized divers in the Persian Gulf and near Sri Lanka, very far from Rome. Pearls were therefore a highly coveted form of wealth;

one of the most famous stories from antiquity is that the Egyptian queen Cleopatra dissolved a large, precious pearl in wine and drank it, to satisfy a bet with her lover, Mark Antony. But beyond their material value, the pearl evidently served as a symbol for the human soul, or more properly, for spiritual salvation. It is this symbolic meaning that the "pearl" serves in the *ActsP12*, just as it does in another famous text from antiquity, the *Hymn of the Pearl* from another apocryphal book, the *Acts of Thomas*.

the movie, *The Matrix*. So it is a very ancient allegory, and inasmuch as it is about recognizing one's spiritual self as identical with the divine, it is very Gnostic.

The allegory in *ActsP12* is not Gnostic, however. There is also a pearl in this text, but unlike in *Hymn of the Pearl*, the pearl doesn't stand for self-knowledge or *gnosis*; it represents Jesus's teachings. The pearl merchant, Lithargoel, tells Peter and the other disciples that they must go to his city to spread their teachings, but that only those who have renounced everything can reach it (5:19–25). The pearl, here, is that it (i.e., Jesus's teachings) is precious, must be defended, and those who want to possess it must face dangers and renounce everything. There is nothing in this allegory to associate these teachings with *gnosis* as it is classically defined (see chap. 1).

APOCALYPSE OF PETER: BACKGROUND

In typically confusing manner, we have a couple of ancient texts with the name *Apocalypse of Peter*. We call this one the *Nag Hammadi Apocalypse of Peter* or the *Coptic Apocalypse of Peter* to distinguish it from the *Greek Apocalypse of Peter*, although (also confusingly) the best manuscript of the Greek document is in Ethiopic. The *Coptic Apocalypse of Peter* is one of the best preserved of all the writings from Nag Hammadi; only a few letters are missing. The Coptic translation is not very good, however, so even though the document is well preserved, we can't always understand what the text itself actually says. Although it appears to have been written in Greek, some scholars think this text originally came from Syria, where other texts about Peter also originated and where there was at one time considerable interest in this particular disciple. When it was written is another mystery, but it probably dates to the third century, because the author speaks out so harshly against Christian dogmas that came to be more dominant around that time.

Unlike the *Greek Apocalypse of Peter*, the *Coptic Apocalypse of Peter* isn't an apocalypse at all. It is a revelation dialogue, in which the resurrected Christ comes and speaks with his disciple Peter. Unlike an apocalypse in which secrets of the cosmos are revealed to a seer (see chap. 18), Christ speaks to Peter about the true story of the crucifixion.

Peter in the *Apocalypse of Peter*

There can be no doubt that whoever wrote this text revered Peter as Jesus's chosen disciple. Although Peter is fearful that the angry mob arrayed against Jesus will kill both of them, and although he will deny Jesus three times, Jesus gives him courage, vision, and insight into what is to come. In this way, Peter's bad behavior in the canonical gospels (especially Mark) is explained: he denied Jesus because it was part of the divine plan. The *ApocPeter* shares this view of Peter with other Petrine texts, but most significantly with the *Letter of Peter to Philip*.

Jesus in the *Apocalypse of Peter*

Although Peter in the *Apocalypse of Peter* behaves as we might expect a chief disciple to behave, Jesus in this text may surprise, even shock, some readers. In this text, Jesus acts as a divine mediator or revealer, giving Peter a "tour" of the events surrounding the crucifixion. (A careful reader may notice that he is never called Jesus or Christ in the *ApocPeter* but Savior.) Now things get substantially more confusing; the Savior is having a conversation with Peter *in the middle of the crucifixion*, but it is not the Savior who is being crucified, but the "living Jesus." Peter speaks:

What do I see, O Lord? That it is you yourself whom they take, and that you are grasping me? Or who is this one, glad and laughing on the tree? And is it another one whose feet and hands they are striking?

The Savior said to me, "He whom you saw on the tree, glad and laughing, this is the living Jesus. But this one into whose hands and feet they drive the nails is his fleshly part, which is the substitute being put to shame, the one who came into being in his likeness. But look at him and me." (81:6–24, trans. Roger Bullard, in James Robinson, editor, *The Nag Hammadi Library in English* [San Francisco: Harper & Row, 1988]: 344)

Christ laughing on the cross? It is a striking image but actually not that rare; we find the same thing happening in another NH text, the *Second Treatise of the Great Seth*. The Savior laughs at the stupidity of those who preach among themselves "Christ crucified." We'll come back to why Christ laughs momentarily; in the meantime, something else in this text is quite remarkable. As he stands there with the Savior Jesus, watching the living Jesus laughing as he is crucified, Peter continues his narration.

And I saw someone about to approach us resembling him, even him who was laughing on the tree. And he was [filled] with a Holy Spirit, and he is the Savior. And there was a great, ineffable light around them, and the multitude of ineffable and invisible angels blessing them. And when I looked at him, the one who gives praise was revealed. (82:4–16, trans. Roger Bullard, in James Robinson, editor, *The Nag Hammadi Library in English* [San Francisco: Harper & Row, 1988]: 344)

Remarkably, there seems to be a *third* Christ here: first, the "fleshly" Jesus hanging on the cross, whose hands, feet, and sides are being pierced; second, the Savior talking to Peter, and third, this light-being Savior "filled with a Holy Spirit." This multiplication of Jesus into various divine Christ-beings is a feature of some **Sethian Christologies**, where we find earthly Jesuses, a heavenly Christ, and then the heavenly Seth who is the Christ (look, for example, at the *GosEg*). The three Christs may also relate to the threefold nature of human beings in Sethian and Valentinian theory. Jesus who is crucified on the cross is the *sarkic* or "person of flesh"; the Savior who speaks to Peter is the *psychic* person (that is to say, this Savior is the soul or ethereal substance of Jesus Christ); and the Christ of light surrounded by angels is the

pneumatic or spiritual Christ. These three "persons" of Jesus Christ correspond to a tripartite division in the ancient Greek and Roman worlds of humans into body, soul, and spirit. Although most people nowadays have only heard of two divisions—body and soul—the soul was in these teachings actually a kind of ethereal body that carried the spirit like a chariot as it traveled from its source in the upper cosmos into the body or as it moved in reverse, after the death of the body. In this way, the soul "serves" the spiritual body, which is why the Savior here speaks of this Christ as his "servant" and his "ethereal body."

ARE THESE PETRINE TEXTS GNOSTIC?

These three texts are useful, grouped together, to help us to think critically about the term "Gnostic" and whether it helps us to understand the Petrine tradition. The *ActsP12* is really not Gnostic, in the sense that there is no focus on hidden knowledge that brings salvation, no mythological framework to the text, no dualism, and no other evident markers of Gnostic thought. Both the *ApocPeter* and the *LPP* could arguably be said to have Gnostic elements, but interestingly these elements are not equally shared in the two documents. Both have **revelation discourses** in which the Savior makes known hidden information about the nature of reality. But while the *ApocPeter* focuses on the crucifixion, the *LPP* records the Savior's teachings about the **archons** and how they came to be. It presents a version of a cosmological myth about **Sophia**'s fall, one that is not quite the same as in any other NH document but which nonetheless follows a general pattern familiar from other Sethian writings.

One prominent theme in these Petrine texts is that Jesus was not actually human and thus did not actually suffer on the cross (**docetism**). Interestingly, it is a position present in a number of writings associated with the apostle Peter. Besides the *ApocPeter*, docetism is also featured in the *LPP*, where Peter insists that contrary to appearances, Jesus did not suffer on the cross (139:13–25). In the *Second Treatise of the Great Seth* (*2ndTreatS*), Peter also talks with Jesus; there, the Savior laughs at the ignorance of those who think that they crucified Christ (51.20–52.3 and 55.16–56.20). And in fact one thing that the heresiologists accused various Gnostic teachers and groups of was being docetists.

Docetism was a hot-button issue among early Christians, because it emerged from different understandings of the nature of divinity. On the one hand, many Christians felt that the idea that humans might cause God to suffer was absurd, even obscene. God cannot suffer, because he is so far up the cosmic chain of being that lowly humans could not effect real suffering. The Petrine writers who ascribed to docetism appeared to have based their ideas on this fundamental principle. On the other hand, some Christians insisted that God had incarnated into flesh, and that flesh was fully human: thus Jesus suffered as a human would have suffered (and more, in fact, because much of that suffering was existential and spiritual). This was the position of proto-orthodox Christians. But to say that all docetists were Gnostic is a gross over-simplification. There is one NH text, *Melchizedek*, a Sethian Christian revelation discourse (and thus, technically Gnostic) but which is stridently anti-docetic, polemicizing against those who erroneously say that Jesus was not really crucified. The truth is, a variety of Christian groups debated the question of whether God could suffer, and what this suffering really meant.

The *LPP* offers a sophisticated take on the problem of suffering. It assumes a docetic position, in that it appears to argue that Jesus was "a stranger to his suffering" (139:21–22). But at the same time, Peter asserts that Jesus's suffering was indeed real: not only at his death but from the time he was incarnated into flesh. The source of

this suffering—not only for Jesus but also for his followers—was the "transgression of the Mother" (139:23). In this document Original Sin did not start with Adam and Eve's disobedience in the garden of Eden; it started with Sophia's disobedience in the Pleroma when she gave birth to the misshapen **Ialdabaoth** without the permission and participation of the Father. At issue, it seems, was the importance of a "suffering Savior" for the morale of this author's Christian community. Rather than brushing off the suffering of the crucifixion as a monstrous but futile act of the authorities of darkness, the *ApocPeter* sees the cosmos as shot through with suffering originating in a primordial act of divine sin. This myth of evil's origin gave meaning to the sufferings of the readers of the *ApocPeter*.

AUTHORITY AND VISIONS: THE POST-RESURRECTION APPEARANCES

Various Christian accounts all concur that after the crucifixion, the resurrected Jesus appeared to his disciples. This was indeed a miraculous event, but it was not a neutral one: the question of to whom Jesus appeared, what form he took, and what he said at the appearance (or appearances) was hotly contested between early Christians, and indeed we find absolutely no signs of agreement from our earliest sources on these details. But they were important, because Jesus's post-resurrection appearances conferred considerable authority on those who had them. Consider this fascinating passage from Paul's First Letter to the Corinthians, where he talks about his own experience of the risen Christ:

> For I handed on to you as of first importance what I in turn had received: that Christ died for our sins in accordance with the scriptures, and that he was buried, and that he was raised on the third day in accordance with the scriptures, and that he appeared to Cephas [Peter], then to the twelve. Then he

appeared to more than five hundred brothers and sisters at one time, most of whom are still alive, though some have died. Then he appeared to James, then to all the apostles. Last of all, as to one untimely born, he appeared also to me. (1 Cor 15:3–8, NRSV)

This passage does a lot of work. Here, Paul is speaking to his community of Christ-followers in Corinth, around the middle of the first century. Jesus had been dead, by that time, for about thirty years. In telling them all this, he is, first of all, justifying where his authority comes from. Paul needed to do this, because unlike Peter and the other disciples, he did not know Jesus when he was alive. What gives him his unique authority, his zeal, is his experience of Jesus. That vision was the end point to Paul's most glorious truth: that Christ died to redeem humankind from sinfulness and that he was resurrected. Paul also notes here, interestingly, that Peter was the first to witness the risen Christ (although if you look carefully at the post-resurrection stories in the four NT gospels, you may find something a bit different). He also says that Christ appeared to Peter and then to the Twelve, as if Peter were not in fact part of the Twelve, but probably he meant Christ appeared first to Peter alone, and then to Peter as part of the Twelve (the title *Acts of Peter and the Twelve Apostles* assumes the same thing). After a good number of other impressive appearances, Christ finally appears to Paul (his curious self-description "as to one untimely born" conveys his humility).

But let's focus on the first part of Paul's words, here: that Christ appeared first to Peter. This, indeed, is the Petrine position we find reflected (even assumed) in the *LPP* and the *ApocPeter*. We find the same thing in two other NH writings that don't mention Peter in their title but which are nevertheless Petrine: the *Second Treatise of the Great Seth* and the *Apocryphon of James*. Peter most certainly does not receive the important first appearance of Christ in other ancient texts, such as the *Gospel of Mary* (see chap. 20).

From all this, we know that there was substantial anxiety as well as controversy about who first saw the resurrected Jesus, and what that meant for the recipient of these visions or experiences.

The controversy about who was really the most significant disciple is also reflected in the *ApocPeter*, which contains (along with the Petrine *2ndTreatS*) some of the most brutal condemnation of other Christians in all our ancient literature. There are clear polemics against someone or something called Hermas (78:18), which is probably a reference to a popular second-century apocalyptic text known as the *Shepherd of Hermas*, mentioned earlier. The author also rails against those Christians who are appointing for themselves bishops and deacons, "as though they had received their authority from God" (79:22–31). But most saliently, we find polemics against Pauline theology. It was Paul, after all, who insisted on teaching a doctrine centered around "Christ, crucified," as he himself puts it: "I decided to know nothing among you except Jesus Christ, and him crucified" (1 Cor 2:2, RSV). This teaching—with its focus on Jesus's suffering and death—appalled Petrine Christians, who saw their own version of Christ's significance diminished by the powerfully popular Pauline Christianity. The bitter enmity between these two factions of Christians had provoked, at the close of the first century, the author of Acts to try to reconcile the two figures. But his attempt failed, and in these NH Petrine texts we get to witness the slow death of once-vital Christian schools that saw Peter as the first, and best, of the apostles. Other schools argued the same thing, namely that Peter was foremost among the apostles. What made the difference between those groups of Peter-followers that thrived and those groups that failed was a matter of theology, or, more precisely, of Christology: those Petrine groups that argued that Christ had not really suffered and died were overcome by the voices of Petrine Christians who saw the reality of the crucifixion and resurrection as the center of Christian faith.

QUESTIONS TO CONSIDER

1. In *Against Heresies (Adv. Haer.)*, the great heresiologist of the second century, Irenaeus of Lyons, defines Gnosticism according to the following theological or cosmological principles:

   - Gnosticism proposes two gods, not one
   - Gnostics believed that the world was made by angels
   - Gnostics believed that the world was created by defect or ignorance

   - God created all things from preexistent matter.

   How do these three texts from the NHL, a collection of supposedly Gnostic texts, do against Irenaeus's criteria?

2. Which of Jesus's disciples do the NH texts tend to hold in high regard? Any idea why? What are the sorts of things that these disciples learn in these texts?

3. Do you detect any differences between NH Petrine texts and NH Pauline texts (Pauline texts include *ApocPaul*, and *InterpKnow*)?

KEY TERMS

apostolic succession	Petrine	Sophia
Ogdoad	pseudepigrapha	revelation discourse
heresiologists	*sarkic*	Paul
pagan	archons	*pneumatic*
cosmology	Codex Tchacos	docetism
demiurge	apocrypha	Ialdabaoth
Pleroma	*psychic*	

FOR FURTHER READING

Barnstone, Willis, ed. *The Other Bible*. San Francisco: HarperOne, 2005.

Schneemelcher, Wilhelm, and Robert McL. Wilson, eds., *The New Testament Apocrypha*. Vol. 2, *Writings Related to the Apostles*. Louisville: John Knox Press, 1992.

For studies about some of these texts

Davies, Stevan. *The Revolt of the Widows: The Social World of the Apocryphal Acts*. Southern Illinois University Press, 1980. An interesting and accessible book about the social setting of the apocryphal Acts, which Davies sees as coming from oral literature often passed along by women.

Molinari, Andrea Lorenzo. *The Acts of Peter and the Twelve Apostles (NHC 6.1): Allegory, Ascent, and Ministry in the Wake of the Decian Persecution*. Leiden: Brill, 2000. A revision of a PhD dissertation, this is the most comprehensive study of the *ActsP12*. For advanced students only.

Pagels, Elaine. *The Gnostic Gospels*. New York: Random House, 1979. A very readable source on the conflicts between various Christian groups all aligning themselves in the names of various disciples and traditions.

18

Apocalypse! Visions of the End

APOCALYPSE OF PAUL (NHC V,2) AND APOCALYPSE OF ADAM (NHC V,5)

In this chapter we look at two of the apocalyptic texts that bear the name **apocalypse** in their titles: the *Apocalypse of Paul* (*ApocPaul*) and the *Apocalypse of Adam* (*ApocAdam*). Then we consider a few apocalyptic passages embedded in other generally non-apocalyptic texts to determine what the literary function of these passages might be. First, though, it is important to go over what makes an apocalypse an apocalypse, and where the genre comes from. Let's start by placing ourselves back in the immediate social context of the first century CE.

BUILDING A SOCIAL CONTEXT

Imagine a world where demons are in control of the government, war is constant, and the enemy appears to be gaining an upper hand. Your holy places are defiled and razed; your most revered political figure publicly tortured and assassinated. Public assembly for protest is forbidden, and those who speak out against the government are arrested, tortured, and put to death in full public view. For many Jews and Christians, this is the world of the first and second centuries. It is no wonder that so many of them speculated that the world might be coming to an end.

In this atmosphere of violence and political oppression, Jews, and then Christians, began to circulate a special kind of writing we call apocalypses or **apocalyptic literature**. The word "apocalypse" means, literally, an "unveiling" (Gk *apo* = "away" + *kalyptos* = "veil"). The word is similar to the Latin "revelation," which contains both the words "veil" and "to reveal." (This is why the NT's book of Revelation is also called the Apocalypse of John.) Although the word "apocalypse" conjures images for most of us of the end of the world, the term itself does not precisely mean only that. It refers more to knowledge that is unveiled, often knowledge of the nature and shape of the heavens. This knowledge includes, usually, information on the structure or geography of the heavens: what is found where, such as where the sun and moon go when you cannot see them; the storehouses of wind and rain; angels and other celestial beings; where human souls go after death; or where to locate things like heavenly temples and cities that mirror those most holy places on earth. Then there are also other things you might see in the heavens:

- Angels and other celestial beings
- The divine throne on which God sits, sometimes located in the heavenly temple in the heavenly Jerusalem
- Paradise or Eden (thought to be in the heavens, not on earth)
- Blessed souls and cursed souls making their way through the cosmos, either to be reincarnated into human bodies, or released into the highest cosmic realm

An apocalypse, then, is really an ancient tour guide, a sort of *Lonely Planet* or *Let's Go: Cosmos* that one might want to consult if just for the pleasure of dreaming of a trip. But sometimes people actually did take them with them, or at any rate they tried: a number of apocalyptic texts have been found in the graves of ancient Egyptian Christian monks. Did these monks deliberately have themselves buried with apocalyptic "tour of the heavens" texts in order to guide them through the afterlife? It is a compelling thought!

JUDAISM AND APOCALYPTIC LITERATURE

Although it is well attested in early Christian literature, the apocalyptic genre actually derives from Judaism. Our earliest apocalypse is a noncanonical Jewish text called 1 Enoch, and the oldest parts of that text derive from the third century BCE. Another early apocalypse, the Hebrew Bible's book of Daniel, was written around 165 BCE. Another book in the Hebrew Bible, the book of Ezekiel, may be even older. Although Ezekiel is not an apocalypse, it has many apocalyptic elements that were influential on later authors,

especially those writing the texts found in the NHL. If you haven't read Ezekiel and Daniel, you might take a look; they are fascinating texts full of extraordinary images.

Although Ezekiel and Daniel, as canonical texts, are our best-known examples of Jewish apocalyptic, there are many similar texts that still survive. Other influential Jewish apocalypses include 1 Enoch, 4 Ezra, and 2 Baruch; if you were raised in the Roman Catholic or Eastern Orthodox traditions you may be familiar with 4 Ezra; in some English Bibles, this text is called 2 Esdras. First Enoch is an ancient Jewish text composed in Greek sometime around the third century BCE. It tells of the heavenly journey of its hero, Enoch (in Gen 5:1–24, Enoch is the father of Methuselah and the great-grandfather of Noah. A righteous man, Enoch does not die but is taken away to heaven at the age of 365). The book of 1 Enoch records the details of Enoch's heavenly tour and includes a fascinating (and in the ancient world, highly influential) story of the fall of the angels. Many of the Nag Hammadi writers appear to have known, and used, 1 Enoch, as well as the book of Ezekiel; imagery from these two texts appears prominently in a wide variety of NHL texts, such as *HypArch* and the *ApJn*. Thus we know that whether or not the writers of apocalyptic literature in the NHL were themselves Jewish, they were intimately familiar with Jewish apocalyptic texts and traditions.

FEATURES OF ANCIENT APOCALYPTIC LITERATURE

One consistent feature of an apocalyptic text is that it always includes at least two characters: (1) a divine revealer sent from the heavens to disclose heavenly knowledge or to act as a celestial tour guide; and (2) a recipient of the revelation, sometimes called a **seer**. There is often a dialogue between revealer and seer, and these texts can be extremely visually oriented, consisting of a lot of description of what the seer sees. Sometimes the heavenly revealer explains to the seer (and thus to the reader) the meaning of the curious sights that the seer encounters on his trip (I say "his" here with good reason: in virtually all our extant Jewish and Christian apocalyptic texts, the seer is male, with the possible exception of Mary Magdalene in the *Gospel of Mary* and the *Books of Jeu*, neither of which is from Nag Hammadi).

Another consistent feature is *conflict*: the setting for an apocalypse is always a war in the heavens, or else the war is between heaven and earth. But there is, always, hope. Although things look grim, there is a portion or remnant of humanity who will be spared, while the rest will suffer horrible fates. God controls this process of judgment, and in the end, righteous people who suffer now will be vindicated and emerge victorious. Part of the point of the apocalyptic text, therefore, is to provide hope and reassurance alongside cosmic knowledge.

In 1978 a conference of religious studies scholars convened to discuss the topic of apocalypticism and produced, from that conference, an influential collection of studies published by an academic journal, *Semeia*. Scholars together composed what came to be, in the field, a famous formulation (the **Semeia Definition**) concerning what constituted apocalyptic. It was:

> A genre of revelatory literature with a narrative framework in which revelation is mediated by an otherworldly being to a human recipient, disclosing a transcendent reality.

To unpack this a bit, an apocalypse is a form of literature (not, for example, a kind of historical writing, or a prophecy). It has a story (a "narrative framework") in which a human seer gains secret knowledge about the cosmos from an encounter with an "otherworldly being."

There are two types of apocalypses: *heavenly journeys* and *historical sketches*, although a single apocalyptic text can contain elements of both. Here are the basic features of each type:

1. The *Heavenly Journey* recounts the trip of a seer, who is taken on a tour by a heavenly revealer of some sort, usually an angel. This type focuses on the revelation of certain secrets about the true nature of the world.

2. The *Historical Sketch* uses symbols and cryptic language to express in veiled terms the political realities of the author's day. For instance, in chapter 2 of the book of Daniel, a statue or image crafted of four different materials symbolizes four successive earthly kingdoms. Sometimes these symbols are explicitly explained; sometimes it remains difficult to know to what a symbol refers, particularly for readers outside the author's immediate political situation. For example, the city of Babylon that sits upon a beast with seven heads in the book of Revelation is never explained, but it nonetheless symbolizes the city of Rome and its seven hills. This guarded, symbolic language to discuss political realities likely provided a safeguard lest these books be discovered by the enemy. This second type of apocalypse is rarer than the first, and is not represented in the NHL.

According to one prominent theory, most ancient Jewish apocalypses were written under specific conditions of stress; the language and elaborate symbolism was necessary to speak in covert terms to avoid persecution. For example, the great beast rising out of the sea bearing the number 666 in Revelation 13:17–18 was probably a coded reference to the Roman Emperor Nero, who persecuted Jews and Christians in the first century (see chap. 3). But many scholars argue that the real meaning of some of these coded symbols would have been fairly obvious to Jews, Christians, and Romans of the time, and apocalyptic coded references were more about participating in a particular style of writing (that is, you use symbols and codes because that's what you do when you are writing an apocalypse) than it is about trying to keep the true meaning of the text a secret from outsiders.

OTHER APOCALYPSES

Although many people have heard of the book of Revelation (note that it is *"Revelation,"* in the singular, not Revelations, in the plural), they don't realize that we actually have scores of apocalyptic texts from Jewish and Christian antiquity that still survive. These include:

- The *Sibylline Oracles* (ca. 150 BCE and forward)
- The *Testament of the Twelve Patriarchs* (late 2nd c. BCE)

- The *Assumption of Moses* (6–36 CE)
- The *Martyrdom of Isaiah* (1st c. CE)
- The *Apocalypse of Moses* (ca. 70 CE)
- The *Testament of Abraham* (1st c. CE)
- The *Book of the Secrets of Enoch* (1st c. CE)
- The *Apocalypse of Abraham* (70–100 CE)
- The *Shepherd of Hermas* (early 2nd c. CE)

THE END OF THE WORLD AS WE KNOW IT?

Most of us associate the world "apocalypse" with the end of the world. And in fact "end of the world" apocalypses form a distinct subcategory of ancient literature. In these apocalyptic texts, the end is heralded by thunder and other cosmic disturbances, disease and depopulation, war, and the eventual return of a faithful remnant to the realm of the first Parent. Some of these end-of-the-world apocalypses found their way into the NHL, although none is as spectacular as the NT's book of Revelation. This is probably because by the second or even third century CE when apocalyptic texts were being written, fewer and fewer people still believed that the world was coming to an end. The second century was actually generally a time of peace and economic and political stability. Christians of the era might not have all seen it this way, since the second century was also a time of the persecution and martyrdom. Still, during this period, apocalyptic speculation became less about imagining the end times as a great cataclysmic event. By the third century, the "heavenly journal" apocalyptic type became far more prominent than the "historical sketch" apocalyptic type that more often featured an end-of-the-world scenario. At any rate, when Christians and Jews envisioned the end of the world they did not think of it in modern terms such as we find in movies like *Armageddon* or *2012*; they thought of it more as the fundamental disruption of the dominant political entity of the day (e.g., in the second century, the Roman Empire) and the initiation of a new age of righteousness, however that was understood.

APOCALYPSES AT NAG HAMMADI

There are a number of apocalypses in the NHL. There are four in Codex V alone, which make the entire codex a sort of "book of revelation." Five of these apocalypses bear the title "apocalypse": the *Apocalypse of Paul*, the *Apocalypse of Adam*, the *Apocalypse of Peter*, the *(First) Apocalypse of James* and the *(Second) Apocalypse of James*. Confusingly, however, three of these named apocalypses (the *Apocalypse of Peter*, and the two apocalypses of James) are not apocalypses at all, but **revelation dialogues** between the resurrected Jesus and a disciple. A revelation dialogue includes a speech that a heavenly revealer makes about the nature of the cosmos, but it does not have to do with a heavenly journey and does not concern the eschaton. However, there are enough points of overlap between the two genres to make a distinction between the two sometimes unhelpful. To make matters even more

ESCHATOLOGY

The English word "**eschatology**" derives from the Gk *eschaton*, the end of time. Some Jews in the Hellenistic and Roman periods appear to have had a particular concern that they were living in the end of days. This kind of eschatological expectation is clear from many of the writings in the NT, particularly the letters of Paul. It is difficult to tell whether Jesus was an apocalyptic prophet who preached an eschatological vision of the world (see, for instance, the "little apocalypse" in Mk:13); it is clearer, though, from what the gospels say of John the Baptist, who preached a doctrine of repentance in preparation for a day of wrath (e.g., Lk 3:7).

Technically, there are two kinds of eschatology we find in the NH writings: *future eschatology* and *individual eschatology*. While future eschatology concerns the fate of the cosmos as a whole, individual eschatology deals with the fates of individual souls. An example of future eschatology would be the disruption of the cosmos at the end of treatises such as the *Trimorphic Protennoia* and *On the Origin of the World*. Examples of individual eschatology would be the passage in the *(First) Apocalypse of James* 33.2–36.1 on the post-mortem judgment of souls, or the description of souls being tortured in the afterlife in the *Book of Thomas the Contender* 142–43.

bewildering, there are a few more apocalypses among the NHL that are not specifically called apocalypses in their titles but are nonetheless apocalypses. Finally, there are apocalyptic passages embedded in texts that are not themselves apocalypses. Table 18.1 on the next page may be helpful in keeping all this straight.

But things are still more complicated than this. Of the texts at NH that are apocalyptic, we can further subdivide these into apocalyptic texts that feature a heavenly journey, and those that do not (see table 18.2). Some of these revelation texts are *discourses* that simply describe a situation, and some are *dialogues* that ostensibly record a conversation or dialogue between the resurrected Jesus and his disciples.

With all this cleared up (!), let's turn to two classic, titled apocalyptic texts from Nag Hammadi: The *Apocalypse of Paul* and the *Apocalypse of Adam*. You'll notice, despite sharing a literary genre, that they are very different from one another. We will start with the *ApocPaul*.

The Apocalypse of Paul (NHC V, 2)

In the apostle **Paul**'s second letter to the Corinthians (**2 Cor**) he says a curious thing: "I

know a man in Christ who fourteen years ago was caught up to the third heaven. Whether it was in the body or out of the body I do not know, God knows" (2 Cor 12:2–4). This curious little passage (which many agree that Paul himself was the man in question but describes himself in the third person) offered a kind of jumping-off point for later writers: What did Paul see and do during his heavenly journey? Thus, a number of apocalyptic texts explore this theme, including a Greek *Apocalypse of Paul*, the *Apocalypse of Paul* from Nag Hammadi (also called the *Coptic Apocalypse of Paul*), and apparently an *Ascension of Paul*, a lost text still to be discovered. The Greek *ApPaul* was well known in the Middle Ages, so much so that Dante came to use it as a model when he composed his *Divine Comedy*.

The NH *ApocPaul* is short, only seven pages long, and is found in a single copy in Codex V. The title is written at both the beginning and the end of the document. It describes Paul's ascent from its onset in the third heavens to his journey through the fourth to the tenth heaven. As he ascends he witnesses the afterlife fate of souls in the heavenly sphere, as they are judged, punished, and send back down to be reincarnated or left to ascend to the highest heaven. Paul himself

TABLE 18.1: Apocalypses at Nag Hammadi

I. Explicitly titled apocalypses		
	a. Properly titled:	
		Apocalypse of Adam (NHC V, 5)
		Apocalypse of Paul (NHC V, 20)
	b. Improperly titled:	
		Apocalypse of Peter (NHC VII, 3)
		First Apocalypse of James (NHC V, 3)
		Second Apocalypse of James (NHC V, 4)
II. Apocalypses without being explicitly so titled		
	Concept of our Great Power (NHC VI, 4)	
	Paraphrase of Shem (NHC VII, 1)	
	Allogenes (NHC XI, 3)	
	Marsanes (NHC X, 1)	
	Zostrianos (NHC VIII, 1)	
III. Other texts with apocalyptic portions		
	Asclepius (NHC VI, 8; 70.3–74.17)	
	On the Origin of the World (NHC II, 5) (126.32–127.17)	
	Trimorphic Protennoia (NHC XIII, 1) (43.4–44.29)	

Modified from Martin Krause, "Die literarischen Gattungen der Apokalypsen von Nag Hammadi," in *Apocalypticism in the Mediterranean World and the Near East: Proceedings of the International Colloquium on Apocalypticism Uppsala, August 12-17, 1979,* ed. David Hellholm, 621, 621–37 (Tübingen: Mohr Siebeck, 1983), 625.

TABLE 18.2: Nag Hammadi Apocalypses by Type

I. Revelations without a journey:		
	a. Discourses	
		Apocalypse of Adam (NHC V, 5)
		Allogenes (NHC XI, 3)
		2nd Apocalypse of James (NHC V, 4)
		Melchizedek (NHC XI, 1)
	b. Dialogues	
		Sophia of Jesus Christ (NHC III, 4 and BG)
		Apocryphon of John (NHC II, 1; III, 1; IV, 1, BG)
		1st Apocalypse of James (NHC V, 3)
		Apocalypse of Peter (NHC VII, 3)
		Letter of Peter to Philip (NHC VIII, 3)
		Hypsiphrone (NHC IX, 4)
II. Revelations with journeys:		
	a. Discourses	
		Paraphrase of Shem (NHC VII, 1)
		Marsanes (NHC X, 10)
	b. Dialogues	
		Zostrianos (NHC VIII, 1)
		Apocalypse of Paul (NHC V, 2)

Adapted from Francis Fallon, "The Gnostic Apocalypses," *Semeia* 14 (1979): 123–58.

joins the souls of the blessed in the tenth heaven, at which point the text ends abruptly.

There are a few notable moments in the *ApocPaul*. As in the NT book of Acts, Paul travels to the city of Jerusalem to meet Jesus's disciples, where he is guided by the Holy Spirit in the guise of a child to meet the twelve apostles. But here, the apostles are not humans but purely spiritual beings who live in the **Ogdoad**, the eighth heaven. We do not know what was meant by this, exactly. Are these apostles the spiritual counterparts of Jesus's earthly disciples? This seems to be the case, since in the fourth heaven Paul looks down and sees "the twelve apostles at his right and left in the creation [i.e., on earth]." Why are there apostle "doubles" in the eighth heaven? One answer might be that the eighth heaven was the first of the heavens to be *outside* the seven planetary spheres (see chaps. 17 and 20); thus the eighth heaven was beyond the reach of destiny or fate, since fate was administered by the planets. Another more complicated

HOW MANY HEAVENS?

We have all heard the expression "being in seventh heaven" as a metaphor for being extremely happy. It is a relic from an old way of thinking about the heavens as multilayered. In this case, it is probably originally Greek (since the Greek way of thinking of the heavens consisted of a seven-planet system (sun, moon, Mercury, Mars, Venus, Jupiter, Saturn), with each planet located in its own sphere. In the Greek astronomical sense, however, one planetary sphere is not a luckier or happier place to be than any other. Certainly the realm of Saturn is not associated with the realm of the blessed; this idea might have derived from ancient Judaism, which also held to a many-layered cosmos. But the curious thing is that there was apparently no consensus on just how many heavens there were. Different texts—even those from Nag Hammadi—give various numbers of heavens, from the conventional three heavens to ten (*ApocPaul*), seventy-two (*1ApocJas*), and even 365!

possibility is that the twelve apostles are associated with the twelve signs of the zodiac, since in some models of the cosmos the zodiac resides in the realm beyond the seven planetary spheres. This association of the apostles with the signs of the zodiac is apparently quite old and not uncommon, and formed the basis of esoteric Christian teachings throughout the Middle Ages and the Renaissance.

Here is what Paul sees:

- Fourth heaven: angels resembling the gods, who oversee the judgment of the dead
- Fifth heaven: a great angel with an iron rod, accompanied by three other angels with whips, "goading the souls on to the judgment" (for other punishing angels in the NHL, compare *Perfect Discourse* 78:24–32; *Book of Thomas the Contender* 141:36–39).
- Sixth heaven: no account of what happens here; Paul is looking up to the next heaven
- Seventh heaven: an old man garbed in white seated on a throne (identified, perhaps, as Yahweh, the God of the Jews) (compare Dan 7:13; 1 Enoch 46–47)
- Eighth heaven (the Ogdoad): the apostles
- Ninth heaven: heavenly beings
- Tenth heaven: spirits of the blessed

The judgment of the dead motif here is significant; the theme of the judgment of the dead enters Christian texts at some point around the end of the first century CE. Note that the judgment here takes place not in hell, as in later Christian theology, but in the heavens; it will be some time in the Christian tradition before souls are judged and tormented in a lower realm. The motif of the soul's torment derives from Greek sources such as Book IX of Homer's *Odyssey*. Some have seen the image of the three flagellating angels as a version of the Furies or Erinyes of Greek mythology. There are also Jewish apocalyptic texts where souls are punished post-mortem, such as in the tenth chapter of the *Testament of Abraham*. But the motif of the judgment of the soul derives from Egyptian funerary texts such as the *Book of Gates* where each realm of the afterlife is separated by a gate guarded by a goddess. In these ancient Egyptian sources, the heart of the dead is judged for its purity by it being weighed on a scale against a feather of the goddess Ma'at. The scene is like that of a law court, and witnesses can be brought forward. If the heart is found to be too heavy (and thus impure), Ammit the Bone Eater, a fearsome creature that is part leopard, part alligator, and part hippopotamus, will gobble it up. Other Egyptian elements in the *ApocPaul* include the role of the "toll-collector" at each gate, and the use of statements or "passwords" along with signs or symbols in order to move through each gate into another heavenly realm.

In the *ApocPaul*, resonances of Egyptian themes such as judgment are found side by side with a theme drawn from Greek moral philosophy: the soul is examined not for impurity but for whether it fell into the negative passions (anger, rage, envy, and desire). When this text was written there was already developed an idea of human sinfulness and how we ought to abstain from sin in order to be positively judged after death. Notice what happens to the souls that had sinned, though: they are cast down to be reincarnated into different bodies that had been "prepared" for them. These might be human or animal bodies; one other Christian text talks about sinful souls cast into the bodies of pigs. Reincarnation is also an idea drawn from ancient Greece; it is interesting to find evidence of it here.

A striking element of the *ApocPaul* is what Paul finds in the seventh heaven (see bulleted list). This image derives from Jewish traditions about Yahweh, seated on a great throne, wearing a dazzling white raiment. Compare, for instance, this passage from the book of Daniel:

> As I looked, thrones were placed and one that was ancient of days took his seat; his raiment was white as snow, and the hair of his head like pure wool; his throne was fiery flames, its wheels were burning fire. A stream of fire issued and came forth from before him; a thousand thousands served him, and ten thousand times ten thousand stood before him; the court sat in judgment, and the books were opened. (Dan 7:9–10)

What is still more remarkable is the way that the Yahweh figure in the *ApocPaul* behaves: rather than acting like the highest god of the Bible, this old man interrogates Paul in the manner of one of the gatekeeping deities; he behaves more like a minor celestial demon. The short dialogue that follows, where the old man asks Paul where he is going, follows a standard pattern that we find in other texts featuring the soul's interrogation

(including the *Gospel of Mary*, the *1stApocJas* and the *GThom*'s logion #50). The *ApocPaul* text leaves no room for ambiguity: the god of the Jews is here a weak and ignorant demon who, despite his best efforts, is unable to trap the souls of the blessed on their ascent to heaven. This image is shocking enough that some scholars surmise that the treatise was written by someone with inside knowledge of Judaism and for a community that had been disaffected from Judaism, thus the tendency to devalue the Jewish god. The place of composition was probably Egypt, because of the author's familiarity with both Egyptian and Jewish traditions.

The Apocalypse of Adam (NHC V, 5)

The *Apocalypse of Adam* is the final text in Codex V, the "book of revelation" codex. Written on poor-quality papyrus, this twenty-one-page text was the sole production of a single scribe, whose handwriting is not found anywhere else among the NH codices. The title is written at the beginning and end of the document.

Unlike the apocalypses of the Christian disciples Paul and James, the *ApAdam* is a **pseudepigraphical** text that takes as its hero a figure from the Hebrew Bible, not the New Testament. And since Adam was the first human being, the *ApAdam* gives a partial account of events at the beginning of biblical history. Here, Adam narrates this history to his son **Seth**. We have only one copy of this text, from Nag Hammadi, although **heresiological** sources do mention an "Apocalypse of Adam." We do not know, though, if this is the same lost text to which Epiphanius refers in the fourth century CE. There were a number of ancient writings about Adam circulating in the ancient world, including the *Testament of Adam*, the *Struggle of Adam*, and the *Life of Adam and Eve*.

The longest part of the *ApAdam* is a long hymnic passage (77:27–83:4), which may have come from an earlier source. In it, thirteen explanations are provided for the coming of a savior figure (he is never identified as Jesus in this text, which is standard for so-called Sethian documents). All these explanations are deficient. Instead, the "true story" is given by a group called the "kingless generation."

The *Apocalypse of Adam* is actually not a true apocalypse but falls into the "last testament" genre. Deriving from ancient Jewish literature, the most famous example of this genre is a series of books known as the *Testament of the Twelve Patriarchs*. Each book gives the "last will and testament" dictated by one of the twelve Jewish patriarchs to his sons. This deathbed literature can be explicitly apocalyptic; it certainly draws on the theme of a father revealing crucial secrets about the world to his son.

The *ApocAdam* draws on Genesis but not as directly as other Nag Hammadi texts such as *HypArch* or *OrigWld*. While those works were more properly **exegesis**, meaning a close textual study, there is no indication here that whoever composed this work necessarily had the book of Genesis in front of him. Rather, the author might merely have been familiar with the basic contours of Genesis's early chapters. The *ApocAdam* therefore gives a "spiritual" account of Genesis's myth of origins. **Adam** and **Eve** are joined together, created together from earth as a primordial **androgyne** (this sounds strange to us, but the first human being described in Plato's *Timaeus* is also androgynous). Yahweh is replaced by the chief ruler **Saklas** or **Sakla**, who divides Adam and Eve into two separate beings "in his wrath" because they are spiritually superior to him. Their "glory," their divine part, leaves them and returns to the **Pleroma**, where it will eventually come to settle into the generation of Seth. The "ordinary" Adam and Eve, severed from one another and stripped of their divine part, serve God "in fear and slavery" (65:20). But the first step to salvation comes in the revelation of three angelic beings (**Abrasaks, Sablo,** and **Gamaliel**), who awaken Adam and

Eve to spiritual knowledge. Unfortunately, the illumination does not last, and the pair fall back into spiritual darkness and sleep. Eve and the creator god conceive Cain, and then Abel is conceived by Eve and Adam, through Adam's "sweet desire for [Seth's] mother" (67:3) (note that this is a remarkably positive way to talk about sexuality for an early Christian text). The text also follows Genesis with a reference to the flood and the narrative of Noah and the ark, although Noah is identified as in this text as Deucalion, a hero from Greek mythology who, like Noah, survives a flood sent by Zeus.

The *ApocAdam* is really about origins, and like other texts from Nag Hammadi, it aims to sort out who descends from whom. The offspring of Cain, Abel, and Seth all have different destinies and different degrees of blessedness; the descendants of Cain and Abel later connect to the offspring of Noah's two sons Ham and Japheth, and who eventually form "twelve kingdoms" (possibly the twelve tribes of Israel). The children of these twelve kingdoms worship Sakla, the chief archon of Sethian mythology (see, for instance, the *GosEg* and the *HypArch*). In the end, there appears to be a threefold genealogy:

1. The descendents of Seth who are destined for salvation and associated with the community behind this text;
2. The descendents of Noah, Ham and Japheth, the children of Israel;
3. Apostates from the children of Israel who come to join the descendents of Seth.

Is this text Christian? Like many others at Nag Hammadi, it shows no indication of being Christian. There is no Jesus; no mention of any other figures around Jesus; no setting in the New Testament era. Some scholars have argued that it is related to the *Gospel of the Egyptians*, but the *GosEg* is a "Christianized" version of what we have here (although the *GosEg* does a lot of things the *ApocAdam* does not). Others point out that although the savior figure (described here as the "third illuminator") is associated with Adam's son Seth, Seth might be a "cover" for, or version of, Jesus. He is not referred to directly because this is typical of the apocalyptic genre; if you are familiar with the New Testament book of Revelation, you will already know that Jesus is rarely mentioned by name in that text, too.

It remains an intriguing possibility, however, that perhaps the "third illuminator" was not meant to be Christ at all. Watch what happens to him: he comes in glory, reveals knowledge of the eternal God, and performs miracles upon the earth. These details *do* make the savior of *ApocAdam* sound like Jesus, especially Jesus in the Gospel of John. But then other details seem not quite right for Jesus: the archons become angry at the activities of the illuminator, and he then withdraws his glory. The archons punish the illuminator's flesh (i.e., his body). There are no specific details furnished, and although this might be a reference to Jesus's arrest, torture, and execution, note that it is an unusual account of events. At what point in the NT gospels does Jesus's "glory" (his divine power) "withdraw" back to the heavens? And does the body of the illuminator die from the ruler's punishment (the text does not make it explicit)? These are just some of the mysteries that the text evokes without providing us with a clear answer.

The Thirteen Kingdoms in *Apocalypse of Adam*

At one point in the middle of the *ApocAdam*, the angels ask, "from where did the words of deception, which all the powers have failed to discover, come?" (77:25–26). Here, the text begins a new section, where thirteen "kingdoms" are listed. The form is a bit curious: each "kingdom" (which seems to be a technical word for a type of archon) posits an answer, which amounts to what we call a **Christological** position—a theory on the nature and origins of an unnamed savior and how this savior "came to the water" (a reference to baptism, which initiated his career on the earth [see Table 18.3]).

The first twelve scenarios are given by the offspring of Cain and Abel; the thirteenth, by contrast, comes from the "400,000 apostates from the Twelve Kingdoms"; it is interesting to note that it resembles, in its way, the **Logos** theology from the beginning of the Gospel of John. This may be a clue that the "apostates" (people who turn away from their religion) were Jewish Christians who had once identified with Johannine groups in the Empire. It is difficult to know how this list was meant to be received by its listeners, other than they are all clearly meant to be erroneous positions. But they are not altogether preposterous stories of origins of divine heroes and saviors. Some resemble Jewish accounts of a messiah. The second kingdom states that the messiah will be a prophet (this, incidentally, will come to be the Muslim view of Jesus, although Islam will not begin for another five hundred or so years after this text was written), and the fourth kingdom traces the origins of the messiah to Solomon and, thus, to his father David. Both of these views of the messiah—that he will be a prophet and from the Davidic line—were current in Jewish communities in the first century of the Common Era; in fact, the depictions of Jesus in the NT gospels make it quite clear that Jesus was both of those things.

Some accounts here are also clearly drawn from Greek and Roman mythology. The fifth kingdom gives a version similar to the birth of the Greek goddess of desire, Aphrodite (in Roman mythology, Venus). Aphrodite, whose name means "arisen from sea foam," was born when the severed genitals of the god Ouranos were cast into the sea. The sixth kingdom's version is reminiscent of the rape of Persephone, a young virgin who is plucking flowers when she is abducted down to

TABLE 18.3: The Thirteen Kingdoms of the *Apocalypse of Adam*

1st Kingdom	He was preexistent, received the glory, and came to "the bosom of his mother" (this might be a reference to the incarnation where Jesus has a human mother, or "his mother" could be the heavenly Sophia who gives him knowledge).
2nd Kingdom	He was a great prophet who received a revelation from an angel, along with glory and strength.
3rd Kingdom	He came from a virgin womb, was born in exile in the desert, where he was "nourished" (could be "raised," or might be nourished as an infant).
4th Kingdom	He was the offspring of king Solomon and a virgin, was raised on the edge of a desert, and received his power and glory from his father's side of the family.
5th Kingdom	He came from heaven as a drop into the sea; he was raised in the abyss and returned to heaven.
6th Kingdom	A maiden picking flowers on the edge of the underworld became pregnant from the "desire of the flowers." The angels of the flowers nourish him, so that he received power and glory.
7th Kingdom	He is a drop from heaven, raised by dragons in caves until a spirit comes upon him and raises him to a high place, where he receives glory and power.
8th Kingdom	A cloud overshadows a rock, and the child is born from that rock. He receives glory and power from the angels above the cloud.
9th Kingdom	One of the nine Muses separates herself from her sisters and goes to a high mountain alone. There, she becomes pregnant from her own desire; the angels who preside over that desire nourish him and give him their glory and power.
10th Kingdom	His father god loved a cloud of desire, masturbated, and cast his semen on a cloud, from which he was born.
11th Kingdom	A father desired his own daughter, impregnated her, and he was born out in the desert, where he was nourished by an angel.
12th Kingdom	He came from two Illuminators, was nourished in the heavens, where he received glory and power.
13th Kingdom	He came in the form of the logos (Word) from an archon, and was mandated to be sent to earth.

the Underworld by Hades. The ninth kingdom with its reference to the nine Muses is also clearly Greek, while the birth of the eighth kingdom is a variant on the myth of the Roman god **Mithras**, who was said to have been born from a rock. The tenth kingdom's myth of creation through a god's masturbation was known in Egypt, where the god Atum masturbates, ejaculates semen into his own mouth, and spits out the god Shu and the goddess Tefnut. So it is likely that all these thirteen positions correspond, to some degree, to myths of origins for various gods and heroes that were already well known, if not necessarily attached to stories about Jesus.

It is clear is that the author of *ApocAd* considers all these positions to be clearly erroneous, if not ridiculous. The true origins of the Redeemer are heavenly, as the offspring of Seth (the fourteenth kingdom) relate: God chose him from all the other celestial beings and gave him knowledge to illuminate. All his spiritual offspring (**seed**), after they are baptized into his sacred secret name, will contend against adversaries until they are brought into the shadow of darkness. Salvation comes when the seed come together and renounce their sinfulness.

A last point about this apocalypse is the emphasis that it places upon baptism. In fact, the last section is probably part of a baptismal ritual and was therefore meant to be recited. The thirteen positions all end with the savior being brought to the water, and it is easy to imagine someone ready for baptism listening to the account of the thirteen kingdoms as a kind of litany. There are also the names given of three beings who preside over baptism: **Micheu, Michar, and Mnesimous.** These three are also mentioned in the baptismal ritual recounted in the *GosEg*; three more illuminators are given in the final line of the document: **Yesseus, Mazareus, and Yessedekeus**, the Living Water. These beings are also mentioned in the *GosEg*. This tells us that communities who read Sethian texts such as the *ApAdam* and the *GosEg* likely had a well-developed baptismal theology and practice. It also seems that they rejected the baptism of other Christian groups (note the reference to the "water of life" being "defiled" in 84:18) and may have replaced actual baptism with a kind of spiritual rite where the initiate is "baptized" symbolically without being immersed in water that was considered to have been defiled. This spiritual baptism took place in the heavens. Finally, an observant reader might have noticed that the final three illuminators who preside over the heavenly waters of baptism, Yesseus, Mazareus, and Yessedekeus, have names that sound suspiciously like "Jesus" and "Nazareth." In fact, this is the most "Christian"

part of the *ApAdam*. What do we make of it? Is this a group that knowingly corrupted the name "Jesus of Nazareth" and turned it into the name of separate celestial beings? Or did it happen accidentally, and this Jewish community of apocalypticists revere three deities whose names were a corrupted form of a new savior who had appeared in first-century Judaea? What do you think?

APOCALYPTIC PASSAGES IN OTHER NAG HAMMADI WRITINGS

Although a number of tractates at Nag Hammadi are either apocalypses and/or bear the title "Apocalypse," there are actually a few other texts in the collection that have substantial apocalyptic sections. For example, *OrigWld*, *Hyp Archons*, and the *TriPro* all end with an eschatological apocalypse. The *Concept of Our Great Power*, by contrast, *begins* with an apocalypse. Thus apocalyptic material might be anywhere in a particular NH tractate, and it takes quite different forms, from end-of-the-world scenarios to the ecstatic ascent of a visionary through cosmic geography.

The NH authors also appeared to have drawn upon a variety of different apocalyptic sources. In *OrigWld*, the author appears to have cobbled together imagery drawn from the NT and Jewish scriptures; for instance, it speaks about kings at war (compare Mt 24:7; Rev 16:14–21); and describes the earth as drunk with blood (compare Isa 34:7). But while many ancient apocalyptic texts discuss wars between human kings, most NH apocalypses remain firmly of the conviction that the final eschatological war will happen in the heavens. The malevolent celestial powers will be conquered by the positive powers, and the righteous human generations will be freed from their earthly bodies and restored to their place of power in the upper cosmos. Consider, for example, this passage from the *HypArch*:

> Then they [members of the "undominated generation"] will be freed of blind thought: And they will trample under foot Death, which is of the Authorities: And they will ascend into the limitless Light, where this Sown Element belongs. Then the Authorities will relinquish their aeons: And their angels will weep over their destruction: And their demons will lament their death. Then all the children of the Light will be truly acquainted with the truth and their root, and the Father of the entirety and the Holy Spirit: They will all say with a single voice, "The Father's truth is just, and the son presides over the entirety": And from everyone unto the ages of ages, "Holy holy holy! Amen!" (97:15–81, trans. Bentley Layton, in James Robinson, editor, *The Nag Hammadi Library in English* [San Francisco: Harper & Row, 1988]: 159–60)

The conviction that there would be a war in the heavens is indeed ancient, but it seems to have had particular potency in the second century; this kind of "cosmic pessimism" is often cited as one of the chief characteristics of second-century Gnosticism. Nevertheless, many proto-orthodox writings were also somewhat bleak in their outlook (consider, for example, the opening of the Gospel of John, where the Word descends into the cosmos but no one acknowledges him; or Paul's words in his letter to the Romans). And in the end, the message of these texts remains the same: a savior will come, set a disordered and chaotic cosmos right, and save his children. This message is in no way different from what we find in the Gospel of John, or in Revelation.

In summary, there are many texts from NH that are either explicitly apocalyptic, or which contain apocalyptic passages. Both types of apocalypses—heavenly journey apocalypses and eschatological apocalypses—are represented. Occasionally, these two are even combined. What this tells us is that apocalyptic literature was still being produced in the second century, and it appears not to have lost popularity even into the third century. Why this is so is more difficult to figure out. Did those who wrote the apocalypses do so because they really believed that the world was coming to an end? Did they do so because they were writing in a time of crisis, and because they believed that however bad things were, that God would vindicate them in the end?

Of course, not all apocalypses warn of a wrathful deity and the descent of a savior to redeem the righteous remnant. Some focus on the theme of a heavenly journey for a single, privileged seer. It is intriguing that many of these apocalyptic texts from NH are grouped together in a single codex: Codex V contains five texts, four of which are named apocalypses: the *ApocPaul*, the *1stApocJas*; the *2ndApocJas*, and the *ApocAdam*. This suggests that a scribe was intentionally ordering the material he received to copy, and that he produced, in turn, a "Book of Apocalypses" for someone or some community. How they used such a book remains a mystery.

QUESTIONS TO CONSIDER

1. Which of these apocalyptic texts from Nag Hammadi look the most like apocalypses to you? On what grounds do you make your determination? What about other portions of other Nag Hammadi texts that aren't called apocalypses but nevertheless contain apocalyptic material (for instance, the middle sections of the *TriProt*)? Which strikes you as the best example of the genre, as it is set out in this chapter?

2. Does the theory that apocalyptic texts were written at times of social crisis make sense to you? Why or why not?

3. This chapter outlines two different types of apocalypses: heavenly journeys and historical apocalypses. Which type is better represented at Nag Hammadi? Any theories as to why this might be?

KEY TERMS

Seth

heresiological (heresiology)

Adam

Eve

Logos

Mithras

Apocalypse

Semeia Definition

revelation dialogue

Paul

Abrasaks, Samblo, and Gamaliel

androgyne

Pleroma

Seed

Yesseus, Mazareus, and Yessedekeus

seer

eschatology

2 Corinthians (Corinthians, Second Letter to the)

pseudepigraphical

exegesis

Sakla/s

Christological

Micheu, Michar, and Mnesimous

Ogdoad

FOR FURTHER READING

Attridge, Harold W. "Valentinian and Sethian Apocalyptic Traditions." *Journal of Early Christian Studies* 8/2 (2000): 173–211. This long article offers a very useful overview of ancient Gnostic apocalypses, for intermediate and advanced students.

Fallon, Francis. "The Gnostic Apocalypses." *Semeia* 14 (1979): 123–58. An older but very clear article, which draws directly on the Semeia Definition to discuss and analyze the NH apocalypses.

Frankfurter, David. "Early Christian Apocalypticism: Literature and Social World." In *The Encyclopedia of Apocalypticism*. Vol. 2, *Apocalypticism in Western History and Culture,* edited by John J. Collins, 1–47. New York: Continuum, 1997. The focus on this informative article is not on literature but on the social context of apocalypticism. For intermediate students.

Gruenwald, Ithamar. *From Apocalypticism to Gnosticism: Studies in Apocalypticism, Merkavah Mysticism and Gnosticism.* Frankfurt am Main: Lang, 1988. This collection of essays offers some fascinating insights. For the advanced student only.

MacRae, George. "Apocalyptic Eschatology in Gnosticism." In *Apocalypticism in the Mediterranean World and the Near East: Proceedings of the International Colloquium on Apocalypticism Uppsala, August 12–17, 1979,* edited by David Hellholm, 317–25. Tübingen: Mohr Siebeck, 1983. This article is difficult to find but can pay off for more advanced students who wish to know more about the apocalyptic genre at Nag Hammadi.

19

The Sethian Platonizing Apocalypses
ZOSTRIANOS (NHC VIII, 1), *ALLOGENES* (NHC XI, 3), AND *MARSANES* (NHC X, 1)

Imagine that we are back in the third century, perhaps in the city of Rome. A small group of men and women are gathering at a private residence, to sit at the feet of **Plotinus**, a famous pagan philosopher. Plotinus, a specialist in ancient Greek philosophy (particularly the works of **Plato**) begins to expound his teachings on the nature of the cosmos, and his students crowd in eagerly, taking notes and preparing their questions. The students are relatively diverse; they are upper class, wealthy, and worldly. Although they are all interested in the same philosophical and spiritual questions, they come from diverse religious traditions: some are Christian, some are not, and some of them apparently self-identify as **Gnostic**.

At this point, one of the Gnostic students speaks up. If the highest God—the one everyone is calling the **First Principle**—is beyond all things, beyond the human intellect and the human capacity to even understand, how can it be known? The question irritates Plotinus, but he has heard it before. It *can* be known, he intimates, but these are the deep mysteries of mystical practice,

not to be discussed lightly. So deep was the veil of secrecy around these mystical practices to "know the One" that it is still difficult to determine how precisely they worked. But suffice it to say that some **Sethian** Gnostics believed that through meditative techniques, one could approach a mystical union with the First Principle. Plotinus did not exactly disagree, but he disliked the way in which these students in his circle conceptualized the heavens as a complicated place full of terrors. They had taken this model of the cosmos not from Plato—the most authoritative source from Plotinus's point of view—but from earlier Jewish, Christian, and native Egyptian texts, which they perceived as authoritative. Some of these texts may even have been ones that we have read from the Nag Hammadi collection of Sethian writings.

In this chapter, we look at three specific Sethian texts from Nag Hammadi: *Zostrianos*, *Allogenes*, and *Marsanes*. All these texts share a few things in common. First, they are extremely difficult to understand, in part because the manuscripts in which they are written are in particularly bad shape. Second, they are all **apoc-alyptic** texts—that is, they concern the vision-ary experiences of a seer, who travels through the cosmos and returns to earth to record his experiences. Third, none of them has a specific narrative or tells a story. Fourth, it is difficult to identify these texts as either Jewish or Christian. The language and imagery on which they rely are drawn from pagan sources. This is not to say that their authors (or readers) were not Christian, but that they promulgated a metaphysical system drawn from pagan philosophical texts rather than from the Jewish and Christian scriptures. Fifth, all of these texts are considered Sethian because of their complex **cosmology**, which they share with other texts that more explicitly invoke Seth as a divine savior (for more on Sethian Gnosticism, see chap. 10). Finally, all of them feature a seer who engages in a mystical practice, the goal of which is a vision of the First Principle.

It is clear that Plotinus knew of these Sethian apocalyptic texts, because one of his chief stu-dents, **Porphyry of Tyre**, tells us that he did:

> There were in his time many Christians and others, and sectarians [*heretikoi*] who had abandoned the old Philosophy (i.e., Platonism), men of the schools of Adelphius and Aculinus, who possessed a great many treatises of Alexander the Libyan and Philocomus and Demostratus and Lydus, and produced apocalypses by Zoroaster and Zostrianos and Nicotheos and Allogenes and Messus and other people of the kind, deceived themselves and deceiving many, alleging that Plato had not penetrated into the depths of intelligible reality. (*Life of Plotinus* 16, trans. A. H. Armstrong, *Plotinus: Enneads*, vol. 1. Loeb Classical Library [Cambridge, MA: Harvard University Press, 1966])

Porphyry tells us that to counter the ideas of these men, Plotinus wrote a treatise called "Against the Gnostics" (you can still read this treatise as *Enneads*, 2.9), and another pagan philosopher, Amelius, wrote an astonishing forty volumes against the book *Zostrianos*. Porphyry himself wrote many pages refuting *Zostrianos*, particularly the idea that it was an authentic revelation from

the ancient sage Zostrianos. These pagan philoso-phers of the third century regarded the Sethian apocalypses as forgeries, and they considered their ideas to be insulting, since they presumed that Plato—whose writings achieved virtually scriptural status in antiquity—had himself fallen short of the mystic's goal: to have a vision of the One. For traditionalist, conservative pagan phi-losophers like Plotinus, saying such a thing was indeed **heresy**.

From our perspective, Porphyry's mention of these so-called heretics circulating apocalyp-tic texts is important and exciting. Since the apocalypses he mentions—"those by Zoroaster and Zostrianos and Nicotheos and Allogenes and Messos"—were unknown to us outside this brief mention, imagine how amazing it was to discover copies of two of these, *Zostrianos* and *Allogenes*, in the NHL. We learned, first of all, that Plotinus and Porphyry were telling the truth, not simply making up scandalous things about their philo-sophical opponents. Second, it helped us to date these Nag Hammadi texts—we now had secure evidence that *Zostrianos* and *Allogenes* had been composed at least by the 270s CE, the time when Plotinus and Porphyry were writing. Third, we could now see for ourselves what Platonist sec-tarians were writing about, and could figure out for ourselves what irritated Plotinus and his stu-dents. Fourth, we get a very brief, but otherwise unprecedented, glimpse into what the life-setting of texts like *Zostrianos* was. We can know who knew about them, where they lived, what kind of education and social class they had, and so on.

It is a good guess that Sethians of the late second century had aligned themselves with other Christians but that, by the third cen-tury, those relations had become strained. At that point, Sethians began to incorporate more Platonist philosophy into their writings, to the point where any overtly Christian elements dropped out. What took their place was Platonist jargon and concepts, particularly Platonist

PLATONISM, MIDDLE PLATONISM, AND NEOPLATONISM

The Greek philosopher **Plato** (423–347 BCE) was a giant figure in the intellectual world of Greco-Roman antiquity. Following his death, Plato's successors continued to develop an intellectual system that reflected his philosophy. Scholars now distinguish between **Platonic philosophy** (a philosophical system drawn from Plato's writings) and **Platonist philosophy** (a philosophical system that follows from Plato's writings but which also incorporates other prominent ancient philosophers such as Aristotle).

Platonism is the name we give to this later school of philosophy based around the ideas of Plato but also incorporating other ideas not found in Plato's works. In turn, Platonism is often divided into two main intellectual schools, **Middle Platonism** and **Neoplatonism**.

Middle Platonism refers to the dominant school of Platonist thought that existed in the first and second centuries. Prominent proponents included Numenius of Apamea, Plutarch, and Maximus of Tyre. The Jewish philosopher Philo of Alexandria also had close connections with Middle Platonist thought, which he sought to reconcile with Judaism.

Neoplatonism emerges in the third century with its founder, **Plotinus**. It continues well into the sixth century and heavily influences later Christian theology, particularly in figures such as Augustine of Hippo.

metaphysics. Some of the typical jargon you find from Platonism includes:

- "being" versus "non-being"

- "intellect" as divine

- the triad of Existence, Life, and Intelligence (*3StelesSeth* 125,28–32; *Zostrianos* 15, 2–12; *Marsanes* 9, 16–18)

Some key Platonist ideas now incorporated into Sethianism included:

- The existence of two separate domains or worlds: the "intelligible world" (also called the "noetic world") and the "sense-perceptible world"

- The noetic world was the world of Pure Being. In the noetic world dwelt Plato's intelligible "Ideas" or forms. These formed the patterns for the material world.

- The "sense-perceptible world" was also known as the realm of Becoming, and it is where we ordinarily dwell in our fleshly bodies.

- Existence manifests itself in a series of triads, or even as triads within triads. As an example, the Christian notion of the Trinity is one

of the lasting legacies of Platonism: the tendency to conceptualize the Divine as Three-in-One.

GREEK PHILOSOPHY AND GNOSTICISM

The study of philosophy in the Roman Empire was not a purely intellectual endeavor, like reading literature or studying biology. Philosophy was a spiritual discipline, akin to what many people today would call a religion. Like religious groups, philosophical study circles had sacred scripture, community, and ritual. Members would congregate on regular occasions, celebrate rituals together, and discuss spiritual or religious beliefs: beliefs about the gods, about human spiritual possibilities, about ways of living in accordance with the will of the gods. Some pagan philosophers were polytheists, honoring a variety of gods. Others were **monotheists**, however, and emphasized belief in one God.

By the third century, Platonism was the dominant philosophical school of the Roman Empire and had the greatest impact on what some scholars

STOICISM, PLATONISM, AND PYTHAGOREANISM

The three most famous ancient schools of philosophy in the Graeco-Roman world, Stoicism, Platonism, and Pythagoreanism, were all different and distinct. Here are some key identifying factors for each:

1. Stoicism receives its name from a building in Greece called the Stoa, where the original group of philosophers first met as a "school." Stoicism taught that everything in the cosmos shared a common energy that was called **pneuma** or, sometimes, **logos**. In this way, Stoics taught, all things are essentially connected through this positive energy. Early Christians picked up on these teachings, modifying Stoic teachings on pneuma into teachings on the Holy Spirit, and the Stoic logos into Christ in his manifestation as the Word of God (Jn 1:1–14).

   Stoics also taught that to live a good life, one had to refrain from expressing negative emotions such as anger, fear, and lust. These emotions they called passions, described as the result of the soul, logos, or pneuma being held inside the human body. Restraining the passions could allow the Stoic sage to be more aware of the inner divine spark (for this reason, we still label people who have a high degree of control over pain, physical or emotional, as stoic). Christians borrowed from Stoicism the idea of restraining the passions through moral teachings and ascetic exercises.

2. Platonism began with the Greek philosopher Plato, but by the turn of the Common Era, it had incorporated some of the teachings of other philosophers such as Aristotle and Pythagoras. Platonism introduced key ideas that also became incorporated into early Christianity: the idea of God as "the Good," and as an omniscient, omnipresent deity; and the division between "body" and "soul" or "body," "soul," and "spirit."

3. **Pythagoreanism** was a religious movement in the early Roman Empire loosely organized around the teachings of the Greek philosopher and polymath Pythagoras. Pythagoreans in the Roman Empire wore special white robes and kept to a strict vegan diet, because they believed that animals were ensouled beings and as such should not be eaten. Pythagorean teachings incorporated the study of music, geometry, and number theory. Gnostic Christians incorporated Pythagorean numerological terms such as monad, dyad, triad, tetrad, and pentad into their cosmologies.

call Gnosticism. Modern scholars have long recognized this relationship between Gnosticism and Platonism, though not always fairly. One scholar, Willy Theiler, called Gnosticism "Proletariat Platonism," meaning a watered-down form of Platonism accessible to ordinary people. The great Harvard classicist A. D. Nock famously described Gnosticism as "Platonism run wild." These scholars acknowledged some relationship between the two schools of thought, but could see that association as one in which Gnosticism "got philosophy wrong." They justified this perception by pointing to Plotinus's and Porphyry's scorn for the Gnostics (actually Plotinus and Porphyry do not call them Gnostics but heretics). These ancient

Neoplatonists strenuously objected to what they read in texts such as *Zostrianos* and *Allogenes*: that their authors envisioned a cosmos full of different levels and various kinds of beings. By contrast, Plato's model of the cosmos was streamlined and harmonious, and looked something like this:

THE GOOD

Forms (Realm of Being)

Visible Cosmos (Realm of Becoming)

If we treat this diagram as a sort of rudimentary map (which Plato likely did not), the little "you are here" arrow would be located in the visible cosmos, the Realm of Becoming. Everything in the realm of Becoming is material modeled on ideal forms, which exist in the Realm of Being. Beyond that realm lies the Good, the highest realm.

The Platonizing Sethians did not really dispute this Platonic model, but by the time they learned of it, Middle Platonists had modified the model such that the realm of the Good was far, far away from the lower two realms. This distancing of the Good made room for all kinds of other things to be going on in the space between the Good and the Realm of Being. Consequently, the people who wrote those texts considered that the cosmos were complicated places of terror, rather than (as Plato asserted) a place that reflected the essential goodness and harmony of God.

The people who wrote *Zostrianos* and the other Sethian apocalypses also believed that Plato had gotten things correct to a certain extent, but that he, and the Platonists who followed Plato's teachings, failed to penetrate the depth of cosmic profundities. In other words, they considered their pagan (and likely, Christian) contemporaries a little on the shallow side, and boasted that they themselves knew more secrets about the cosmos than their teachers, the leading intellectuals in the Roman Empire. It is easy to imagine why this attitude infuriated people like Plotinus and Porphyry.

Let's step back for a moment and reevaluate what these Platonizing Sethians were really up to, without accusing them of wrecking Plato's system. Above all, they were attempting to reconcile their understanding of Plato with their own Judeo-Christian intellectual heritage. Although the Platonic cosmos may have been simple, by the third century certain Christians thought of the cosmos as much more complicated, mostly because of the influence of Jewish apocalyptic texts. These texts were still conceptually important to them, just as Genesis and other Hebrew Scriptures had been to earlier generations of Sethians. Meanwhile, speculation in Middle Platonism had produced metaphysical systems

in which a larger and larger conceptual space had opened up between the Realm of Becoming, where we ordinarily dwell, and the larger dimension of the Good. Put differently, God became more and more distant and thus harder to reach. At the same time, the second century witnessed a proliferation of religious movements and texts based on the idea that it was indeed possible for a specially prepared individual to have an experience of the Good, the First Principle. The idea that one could ascend through the cosmos to have a vision of the First Principle coincided particularly well with earlier Jewish apocalyptic texts, where a seer ascends through the cosmos and experiences a vision of God.

WHAT'S APOCALYPTIC ABOUT SETHIAN APOCALYPSES

Zostrianos, Allogenes, and *Marsanes* can all be classified as apocalyptic literature. But they are a special kind of apocalyptic literature, so to understand how and why they are, we need to go back to the **Semeia definition** of apocalyptic (see chap. 18). According to a group of experts in biblical and ancient literature, apocalyptic is defined as:

> a genre of revelatory literature with a narrative framework in which revelation is mediated by an otherworldly being to a human recipient (seer), disclosing a transcendent reality.

All four Sethian apocalypses feature a seer, otherwordly beings, and a transcendent reality. All of them are pseudonymous, their authorship having been ascribed to an ancient sage. The goal, in all cases, is a vision of the highest possible level of being. In the oldest Jewish apocalypses, the highest revelation is a vision of God, pictured on his throne chariot (e.g., Ezek 1; Rev 4:1–11). In the Sethian apocalypses, one can ascend higher than the Old Testament God; the ultimate vision is the First Principle, the source and core of the whole world.

At the same time, while these four texts fall nicely into the apocalyptic genre, we can see certain significant new developments that distinguish these texts from earlier Jewish, Christian, and even other Nag Hammadi apocalypses:

1. A distinct cosmology, which Sethian texts do not share with any other school in the Roman Empire. Their cosmos is multileveled but not structurally complex; it is also highly conceptual, drawing on Platonist language rather than more familiar language of the heavens taken from Jewish and Christian apocalyptic.

2. If Jewish apocalyptic texts are, on some level, a literary response to a social situation of crisis or persecution (see chap. 18), it is hard to make a similar argument with these Sethian apocalypses. For instance, the theme of judgment, of persecution then vindication of the righteous, is entirely absent. Instead you find an obsessive listing of cosmic rites; it is clear something is going on in terms of a ritual context, but it is unclear what that is. These texts are therefore truly esoteric—written for a small circle of educated elites who are not concerned about disseminating their knowledge but instead with ritual or mystical practice. The nature of this mystical practice appears to have involved some sort of ecstatic "ascent" of individual practitioners through the cosmic spheres during one's lifetime (as opposed to post-mortem ascents of the soul, such as we see in texts such as the *1stApocJas*). The people who circulated these texts, then, may have practiced something akin to shamanism: a mystical practice of separating one's consciousness from the body in order to discover profound truths about the cosmos. This practice was not exclusively Sethian; we find evidence for it in other traditions and texts from the first to the fourth century. It was, however, a

step beyond anything that Plato had developed as a spiritual technique. It also marked a profound shift from Jewish apocalypticism, in which the visionary ascent of the seer was a mark of literary genre, to a new kind of writing based on a description of spiritual practice, which could also serve as a practical guide to such practice.

3. Another major development that separates Sethian apocalypticism from classical Jewish apocalypticism is a focus on interiority. A journey up through the cosmos was also understood, simultaneously, to be a journey within one's own psyche. This was possible because of the Stoic and Platonist teaching that the human being was a microcosm, which mirrored in physical form the macrocosm that was the cosmos. Thus the technique of spiritual ascent through the cosmos was also a spiritual turning inward until one reached one's deepest, core self. At that level, the self was identical with the Good, the highest and most profound reality. But since this ascent was achieved during the lifetime of an individual (unlike post-death, one-way ascents we find in other texts), the ascent was necessarily coupled with a descent back through those cosmic realms, or a movement back out of a deep state of consciousness through various conceptual layers and back into waking consciousness. Nevertheless, the individual is not the same after this ascent and descent, but has been transformed through the experience.

Zostrianos

Found in Codex VIII, *Zostrianos*, at around 125 pages, is the longest document in the NHL. Unfortunately, it is quite corrupt, so it is extremely difficult to reconstruct since many pages are fragmentary. What we know is that it is a long account of a celestial vision granted to a seer by the name of **Zostrianos**, son of Iolaos.

WHO WAS ZOSTRIANOS?

The character who gives the tractate *Zostrianos* its name was a mythical hero of combined Greek and Persian origin. He is named as the son of Iolaos, a Greek, and grandfather to another Greek hero called Er the Pamphylian (Plato, *Republic* X 614b). In later tradition Er is assimilated with a Persian figure, the great holy man Zoroaster, the founder of Zoroastrianism (a religion originating in ancient Persia and that still has many adherents today). You may have heard of him by his other name, Zarathustra. Zostrianos is the ostensible author of this text, which is written as a first-person account. Because of this, *Zostrianos* counts as a **pseudepigraphical** text. Because Zostrianos lived long before Plato, it is probably the case that whoever wrote this text believed that as much as Plato had understood profound truths, those of Zostrianos were even more precious. In fact, even the copyist felt the same way: he uses a special Greek/Coptic alphabetical cipher—undecipherable to uninitiated readers—to write a secret subtitle for *Zostrianos*: "the Oracles of Truth of Zoroaster" in the tractate's colophon.

Zostrianos brings back knowledge of what he sees in the heavens in order to "save those who are worthy." The cosmos that Zostrianos sees is remarkably similar to the one outlined in the *GosEg*, featuring the Invisible Spirit and **Barbēlō**, the four luminaries, **Adamas** and the great Seth.

What makes *Zostrianos* distinctive is its emphasis on the mystical, visionary ascent of a single seer or, more properly, a practitioner. This gives it a different flavor from other Sethian ascent texts such as *3StelesSeth* or *GosEg*, which seem to suggest that ritual, contemplative ascent is done collectively (hence they use first-person plural rather than *Zost*'s first-person singular). Interestingly, the narrative starts with Zostrianos caught in the depths of a depression and seeking to commit suicide. At this point, an angel of light treats him to a tour of the cosmos. In essence, Zostrianos is a mystic, who through a process akin to meditation, leaves his body on earth while his mind goes on a tour of the cosmos. In the course of this ascent, Zostrianos ascends through countless cosmic levels, encounters various angelic guides and other residents of each level, until he ultimately receives enlightenment and returns to the physical world. He then records what he witnessed for the benefit of Seth's **Seed**.

At the highest cosmic level exists the Great Invisible Spirit, from whom the rest of the cosmos and its inhabitants have emanated. Each cosmic level is farther removed and thus less perfect than the one above it (see Table 19-1 on the next page).

In keeping with Zostrianos's interest in cosmic architecture, we encounter in *Zostrianos* many different kinds of divine revealers populating the cosmos. Each one reveals to Zostrianos a part of the divine whole. There are dozens of names here, some of them matching what we find in the *GosEg* but others that are unique to *Zostrianos*. Characters we've seen before include:

- The beings associated with celestial baptism: **Michar and Micheus**, Barpharanges, and **Yesseus Mazareus Yessedekeus**
- The **aeon**s of the upper realms, including: **Geradamas, Autogenes, Seth, Adamas, Mirothea**, Prophania, **Sophia, Protophanes, Kalyptos**, and Yoel
- The **Four Luminaries**: Oroael, Daveithai, Harmozel, and Eleleth
- Gamaliel, a guardian of the immortal soul
- Theopemptos, a guardian of the glory
- Samblo
- Salamex, Semen, and Arme (also in *Allogenes*, not in *GosEg*)

TABLE 19.1: The Cosmic Architecture of *Zostrianos*

↑	REALM OF THE SELF-GENERATED AEONS	Zostrianos is baptized five times in the name of Autogenes by Michar and Micheus. He is purified by Barpharanges. Then he is sealed (anointed with oil) by Michar, Micheus, Seldao, Elenos, and Zogenethlos. When the all-glorious virgin Youel baptizes Zostrianos for the fifth time, Zostrianos becomes divine, and stands upon the Fifth Aeon.
	THE TRULY EXISTENT REPENTANCE • Where immortal souls who have embraced gnosis and renounced worldly things reside • This level contains six subaeons arranged according to different kinds of sins that the souls had committed on earth	Zostrianos is baptized here four times.
	THE TRULY EXISTENT SOJOURN (OR EXILE) • Where disembodied souls reside after the death of the body. • These souls can avoid reincarnation if they pursue knowledge and keep themselves separate from evil people and beings	Zostrianos is baptized.
	REALM OF THE AEONIC COPIES • Also called the "airy earth"	Zostrianos is baptized, receives the image of the glories, becoming like one of them.
Direction of Ascent	REALM OF THE THIRTEEN AEONS • This is the realm administered by the Archon of Creation and his angelic host • The realm of embodiment, where the soul begins its journey	

Beings that are only in *Zostrianos* include:

- Seldao, Elenos, and Zogenethlos
- Authrounios
- Ephesek, the Child of the Child (who reveals knowledge to Zostrianos)
- Guardians of the immortal soul: Strempsouchos, Akramas, and Loel
- Ormos, Seisauel, and Audael
- The "myriads" (presumably a class of angels): Phaleris, Phalses, and Eurios
- The guardians of the glory: Stetheus, Eurumeneus, and Olsen
- The assistants: Lalmeus and Eidomeneus (other names are too fragmented to reconstruct)

- The judges: Sumphthar, Eukrebos, and Keilar
- The angels who guide the clouds: Sappho and Thouro
- The god-revealers: Selmen, Zachthos, Yachthos, Setheus, Antiphantes, Seldao, and Elennos
- The concealed aeons: Harmedon, Diphanes, and Malsedon
- The first-manifest aeons: Solmis, Akremon, and Ambrosios

Zostrianos, like its sister Sethian text *GosEg*, presents a picture of a complicated cosmic architecture in the lower realms. The text draws on a range of philosophical sources and terminology from Middle Platonism, but also apparently introduces some of its own. However, the upper realms are more streamlined (see Diagram 19.1).

The highest component of this structure, the Triple-Powered Invisible Spirit, is not actually in the cosmos at all, but is completely transcendent and unknowable. This deity has three active powers, Existence, Vitality (or Life), and Blessedness (or Mentality). Together these three powers generate the **Barbēlō** aeon, a transcendent divine Intellect. Here are found the archetypes or forms of all things; it corresponds to the Platonic realm of Being. The **Barbēlō** aeon in turn has three sublevels: **Kalyptos** ("Hidden"), **Protophanes** ("First Appearing"), and **Autogenes** ("Self-Generating").

At the level of the Barbēlō aeon, the Kalyptos aeon is the domain of intelligible reality—where "those who truly exist" exist. These correspond to the Platonic forms or archetypes. The aeon of Protophanes is called the Perfect Male Mind, the domain of "the all-perfect ones who are unified." It appears to be the place where individual minds or intelligences unite with their ideal forms. At the aeon of Autogenes dwell the "perfect individuals" or differentiated souls.

In each aeon, Zostrianos also encounters a range of angels, attendants, lights, glories, and other beings.

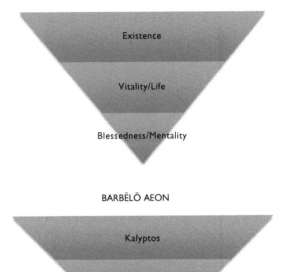

DIAGRAM 19.1: The Upper Cosmic Realms of *Zostrianos*

Zostrianos is not much of a Christian text; it is tempting, in fact, to call it "post-Christian." Although some Sethian texts seem to predate Christianity (see chap. 10), this one probably comes from a phase when Sethians had broken with Christian groups. Since Porphyry and Plotinus know of it, *Zostrianos* had to have been written by 268 CE, when Porphyry mentions it. Its author seems to see himself as a Platonist primarily, since he keeps coming back to key philosophical issues such as the nature of existence and the different kinds of souls. Various themes from many of Plato's dialogues appear here, particularly those from the *Phaedo*, *Phaedrus*, *Timaeus*, the *Republic*, and *Parmenides*. At the same time, *Zostrianos* is a very eclectic text that reflects a view of the cosmos different from anything we see in Plato's own writing. The references to baptisms, liturgical formulae, and **voces magicae** all suggest that the text was meant to be used by a worship community, but we have no evidence for where or how this happened. It also ensured that strict Platonists in the third century—who did not believe that the cosmic architecture was so very complex—treated the text with scorn. In fact, Porphyry mentions that his fellow philosopher Amelius composed a multivolume refutation of *Zostrianos*, which unfortunately no longer exists.

Allogenes

Allogenes is a relatively short **revelation discourse** from Codex XI, an eclectic volume containing both Sethian and Valentinian writings. To complicate matters, we now have another text—completely different from the Nag Hammadi *Allogenes* that we are considering here—also called *Allogenes*, from a separate manuscript (the recently discovered **Codex Tchacos**, which contains the *Gospel of Judas*).

The word "Allogenes" means "stranger," or literally "born elsewhere," in Greek, and we are fairly sure that the "stranger" referred to in this text is Seth. *Allogenes* is another one of the apocalypses that Porphyry mentions (although, in fairness, he could have been talking about the other *Allogenes* text in CT). In *Allogenes* from the NHL, Allogenes reveals cosmic knowledge to his son Messos (notice that Porphyry bitterly complains about an apocalypse in the names of Allogenes and Messos). Because of this style of father-to-son address, *Allogenes* looks a little more like a Hermetic writing (see chap. 16) than a classic Jewish apocalypse. In fact, there is really nothing particularly Jewish or Christian about it, making it a typical example of late Sethianism. However, it is certainly an apocalypse, with a great deal of cosmic revelation; it is unclear, however, whether it counts as a **pseudepigraphon**, since Allogenes is not an ancient, historical (or even quasi-historical) person. The text ends with an order that Allogenes/Seth write down the revealed knowledge he received in a

book, and to deposit this book on a mountain, where it will be guarded for Seth's posterity, his "seed." We've seen this pattern before in slightly different forms, particularly at the beginning of *3StelesSeth* and the end of the *GosEg* and *Zostrianos*.

Curiously, *Allogenes* has *two* heavenly revealers. Although Allogenes reveals cosmic knowledge to Messos, he himself learns it from the divine feminine revealer Youel. We've encountered Youel in Sethian cosmologies before, in both *Zostrianos* and *GosEg*, but she plays a greater role here. Still, Youel isn't really an interpreting angel who explains to Allogenes what he sees; she is a mouthpiece for describing the mythic, narrative sections of the text.

In terms of cosmic architecture, *Allogenes* is a streamlined version of its sister apocalypse, *Zostrianos*. At the top of the hierarchy stands the Great Invisible Spirit. Beneath is the Barbēlō aeon, with Kalyptos, Protophanes, and Autogenes that have been generated by Vitality, Existence, and Blessedness, the Triple Powers. However, in a significant departure from *Zostrianos*, each stage of ascent is not marked with a baptism, nor is Allogenes guided by an interpreting angel. In fact, *Allogenes* is not really an ascent text at all but a sort of inward journey through various stages of ecstatic contemplation and interiority. There is no return journey given. Thus *Allogenes* really recounts a specific type of spiritual exercise, which we learn is the result of the eponymous seer's century of "deliberation" or deliberate spiritual practice.

You might notice something else here: there are passages from *Allogenes* that are virtually identical to those in *ApJn*, particularly on the nature of the Great Invisible Spirit as unknowable. It is clear that there is some sort of literary relationship between the two texts, but we are not sure quite what it might be. Most likely, the author of this text read *ApJn* and then borrowed passages from it, dropping them in more of a Platonizing framework, as if to update them in a new context where Platonizing traditions had become more fashionable. He also transforms *ApJn* into "a psychology of the individual Gnostic—macrocosm into microcosm, myth into philosophical mysticism" (Layton, *Gnostic Scriptures*, 141).

Marsanes

The writing called *Marsanes* comes to us in the NHL in a particularly fragmented form in Codex X, all of which is severely damaged. The damage is so bad, in fact, that we do not know for sure how extensive the codex was originally, nor do we know how many writings it contained. At this point it contains only *Marsanes*. Furthermore, the sole copy of *Marsanes* to exist from antiquity is corrupt—that is, the scribe charged with the task of copying out the text was probably illiterate and did not have much of a sense of what the text was about—not a very good state of affairs for a scribe. Luckily, the first ten pages of the document remained more or less intact, so at least we have a sense of this writing. As we have it, it now runs about sixty-eight pages.

In some circles, the hero of *Marsanes* was known as a powerful prophet or "perfect man" (**Bruce Codex** 7). **Epiphanius of Salamis** writes that a group called the Archontics venerate a "Marsianos, who had been snatched up into the heavens and had come back after three days (*Pan.* 40.7.6); we suspect Marsianos and Marsanes are identical. In this NH text, Marsanes goes on a sort of tour of the heavens. Since Marsanes was a fictional character, the apocalypse bearing his name is a pseudepigraphon, much like *Zostrianos*. Beyond that, we do not know very much about the character Marsanes. The word "Mar," however, is Syriac for "master," so it is possible that the name was originally "Master Sanes." This gives us a clue that the text might have originated in Syria, rather than in Alexandria like so many other NH writings.

Marsanes was probably written later than its sister texts *Zostrianos* and *Allogenes*, possibly as late as the end of the third century or the beginning of the fourth. And it is likely that its author was familiar with those earlier texts. Rather than repeating them, the author assumes knowledge of them and focuses instead on doctrine not covered in the earlier treatises. While the first twenty pages begin with cosmological information, it then takes a rather abrupt turn into other sorts of knowledge, including the judgment of souls, the power of language, astrology and astral phenomena, arithmology, and ritual practice. Let's consider the text's cosmology first.

The author of *Marsanes* doesn't spend much time laying out the cosmos and its various beings but does posit thirteen "seals" or levels of being (see Table 19-2).

It is important not to try to resolve the differences between *Marsanes*, on the one hand, and *Zostrianos* and *Allogenes*, on the other. Those differences represent points of controversy that were actively disputed in antiquity. And do you notice the most glaring difference between them? Unlike virtually all Sethian cosmologies, the highest being

TABLE 19.2: The Thirteen Seals of Marsanes

Seal 13	The Unknowable Silent One
Seal 12	The Great Invisible Spirit
Seal 11	The Triple-Powered One
Seal 10	The Barbēlō Aeon
Seal 9	Kalyptos
Seal 8	Protophanes
Seal 7	Autogenes
Seal 6	The Self-Generated Aeons
Seal 5	The Repentance
Seal 4	The Sojourn
Seal 3	The Third
Seal 2	The Second
Seal 1	The First

Source: John D. Turner in Marvin Meyer, ed., *The Nag Hammadi Scriptures* (San Francisco: HarperOne, 2007), 630–31.

in *Marsanes* is not the Great Invisible Spirit but the Unknowable Silent One. Although this is an innovation for Sethianism, it reflects discussions in late-third-century Platonism; we find a similar concept in monistic pagan philosophical texts. This is one way we can date *Marsanes* as relatively late.

It is also interesting that although salvation in *Marsanes* comes from contemplative ascent of the mystic through the cosmos, there is also a salvific descent of Autogenes into the lower world. It is possible that this connects *Marsanes* with other Sethian texts such as the *ApJn* or the *TriProt*; on the other hand, perhaps Autogenes's ascent is meant as a sort of prototype of Marsanes's own salvific action in the world. However, the main orientation of this text is not around these descents or even ascents but around various types of knowledge.

The sections of *Marsanes* that offer speculative knowledge on such things as vowel sounds and number theory are some of the most inscrutable in the entire NHL. The author shows himself (or, perhaps, herself) to be in dialogue with other Neoplatonists who were much occupied with these topics. Neoplatonists were not only bookish intellectuals; they were also deeply involved with a set of ritual practices classified as **theurgy**. Theurgical rites could include the invocation of the gods through vowel sounds, the use of special stones, and perhaps the ritual animation of statues. As a highly secret practice, however, we do not know much about it—other than that Marsanes's long account of the power of vowel sounds, the discussion of configurations of the soul and their relationship to certain astral powers. The brief mention of wax images and emerald stones (36:1–6) seems to suggest that whoever wrote this text was engaged in the very same set of practices as other pagan Neoplatonists.

BAPTISM IN SETHIAN APOCALYPSES

In some Sethian apocalyptic texts—especially *Zostrianos*—you might have noticed that the language of baptism is consistently paired with the language of ascent through the cosmic spheres. It goes something like this: an ancient seer travels up through the cosmos, reaching one level or "heaven" where he receives a "baptism." In the *ApocAdam*, for instance, the initiate moves through twelve different celestial "kingdoms." In each kingdom, he or she receives instruction and increases his or her level of *gnosis*, until finally in the **Thirteenth Kingdom** the initiate is brought "to the water" and receives "glory and power." In *Zostrianos*, the pattern is a little different; the initiate continues upward through a succession of levels, receiving "baptism" on each level. This process continues, until Zostrianos has received twenty-two baptisms. In *Marsanes*, as in the *ApocAdam*, the number thirteen emerges, but here, the initiate receives thirteen "**seals**," with the word "seal" (Gk *sphragis*) associated with baptism; there is no overt use of the term "baptism" otherwise.

First of all, scholars have debated whether baptisms in texts such as *Zostrianos* really happened as actual ritual events. Perhaps the authors or communities who used these texts had completely rejected the actual earthly rite of baptism and replaced it with an idealized rite that existed only as a literary device. In other words, baptism did not really exist in these communities at all; it was something that happened only to characters in their sacred scriptures, and only in the heavens. This may explain what Zostrianos preaches at the very end of *Zostrianos*: "Do not baptize yourselves with Death, nor entrust yourselves to things inferior to you as if they were superior beings" (131). A second theory is that baptism was performed in Sethian communities but not as a water baptism. Instead, it was most likely actually an act of anointing with oil rather than water—something technically called **chrismation**, but called "baptism" by Sethians. While it happened on earth, it was simultaneously thought to mirror what was happening in the cosmos. Think of it a bit like this: all people have a sort of angel "double," and significant actions that happen to you on earth mirror or replicate, simultaneously, what happens to your angel double in the heavens.

The curious baptismal language in these Sethian apocalypses confounds even the most confident scholars of Sethianism. We are not sure why these texts equate celestial ascent with baptism; it wasn't necessary or logical. For instance, the Sethian ascent language in the *3StelesSeth* (see chap. 10) never equates ascent with baptism, and other Sethian texts that mention the baptismal rite of the **Five Seals** do not talk about ascent. But at some point, the rite of baptism becomes combined with rituals of ascent. More than that remains a secret, which those who read and understood these texts took to their graves.

The later Platonizing Sethian apocalypses that we have examined in this chapter represent some of the most difficult writings to understand in the entire Nag Hammadi corpus. They are problematic for a couple of reasons. First, they build upon pagan philosophical streams and conversations, which are studied these days only by a small number of scholars. Neoplatonist texts are, on the whole, extraordinarily hard to grasp. It is not so much that the ideas they contain are particularly challenging; it is more the case that they were in dialogue with other texts and ideas, which have not survived the centuries. Another difficulty with the Sethian Platonizing apocalypses has to do with the physical shape of the manuscripts that contain these works; the sole manuscripts of many of these writings are so full of lacunae that we have no way of reconstructing them. Nevertheless, these writings have the unusual advantage of being cited by two known historical figures: Plotinus and his student Porphyry. At least we have a rare opportunity to see how one prominent intellectual thought about these texts, and to see, for a brief moment, those who read and believed in the spiritual systems of these texts from the faraway world of the third century.

QUESTIONS TO CONSIDER

1. Judging by the Semeia Definition of the apocalyptic genre (see chap. 18), are these Sethian apocalypses really apocalypses, or a new kind of writing?

2. What are the key themes that these three texts share?

3. Why does Plotinus get so upset about what the Platonizing Sethians he met were doing?

KEY TERMS

Plotinus	Kalyptos	Epiphanius of Salamis
First Principle	seal	Geradamas/Adamas
cosmology	pseudepigraphical (see: pseudepigrapha)	Sophia
heresy	*voces magicae*	Sethian
pneuma	Yesseus, Mazareus, and Yessedekeus	Plotinus
logos	Mirothea	Stoicism
Semeia definition	theurgy	chrismation
Adamas	Platonic philosophy/ Platonist philosophy/Platonism	Autogenes

revelation discourse	Neoplatonism	Five Seals
Codex Tchacos	monotheists	Barbēlō
Plato	Zostrianos	Michar and Micheus
Middle Platonism	Protophanes	Seth
Porphyry	Thirteenth Kingdom	Four Luminaries
Pythagoreanism	Seed (of Seth)	

FOR FURTHER READING

Armstrong, A. H. "Gnosis and Greek Philosophy." In *Gnosis: Festschrift für Hans Jonas*, 87–124. Göttingen: Vandenhoeck & Ruprecht, 1978. A broad-brushed and dismissive study of Gnosticism, from the perspective of a prominent scholar of Plotinus and Neoplatonism.

Pearson, Birger. "Gnosticism as Platonism: With Special Reference to *Marsanes* (NHC 10,1)." *Harvard Theological Review* 77/1 (1984): 55–72. A technical essay by a very good scholar of Gnosticism that focuses on *Marsanes*, a severely neglected text. For intermediate students.

Turner, John D. "Gnosticism and Platonism: The Platonizing Sethian Texts from Nag Hammadi and Their Relation to Later Platonic Literature." In *Gnosticism and Neoplatonism*, edited by R. T. Wallis and J. Bregman, 425–59. Studies in Neoplatonism 6. Albany: SUNY Press, 1992. Another fine, detailed study of the Sethian apocalyptic texts from the world's top scholar of Sethian Platonism. This is difficult reading but recommended for advanced students.

Turner, John D., and Ruth Majercik, eds. *Gnosticism and Later Platonism: Themes, Figures, and Texts*. Atlanta: Society of Biblical Literature, 2000. This collection of essays is fairly recent and a state-of-the-art treatise. Recommended for advanced readers.

20

Beyond Nag Hammadi

THE *GOSPEL OF JUDAS* AND THE *GOSPEL OF MARY MAGDALENE*

There are two more, last ancient Christian texts that remain to be discussed in any book on "Gnosticism." Neither was found at Nag Hammadi, yet they have considerable importance and certainly a great deal of notoriety. Traditionally, both are classified as Gnostic writings, and because of this, both tend to be grouped with the NHL. Since they feature two so-called underdogs of the early Christian tradition—Mary Magdalene and Judas Iscariot—people have been more fascinated by these two writings than by any other Gnostic text from antiquity. In terms of offering new knowledge about Jesus, which is how these texts were marketed to the public, the *Gospel of Judas* and the *Gospel of Mary* are useless; both of them are second-century texts, composed long after Jesus's life and death. On the other hand, they are interesting documents for the study of second-century Christianity, offering us some tantalizing views into the perspective of authors who felt that they, alone, had interpreted Jesus's teachings correctly. These two texts provide sharp answers to **Irenaeus** and his fellow **heresiologists**, giving us the "other half of the conversation" from that which we read from the perspective of early Roman Catholic Christianity. In this final chapter, we'll look at these two surprising "gospels," and think more about the very diverse nature of Christianity in the Roman Empire.

BACKGROUND OF THE CODEX TCHACOS

Rumors circulated that an ancient manuscript of Coptic writings—including, possibly, the heretofore lost *Gospel of Judas*—had been for sale on the antiquities market since the late 1970s and on three different continents. In 1983 the Coptologist Stephen Emmel was sent to Geneva, Switzerland, to examine an ancient Coptic codex to decide whether it should be purchased. But the asking price was too high, and there remained serious questions about whether the codex had been obtained illegally. Without a buyer, an art dealer involved with the sale deposited the manuscript in a bank vault, where it languished for sixteen years. By this time the codex had fallen into disrepair, yet the Maecenas Foundation for Ancient Art and the Waitt Institute for Historical Discovery recognized its value and purchased the book in early 2006. The Maecenas Foundation, upon finding out that it possessed the lost *GosJud*, quickly struck a deal with National Geographic to produce documentaries, magazines, and a critical translation in book form, all of which meant that the *GosJud* was given a spectacular public debut in May 2006.

Codex Tchacos (CT) was named after the father of an antiquities dealer, Frieda Tchacos-Nussberger, who bought the book in 2000 before knowing its importance. Carbon-dated to 280 CE, the CT is a relatively early manuscript, perhaps as much as a century older than the NH codices. It supposedly surfaced in the town of El-Minya, Egypt, which has many unexcavated early Egyptian monastic sites and Roman-Egyptian tombs; apparently, the book had been found in a limestone box in a burial cave. It was written in **Sahidic**, the most common of the Coptic dialects, although it, like all NH documents, was probably first composed in Greek.

The CT contains four separate works:

- *Letter of Peter to Philip*
- *First Apocalypse of James*
- *Allogenes* (usually called *Allogenes the Stranger* to distinguish it from *Allogenes* in the NHL)
- *Gospel of Judas*

Two of these texts, *Letter of Peter to Philip* (LPP) and the *First Apocalypse of James* (1stApocJas), were already known to us from Nag Hammadi. Their presence in two different codices from two different parts of Egypt strengthens the argument that these treatises were important and probably circulated widely. It is also interesting that both Codex I and CT begin with *LPP*; it is not certain what this arrangement means, but the letter appeared to be something that Egyptian scribes put at the front of collections. The copy of *1stApocJas* in CT is much less fragmentary than the

copy from Nag Hammadi, so it fills in some of the blanks in that treatise, a rare and exciting opportunity. The treatise *Allogenes* is also known from the NHL, but the version in Codex Tchacos is different from the one in the NHL, so one of the tasks that remains is to figure out the relationship between them. And finally, of course, the one text that was completely unknown before the Codex Tchacos's discovery is the *Gospel of Judas*.

Because of years of neglect—kept in a bank vault and, at one point, frozen in a botched attempt to preserve it—the CT splintered literally into a thousand pieces. It will take many years to place all the fragments, and so modern critical translations released at the end of the first decade of the twenty-first century are much like snapshots in time: they are based on partial reconstructions of the text. These reconstructions will all need to be changed as fragments are restored to their proper place. In the meantime, one of the vexing things about the *GosJud* is that different English translations of the text available on the market sometimes say quite different things from one another.

GOSPEL OF JUDAS: BACKGROUND

The *GosJud* exists only in a single version from CT. The title states that this gospel is about Judas, not by him, thus the Gospel *of* Judas, not the Gospel *According to* Judas. It is therefore a little different from the canonical gospels or even some noncanonical gospels: for example, the *Gospel According to Thomas*, which bear the traditional names of their authors. As it now stands, we have only a portion of the original text. On November 22, 2009, at a meeting of the Society of Biblical Literature, the scholar Marvin Meyer announced that the remaining portion of the Codex Tchacos has been recovered, and that when the fragments are replaced and the text restored, we will have 90 to 95 percent of the gospel.

In *GosJud*, Jesus acts as a heavenly revealer to Judas, making this text a **revelation dialogue**. You may note that the *GosJud* reads a bit like Jesus's "farewell discourses" in the Gospel of John (chaps. 14–17). The opening lines of *GosJud* make it clear that this dialogue was meant to be secret (33:1–2). In terms of literary genre, the text is also an apocalypse, in that Jesus acts in it as a sort of tour-guide to the heavens, revealing secret or hidden truths to him.

We knew that a text called the *Gospel of Judas* was written in antiquity, because around the year 180 CE, **Irenaeus of Lyons** tells us about it. He says that the text in his possession claims that Judas had access to special salvific knowledge, and that Judas betrayed Jesus because he knew that doing so "accomplished the mystery of betrayal." Through Judas's actions, Irenaeus continues, all things on heaven and earth were thrown into confusion (*Adv. Haer.* 1.31). Irenaeus's account is supported by **Epiphanius of Salamis**, who also knew the *Gospel of Judas*. Epiphanius loathed the work because it made a hero of the man who betrayed Jesus in that he "performed a good work for our salvation," according to Epiphanius's assessment of the text (*Pan.* 38). These details conform enough to our copy of *GosJud* that we are fairly sure we now have the ancient document that Irenaeus and Epiphanius treated with great disapprobation. The CT *GosJud* features Judas in the position of the most privileged of the disciples, one who alone recognizes who Jesus is and what he has come to accomplish. And Jesus, in this gospel, more or less commissions Judas to do what he has to do: to betray him because that is his destiny.

Who Was Judas?

Judas Iscariot (Iscariot is not his surname; it is an indication of the region from which he came) appears in all four gospels of the NT. At first a trusted disciple of Jesus, Judas is corrupted by Jewish authorities and accepts their bribe to surrender Jesus to the religious and political authorities of Jerusalem. In the pivotal Last Supper scenes in the NT gospels, Jesus tells his disciples that one among them will betray him. And indeed, later, Judas leads the authorities to Jesus, having told them that the man whom he kisses is the man whom they should seize—a "Judas kiss" is therefore a colloquial expression for an act of betrayal.

Interestingly, Judas is said in the NT tradition to suffer from terrible guilt for his part in Jesus's death. The NT actually preserves two very different stories of what happens to Judas. In Matthew 27:3–8, Judas is so tormented by his guilt that he hangs himself. In the book of Acts 1:16–19, however, Judas trips in an area just outside of Jerusalem called the "Field of Blood," falling so badly that his belly splits open and his guts fall onto the ground. Although this story is not told as frequently as the story of Judas's hanging, in antiquity it was quite popular, and we have a number of stories of famous **heretics** from the fourth century where they share a similar or identical fate.

Villain or Hero?

The story of Judas has held a kind of popular mystique in popular culture. More often than not, Judas appears as a sort of sympathetic figure, a mere pawn in cosmic events. In this way of understanding him, Judas had no choice over the terrible role he had to play: someone had to betray Jesus in order for salvation history to be initiated. As Jesus urges him in the Gospel of John, "Do quickly what you are going to do" (Jn 13:27, NRSV). In Nikos Kazantzakis's 1951 novel *The Last Temptation of Christ*—as in the 1987 movie of the same name directed by Martin Scorsese—Judas is Jesus's best friend whom Jesus directly asks, privately, to betray him so that destiny may be fulfilled. Judas initially resists but, finally and mournfully, relents. Jesus acknowledges that Judas's job—to betray a dear friend—is the harder thing to do than dying.

One issue that emerged when the *Gospel of Judas* had been discovered was whether it, like modern renditions of the character, would be sympathetic to Judas. After all, as a kind of arch-heretic in a heretical corpus of writing known for surprising turns and inversions, Judas-as-hero would hardly have been surprising. In reality, whether Judas is a villain or a hero in *GosJud* is far from clear. The interpretation hinges around certain places in the manuscript where, unfortunately, reconstructions are uncertain. Modern English translators thus offer quite different pictures of Judas; in table 20.1, four modern editions of this gospel reconstruct or translate the Coptic text very differently.

These points of controversy can be summarized:

1. *GosJud* 44:21: What does it mean that Jesus calls Judas the "thirteenth ***daimōn***"? A *daimōn* is kind of powerful celestial being. The problem is whether the person who wrote *GosJud* understood that being to be neutral (as the word was usually used in the Graeco-Roman world) or evil (as Christians came to use the word). The first English edition of the text, done by Rudolphe Kasser, Marvin Meyer, Gregor Wurst, and François Gaudard, doesn't translate the word but *transliterates* it—that is, changes Coptic characters into their English equivalents. Thus the team chose to leave "thirteenth *daimōn*" ambiguous. Marvin Meyer chooses the equally vague word "spirit." Elaine Pagels and Karen King chose to translate the word as "god," which is more or less

TABLE 20.1: Table of Some Alternate Text Readings for the *Gospel of Judas*

GosJudas	Pagels/King	Meyer	DeConick	Kasser et al
35: 23–27	"it is possible for you to reach that place, but you will suffer much grief."	"you can attain it, but you will go through a great deal of grief."	"I shall tell you the mysteries of the Kingdom, not so that you will go there, but so that you will grieve greatly."	"I shall tell you the mysteries of the kingdom, not so that you will go there, but you will grieve a great deal."
44: 21	Judas is the "thirteenth god."	Judas is the "thirteenth spirit."	Judas is the "thirteenth demon."	Judas is the "thirteenth *daimōn*."
46: 5–7	Judas said, "Teacher, surely the rulers are not subject to my seed?"	"Master, is it possible that my seed is subject to the rulers?"	Judas said, "Teacher, enough! At no time may my seed control the Archons!"	"Master, could it be that my seed is under the control of the rulers?"
52: 5–6	"the first is Seth, who is called 'Christ.'"	"the first is Seth, who is called Christ."	"the first is called Atheth, who is called the 'Good One.'"	"the first is Seth, who is called the Christ."
56: 17–21	"As for you, you will surpass them all. For you will sacrifice the human being who bears me."	"But you will exceed all of them. For you will sacrifice the man who bears me."	"But you will do worse than all of them. For the man who clothes me, you will sacrifice him."	"But you will exceed all of them. For you will sacrifice the man who bears me."

neutral; certainly it is a lot more positive than "demon," which is the favored translation of April DeConick.

2. *GosJud* 35:23–27: In this passage Jesus talks to Judas about the "mysteries of the Kingdom." Will Judas *see* that kingdom, though? Elaine Pagels and Karen King agree with Marvin Meyer's reading: Judas can in fact enter the kingdom, but (first? while there?) he will suffer greatly for the privilege. By contrast, DeConick agrees with Kasser's team: Judas can hear about the kingdom, but hearing about it will cause him much suffering and grief because he is not permitted to go there after his act of betrayal.

3. *GosJud* 56:17–21: Is Judas's act heroic or villainous? Unfortunately, the lines right before this passage are too corrupt to reconstruct, so context can't help us out. The reference is giving Jesus up ("sacrificing") to the authorities, but this author (like others in Christian antiquity) held a **docetic** view of Jesus: that it was only Jesus's human body that was put to death; the preexistent Christ returned to heaven at the crucifixion, unharmed. On that much, there is agreement; what scholars dispute is whether Judas's act of betrayal was a necessary evil or a very bad thing. On the one hand, Pagels/King, Meyer, and Kasser's team all choose "But you will exceed all of them. For you will sacrifice the one who bears me." Together, they see Judas as fulfilling a positive (perhaps even necessary) role: in essence, he plays a crucial part in the unfolding of the cosmic drama that was Jesus's appearance on earth. On the other hand, April DeConick reads this as an indication that Judas will be *more* evil than the evil people referred to in the corrupt previous line; what he does will be *worse* than any other kind of evil.

4. *GosJud* 55:10–11: All the English translations agree here, but the issue is one of interpretation. Jesus tells Judas that his star will rule over the "thirteenth aeon." Is this a good thing or a bad thing? Some see anything associated with the number thirteen as unlucky or bad: the thirteenth aeon is a place of exile, quite apart from the twelve cosmic realms associated here with the twelve disciples. In other Gnostic texts that date to the same era as *GosJud*, the thirteenth aeon is the dwelling place of **Sophia** in her repentance, and thus, certainly not wicked. In fact, if the thirteenth aeon was associated with repentance, this would be a rather logical place for Judas to end up, since the NT writings make it quite clear that Judas was repentant for what he had done.

So is Judas a hero or a villain? Here's how the four modern English translations cited here come down on the issue:

- Pagels/King: HERO
- DeConick: VILLAIN
- Meyer: the Judas character is more COMPLEX; he does what he needs to do
- Kasser team: NEUTRAL, but leaning toward villain.

What is the right interpretation? If Judas is the bad guy, then this gospel tells a story that is in line with mainstream Christian tradition that sees Judas as a villain and traitor.

A slightly more nuanced view is that the author of *GosJud* did not believe that Judas actually harmed Jesus by colluding in his death; Judas was compelled to behave according to his destiny as controlled by the stars. In fact, the entire event of the arrest, trial, and crucifixion was, in a sense, foreordained in the sense that all involved—with the exception of Jesus—were merely puppets of destiny. Jesus alone was free of this destiny. As a superior being, Jesus laughs at Judas because he recognizes, as Judas does not, Judas's ultimate powerlessness. Judas is identified as a demon for his malevolent intent and removed to the thirteenth aeon far from Jesus, where he is alone and there is no repentance for him. Thus Judas is bad, but not super bad; he is just part of a very flawed cosmos in which there is no salvation.

The opposite argument—that Judas was in fact Jesus's most trusted friend and confidant who does not actually betray him—was greeted with shock and disgust by some modern readers, who saw this gospel as denigrating the true story of Jesus's betrayal. In this interpretation, Jesus recognizes Judas's understanding of the other disciples as engaged in corrupt practices, and installs him as a sort of reward in a higher celestial realm than the others, where he may rule over them as a *daimōn*—a celestial power that is neither good nor bad. In this second, more radical interpretation, Jesus and Judas are both "good" people, but the twelve disciples are evil.

It is important to be clear that with the text of the *GosJud* as corrupted as it is, there's no way we can be sure which reading is correct. Perhaps, when all the fragments are pieced together, we'll finally know how the author of this writing understood Judas.

THE COSMOLOGY OF THE GOSPEL OF JUDAS

One thing that might help us to determine more about Judas in this writing is to find out how he fits into the "bigger picture" of the cosmos, since the author understood Christian salvation in cosmic terms. It is significant that in the classic style of an **apocalypse**, Jesus reveals to Judas the nature and shape of the cosmos. This is privileged secret information that the other disciples do not have, so it would be strange for Jesus to share it with a villain. In the apocalyptic genre—and *GosJud* qualifies as an apocalypse—the person receiving knowledge about the cosmos is *always* privileged, and thus always the hero of the text.

In many key ways, the *GosJud* shares conceptual material with some **Sethian** texts, especially the *GosEg* and the *ApJn*. The Great Invisible Spirit figures as the chief deity in the cosmos, from which other beings issue forth as light clouds (see the *Paraphrase of Shem* [*PShem*] for another NH text with scores of beings coming forth from light clouds). Other familiar beings are **Autogenes, Adamas**, and the **Four Luminaries**, Oroael, Harmozel, Daveithai and Eleleth. Jesus is described as child of the **Barbēlō**, the Mother in the Sethian triad Father/Barbēlō/Autogenes (35:17–18). This is a complex, courtly vision of the cosmos, full of light and scores of angels. Numerology—specifically the numbers 12, 24, 72, and 360—feature prominently.

It is noteworthy that the revelatory section of *GosJud* (47:1–55:20) contains virtually no overtly Christian elements but appears to derive from Hellenistic Jewish sources on the nature of the world. For instance, this section uses the word "luminaries" and talks about beings emerging from light clouds; these words and concepts derive from Jewish texts rather than from any Greek idea of nested planetary spheres. In fact, it may be that the entire cosmological section was once part of an earlier Jewish Sethian tradition that then was reused here.

IS THE GOSPEL OF JUDAS SETHIAN?

Scholars dispute whether the *GosJud* is in fact a Sethian text. On the one hand, the cosmology of the text looks very Sethian. We find characters we would expect to find in a Sethian text: for instance, the Great Invisible Spirit, Saklas, and Autogenes appear here, as they do in classic Sethian texts such as *GosEg*.

If this text is Sethian, on the other hand, we run into two big problems. First, Seth is virtually absent from this text's **cosmology** or **soteriology**. There may be a few explanations:

• Maybe the part about Seth is simply missing from the single, incomplete manuscript we have.

- Maybe Seth's presence was simply taken for granted.
- Maybe this particular cosmology is not Sethian but draws on Sethian traditions, perhaps even refutes them by de-emphasizing the Sethian savior.

Many people have noted that Seth plays no role in the *ApJn*, which is undisputedly Sethian, nor in *HypArch*, another undisputedly Sethian text. In this case, then, what makes *GosJud* Sethian is that it shares typological connections with other known Sethian texts (for a list of these connections, see chap. 10, "Sethian Gnosticism.") There are other Sethian characters missing, too, notably Barbēlō and Sophia, making *GosJud* a very "male-oriented" text but not necessarily a non-Sethian text (*HypArch* is a good example of a Sethian text that gives great importance to female characters; *GosEg* is a good example of a Sethian text that is male-oriented). This teaches us that Sethianism was a broad and flexible school of thought, with few rigid doctrines concerning cosmic architecture.

However, there is one place where the name of Seth actually does appear. Or, better, where it *possibly* occurs. In *GosJud* 52:5–6, there is a list of the **archons** who rule over the underworld:

- The first one, [. . .]th, who is called the [. . .]
- The [second] is Harmathoth, who is [. . .]
- The [third] is Galila
- The fourth is Iobel
- The fifth is Adonaios

As you can see, there are some holes in this list, and the most vexing hole of all conceals the name and identity of the first ruler (see fig. 20-1).

To reconstruct the list, we start by comparing it with two very similar lists of archon names in the *GosEg* and the *ApJn*. On this basis, the first archon should be called Athoth. The problem with this reconstruction, however, is that enough of the CT manuscript remains around the last "th" in the name that we know that the letters "ATHO" don't fit. In fact if you look very hard at the page in question—and all those who work on the *GosJud* have looked *very* hard at it—the most plausible letters to restore in the lacuna are "SE," thus:

"The first one, Seth, who is called the [. . .]"

If this is correct, though, it poses a huge problem: what is Seth—the most important and holy figure in the Sethian pantheon—doing right here at the top of the list of minor, lower *daimones*, the rulers of Chaos and the Underworld?

And the problem continues when we try to restore the next part of the line. What appears here are four Coptic letters with a line over the tops of the letters. The presence of this line indicates, in Coptic, a sacred name, and also that that sacred name is abbreviated. The most obvious way to interpret it, following scores of other Coptic texts, is as a contraction for "the Christ." So we would have what most of the modern English translators of the text have reconstructed:

"The first one, Seth, who is called the [Christ]."

But how could this be? Even if it makes sense that Seth's other name is "the Christ"—not entirely surprising for a Sethian text—why, or how, could Seth/Christ be found here, as a demon of the abyss, in a text that already features Jesus as the revealer figure? This is a puzzle that has not yet been solved. Perhaps the scribe copying out the manuscript a century or two after it was originally composed simply made an error. Perhaps he meant to write "Athoth" but for whatever reason substituted "Seth" by mistake. Perhaps as a fourth-century scribe he knew absolutely nothing about second-century Sethianism, and therefore did not catch his own error.

The most radical solution is that the reconstruction "Seth, who is the Christ" is correct, and the scribe copied what he saw accurately.

FIGURE 20.1 Folio 52 of Codex Tchacos, which gives the names of the five angels who rule over the abyss. Circled is the area where scholars debate the missing words. Is the first angel Seth, or someone else? And is Seth "the Christ"?

The original author may have been a part of a Sethian group but, for some reason, broke from that group and came to disavow their ideas. Thus he composed a so-called Sethian gospel, but one that is all wrong for a Sethian text. He left Seth out of the divine structure of the higher cosmos, and instead substituted Jesus as the main revealer. He thus demoted Seth to the status of a minor,

STAR LANGUAGE IN THE *GOSPEL OF JUDAS*

More than any other ancient Christian text, the *GosJud* uses the word "star" repeatedly. We learn that each disciple is assigned a star (42:7–8), and that stars are somehow associated with angels (37:4–5; 40:16–17; 41:5). Judas's star, furthermore, has "led him astray" (45:13). What does this mean? Apparently the *GosJud* is drawing upon ancient Greek and Jewish ideas that linked stars to fate. Destiny worked two ways. First, all people were born under one of the twelve signs of the zodiac, and these signs determined character and fate.

Second, the seven planets also controlled human behavior. In fact, when Jesus tells Judas that his star has led him *astray*, he's actually making a pun: the Greek verb here, *planein*, means "to wander" and "to err" but also "to be a planet" (it is the basis for the English word "planet," which means, literally, a "wandering star"). Early Christians believed that not only did the planets "wander," they also erred; people could be drawn into sin by the stars, but then set back on the right path by Jesus Christ.

even hostile divinity. Furthermore, "Seth, who is called the Christ" could have been a way of castigating Sethian Christians. The line suggests (as does the entire gospel) that these people misunderstood the name Jesus; they do not call him Jesus, but Christ, and by Christ, they actually mean Seth. And by Seth, they do not mean the highest being in the cosmos, but when they pray to Christ, as of course many Christians must have done, they are actually invoking a demon of chaos.

WHAT THE *GOSPEL OF JUDAS* TELLS US ABOUT PROTO-ORTHODOX CHRISTIANITY

Whoever wrote the *GosJud* apparently suffered an intense hatred for some of the Christians of his day. How do we know this? First of all, it is hard not to notice that Jesus's disciples come across quite badly right from the start. When Jesus encounters them for the first time celebrating the **Eucharist**, he laughs derisively at them. When they ask him why, he tells them that they are not honoring him, as they believe they are, but actually their own god (not directly named here, but almost certainly **Sakla**). The disciples react with irrational anger, almost as if they themselves are archons. Blaspheming him to themselves, they

are unable to face him. Only Judas has the courage of heart.

The most disturbing image in the entire *GosJud*, however, is the disciples' collective vision of a huge building with an altar (38:1–39:5). Twelve men offer sacrifices in front of a crowd. It is not an animal sacrifice, like you might expect at the Jerusalem Temple or a Roman temple; it is a human sacrifice, and the victims are none other than the priests' wives and children. As these priests sacrifice, they invoke Jesus's name. What is the meaning of this?

As it happens, Jesus provides an explanation of the disciples' vision: *they* are the evil sacrificing priests. The cattle in the vision are those Christians whom they had led astray in their teachings. And what are those teachings? The author sees the focus on Jesus's crucifixion—and ways of talking about it as an ultimate "sacrifice"—as a monstrous doctrine. A benevolent god cannot ask for human sacrifices; even the God of Abraham stays Abraham's hand before he sacrifices his only son Isaac (Gen 22:1–14). The *GosJud* text makes it clear that Jesus was not actually crucified; only his body was killed, not his divine, preexistent self. To make the doctrine of "Christ, crucified" the centerpiece of Christian theology was to horribly

THE JERUSALEM TEMPLE

The Jerusalem Temple was the centerpiece for Jewish religion until Roman troops destroyed it in 70 CE. The main function of the Temple was for the faithful to come to offer sacrifices, as outlined in the Torah. Sacrifices were performed daily by a priestly organization, the Levites.

Not all people approved of the Temple system; some Jews believed that the Levites had become corrupt, perhaps by pandering too much to the Greeks and Romans who held the city of Jerusalem under their power. Some of them withdrew to the desert to form communities of Jews who rejected Temple sacrifice as impure; there they established their own systems of prayer and "pure" (i.e., bloodless) sacrifice. It appears that the author of the *GosJud* agreed with these Jews, because the language he uses to describe the disciple/priests is virtually identical to the language that these Jews used to describe the corrupt Levites as murderers and adulterers who had defiled God's Temple on earth.

Furthermore, the Jews who believed that the Jerusalem Temple was corrupt shared something else with the author of *GosJud*: both believed that there existed in the cosmos a pure, undefiled heavenly temple. This is the temple that Judas sees in his vision (44:15–46:4) but which Jesus prevents him from entering because, as a mortal, he is unworthy. In other words, whoever wrote this text had a very Jewish mind-set, which is interesting: he was also very clearly Christian.

misconstrue what Jesus's appearance on earth was all about.

But there is a second, almost darker element to this author's horror of sacrifice. His insistence that the twelve disciples were performing human sacrifices may allude to Christian martyrdom, which in the middle of the second century had become a public (and ghastly) way for Christians to show their allegiance to Christ. Proto-orthodox Christian teachers such as **Tertullian** claimed that martyrdom was God's will, because it glorified God (*On Fleeing Persecution*, ca. 212 CE). The idea that martyrdom could actually be pleasing to God was a grotesque distortion of true Christianity, as the author of the *GosJud* saw it. Only a demon would demand blood sacrifice; and it is no mistake that the author describes the evil archon **Nebro** as one whose "appearance was defiled with blood" (51:11). Nebro demands blood from those who honor him; what the disciples do not realize, when they call on Jesus's name as they go willingly to their deaths and use Jesus's death as their model, is that they are serving Nebro, not God.

The *GosJud* is not the only second-century text to reject martyrdom. Other texts from the NHL that do so are the *Testimony of Truth* (*TestTruth*) and the *Apocalypse of Peter* (*ApocPeter*). But Christian anti-martyrdom texts are rare, and far more popular was proto-orthodox Christianity's insistence that martyrdom pleased God and brought heavenly rewards to those who underwent such suffering. The *GosJud* reveals that the same sort of heavenly revelations that the martyrs won through self-sacrifice could come to the faithful through a proper understanding of Jesus's role as a savior. Whoever wrote this text felt so disaffected from proto-orthodox Christianity that he rejected all Jesus's disciples as under the blind influence of a blood-thirsty demon; as for himself, he felt so outside these monstrous teachings of "the Twelve" that he could only identify with Judas, the man whom, according to this gospel, had been told all the secrets of the cosmos (57:15).

A GOSPEL WITHOUT SALVATION?

One of the most shocking things about the *GosJud* is that it doesn't have a very uplifting ending. In fact, it ends with Judas handing Jesus over to be crucified. Some people have been so troubled by this that they've reasoned that Judas must be a good guy—because if he were an evil demon, the story would end with evil winning. Not only is that a depressing story, it is also not what a gospel, the meaning of which is "good news," is all about. But those who despair at the depressing end of this text should remember: we only have a portion of this text remaining, and we'll have to wait to find out how it really ends.

GOSPEL OF MARY (MAGDALENE)

Because the *Gospel of Mary* is included in the NHLE, people often mistakenly think that it was found at Nag Hammadi. In fact, it is from another important Coptic manuscript, the Berlin Gnostic Codex (BG 8502), which also contains copies of the *ApJn* and the *Sophia of Jesus Christ* (SJC) (two texts that were also found at NH). The BG dates from around the same time as the NH codices, around the end of the fourth century. Although BG was purchased in 1896 it wasn't actually published until 1955, and so it is in effect a relatively new discovery for many people.

GOSPEL OF MARY: BACKGROUND

Did heresiologists know about this text? No one refers to it directly, but there are some references to documents that were known as the *Greater and Lesser Questions of Mary*. Since the heresiologists don't quote from those writings, it is hard to know if they come from the *Gospel of Mary*. And, at any rate, it would be hard to know for sure because the only extant copy is missing pages 1–6 and 11–14. We're not really much helped in our reconstructions of the missing parts by the discovery at **Oxyrhynchus** of three, small, papyrus fragments of the text in Greek. The fragments do indicate that this gospel circulated quite widely in antiquity, because it is very unusual to find

multiple copies of an ancient text. As we have it now, the text is less than eight pages long.

Who Was Mary?

Although the NT states that there were many women named Mary around Jesus, the Mary in this particular document is Mary of Magdala, usually known as Mary Magdalene. We know very little about this person; we know she was from the city of Magdala in Palestine, and we know that she was not married, because she takes her name after her city rather than after her husband. According to the Gospel of Luke, this Mary was a financial supporter of Jesus and his followers.

Most people do not realize that much of what they think they know about Mary Magdalene is not really biblical; it derives from later Christian tradition. For instance, most people perceive Mary Magdalene as a prostitute. But you will not find this anywhere in the NT. What you will find in Luke 7:36–50 is an account of a woman who "was a sinner" and who anoints Jesus's feet with precious ointment. This woman is not identified as Mary Magdalene; the only thing she is called is "a sinner." Nevertheless, this woman was combined by early Western medieval theologians with the figure of Mary of Magdala to fill out her character... and, very possibly, to denigrate Mary Magdalene's importance to many faithful Christians who considered her Jesus's favored disciple. It is interesting that in Eastern Orthodoxy, Mary Magdalene is never considered a prostitute or confused with the woman who was a "sinner."

In recent decades, thanks to popular (and fictional) renditions of Christian tradition such as novelist Dan Brown's hugely popular *The Da Vinci Code*, some people were led to believe that Jesus and Mary were, if not married, then lovers, and that this "secret" was intentionally covered up by the Roman Catholic Church. Gnostic texts and, in particular, the *Gospel of Mary* are often cited as containing proof of this secret, sexual relationship. Those coming to these texts for this reason are sure to be disappointed; there is no proof, either in the *Gospel of Mary* or any other ancient text, that Jesus and Mary were a couple (see the boxed item: "Jesus and Mary, Sitting in a Tree…" on p. 98 of chap. 8). What does come across from both the canonical and noncanonical early Christian material was that Mary was prominent among Jesus's followers. In all four NT gospels, Mary Magdalene is mentioned in the accounts of Jesus's resurrection as a significant witness. At the end of the Gospel of John, she plays a particularly important role as the one who first sees the resurrected Christ, although she does not recognize him. In the *Gospel of Philip*, she is mentioned as Jesus's favored disciple. Probably it is likely that her prominence in the resurrection accounts gave rise to statements such as that which we find in the *GosPhil*, and to later, second-century accounts of her as privy to secret knowledge that Jesus imparted only to her.

Did Mary Magdalene actually write the *Gospel of Mary*? Recently, this idea has gained favor, especially among those who want to see Mary Magdalene as Jesus's partner and most vital disciple. The answer, however, is no: we can tell from both the style of the text and its theology that it dates from no earlier than the second century. By that time, the real Mary Magdala was long gone. It is clear, though, that she had a real following; Mary is the favored disciple in a range of second-century texts, from NH's *GosPhil* to lesser-known writings such as the **Pistis Sophia**. Whoever wrote the *GosMary* chose to write in Mary's name, and chose, too, to preserve what they believed to be true: that this woman was Jesus's disciple who "understood the All." That makes the *GosMary* our only Christian gospel ascribed to a woman, even if she did not write it.

THE COSMOLOGY OF THE GOSPEL OF MARY

Like the *GosJud* and so many texts at NH, the *GosMary* is an apocalypse, in which a seer (in this case, Mary) is given a tour of the cosmos by a privileged being (in this case, Jesus as the Savior). This text is also a **revelation dialogue**, in which Jesus reveals information about the cosmos to a recipient on earth. What Mary has seen is a multileveled cosmos, with each area controlled by a planetary power. In this text, these powers are known collectively as the Power of Darkness: Ignorance, Desire, and Wrath.

JESUS IN THE GOSPEL OF MARY

In the *Gospel of Mary*, Jesus is named only as Savior, Lord, and Blessed One. All these terms are originally Greek, and the image of the cosmos and the conception of human beings as connected integrally to that cosmos that the author of this text describes also comes from Greek philosophy (particularly Stoicism) and astronomy. In this way, *GosMary* is markedly different from the *GosJud*, which conceptualizes the cosmos in essentially Jewish terms.

While we encounter Jesus on earth in the *GosJud* in the days leading up to Passover and the crucifixion, the Jesus in *GosMary* is the post-resurrection Savior. He joins his gathered disciples to answer questions and to send them out as apostles. Jesus's teachings concern the nature of salvation. People, he teaches, need to understand that they bear the Image of the Good within. This Image is also called, in this text, the Son of man and the Perfect Man.

Part of Jesus's teachings concern the nature of sin. Remarkably, the Savior in this text remarks, "There is no such thing as sin." What he means is that since God is Good and made all things, he could not have made sin. People sin when they become alienated from the Good and caught up in their emotions and passions, which are imposed on humans by imperfect celestial beings. Proper teaching can instruct the soul in how to master these passions.

SALVATION IN THE *GOSPEL OF MARY*

Mary shares with the other disciples her knowledge of the ascent of the soul after death through the planetary spheres. At each level, the soul will be interrogated; in keeping with their natures, each Power of Darkness asks a particular question: Ignorance asks a stupid question, Desire desires to covet the soul, and Wrath angrily interrogates the soul. One way to achieve ultimate salvation, therefore, is to know what to say and do when the powers interrogate you. This was a common theme in second-century writings, as we can see from texts such as NH's *First Apocalypse of James* (see chap. 14). Even before death, however, people could be saved by turning and searching within for the image of God. One must understand that the soul is spiritual and belongs, ultimately, to the Good, with which it shares its nature.

WHAT THE *GOSPEL OF MARY* TELLS US ABOUT PROTO-ORTHODOX CHRISTIANITY

It would not be wrong to say that despite being Jesus's favored disciple, Mary in this text gets no respect from her fellow male disciples. After she discloses the mysteries of the cosmos to them, the apostle Andrew, in particular, launches an attack on her. Peter picks up the charge, finding it offensive that Jesus would select a woman to be a favored disciple and reveal to her mysteries that he had kept from the men; he is so belligerent and accusing that he reduces Mary to tears. Another apostle, Levi, steps in to defend her, but

the damage had been done. Peter's behavior here mirrors that in the *GThom* #114, where Peter demands that Jesus make Mary depart from them, "for women are not worthy of life." Whoever wrote *GosMary* considered Peter an ignorant bigot, one who did not have "ears to hear" the truths that Jesus had conveyed only to a woman. In fact Peter's outbursts proved that he was still enslaved to the Powers of Darkness: Ignorance, Desire, and Wrath.

As Karen King has indicated in her study of this gospel, the characterization of all the disciples in *GosMary* indicates diverse views on who was best qualified to lead the Christian movement forward. According to this text, leadership should be based on discerning which disciples best understood Jesus's teachings, especially ones that were difficult to understand. Only those with considerable spiritual wisdom and discernment were able to transcend the influence of the cosmos, and to lead their flock away from sin and to salvation.

In summary, both the GosJud and GosMary share heroes who were vilified by mainstream Christian tradition in the West—the underdogs or antiheroes. This gives us a sense of their respective authors, who may have seen themselves as profoundly disaffected from apostolic Christianity as it developed. Certainly this is clear from the *GosJud*, but the apostle Peter's callous behavior toward Mary Magdalene speaks to the same problems. In the final analysis, these two texts highlight points of conflict between Christianity and Judaism, Christianity and paganism, and most importantly, between Christians themselves.

QUESTIONS TO CONSIDER

1. As you understand the *Gospel of Judas*, is Judas a hero or a villain?

2. In what ways are the *Gospel of Mary* and the *Gospel of Judas* alike? In what way are they different? Why would anyone write a gospel in the name of Mary or Judas? Any ideas?

3. The *Gospel of Mary* appears to draw on Greek traditions, whereas the *Gospel of Judas* draws on Jewish traditions. Can you identify some of these traditions, in both cases?

KEY TERMS

heresiologist	Autogenes	*Pistis Sophia*
heretic	cosmology	Four Luminaries
Sethian	Tertullian	revelation discourse
archon	Oxyrhynchus	*daimōn*
Sakla	Sahidic	apocalypse
revelation dialogue	Epiphanius of Salamis	Barbēlō
Codex Tchacos	Sophia	Eucharist
Irenaeus of Lyons	Adamas	Nebro
docetic	soteriology	

FOR FURTHER READING

Brock, Ann Graham. *Mary Magdalene, The First Apostle: The Struggle for Authority*. Cambridge, MA: Harvard University Press, 2003. A very readable introduction to the figure of Mary Magdalene.

DeConick, April D. *The Thirteenth Apostle: What the Gospel of Judas Really Says*. London: Continuum, 2007. An independent translation of the Gospel of Judas with explanatory chapters. For a general educated audience.

Kasser, Rudolphe, Marvin Meyer, and Gregor Wurst. *The Gospel of Judas*. Commentary by Bart D. Ehrman. Washington, DC: National Geographic, 2006. A critical edition and commentary of solely the *Gospel of Judas*. Good for readers interested in this text, with very readable commentary by Bart Ehrman.

Kasser, Rudolphe, and Gregor Wurst. *The Gospel of Judas, Critical Edition: Together with the Letter of Peter to Philip, James, and a Book of Allogenes from Codex Tchacos*. Washington, DC: National Geographic, 2007. A Coptic edition of the CT, with translations into French and English. Very useful for serious scholarship.

King, Karen L. *The Gospel of Mary of Magdala: Jesus and the First Woman Apostle*. Santa Rosa, CA: Polebridge Press, 2003. A new edition of the *Gospel of Mary*, with an introduction and notes. For a general, interested audience.

Krosney, Herbert. *The Lost Gospel: The Quest for the Gospel of Judas Iscariot*. Washington, DC: National Geographic, 2006. A very readable account of the discovery of Codex Tchacos, along with a translation and commentary. For nonspecialist audiences.

Pagels, Elaine, and Karen L. King. *Reading Judas: The Gospel of Judas and the Shaping of Christianity*. New York: Viking, 2007. This translation follows a wonderful discussion of the text in its historical context, with emphasis placed on the author of the *GosJud*'s relationship to proto-orthodox Christianity.

Schaberg, Jane. *The Resurrection of Mary Magdalene: Legends, Apocrypha, and the Christian Testament*. Continuum, 2002. A comprehensive study by a top feminist scholar.

In popular culture

The Philadelphia-based hip-hop trio Jedi Mind Tricks mention the *Gospel of Judas* in their song "Heavy Metal Kings."

National Geographic maintains a beautiful website on the *Gospel of Judas*, with English and Coptic versions of the text and downloadable, high resolutions of the entire Codex Tchacos: http://www.nationalgeographic.com/lostgospel/index.html

Table of Parallels from Our Three Nag Hammadi Creation Myths

H aving trouble keeping straight what things happen when and to whom in *Hypostasis of the Archons*, the *Apocryphon of John*, and *On the Origin* of the World? You're not alone! It can be challenging to keep the details straight in these texts, because they are so similar and draw on the book of Genesis so similarly. This table should help.

Biblical Reference	HypArch	ApJn	OrigWld
	Chief **archon** is named Samael	Chief archon is named Ialtabaoth and later, **Samael**	Chief archon is Yaldabaoth
Isa 46:9	"It is I who am God" blasphemy.		"It is I who am God, and there is no other one that exists apart from me."
Ex 20:5 Deut 49:9		"I am a jealous god. And there is no other god apart from me."	
		Repentance of the mother for creating Ialtabaoth	
	Blasphemous utterance becomes hypostasized, and Samael chases it to chaos and the abyss.		**Pistis** sends Samael into the abyss and withdraws into the light.
			Enthronement of **Sabaoth** by Pistis Sophia.

continued

Gen 1:1 (light over the face of the abyss)	Incorruptibility gazes into the waters, creating an image, which the archons desire.	The holy mother-father and Forethought show the rulers an image "like a portrait statue." The archons see the image reflected in the waters.	To prove Samael wrong about being the only god, a light appears with a human likeness, the Light **Adam**. This happens on the first day of creation.
Gen 1:26	Archons say "Come, let us create a human being that will be soil from the earth."	Archons say "come, let us make a human being after the image of god and after our images, so that the human being's image might serve as a light for us."	Samael tells the authorities, "If you do not want him (the Light Adam) to destroy our work, come let us create a man out of earth, according to the image of our body and according to the likeness of this being."
		Creation of the first Adam "by means of one another's power" collectively.	
			Creation of the second Adam who is soul-endowed, on the sixth day (we don't know who creates him).
Gen 2:7	Creation of first human from mud, after the image of God. It lies inert.	The Adam is an animate body, inactive and immovable.	The archons masturbate onto the earth and create a man from the soil with a body that resembles theirs but a likeness resembling the Light Adam on the eighth day.
Gen 2:7	Samael breathes into the human's face, and it becomes animate (i.e., possess psyche) but inert.	Ialtabaoth blows his spirit into Adam, and it transfers from him to Adam, leaving Ialtabaoth devoid of the mother's spirit.	"He became a soul-endowed man." But he has no spirit and lies for forty days inanimate.
		The being shines with the spirit, so the archons cast him down into matter.	
		The Mother sends Adam a "helper," called Life (**Zoe**), to teach him about salvation. The helper hides within Adam to evade the rulers and to undo the damage the Mother did.	**Sophia** lets fall a droplet of light onto the water, and an androgynous being emerges, which she molds into a female body in the likeness of the Mother. She is called the Eve of Life, but the authorities call her "the Beast."

continued

Gen 2:7	The Spirit descends and dwells within the being (i.e., Adam becomes pneumatic).		Sophia Zoe sends her breath into Adam on the fortieth day of him lying inert.
	The Spirit calls the being "Adam."	"Let us call him Adam, so that we might have his name as a luminous power."	"And he was called Adam, that is, 'father,' according to the name of the one that existed before him."
		The archons create a second Adam out of matter, to create a mortal human being.	
Gen 2:18–19	The rulers bring animals and birds of the sky to Adam to name.		
Gen 2:15	Adam set in the garden by archons.	The rulers bring their mortal Adam into the garden.	The authorities take Adam to paradise.
Gen 3:3	Archons tell Adam "From every tree in the garden you shall eat, yet from the tree of knowledge of good and evil do not eat, nor touch it, for the day you eat from it, with death you are going to die."	The archons say "eat!" In the middle of the garden they put the "tree of their life." They keep the tree of the knowledge of good and evil hidden, lest the mortal Adam eat and "recognize the nakedness of his shame."	The seven archons tell Adam and Eve timidly, "The fruit of all the trees created for you in paradise shall be eaten; but as for the tree of knowledge, control yourselves and do not eat from it. If you eat you will die."
		The Savior causes "them" to eat the fruit of the tree of knowledge.	
Gen 2:21	Rulers say "Come let us cause a deep sleep to fall upon Adam."	The snake causes a deep sleep to fall on Adam.	The authorities cause a deep sleep over Adam, teaching him in sleep that Eve really came from his rib (rather than from above) so that women are forced to obey their husbands and husbands lord their power over their wives.
	Sleep = lack of *gnosis*	Sleep = a lack of *gnosis* and spiritual perception.	
	Woman created from Adam's side, leaving him merely psychic (the **pneumatic** element leaves with the woman.)	Woman created from Adam's side, because Ialdabaoth wants to extract the light within him. He models the woman after the image of the Afterthought he had seen reflected in the waters.	

continued

	Spirit-endowed (pneumatic) woman says "Arise, Adam."		Sophia sends Zoe Eve on the eighth day (after the day the archons call "rest"). She calls out "Adam! Become alive! Arise upon the Earth!"
Gen 3:20	"It is you who has given me life; you will be called 'mother of the living.'"		"You shall be called 'mother of the living.' For it is you who have given me life."
Gen 2:23		Adam recognizes the woman beside him, shaking off his perceptual sleep: "This now is bone of my bones and flesh of my flesh."	
		The Savior shows himself as an eagle on the tree of knowledge, in order to raise them out of the deep sleep.	
Gen 3:17		Ialdabaoth comes upon the female preparing herself for her male, "for he was not acquainted with the mystery that had come to pass from the holy plan."	
	Archons desire to rape Adam's counterpart.		Archons: "What sort of thing is this luminous woman? For she resembles that likeness which appear to us in the light. Now come, let us lay hold of her and cast our seed into her, so that when she becomes soiled she many not be able to ascend into her light."
	The woman flees and becomes a tree.		Eve puts a "mist" into the authorities' eyes, leaving only her likeness with Adam. She withdraws into the tree of knowledge.
	Archons rape the woman's "shadow."	Ialdabaoth rapes Eve, but the forethought of the entirety snatches up Zoe out of Eve.	The archons rape Eve's likeness violently and "wickedly," in both "natural" and "unnatural" ways.

continued

	The female spiritual principle enters the snake, "the instructor."	The snake is associated with the archons.	The female spiritual principle, the Instructor, appears. She is the wisest of all creatures and called "the Beast" by the archons.
Gen 3:1 and following	The snake asks the (now carnal) woman what the archons said about the fruit of the tree.		The Beast asks Eve, "What did God say to you? Was it 'do not eat from the tree of *gnosis*?.'"
Gen 3:4	Snake: "With death you shall not die, for it was out of envy that it said this to you. Rather, your eyes shall open and you shall come to be like gods, recognizing good and evil."	The snake encourages them to eat so as to sow in them "a desire for corruption" (i.e., sex) so that Adam will be useful to the archons.	"Do not be afraid. In death you shall not die. For he knows that when you eat from it, your intellect will become sober and you will come to be like gods, recognizing the difference that obtains between evil men and good ones."
Gen 3:6	The carnal woman eats the fruit and gives it to her husband; they recognize they are "naked" of the spiritual element.		Eve eats the fruit and gives it to her husband, "then their intellect became open. For when they had eaten, the light of *gnosis* had shone upon them."
Gen 3:9	The chief archon looks for Adam in the garden.		The rulers look for Adam in paradise.
Gen 3:13ff.	Adam and the woman offer their explanations to the ruler.		Adam and Eve offer their explanations to the ruler.
	The archons curse the snake's "shadow."		The rulers are not able to do anything to the instructor, so they curse him.
Gen 3:24	Archons expel Adam from the garden, throwing humankind into "distraction and toil."	Ialdabaoth expels Adam and his wife from the garden, clothing them in "obscure darkness."	In fear of what the enlightened Adam will do, the rulers expel Adam and Eve from paradise, guarding the tree of life with cherubim with fiery swords.
Gen 4:1	The woman gives birth to Cain, the archons' child.	Eve gives birth to Eloim and Iaue or Cain and Abel, the children of Ialdabaoth.	
	The woman bears Abel, Adam's child.		The likeness Eve bears Abel from the first ruler.

continued

Gen 4:25	The woman bears Seth to Adam.	Adam begets Seth after the "image of the son of man."	
	Eve becomes pregnant (no mention of a father) and bears **Norea**, "the virgin whom the powers did not defile."	The Mother sends down her spirit in the image of a "female being who resembled her" (presumably Norea, but she is not named)	
			Eve bears many other unnamed children from the authorities.

Note that in *HypArch* the chief archon is never called Ialdabaoth; *ApJn* actually has Adam created *twice*, as a celestial Adam (associated with various demons) and then as Adam made of *matter* (not mud). In *HypArch*, the snake is a spiritual being, but in *ApJn*, he's in league with the evil archons. The *ApJn* includes the drama of Sophia's repentance, but this is absent in *HypArch*.

In *ApJn*, Cain and Abel are both Ialdabaoth's children. In *HypArch*, Cain is the child of the rulers (which one is not specified); Abel and Seth are Adam's children, and Norea is the result of Eve's "virgin" birth. In *OrigWld*, Eve is actually created and named *first*, before Adam. Furthermore, she animates Adam by commandment/word, not by inspiration (breathing spirit into him). Eve is not created from Adam's rib—according to *OrigWld* this is a lie that the archons tell Adam so that women are forced to obey men and that men are allowed to lord over women.

Another way to look at this chart is that it highlights "points of conflict" in the second century about how to interpret Genesis properly. Read this way, we do not need these sources to all agree nor do we want to reconcile them. We want to see where the disagreements were at the time that Genesis was used. For example, here are some of the issues that Christians were actively disputing:

- Was the snake really sent from higher forces to help initiate salvation (allowing Adam and Eve to become awakened to their true situation and break from the archon's clutches), or was he actually the archons' instrument (because through his encouragement Adam and Eve lost their innocence and became sexual beings)?

- When God says in Gen 1:26, "Let us create humankind in our image?" what image is this? Whose image? Are humans created in the image of the highest God, or in the image of the archons? Are both women and men made in God's image, or just men, with women as "secondary" creatures?

- How many Adams were there, really? In Gen 1:26 there is mention of one human creation; in Gen 2:7 there is another. Does this mean there were two separate Adams, a heavenly one and an earthly one? How could Adam the "mud man" (Gen 2:7) be superior to the Adam of 1:26, who is explicitly said to be created in the image of God?

- What about Adam and Eve's children? Where did they really come from? If Cain was born with a murderous nature and he is only the third human being (and human beings are created in the image of God), how could he be evil?

Can you find other possible points of conflict from these three accounts placed side by side?

Glossary

The terms in boldface here are collected from individual chapters of this book and, on occasion, from the NH writings themselves. For fuller definitions and more terms, the reader is advised to consult Andrew Philip Smith, *A Dictionary of Gnosticism* (Wheaton, IL: Quest, 2009).

Abel: In Genesis, the second son of Adam and Eve. In the *ApJn*, Abel/Yave is the offspring that results from Ialdabaoth's rape of Eve. He appears also as one of the seven archons in the *ApJn*, and the seventh of twelve archons in the *GosEg*.

Abrasaks: In *ApocAdam*, one of three savior angels, along with Sablo and Gamaliel. The name Abrasaks is well known from magical spells and amulets; sometimes ABRASAX.

Achamoth: A name for the feminine manifestation of the **First Principle**, sometimes identical with **Sophia**. The name "Achamoth" is a corruption of the Hebrew "Hokhma" or "wisdom" (just as Sophia is Greek for "wisdom.")

Adam: The first man in some Gnostic cosmologies, from the Hebrew word "man" and "ground, soil." Adam is not always a human being in Nag Hammadi texts; there is often reference to a celestial Adam who precedes the creation of the earthly Adam and remains superior to him. See **Adamas**.

Adamas/Ger-Adamas: The primordial being in Sethian cosmology upon whom the earthly first man, Adam, is modeled. Also called the Heavenly Adam.

Aeon: An emanation from the **First Principle**. An aeon can be spatial, as in a realm; it can be personified, as in Truth or Wisdom; and finally (but more rarely in second-century CE usage) it can designate a period of time.

Aetiological: An adjective to describe a story, passage, or phrase that explains the origins of something.

Affusion: An early form of baptismal ritual, in which water is poured over the head of the person being baptized.

Akhmimic: A dialect of Coptic used in the Egyptian town of Akhmim in the fourth and fifth centuries.

Alexandria: A large city in northern Egypt founded by Alexander the Great. Alexandria, as a seat of learning and culture, drew intellectuals from all over the Roman Empire. It is believed that many of the Nag Hammadi writings were originally composed in Alexandria.

Allogenes: From a Greek word meaning "of foreign birth" so sometimes translated as "stranger" or "foreigner." Also: the title of two different ancient texts, one found at Nag Hammadi, the other in the **Codex Tchacos**.

Androgyne: A being that is both male and female. Androgyny was often considered a divine state, since sexual difference implied a division of a primordial state which transcended gender. Many NH texts feature an androgynous primal being, sometimes given names such as the Mother-Father or Metropator. The archons are technically androgynous, although they often behave as if they were male beings. The first Adam, a mud being, is technically an androgyne until Eve is removed from it and sexual difference is thereby initiated.

Angels of the Entirety: In Sethian cosmology, the four angels Harmozel, Daveithai, Oroael, and Eleleth. These are beneficent angels or **aeons** who assist in the process of salvation. Also known as the **Four Luminaries**.

Apocalypse: A literary genre, from a Greek word meaning "unveiled." In apocalyptic texts, heavenly knowledge is revealed to a human recipient or "seer." This knowledge can be of various sorts, but in the Christian period, apocalyptic texts tend to focus on revelations or predictions of the end of the world.

Apocalyptic literature: A class or genre of writings which make central the revelation of knowledge, generally about the nature or structure of the cosmos. Originally a Jewish literary genre, apocalyptic literature became tremendously popular in early Christianity.

Apocryphon (pl.: apocrypha): Greek for "secret thing." A word for a document or books, which are not usually part of the Jewish or Christian **canon** or list of approved books.

Apolytrosis: From the Greek "untying" or "loosening." A Valentinian sacrament about which we know little; Irenaeus of Lyons tells us that it could take different forms in different communities. Its ultimate goal was probably to facilitate the soul or spirit becoming "untied" from the body after death.

Apophatic theology: Also called "negative theology." A way of describing or conceptualizing God in privative terms: God is *un*knowable, *un*limited, *in*visible, etc.

apostolic authority: The authority to found Christian communities, to heal the sick, teach, and missionize given by Jesus to his apostles.

Aramaic: A form of Hebrew and the language of Jesus and his disciples. Although none of the Nag Hammadi texts were written in Aramaic, a few (e.g., *GosPhil*) show evidence of puns and wordplays that make sense only in Aramaic, indicating that the authors of these texts had some familiarity with this ancient language.

Archigenetor: From the Greek for First Parent or Primal Parent. The highest being in some Gnostic cosmologies.

Archon: Greek word for "prince" or "ruler." A term for a secular ruler, which becomes in these texts the name for powerful but deeply flawed celestial beings. Archons are always negative characters.

Aretalogy: A form of speech where the speaker expresses him- or herself in first-person declarations, beginning with "I am . . ."

Ascent formula(e): Words spoken by the soul to specific celestial gatekeepers in order to escape their clutches. These formulae contain statements about the soul's true origin in the **Pleroma.**

Asceticism (Ascetic, adj.): The suppression and mastery of the body's physical desires, particularly hunger, thirst, and sexual appetite.

Aspersion: The baptismal practice of sprinkling water over the heads of individuals being baptized.

Athanasius: An influential bishop in fourth-century Alexandria. Athanasius issued a list of books he considered acceptable as forming the canon of approved Christian writings; see **Festal Letter of 367.** Some speculate that the NH codices were hidden in response to Athanasius, although there is no proof of this.

Augustus: The title for the first Roman Emperor (ruled from 27 BCE to 14 CE), by which he was known.

Autogenes: "Self-generated." A name for the second person of the **Sethian** trinity. The highest form is the Unbegotten, followed by the "Self-Generated" and then by the "Begotten."

Barbēlō: A male name for the female aeon **Sophia**. It refers to Sophia in her male or androgynous creative aspect.

Basilides: An early second-century Gnostic Christian teacher based in Alexandria, and whose works have been lost.

Battle at Milvian Bridge: The decisive battle of the Roman emperor Constantine over his enemy, Maxentius, at the Milvian Bridge. Constantine attributed his success to the God of the Christians, and in recognition for victory, adopted Christianity as his new faith.

BCE/CE: The modern academic way of indicating dates. BCE stands for "Before the Common Era" and CE for "the Common Era." These correspond precisely to the Christian dating system, "before Christ," (BC) and "Anno Domini" (AD), "year of Our Lord."

Being, Life, and Intellect: Also translated as Existence, Vitality, and Mentality/Blessedness, a primordial **Sethian** triad found in *3StelesSeth, Marsanes,* and *Zostrianos.*

Books of Jeu: A set of two important **Sethian** cosmological tractates preserved in a single Coptic manuscript, the **Bruce Codex.**

Bridal Chamber: A Valentinian sacrament apparently celebrating the unification of an individual with her or his celestial counterpart or **syzygy**. The nature of the Bridal chamber ritual remains mysterious, but it was apparently the most important of the Valentinian church's sacraments.

Bruce Codex: A book of "Gnostic" writings, discovered by James Bruce in 1769 in Egypt. It is now in the Bodleian Museum, Oxford. It contains five works, most notably the *1st* and *2nd Books of Jeu.*

Cain: Adam and Eve's first child and murderer of his brother **Abel**. In *ApJn*, Cain is one of seven archons; in the *GosEg*, Cain is one of twelve archons.

Canon: List of approved books that comprise the New Testament or Hebrew Bible.

Cartonnage: Pieces of discarded papyrus from trash heaps glued together to form a hard material used to make book covers.

Catechumen: In Christianity, an individual being prepared to receive baptism.

Catholic Church: From the Greek *katholikos*, "universal" or "whole," the name for the largest Christian denomination worldwide. In formation since the second century, Roman Catholic Christianity came to be influential, defining itself as the dominant form of Christianity against various smaller sects or Christian groups.

Chaos: In **Sethian** cosmology, the formless material outside the **Pleroma** before it is populated; often associated with the Abyss. In *OrigWld* Chaos is the shadow of the Pre-existent One and the parent of **Ialdabaoth**. Seven androgynous **aeons** are set over Chaos to rule it.

Choic: From a Greek word meaning "of the soil." The lowest form of being or the lowest of three types of "soul" in human beings.

chrism/chrismation: The practice of anointing with oil. One of five Valentinian sacraments mentioned in the *GosPhil*.

Christ: From the Greek "anointed one," which itself translates the Hebrew *meschiach* or "messiah." A title for Jesus of Nazareth, often used by the apostle **Paul**. In NH documents, Christ is a pre-existent being who is sometimes distinguished from Jesus or the Savior.

Christology (Christological, adj.): An understanding or concept of Jesus's nature and being. Scholars often distinguish between "high Christology" in which Jesus is considered fully divine, and "low Christology" in which Jesus is more of a human teacher. Most Christian texts developed a position somewhere between these two extremes.

Clement of Alexandria (ca. 150–215 CE): A Christian philosopher of the late-second–early-third century. A member of the nascent Christian orthodoxy, he preserves some Gnostic documents in his writings against heretics.

Codex (pl: codices): An ancient book, with papyrus pages and, usually, leather covers. The codex form for documents came to replace the scroll by the third century CE.

Codex Tchacos: A significant manuscript of Coptic writings discovered in El-Minya Egypt in the 1970s. It contains four texts, the most important of which is the *Gospel of Judas*.

Codicology: The study of the formation of codices, including determining dating, provenance, scribal hand, technology, and reasons for the order of individual tractates in a codex.

collegium **(pl.** *collegia***):** In Rome, a formal name for a group of priests but also the name for a voluntary association of ordinary people who band together to offer each other specific social services. Early Christianity is sometimes described as having been a type of collegium, where members offer assistance to one another.

Colophon: A short note written by a scribe at the end of a copied tractate in a codex.

Colossians, letter to the: A letter ascribed to the apostle Paul but probably composed by someone else drawing on Paul's authority. Colossians offers a high Christology and group-identity of a church or assembly as part of Christ's body. Colossians was a popular letter for those who wrote many of the NH documents.

Configurations of the Fate of the Heavens Beneath the Twelve: In *OrigWld*, a lost book of cosmological wisdom.

Constantine I (Constantine the Great): The first Roman emperor to become Christian. Ruled from 306 to 337 CE. Constantine I's conversion greatly helped Christianity to spread.

Coptic Museum: A museum in Cairo, Egypt, that now houses the NH writings.

Coptic: The dominant language of Christian Egypt, written with a modified Greek script. It is the language of all our significant manuscripts of "Gnostic" writings, although it was not the original language of the writings themselves. Coptic has four major dialects, two of which (**Akhmimic** and **Sahidic**) were used in translating the Nag Hammadi writings from Greek.

Corinthians, first letter to the: One of the most significant letters of the apostle **Paul**, composed ca. 53–57 CE, now in the New Testament. First Corinthians is excerpted often in the NH writings.

Corinthians, second letter to the: The second letter written by **Paul** to the Corinthians, although it may be a composite document. In it, Paul claims to have had a visionary journey up to the third heaven (2 Cor 12:1–4), which provided an inspiration for certain writings at NH, most notably the *Apocalypse of Paul*.

Corpus Hermeticum: A collection of pagan philosophical writings revealed by **Hermes Trismegistus**. See also **Hermetica**.

cosmogony: A narrative account of the creation of the cosmos and its inhabitants.

cosmology: The expression of the nature and shape of the cosmos.

Council of Nicaea: The first international assembly of Christian bishops in 325 CE, gathered to develop Christian orthodoxy and combat heresy.

Counterfeit Spirit: In Sethian writings (particularly *ApJn*) a false spirit or force that keeps people spiritually enslaved.

creed: A short statement of Christian belief.

criterion of dissimilarity: A principle developed in New Testament Studies to determine the authenticity of certain of Jesus's sayings. It states that if a saying attributed to Jesus doesn't fit an agenda of early Christian communities, the saying may be traced back to Jesus.

daimōn (pl. daimōnes): A celestial being, distinct from angels but not necessarily evil.

Decad: A collection of ten **aeons** in **Valentinian** cosmology.

Demiurge: Literally, the "maker." The craftsman or creator god in Plato's dialogue *Timaeus*, often identified with **Ialdabaoth** in **Sethian** texts and described in wholly negative terms. In Valentinian writings, the Demiurge is more positively valued.

Derdekeas: Son of the Infinite Light; the revealer figure in the *Paraphrase of Shem*.

docetism (also, docetic, docetist): From the Greek "to seem"; the belief or teaching that Jesus did not incarnate into human flesh, but only appeared to be human. Many people found the idea of God coming down and inhabiting a human body, and then suffering and being put to death repellent or nonsensical. Thus some proposed docetism as a way of preserving Jesus's ultimate divinity. Docetism quickly was declared a heretical teaching by proto-orthodox theologians. Only a few NH texts preserve a docetic Christology.

Dodecad: A collection of twelve **aeons** in **Valentinian** cosmology.

Domedon Doxomedon: In *GosEg*, a heavenly aeon or realm where the chariot-throne can be found. From the Greek "domedon," "Lord of the House," and "Doxomedon," "Lord of Glory."

doxology: Words of praise to a deity, possibly recited aloud in the context of prayers or a religious service.

dualism: A fundamental state based on two balanced opposing principles. These can be: good/evil; human/divine; body/soul. Gnosticism is often mischaracterized as dualistic.

Dyad: A binary pair of **aeons** or beings. The term likely drew from **Pythagorean** number theory.

Edessa: A cosmopolitan city on the eastern fringes of the Roman Empire and a hub of learning. Some scholars speculate that certain "Gnostic" writings, especially those associated with the apostle Thomas (who is said to be buried in Edessa) were written there.

ekklesia: An assembly of people, often misleadingly translated as "church."

Eleleth: A great angel, one of the four great **Angels of the Entirety** mentioned in Sethian texts, along with Daveithai, Oroael and Harmozel. In the *HypArch* and *ApJn*, Eleleth is a revealer and savior, who answers **Norea**'s distress call and reveals to her the truth of her divine origins.

emanation: A kind of "pouring out" or "spilling over" of the first divine realm as a form of asexual creation.

encratism, encratitic (adj.): A practice of containing and controlling bodily appetites such as hunger, thirst, and sexual desire.

Ennead: A group of nine *aeons*, or the ninth realm. In the *Discourse on the Eighth and Ninth*, the Ennead is the highest divine realm, part of the hyper-cosmos or space above the known cosmos.

Ennoia: "Thought." An aeon or primary feminine manifestation of the Unbegotten or highest form of the divine.

Epinoia: "Insight." An aeon or primary feminine manifestation of the Unbegotten.

Epiphanius of Salamis, St.: A fourth-century bishop of Salamis (modern-day Cyprus) and a **heresiologist**. Author of the *Panarion*, a compendium of **Gnostic** groups and how to identify them.

eschatology (eschatological, adj.): Having to do with the eschaton, the end (usually of the world). The word can also describe beliefs about the fate of the soul, rather than the end of the world.

esoteric: Something that is considered hidden or secret from others, particularly a religious teaching.

Eucharist: A Christian sacrament in which bread or some other substance is identified with the savior before being ritually consumed.

Eve: The first woman in many Gnostic cosmologies. Her name is related to the Hebrew word "life."

exegesis: Textual analysis based on drawing out the various layers of meaning in a text, usually a work of scripture.

Festal Letter of 367: An open letter issued at Easter in the year 367 CE by the influential bishop of **Alexandria, Athanasius.** It lists the twenty-seven books of the NT that Athanasius considered authoritative and is our earliest canon list that corresponds to the modern New Testament.

Five Seals: A Sethian baptismal rite, never fully explicated in any of our NH texts.

Four Luminaries: see **Angels of the Entirety.**

Frame story: A secondary narrative added to a treatise in order to "frame" it as something else; for example, a cosmological treatise might be framed by a **revelation dialogue** between Jesus and a disciple.

freedpeople: A class of Roman people who had been freed from slavery during the course of their life. Freedpeople were often educated and wealthy.

geocentric: A model of the cosmos in which the earth stands at the center. This was the prevailing cosmic model in antiquity.

gloss: A brief commentary or explanation introduced by an ancient editor or scribe into a manuscript.

glossolalia: Literally, "tongue-speaking," sounds that certain Christians made while praying that were thought to be inspired by the Holy Spirit.

gnosis: Greek for "knowledge"; a specific knowledge of one's divine origins and that the path to salvation comes through self-knowledge.

Gnosticism: A modern title given to a movement that peaked in the second century CE and which was concerned with *gnosis.* It remains unclear how accurate a term it is for the variety of worldviews often called "Gnostic."

gospel: From the word meaning "good news," literally a message (in this case of salvation). A gospel is a literary text that often tells the story of Jesus's life and death. However, many of our gospels from Nag Hammadi are not biographies but retain the broader sense of "good news" since they present ideas of salvation.

Great Account: Irenaeus' account of **Valentinian** cosmology, from Book 1 of his work, *Against Hereses.*

Hans Jonas (1903–1993): A German Jewish philosopher whose book, *The Gnostic Religion,* had tremendous impact on modern scholars.

Hebdomad: A group of seven archons, usually identified with the seven planets or with the seven days of the week.

Heimarmene: Fate or destiny, a force exerted by the archons to enslave humankind.

Hellenization (also, Hellenized): The process of adopting Greek culture and language in the lands outside Greece, initiated by Alexander the Great.

heresiology; heresiologist: The study of, or someone who studies, heresy. A number of prominent heresiologists from the second through the fourth centuries set the boundaries of who would be considered "Gnostics" or other kinds of heretics. The heresiologists were our sole source of information about those who wrote and used the NH writings until their discovery in 1945.

heresy, heretic: A choice to break away from a bigger movement, from the Greek *hairesis,* "division." A derogatory word leveled by some Christians against others who they believed did not adhere to the doctrines and practices of **Catholic** Christianity.

Hermes Trismegistus: A legendary teacher of wisdom, known as the "thrice-great" ("trismegistus") Hermes. He is featured in a set of ancient writings called the **Hermetica.**

Hermetica: A class of religious, philosophical writings, often in the form of dialogues between Hermes Trismegistus and his sons or students.

Hermetism, hermeticism: A pagan religious movement based in Egypt that drew on various intellectual traditions in the Graeco-Roman world, particularly Middle Platonism and Stoicism. Many texts take the form of a dialogue between Hermes Trismegistus and a disciple. The Nag Hammadi library contains three Hermetic texts, one of which was already known from other sources (*Asclepius*). There are obvious points of contact between some of our Christian Nag Hammadi texts and our pagan Hermetic texts.

hierophany: A manifestation of the divine to a visionary or to people on earth.

Hippolytus of Rome (170 to 235 CE): An important Christian theologian, bishop, and **heresiologist.** Most of his many writings have not survived, including the important *Syntagma,* but one that has is his *Refutation of All Heresies,* which directs itself against Gnosticism.

homily: A commentary after a scriptural reading that acts to provide a moral lesson or example to listeners during the course of a church service.

hylic: From the Greek "hyle," or "matter." The lowest of three possible levels of being, and a synonym for *sarkic* or *choic.*

hypostasis (also hypostasize, hypostasized, hypostasization): An abstract quality which has become concrete. An example would be the quality "wisdom," which in many Gnostic texts becomes personified as the higher being named **Wisdom**. Other common hypostases in Gnostic literature include Life (**Zoe**), Truth (Alethia), and Providence (**Pronoia**).

Ialdabaoth/Yaltabaoth: The most common name for the chief **archon** (*HypArch*; *ApJn*; *OrgWld*). There have been many attempts to derive the translation or meaning of the name, but scholars remain unsure from where it derived or what it meant.

Invisible Spirit: The First Principle in **Sethian** cosmologies, from which all other beings emanate. Also called the Father, the Invisible Spirit is found in a triad with the Mother (**Barbēlō**) and the Son, **Autogenes**.

invocation: A kind of prayer that summons or calls upon a deity.

Irenaeus of Lyons: A proto-orthodox writer and bishop of the city of Lyons in Gaul (now France); his five-volume work, *Against Heresies* (*Adv. Haer.*), is a major source of information about various Christian groups he considered heretical.

Isis: Egyptian goddess revered in the Roman world. A series of inscriptions to Isis mirror some of the content and form of NH's *Thunder: Perfect Mind*.

Jesus Movement: The first generation of Jesus's followers after his death, before the name "Christianity" would be given to the movement.

Johannine Prologue: The first eighteen chapters of the Gospel of John, which are thought to have been an independent writing that John's author incorporated into the gospel. The account of the salvific descent of the **Logos** in the Johannine Prologue forms some of the most important conceptual background to a huge number of NH texts.

Jung Codex: Nag Hammadi Codex I, which was at one time purchased and given to the Swiss psychologist Carl Jung for his birthday. It was eventually removed from the Jung Foundation in Zurich and now has joined the other Nag Hammadi codices in the Coptic Museum, Cairo.

Kalyptos: Greek for "hidden," the highest of the Sethian triad Kalyptos, **Protophanes**, and **Autogenes** in the Upper Realms, and the domain of Intelligible Reality.

lacuna (e): A physical hole in a manuscript page.

leontomorphic: From the Greek *leo* ("lion") and *morphos*, ("form"), a lion-shaped or lion-headed god. **Ialdabaoth** is often described as "lion-headed."

Liturgy: A religious rite, consisting of formal words or formulae, spoken aloud in a particular order. Liturgy comes from a Greek word that means "service."

logion (pl: logia): A brief saying or aphorism, usually of Jesus. The *GThom* is arranged into 114 logia or sayings of Jesus.

Logos: The "Word" or active principle of the Father, who appears in the cosmos to save humankind. In the Gospel of John, the Logos is associated with the pre-existent Christ. The idea of the Logos first appears in **Stoicism** as a positive pervasive force in the cosmos that suffuses all things; in Christian versions, the Logos is freestanding and does not indwell all things.

Manichaeans: Followers of a widespread religious tradition based on the teachings and revelations of Mani (216–276 CE). They taught a radical dualism in which the world was divided into a World of Light and a World of Darkness. With many affinities with so-called Gnostic thought, the Manichaeans were despised in the late Roman Empire as heretics, and persecuted into eventual extinction under the force of a Christian empire.

martyr: From the Greek word for "witness," someone who chooses to die for his or her beliefs.

Merkavah (also, Merkabah): A form of Jewish mysticism arising by the first century BCE that derived from speculation on the Book of Ezekiel's description of God in his chariot (Hebrew: *merkavah*). Elements of Merkavah mysticism appear in certain NH writings, particularly *OrgWld* and *HypArch* where **Sabaoth** sits on a divine chariot in the heavens.

Messina Definition: A formal definition of **Gnosticism**, heavily dependent on the work of Hans Jonas, and developed collaboratively in an international meeting of Gnosticism scholars in Messina, Italy, in 1966.

Micheu, Michar, and Mnesimous: Three beings who preside over celestial baptism in **Sethian** texts (*ApAd*; *GosEg*). They are always mentioned together.

Middle Platonism: The (modern) name given to a philosophical school in the Roman Empire based on principles drawn from **Plato**, but also combining other ancient Greek philosophical ideas, particularly from **Stoicism** and occasionally Aristotelianism and Pythagoreanism.

Midrash: A form of Jewish scriptural interpretation, in which gaps in scriptural narrative are filled out, sometimes creatively. Texts such as *HypArch* and *ApJn* are in part midrashic responses to the book of Genesis.

Mind: See **Nous**.

Mirothea (or Meirothea): An aspect of **Barbēlō**, present in *TriProt*. Her name may connect her with concepts of destiny or fate.

Mithras: A Roman god associated with Persia, worshiped in the Roman Empire in a movement known as Mithraism. Initiates to the Mithraic mysteries met periodically in underground temples, which featured at the front an image of Mithras slaughtering a bull.

Monad: A single, divine principle from which all things issue.

monasticism: A movement, which gained force in the fourth century CE and advocated, among other things, a life largely spent in solitude and the suppression of bodily desires, namely hunger and sex. Egypt and Syria both have strong monastic movements in the ancient world.

monist: A philosophy based upon a single, undivided primary entity.

Monogenes: Greek for the "only begotten," an aspect of the Father in his capacity as Son.

monotheism (also, monotheists): A philosophical or religious system based on the worship of a single god.

mystery cult: A religion in the Roman Empire, which initiated people into secret revelations. The most famous mystery cult was the Eleusinian Mysteries performed for more than a thousand years at Eleusis, Greece. The bond of secrecy was maintained such that we know very little about what happened in these mystery cults.

mystes: An initiate into a **mystery cult.**

mytholegoumena: Mythic or mythological elements that are combined together into a narrative.

Nag Hammadi: A village in upper (southern) Egypt, near the place where the Nag Hammadi Codices were found in 1945.

Nebro: An evil archon in the *GosJud*, whose face is marked with blood and flashes with fire. This archon is probably associated with Nebruel, a female archon in *GosEg* who is paired with Saklas and together generates with him the lower cosmos.

neophyte: a Newlybaptized Christian, from the Greek word for "newborn."

Neoplatonism: A monotheistic philosophical school of the late Roman Empire (third century CE and beyond) heavily concerned with reinterpreting Plato's writings. One of the most famous Neoplatonist teachers from this time was Plotinus, who taught a range of students (including Gnostics) in his study circles in Rome.

New Testament: Christian scripture, twenty-seven books dating from the mid-first to the early second century CE. Our present-day NT was not compiled until well after the fourth century; thus the authors of Nag Hammadi texts did not have access to complete New Testaments. Nonetheless, they certainly knew of many of the writings that comprise the NT, including the gospels and the letters of the apostle **Paul.**

Nicene Creed: A formal statement of belief, developed at the **Council of Nicaea** in 325 CE convened by **Constantine the Great.** The Nicene Creed is still recited in many Christian churches today.

noncanonical: Christian and Jewish texts that did not make it into the official canon or list of approved writings. All the Nag Hammadi texts are noncanonical, but not all noncanonical texts can be called **Gnostic.**

Norea: The fourth child and only daughter of Adam and Eve (see *HypArch*). She is virginal and pure in origin.

Nous: The Divine Mind.

Ogdoad: A set of eight divine beings or *aeons*. The Ogdoad can also be a divine realm.

oligarchy: A system of government where a few select elites (Gk: *oligos*) hold power.

Origen of Alexandria (ca. 284–253 CE): A controversial Christian intellectual and prolific writer of the third century. Origen condemns **Gnosticism** in his work, *Contra Celsum*, but often uses the language of *gnosis* in a positive sense.

Orthodox Christianity: A formal division of Christianity, which emerged in the Byzantine world. The Eastern Orthodox Church is the largest Christian denomination worldwide after Roman Catholicism. Both denominations claim to have been the "original" form of Christianity.

orthodoxy: From the Greek "straight thinking" or "right opinion," a term that designates a dominant group of people holding beliefs they believe to be true and dominant.

Ousiarchs: A class of celestial beings. The name comes from the Greek words "*ousia*," being, and "*archē*," rulers.

Oxyrhynchus: An ancient city in Egypt. Once excavated, it was found to have contained numerous papyri fragments. Some of these fragments have yielded Greek copies of ancient Christian texts, including the *GThom* and the *GosMary*.

Pachomian: A system of monasticism based on the Egyptian Christian Pachomius (292–348). Some scholars believe that Pachomian monks copied out the Nag

Hammadi writings, but there is no evidence to support this theory.

paganism: A loose set of religious beliefs and practices in the Roman Empire other than those that fall under the category "Christian" or "Jewish." The term is not capitalized, however, because it is not a formal movement or religion.

paedagogue: A teacher, usually a slave employed for the purpose of educating boys and young men. In some **Valentinian** documents (*GosPhil*; *InterpKnowledge*) Jesus comes in the form of a paedagogue.

paleography: The study of ancient manuscript writing. One important function is to ascertain the dating of early texts.

papyrus (pl: papyri): Sheets of a pulpy plant material cultivated in Egypt, used before the use of paper or vellum/parchment and the invention of paper. Vellum was derived from animal skin and was thus a luxury good, but papyrus was both cheap and durable.

paraenesis: Moral exhortation or encouragement of an assembly or church leader to her or his congregation.

Paul: Born Saul of Tarsus, Paul has an experience of the resurrected Christ that initiates a period of intense missionization. Paul established communities of Christ-followers, with whom he corresponds in a series of letters, some of which still exist and are in the New Testament. Paul appears to have been in conflict with Jesus's disciples, namely Peter and James, concerning how to follow Jesus.

Pax Romana: "Roman Peace," the governing principle of the Roman Empire that promised various protections and advantages in exchange for submission to Rome.

Peter: Also called Simon Peter, one of Jesus's chief disciples and the leader of the Jerusalem assembly ("church") after Jesus's death.

petition: A form of prayer asking for something to be granted.

Petrine: Having to do with the apostle Peter.

Pistis (or Pistis Sophia, name): From the Greek for "faith," one of the epithets of Sophia (*Pistis Sophia*).

Pistis Sophia: An important early Christian **revelation** text, in which Jesus reveals cosmic knowledge to his chief disciple Mary Magdalene. The *Pistis Sophia* is best known from the surviving version in the Askew Codex, now in the British Museum.

Plato (ca. 423–347 BCE): A major Greek philosopher and student of Socrates. Plato's dialogues and letters formed the foundation for much of Western philosophy. His works were considered by many educated citizens of the second century to be of the highest authority, and shades of them (particularly the *Symposium*, the *Timaeus*, and the *Phaedrus*) underscore much of second-century NH writings.

Platonic philosophy: A system of philosophy based directly on the writings of Plato.

Platonism: A philosophical school of thought in the Roman Empire based mostly on the writings of **Plato**, but also incorporating elements of **Pythagoreanism**. Platonism in the Roman Empire is sometimes divided into **Middle Platonism** (first–third centuries) and **Neoplatonism** (third–fifth centuries).

Pleroma: Greek for the "fullness" or the "entirety." The upper celestial realms where the **aeons** live.

Plotinus (204–270 CE): A major ancient philosopher and interpreter of **Plato** and who initiated **Neoplatonism**. Certain Gnostic students in Plotinus's school introduced the **Sethian** apocalypses *Zostrianos* and *Allogenes* to their fellow Platonists, provoking Plotinus to compose a treatise *Against the Gnostics* (*Enneads* 2.9).

pneuma: An ethereal substance that comes from the **Pleroma** and is translated as "spirit" in English. It also means "breath." The pneuma is what animates the modeled Adam in NH creation stories; many people (but not necessarily all) have pneuma within them that will return to the Pleroma after the death of the body.

pneumatic: Spiritual human beings, from the Greek word "**pneuma**" or "spirit."

Porphyry of Tyre (234–305 CE): Plotinus's biographer and one of his chief students.

praxis: Practice, as in an action done in contrast to something believed (e.g., baptism).

Pronoia: From the Greek for "forethought" or Providence (the Latin translation of the Greek word). One of the female **aeons**, who works to assist the **pneumatic** gain salvation.

Protennoia: From the Greek "first thought," a divine feminine being who emanates from the Primal Parent or First Father. She is similar to other feminine emanations, including *Pronoia* and *Ennoia*.

protest exegesis: A way of interpreting the scriptures subversively, counter to the established interpretation. The reinterpretation of the God of the Jews in Genesis as an evil **archon** (as in *HypArch*) is sometimes understood as the result of disaffected Jewish readers of Genesis engaging in protest **exegesis**.

protology: A study of things that happened at the beginning of time.

Protophanes: A significant **aeon** in **Sethian** cosmologies.

Prunikos: One of the epithets of **Sophia**.

pseudepigrapha (pseudepigraphical, adj.): From the Greek for "false writings," or writings ascribed to someone other than the actual writer in Judaism and Christianity.

Pseudo-Tertullian: The name by which the unknown author of *Adversus Omnes Haereses*, an appendix to the work *De praescriptionem haereticorum* of Tertullian, is known.

psyche: The Greek word for the human soul.

psychic: The middle of three classes of human beings, between **pneumatic** (spiritual) and **sarkic** (fleshly).

psychopomp: A figure, generally a god (and often the god Hermes/Mercury) who leads souls into the afterlife.

Pythagoreanism: A philosophical school in the Roman Empire loosely based on the teachings of the Greek polymath Pythagoras. The school taught music and mathematical theory as well as philosophy, and its adherents wore special clothing and kept to a vegetarian diet. By the third century CE, we call the same movement **Neoplatonism**.

Q: From German "Quelle" or "source," the source used by the gospel writers Matthew and Luke, consisting predominantly of Jesus' sayings. In form, it might have resembled the *GThom*.

realized eschatology: A belief that the end of the world has already arrived, but that it has not taken a radical apocalyptic form.

recension: A version of a text.

redaction: An edited portion or version of a text.

redaction criticism: The modern study of how ancient writers redacted or edited their sources in order to reflect their own understandings and concerns.

Redemption: One of five **Valentinian sacraments** mentioned in the *GPhil*; apparently a rite that allowed the soul to join its source in the **Pleroma** after the death of the body.

Refrigerium: A funerary feast common in the fourth century and beyond, to toast the souls of the dead in the afterlife.

repose (*anapausis*): A state of rest that occurs when the spirits of the "perfect" are restored to their original home in the **Pleroma**.

revelation dialogue/discourse: Words that the risen Jesus as Savior speaks to a chosen disciple, revealing the nature of the cosmos and salvation.

Rome: The largest city in the Roman Empire of the second century and home of the Roman Emperor. There were Christians in Rome since the first century. Later, **Valentinus** came to teach there.

Sabaoth: One of the seven **archons**, and usually identified as the son of **Ialdabaoth**. In various NH cosmogonies, Sabaoth repents and is subsequently enthroned on a throne-chariot in the heavens by his mother, **Sophia**. Sabaoth is featured on many ancient amulets.

sacrament: A ritual of initiation. In the second century, Christian sacraments included **baptism**, anointment or **chrism**, and the **Eucharist**. Certain groups, such as the **Valentinians**, practiced their own sacraments.

Sahidic Coptic: The most common dialect of **Coptic** used in Christian Egypt.

Saklas/Sakla: Aramaic for "fool." One of the names of **Ialdabaoth**, especially in *GosEg*.

Samael: Aramaic for "god of the blind" or "blind god." The given name of the chief **archon** in *Hypostasis of the Archons*. He is called blind because he is ignorant of the existence of higher realms. He is equated with **Ialdabaoth**.

sarkic: From the Greek for "of the flesh." The lowest level in the threefold structure of humanity that corresponds to human spiritual possibilities. The sarkic **Adam** has no spiritual possibility, but is merely an animated body.

sayings collection: A collection of Jesus' sayings, such as the *GThom* or the **Q** source.

Seal: A mark or symbol drawn on the body with oil as part of a **sacrament**.

Seed, Seed of Seth: Technically, the offspring or children of a being, usually Seth. Certain people in the second and third centuries evidently considered themselves the Seed of Seth, who Seth had disseminated throughout the world until all would be gathered together in the upper realms after death or at the end of time.

seer: A human visionary who is given a tour of the cosmos by a divine being in **apocalyptic** literature.

Semeia Definition: A modern scholarly definition of **apocalyptic** literature from 1979, first published in the academic journal *Semeia*.

Septuagint: The Jewish scriptures translated into Greek during the Hellenistic period (ca. third century BCE) and used by Jews and Christians in the Roman Empire, most of whom did not read Hebrew. The abbreviation for this translation, LXX, refers to the number of translators (originally 72, but rounded off to 70).

Seth: The third child of **Adam** and **Eve**. In some Nag Hammadi writings, Seth is a heavenly savior, the originator of the Great Race.

Sethianism (or Sethian Gnosticism): A reconstructed intellectual movement in the second and third centuries based around the savior **Seth** and other shared typologies, such as a cosmology based on a primary triad of Father, Mother (**Barbēlō**), and Son.

Sophia: From the Greek "wisdom," a divine feminine entity and usually the first child of the Primal Parent or First Father. In some Gnostic cosmologies, Sophia acts foolishly by creating her own offspring, the monstrous **Ialdabaoth**. The story of her repentance is central to many **Gnostic** ideas of salvation. She acts beneficently toward humankind, urging them to wake up to their spiritual nature.

Son of man: One of the titles for Jesus often found in NH writings. The term is sometimes translated "child of humanity" by modern scholars.

Soteriology: Teachings or concepts of salvation.

Stoicism: One of the most influential Greek philosophical schools in antiquity. Practitioners or "Stoics" worked to restrain their emotions and cultivate an attitude of non-engagement with the world. Stoic ideas were popular in most strands of early Christianity, and are particularly evident in many Nag Hammadi documents.

Stoics: Adherents of Stoicism, active in the Roman Empire. Stoics cultivated a measured acceptance of death and advocated suppressing emotions and appetites.

subpleromic domain: In **Valentinian** cosmology, the lower cosmic area beneath the **Pleroma** with its celestial **aeons**. The subpleromic domain is ruled by the **Demiurge**.

Subakhmimic Coptic: A dialect of Coptic from around the area of Akhmim (Greek Panopolis) in Egypt, that flourished in the fourth century. Also known as Lycopolitan.

Synoptic Gospels: The NT gospels of Matthew, Mark, and Luke. These three share narrative style and source material.

Syriac: The language of Syrian Christians, closely related to Hebrew and Aramaic. Many early Christian texts are preserved in Syriac and may have been written in that language.

syzygy (also: syzygos): An individual's "yokefellow," a partner of the opposite sex who makes up a complete unit. The Greek word *syzygos* becomes in Latin *coniunx*, the word for "spouse," from which we get the English word "conjugal."

Tertullian (ca. 160– ca. 225 AD): A Christian theologian and writer from Carthage, North Africa. Tertullian wrote polemical works against Gnosticism, but not enough to be counted among the most important **heresiologists**.

Tetrad: A set of the first four primary deities in **Valentinian** systems.

Theodosian Code: A compilation of Christian laws that were put in place between 312 CE and the formal issue of the Code in 438 CE. It receives its name from **Theodosius II,** and contains many laws that limit or persecute non-Catholic Christians.

Theodosian Decrees: A series of imperial decrees issued from 389–391 CE under **Theodosius I**, which effectively outlawed paganism.

Theodosius I (347–395 CE): An important late fourth-century emperor who worked to ensure that all bishops in the Roman Empire adhered to the orthodox Christian position established at the **Council of Nicaea** and followed the primacy of the bishops of *Rome* and **Alexandria**.

theriomorphic: From the Greek "animal-formed," usually used to describe the **archons**.

Theudas: A student of **Paul** the apostle, who taught **Valentinus**.

Thirteenth Kingdom: An **aeon** in **Sethian** cosmology. Various texts offer conflicting opinions on whether this is a blessed realm or not. See: *Allogenes; GosJud; ApocAdam.*

theurgy: A secret ritual practice among **Neoplatonists** involving amulets, images, and invocation of vowel sounds. The goal of theurgy is to call upon the gods to ask for their aid in self-divination or in uniting with the divine One, source of the cosmos. The Sethian apocalypse *Marsanes* appears to allude to theurgical practices.

Thrice-Male Child: A divine **aeon** in Sethian cosmologies who bears some similarities to the Sethian Christ.

Trisagion/Trishagion: From the Greek "three times holy." A standard hymn of the Divine **Liturgy** used in Eastern Orthodox Churches, and found in prayers from Nag Hammadi. It repeats "holy, holy, holy" three times.

Two-Source Hypothesis: In New Testament studies, a hypothesis on the relationship between the three Synoptic Gospels (Matthew, Mark and Luke). The hypothesis states that Matthew and

Luke borrowed much of the material in their gospels from Mark and another source, now lost, that scholars call **Q.**

Uranography: Writings about the nature and shape of the heavens (Gk *ouranos*).

Valentinianism (also, Valentinian, adj.): A form of intellectual or philosophical Christianity in the second and third centuries and beyond based on the teachings of Valentinus. Valentinians came to develop their own bishops and churches, but were eradicated by the early Roman Catholic Church.

Valentinus: A second-century Christian teacher who traced his intellectual pedigree through his teacher **Theudas**, a student of **Paul**. Valentinus was popular and well respected, but all his writings were destroyed by the **Catholic Church** for being heretical.

Voces magicae: Strings of vowels often found in Nag Hammadi manuscripts, meant to evoke divine power.

volumen: A scroll, and the source of the English word "volume."

Wisdom sayings, Wisdom traditions: A class of ancient Jewish literature that often takes the form of aphorisms (short sayings) or proverbs. Wisdom literature emerged from Hellenized (i.e., Greek) Judaism and also incorporates ideas of Wisdom as a divine feminine being present with God at creation.

Yesseus/Iesseus, Mazareus. and Yessedekeus/Iessedekeus, the Living Water: A group of three celestial figures who preside over the final stages of celestial baptism in Sethian texts such as *ApAdam* and *GosEg*. The names are unattested outside this context; it may be that "Yesseus Mazareus" is a corrupted form of "Jesus Nazareus."

Zoe: "Life"; one of the female **aeons**, sometimes associated with **Sophia** as her dynamic principle, sometimes named as the daughter of Sophia (*HypArch*) or else with the spiritual component of **Eve**. **Zostrianos:** The great-grandfather of the Persian holy man Zarathustra/Zoroaster and the son of a Greek, Iolaos. This ancient seer is known in Greek sources as a great holy man and is the pseudepigraphic author of the Sethian apocalypse *Zostrianos*.

Illustration Credits

Index

Page numbers followed by the letter "*d*" indicate diagrams; page numbers followed by the letter "*f*" indicate figures; page numbers followed by the letter "*t*" indicate tables.